任务型语码转换式双语教学系列教材

总主编 刘玉彬 副总主编 杜元虎 总主审 段晓东

电子信息技术

ELECTRONIC INFORMATION TECHNOLOGY

主　编 韩桂英 郑蕊蕊

副主编 刘忠富 李春杰 张维维

主　审 崔 颖

大连理工大学出版社

图书在版编目(CIP)数据

电子信息技术 / 韩桂英，郑蕊蕊主编. — 大连：
大连理工大学出版社，2014.8(2015.9 重印)
任务型语码转换式双语教学系列教材
ISBN 978-7-5611-8129-4

Ⅰ. ①电… Ⅱ. ①韩… ②郑… Ⅲ. ①电子信息－双语教学－高等学校－教材 Ⅳ. ①G203

中国版本图书馆 CIP 数据核字(2013)第 187652 号

大连理工大学出版社出版

地址：大连市软件园路 80 号　邮政编码：116023
发行：0411-84708842　邮购：0411-84703636　传真：0411-84701466
E-mail：dutp@dutp.cn　URL：http://www.dutp.cn

大连美跃彩色印刷有限公司印刷　　大连理工大学出版社发行

幅面尺寸：183mm×233mm　印张：15　字数：486 千字
2014 年 8 月第 1 版　　2015 年 9 月第 2 次印刷

责任编辑：邵　婉　　责任校对：齐　悦
封面设计：波　朗

ISBN 978-7-5611-8129-4　　定　价：26.00 元

总序

PREFACE

2014 年的初夏，我们为广大师生奉上这套“任务型语码转换式双语教学系列教材”。

“任务型语码转换式双语教学”是双语教学内涵建设的成果，主要由两大模块构成：课上，以不影响学科授课进度为前提，根据学生实际、专业特点、学年变化及社会需求等，适时适量地渗透英语专业语汇、语句、语段或语篇，“润物细无声”般地扩大学生专业语汇量，提高学生专业英语能力；课外，可向学生提供多种选择的“用中学”平台，如英语科技文献翻译、英语实验报告、英语学术论文、英语小论文、英语课程设计报告、模拟国际研讨会、英语辩论、工作室英语讨论会等，使学生的专业英语实践及应用达到一定频度和数量，激活英语与学科知识的相互渗透，培养学生用英语学习、科研、工作的能力及适应教育国际化和经济一体化的能力。

为保证“任务型语码转换式双语教学”有计划、系统、高效、科学地持续运行，减少教学的随意性和盲目性，方便师生的教与学，我们编写了这套“任务型语码转换式双语教学系列教材”。

本套教材的全部内容均采用汉英双语编写。

教材按专业组册，涵盖所有主干专业课和专业基础课，力求较为全面地反映各学科领域的知识体系。

分册教材编写以中文版课程教材为单位，即一门课为分册教材的一章，每章内容以中文版教材章节为序，每门课以一本中文教材为蓝本，兼顾其他同类教材内容，蓝本教材绝大部分是面向 21 世纪的国家规划教材。

教材的词汇短语部分，注意体现学科发展的新词、新语，同时考虑课程需求及专业特点，在不同程度灵活渗透了各章节的重要概念、定义，概述了体现章节内容主旨的语句及语段。分册教材还编写了体现各自专业特点的渗透内容，如例题及解题方法，课程的发生、发展及前沿简介，图示，实验原理，合同文本，案例分析，法条，计算机操作错误提示等。

部分教材补充了中文教材未能体现的先进理论、先进工艺、先进材料或先进方法的核心内容，弥补了某些中文教材内容相对滞后的不足；部分教材概述了各自专业常用研究方法、最新研究成果及学术发展的趋势动态；部分教材还选择性地把编者的部分科研成果转化为教材内容，以期启发学生的创新思维，开阔学生的视野，丰富学生的知识结构，从教材角度支持学生参与科研活动。

本套教材大多数分册都编写了对“用中学”任务实施具有指导性的内容，应用性内容的设计及编写比例因专业而异。与专业紧密结合的应用性内容包括英语写作介绍，如英语实验报告写作，英语论文写作，英语论文摘要写作，英语产品、作品或项目的概要介绍写作等。应用性内容的编写旨在降低学生参与各种实践应用活动的难度，提高学生参与“用中学”活动的可实现性，帮助学生提高完成“用中学”任务的质量水平。

考虑学生英语写作和汉译英的方便，多数分册教材都编写了词汇与短语索引。

“任务型语码转换式双语教学系列教材”尚属尝试性首创，是多人辛勤耐心劳作的结果。尽管在编写过程中，我们一边使用一边修改，力求教材的实用性、知识性、先进性融为一体，希望教材能对学生专业语汇积累及专业资料阅读、英语写作、英汉互译能力的提高发挥作用；尽管编者在教材编写的同时也都在实践“任务型语码转换式双语教学”，但由于我们缺乏经验，学识水平和占有资料有限，加上为使学生尽早使用教材，编写时间仓促，在教材内容编写、译文处理、分类体系等方面存在缺点、疏忽和失误，恳请各方专家和广大师生对本套教材提出批评和建议，以期再版时更加完善。

在教材的编写过程中，大量中外出版物中的内容给了我们重要启示和权威性的参考帮助，在此，我们谨向有关资料的编著者致以诚挚的谢意！

编　者
2014 年 5 月

前言

FOREWORD

本书是为推动任务型语码转换式双语教学模式在非英语专业中的应用和实践而编写，是一部本科电子信息工程专业的渗透式双语教学辅助教材。

双语教学是我国高等教育教学改革的一个热门话题。实施双语教学是我国高等教育适应经济全球化趋势，培养具有国际合作意识、国际交流与竞争能力的外向型人才的重要途径。双语教学可分为三个层次，即全英语式教学、整合式双语教学和渗透式双语教学。前两个层次对师资和学生的外语水平要求较高，难以大面积实施，而渗透式双语教学则不受师资和学生的外语水平条件的限制，在教学中易于普及推广。

按照语言认知的规律，根据语码转换和语言附带习得理论，渗透式双语教学是在不影响学科授课进度和课堂信息量的前提下，通过渗透一些与课程教学内容相关的英文语汇，使学生在学习学科课程的同时附带学习一些英文专业单词、短语或语段，似“润物细无声”般地扩大了学生的专业英文语汇量，使学生的外语能力在不知不觉中得到提高。学生掌握和扩大专业英语词汇既有利于今后的专业学习，又有利于提高学生对英语的应用和理解能力，同时有利于学生阅读专业文献，吸收国外先进技术。为此我们编写了这部语码转换式双语教学教材。

本书的编写有如下特点：(1)课程范围广。本书包括电子信息、通信工程等专业的技术基础课及主要的专业课，全书含电路原理、数字电子技术、信号与系统等共三十一章内容。(2)注重先进性。中文教材采用近几年出版的优秀教材，原版教材选自具有较大影响且为知名大学所采用的教材。(3)编排力求系统性。本书以中英文形式印刷出版，每门课程按中英文教材章节顺序给出专业词汇及短语，将每章的重点概念或语段从原版教材中摘出，并译成中文。(4)使用的便捷性。本书按照课程的章节顺序进行查阅。

参加编写的人员有付立军(第1章)、张艳(第1章实验)、薛原(第1、2章)、张俊星(第3章)、于为民(第4章)、刘忠富(第5、13章)、张维维(第6、26章)、李婷(第7章)、于少华(第8章)、石立新(第9章)、李春杰(第10、20章)、孙炎辉(第11、19章)、韩桂英(第12、24、25、27章)、许爽(第14、16章)、刘燕(第15、18章)、李绍民(第17章)、王培昌(第21章)、王都生(第22、28、29、30章)、郑蕊蕊(第22、31章)、崔艳秋(第23章)。全书由崔颖主审，郑蕊蕊统稿，特别感谢崔颖老师参与了部分章节部分内容的撰写和修改工作。

在本书的编写过程中，查阅和参考了大量的文献资料，从中得到了许多有益的启发和教益，在此谨向参考文献的作者致以诚挚的谢意。

编写渗透式双语教学辅助教材是一个尝试，它不同于汉英词典，是按课程进行编排的。不论是课程选择的合理性，还是教材选择的适当性，都有待于通过教学实践来检验。本教材在编写过程中，虽然参考了国内外有关文献，但限于时间仓促，篇幅有限，很难全面反映电子信息工程领域中各学科的内容，书中错误和不足之处在所难免，敬请广大读者批评指正。

编 者

2014 年 7 月

目录 CONTENTS

目录 CONTENTS

第一章　电路原理
Chapter 1　Principle of Electric Circuits
第一部分　电路原理
Part One: Principle of Electric Circuits
课程简介

本课程是电气类本科生的一门非常重要的必修课。课程介绍集总参数电路的基本原理，主要内容有：基本电路元件（电阻、电容、电感以及理想电源和受控电源），电路的基本定律和定理；动态电路的时域分析；使用相量法、阻抗、有功功率、无功功率、视在功率以及复功率进行正弦稳态电路分析；三相电路的分析和计算、测量功率的方法。通过学习本课程，学生将掌握电路分析的基本知识，并有能力解决各种电路相关问题。

Course Summary

This course is a very important compulsory course in the undergraduate electrical engineering curriculum. It introduces the fundamentals of the lumped circuit. Topics covered include: basic circuit elements(resistor, capacitor, inductor, current and voltage sources – both independent and dependent); basic law and theorems of electric circuits; time-domain analysis of dynamics networks; analysis of networks in the sinusoidal steady state by employing phasor, impedance, real-, reactive-, apparent-complex power; methods of analysis, calculation and measurement of power in three-phase networks. When students successfully complete this course, they will have a good command of basic circuit principles and demonstrate an ability to solve a variety of circuit-related problems.

第一节　电路模型和电路定律
Section 1　Circuit Model and Circuit Law

u-i 特性　u-i characteristic
安培　ampere(A)
★ 参考方向　reference direction
超导体　superconductor
代数和　algebraic sum
★ 电导　conductance
★ 电感　inductance
★ 电感元件　inductance element
电荷　charge
★ 电流　current
电流表　ammeter
电路　electric circuit
电路参数　circuit parameter
电路模型　circuit model
电位差(电势差)　potential difference
电路元件　circuit element
★ 电容　capacitance
★ 电容元件 capacitor
电位　potential
电位参考点　potential reference point
电位降　potential drop
电位升　potential rise
★ 电压　voltage
电压表　voltmeter
电压电流关系　voltage-current relation
★ 电源　source
电子　electron
★ 电阻　resistance
★ 电阻元件　resistor
短路　short circuit
法拉　farad
法拉第电磁感应定律　Faraday's law of electromagnetic
非线性电感元件　nonlinear inductor
非线性电路　nonlinear circuit
非线性电容元件　nonlinear capacitor
非线性电阻　nonlinear resistance
非线性电阻元件　nonlinear resistor
★ 伏特　volt(V)
负电荷　negative charge

★ 功率 power
★ 关联参考方向(无源符号约定) passive sign convention
国际单位制 international system of units (SI)
毫亨 millihenry
赫兹(赫) Hertz(Hz)
亨利 Henry
基尔霍夫电流定律 Kirchhoff's current law (KCL)
基尔霍夫电压定律 Kirchhoff's voltage law (KVL)
基尔霍夫定律 Kirchhoff's law
焦耳 Joule(J)
开路 open circuit
库仑 Coulomb
楞次定律 Lenz's law
零电位点 zero potential point
模型 model
能量 energy
欧姆 Ohm
欧姆定律 Ohm's law
皮法 picofarad
千赫 kilohertz
输出 output
输入 input
瓦特 Watt(W)
微法 microfarad
微亨 microhenry
无源元件 passive element
西门子 Siemens(S)
线性电阻 linear resistance
线性电感元件 linear inductor
线性电路 linear circuit
线性电容元件 linear capacitor
线性电阻元件 linear resistor
有源元件 active element
右手螺旋定则 right-handed screw rule
元件 element
正电荷 positive charge

1 An electric circuit consists of electrical elements connected together.
电子电路由若干个相互连接在一起的电路元件组成。

2 Current is the rate of charge flow.

$$i=\frac{dq}{dt}$$

电流是电荷流动的变化率。

$$i=\frac{dq}{dt}$$

3 Voltage is the energy required to move 1C of charge through an element.

$$v=\frac{dw}{dq}$$

电压是移动 1C 电荷流过元件所需要的能量。

$$v=\frac{dw}{dq}$$

4 Power is the energy supplied or absorbed per unit time. It is also the product of voltage and current.

$$p=\frac{dw}{dt}=vi$$

功率是单位时间内所提供(发出)或吸收的能量,也可表达为电压与电流的乘积。

$$p=\frac{dw}{dt}=vi$$

5 According to the passive sign convention, power assumes a positive sign when the current enters an element across the positive polarity of the voltage.
无源符号规则规定,若电流由接电压正端处流入元件,则功率的符号为正。

6 Ohm's law states that the voltage across a resistor is directly proportional to the current flowing through the resistor.
欧姆定律:电阻两端的电压与流经该电阻的电流成正比。

7 The current through a capacitor is directly proportional to the time rate of change of the voltage across it.

$$i=C\frac{dv}{dt}$$

The current through a capacitor is zero unless the voltage is changing. Thus a capacitor acts like an open circuit to a DC source.

流经电容器的电流正比于其两端电压随时间的变化率：

$$i=C\frac{dv}{dt}$$

除非电压随时间正在变化，否则流过电容器的电流为零。所以对直流电源而言，电容器的作用相当于开路。

8 The voltage across a capacitor is directly proportional to the time integral of the current through it.

$$v=\frac{1}{C}\int_{-\infty}^{t} idt=\frac{1}{C}\int_{t_0}^{t} idt+i(t_0)$$

The voltage across a capacitor cannot change instantly.

电容器两端的电压正比于流过它的电流对时间的积分：

$$v=\frac{1}{C}\int_{-\infty}^{t} idt=\frac{1}{C}\int_{t_0}^{t} idt+i(t_0)$$

电容器两端的电压不能突变。

9 The voltage across an inductor is directly proportional to the time rate of change of the current through it.

$$v=L\frac{di}{dt}$$

The voltage across the inductor is zero unless the current is changing. Thus an inductor acts as a short circuit to a DC source.

电感器两端的电压正比于流过它的电流随时间的变化率：

$$v=L\frac{di}{dt}$$

除非电流随时间正在变化，否则电感器两端的电压为零。所以对直流电源而言，电感器的作用相当于短路。

10 The current through an inductor is directly proportional to the time integral of the voltage across it.

$$i=\frac{1}{L}\int_{-\infty}^{t} vdt=\frac{1}{L}\int_{t_0}^{t} vdt+v(t_0)$$

The current through an inductor cannot change instantly.

流过电感器的电流正比于其两端电压对时间的积分：

$$i=\frac{1}{L}\int_{-\infty}^{t} vdt=\frac{1}{L}\int_{t_0}^{t} vdt+v(t_0)$$

流过电感器的电流不能突变。

11 An ideal independent source is an active element that provides a specified voltage or current, and completely independent of other circuit variables. An ideal dependent (or controlled) source is an active element in which the source quantity is controlled by another voltage or current.

理想的独立电源是有源(电源)元件，它独立地提供一定的电压或电流，与电路中的其他参量无关。理想的非独立电源(受控源)是有源元件，它所提供的电压或电流是受别的电压或电流控制的。

12 Kirchhoff's current law states that the algebraic sum of all the currents at any node in a circuit equals zero. In other words, the sum of the currents entering a node is equal to the sum of the currents leaving the node.

基尔霍夫电流定律：在电路中，任何节点上的所有电流的代数和等于零。或者说，流入节点的电流之和等于流出该节点的电流之和。

13 Kirchhoff's voltage law states that the algebraic sum of all the voltages around any closed path in a circuit equals zero. In other words, the sum of voltage rises equals the sum of voltage drops.
基尔霍夫电压定律:在电路中,环绕任何闭合路径的所有电压的代数和等于零。或者说,电压升高之和等于电压下降之和。

第二节 电阻电路的等效变换
Section 2 Equivalent Transformation of Resistive Circuits

Δ-Y 变换 delta-to-wye conversion
并联电路分析 analysis of parallel circuit
并联连接的电路元件 parallel-connected circuit element
串并联电路 series-parallel circuit
★ 串并联电路分析 analysis of series-parallel circuit
串联电路分析 analysis of series circuit
串联连接的电路元件 series-connected circuit element
等效串联电阻 equivalent series resistance
等效电导 equivalent conductance
★ 等效电阻 equivalent resistance
★ 电路分析 circuit analysis
电路理论 circuit theory
电压表的负载效应 voltmeter loading effect
★ 电源变换 source transformation
电阻的并联 resistor in parallel
电阻的串联 resistor in series
电阻电路 resistive circuit
二端网络 two-terminal network
二端元件 two-terminal element
分流电路 current-divider circuit
分压电路 voltage-divider circuit
集中参数 lumped parameter
集中参数电路 lumped circuit
集中参数元件 lumped element
交流电源 alternating current (AC) power supply
理想电路元件 ideal circuit element
三端元件 three-terminal element
星形电阻网络 star-connected resistance network
三角形电阻网络 delta-connected resistance network
★ 输入电阻 input resistance
★ 直流电源 direct current (DC) power supply

1 A linear network consists of linear elements, linear dependent sources, and linear independent sources, etc..
一个线性网络由线性元件、线性受控源和线性独立源等组成。

2 Two elements are in series when they are connected sequentially, end to end. When elements are in series, the current flows through them is the same. They are in parallel if they are connected to the same two nodes. Elements in parallel always have the same voltage across them.
头尾依次连接的两个元件称为串联,流过串联元件的电流相同。两个元件的两端连到相同的两个节点上称为并联,并联元件两端的电压相同。

3 Resistors in series behave as a single resistor whose resistance equals to the sum of the resistances of the individual resistors. Conductances in parallel behave as a single conductance whose value is equal to the sum of the individual conductances.
多个电阻串联的等效电阻值等于各个电阻值的和。多个电阻并联的等效电导等于各个电导之和。

4 A source transformation is the process of replacing a voltage source in series with a resistor by a current source in parallel with a resistor, or vice versa.
电源变换是用带并联电阻的电流源取代带串联电阻的电压源(或者反之)的一种转换过程。

第三节 电阻电路的一般分析
Section 3 Methods of General Analysis in Resistive Circuits

并联电路 parallel circuit
★ 参考节点 reference node
串联电路 series circuit
对称网络 bilateral network
非平面电路 nonplanar circuit
附加方程 supplemented equation

广义节点　supernode
广义网孔　supermesh
★ 互导　mutual conductance
★ 互阻　mutual resistance
回路　loop
回路电流　loop current
★ 回路电流法　loop-current method
回路分析法　loop analysis method
节点　node
节点电压　node voltage
★ 节点电压法　node-voltage method
节点分析法　nodal analysis method
连通图　connected graph
连支　link
路径　path
平面电路　planar circuit
树　tree
树支　tree branch
图　graph
网孔　mesh
网孔电流　mesh current
★ 网孔电流法　mesh-current method
网孔分析法　mesh analysis
有伴电流源　accompanied current source
有伴电压源　accompanied voltage source
支路　branch
支路电流　branch current
支路电流法　branch-current method
支路电压　branch voltage

例1 A branch is a single two-terminal element in an electric circuit. A node is the point of connection between two or more branches. A loop is a closed path in a circuit. The number of branches b, the number of nodes n, and the number of independent loops l in a network are related as

$$b=l+n-1$$

支路是电路中的单个二端元件。节点是两个或两个以上支路的连接点。电路中的闭合路径叫回路。网络中的支路数 b，节点数 n 和独立回路数 l 满足如下关系：

$$b=l+n-1$$

例2 Mesh analysis is the application of Kirchhoff's voltage law around meshes in a planar circuit. We express the result in terms of mesh currents. Solving the simultaneous equations yields the mesh currents.

网孔分析法是平面电路中相连接的网孔电路应用基尔霍夫电压定律的方法，其结果用网孔电流表示。通过解联立方程组可得到各个网孔电流。

例3 Nodal analysis is the application of Kirchhoff's current law at the non-reference nodes. (It is applicable to both planar and nonplanar circuits.) We express the result in terms of the node voltages. Solving the simultaneous equations yields the node voltages.

节点分析法是基尔霍夫电流定律在非参考节点上的应用(它可应用于平面电路和非平面电路)，其结果用节点电压表示。通过解联立方程组可得到各个节点的电压。

例4 Nodal analysis is normally used when a circuit has fewer node equations than mesh equations. Mesh analysis is normally used when a circuit has fewer mesh equations than node equations.

节点分析法一般用于电路中节点方程比网孔方程少的情况。网孔分析法一般应用于电路中网孔方程比节点方程少的情况。

第四节　电路定理
Section 4　Circuit Theorems

原理　principle
定理　theorem
定律　law
变量　variable
★ 戴维宁等效电路　Thevenin equivalent circuit
戴维宁定理　Thevenin's theorem
等效电路　equivalent circuit
等效发电机　equivalent generator
★ 电流控制电流源　current-controlled current source (CCCS)
★ 电流控制电压源　current-controlled voltage source (CCVS)
电流源　current source
★ 电压控制电流源　voltage-controlled current

source (VCCS)
★ 电压控制电压源 voltage-controlled voltage source (VCVS)
电压源 voltage source
电压源内阻 internal resistance of voltage source
叠加原理 superposition principle
★ 独立电源 independent source
★ 对外等效 equivalent external to the conversion
二端电路 two-terminal circuit
非独立(受控)电源 dependent source/controlled source
非线性电路 nonlinear circuit
★ 负载 load
负载效应 loading effect
工作电压 working voltage
互易定理 reciprocity theorem
互易条件 reciprocity condition
互易网络 reciprocity network
激励 excitation
★ 诺顿等效电路 Norton equivalent circuit
诺顿定理 Norton's theorem
匹配 matching
特勒根定理 Tellegen's theorem
特勒根功率定理 Tellegen's power theorem
特勒根似功率定理 Tellegen's quasi-power theorem
替代定理 substitution theorem
线性电路 linear circuit
线性对称电路 linear bilateral circuit
线性值 linear quantity
线性组合 linear combination
响应 response
原电路 original circuit
★ 最大功率传输 maximum power transfer

1 Network theorems are used to reduce a complex circuit to a simpler one, thereby making circuit analysis much simpler.
网络的若干定理用于将复杂电路转化为简单电路，从而使电路分析更为简易。

2 The superposition principle states that the voltage across (or current through) an element in a linear circuit is the algebraic sum of the voltages across (or currents through) that element due to each independent source acting alone.
叠加原理：在线性电路中，任一器件上的电压或电流都是电路中各个独立电源单独作用时在该处产生的电压或电流的叠加。

3 Substitution theorem states that any branch within a circuit may be replaced by an equivalent branch, provided the replacement branch has the same current through it and voltage across it as the original branch.
替代定理：给定电路的任一支路都可由一等效支路来替代，替代支路的电流和电压均与原支路的值相同。

4 Thevenin's theorem states that a linear two-terminal circuit can be replaced by an equivalent circuit consisting of a voltage source V_{Th} in series with a resistor R_{Th}, where V_{Th} is the open-circuit voltage at the terminals and R_{Th} is the input or equivalent resistance at the terminals when the independent sources are turned off.
戴维宁定理：线性二端电路可以由一个等效电路来取代，该电路由一个电压源 V_{Th} 与一个电阻 R_{Th} 串联组成。其中，V_{Th} 等于二端电路的开路电压，R_{Th} 等于独立电源置零后的输入或等效电阻。

5 Norton's theorem states that a linear two-terminal circuit can be replaced by an equivalent circuit consisting of a current source I_N in parallel with a resistor R_N, where I_N is the short-circuit current through the terminals and R_N is the input or equivalent resistance at the terminals when the independent sources are turned off.
诺顿定理：线性二端电路可以被一个由一个电流源 I_N 与一个电阻 R_N 并联组成的等效电路取代，其中，I_N 等于流过端点的短路电流，R_N 等于独立电源置零后的输入或等效电阻。

6 For a given Thevenin equivalent circuit, maximum power transfer occurs when $R_L = R_{Th}$, that is, when the load resistance is equal to the Thevenin resistance.
对于一个给定的戴维宁等效电路，当负载电阻等于戴维宁电阻时，即 $R_L = R_{Th}$，传递到负载上的功率最大。

第五节　含有运算放大器的电阻电路
Section 5　Resistive Circuits with Operational Amplifiers

差动输入　differential mode input
差动输入电压　differential input voltage
★倒向比例电路　inverting-amplifier circuit
反向放大器　inverting amplifier
反向输入端　inverting input terminal
电压传输特性　voltage transfer characteristic
★电压跟随器　voltage follower
反相输入　inverting input
放大电路　amplifier circuit
负电源　negative power supply
负反馈　negative feedback
公共端　common node
集成电路　integrated circuit
加法电路　summing circuit
晶体管　transistor
运算放大器　operational amplifier(op amp)
开环电压增益　open-loop voltage gain
★开环增益　open-loop gain
★理想运算放大器　ideal op amp
★输出电压　output voltage
★输入电压　input voltage
输入阻抗　input impedance
同相输入　noninverting input
同相输入端　noninverting input terminal
线性区　linear region
虚短　virtual short
增益　gain
正电源　positive power supply

1 An op amp is an active circuit element designed to perform mathematical operations of addition, subtraction, multiplication, division, differentiation and integration.
运算放大器是一个有源电路器件,用于进行诸如加减乘除、微分、积分等运算。

2 The op amp is a high-gain amplifier that has high input resistance and low output resistance.
运算放大器是一个高增益放大器,其输入电阻很大,而输出电阻很小。

3 An ideal op amp is an amplifier with infinite open-loop gain, infinite input resistance, and zero output resistance.
理想运算放大器是开环增益为无穷大、输入电阻为无穷大、输出电阻为零的运算放大器。

4 Two important characteristics of the ideal op amp are:
(1) The currents into both input terminals are zero.
(2) The voltage across the input terminals is negligibly small.
理想运算放大器有两个重要特性:
(1)流入两个输入端的电流均为零;
(2)两个输入端之间的电压很小,可以忽略不计。

5 In an inverting amplifier, the output voltage is a negative multiple of the input.
反相放大器中输出电压是输入电压乘以负的倍数。

6 In a noninverting amplifier, the output voltage is a positive multiple of the input.
同相放大器中输出电压是输入电压乘以正的倍数。

7 In a voltage follower, the output follows the input.
电压跟随器:其输出电压等于(跟随)输入电压。

8 Op amp circuits may be cascaded without changing their input-output relationships.
运算放大电路可以级联,且不影响自身的输入-输出关系。

第六节　一阶电路
Section 6　First-order Circuits

★RC(电阻-电容)电路　RC (resistor-capacitor) circuit
★RL(电阻-电感)电路　RL(resistor-inductor) circuit
保险丝　fuse
超前　advance/ lead
冲激函数　impulse function

冲激响应　impulse response
初始电压　initial voltage
初值　initial value
储能元件　storage element/energy-storage element
单位冲激函数　unit impulse function
单位阶跃函数　unit step function
电池　battery cell
电介质　dielectric
电路符号　circuit symbol
电路图　circuit diagram
电通量　electric flux
动态元件　dynamic element
断路器　circuit breaker
发电机　generator
干电池　dry cell
换路　switching
记忆元件　memory element
奇函数　odd function
阶跃函数　step function
★ 阶跃响应　step response
介电常数　permittivity
绝缘体　insulator
开关　switch
开关函数　switching function
连续的　continuous
★ 零输入响应　source-free response
零状态　zero state
★ 零状态响应　zero-state response
偶函数　even function
奇异函数　singularity function
★ 强迫响应　forced response
强制分量　forced component
取样性质　sampling property
★ 全响应　complete response
筛分性质　sifting property
时间常数　time constant
衰减　decay
衰减常数　attenuation constant
特解　particular solution
特征方程　characteristic equation
特征根　characteristic root
★ 稳态响应　steady-state response
稳态值　steady-state value
无记忆元件　memoryless element
★ 无源/零输入 RC 电路　source-free RC circuit
★ 无源/零输入 RL 电路　source-free RL circuit
无源电路元件　passive circuit element
无源线性元件　passive linear element
线性元件　linear element
一阶常微分方程式　first-order ordinary differential equation
一阶电路　first-order circuit
云母　mica
暂态/瞬变状态　transient state
暂态分量　transient component
暂态分析　transient analysis
★ 暂态响应　transient response
直流电流源　DC current source
直流电压源　DC voltage source
指数规律衰减　exponential decay
滞后　delay/ lag
终值　final value
★ 自然响应　natural response
自由分量　free component

The analysis in this section is applicable to any circuit that can be reduced to an equivalent circuit that is made up of a resistor and a single energy-storage element (inductor or capacitor). Such a circuit is first-order because its behavior is described by a first-order differential equation. When analyzing RC and RL circuits, one must always keep in mind that the capacitor is an open circuit in steady-state DC conditions while the inductor is a short circuit to steady-state DC conditions.

本节对电路的分析方法适用于任何电路，即最终可简化为由一个电阻和一个储能元件(电感或电容)组成的等效电路的任何电路。这种电路是一阶电路，因为其特性可以用一阶微分方程来描述。分析 RC 和 RL 电路时，不要忘记，在稳态直流条件下的电容器相当于开路，而电感器则相当于短路。

The time constant of a circuit is the time required for the response to decay by a factor of 1/e or 36.8 percent of its initial value. The time constant of an RL circuit equals the equivalent inductance divided by the Thevenin resistance as viewed from the terminals of the equivalent inductor. The time constant of an RC circuit equals the equivalent capacitance multiplied by the Thevenin resistance as viewed from the terminals of the equivalent capacitor.

电路的时间常数是电路响应衰减到初始值的 1/e 或 36.8%时所需要的时间。RL 电路的时间常数等于等效电感除以等效电感两端看到的戴维宁电阻。RC 电路的时间常数等于等效电容乘以等效电容两端看到的戴维宁电阻。

3. In the presence of a DC current, an inductor behaves like a short circuit. In the presence of a DC voltage, a capacitor behaves like an open circuit.
对于直流电流，电感表现为短路。对于直流电压，电容表现为开路。

4. Capacitive voltages and inductive currents are continuous; that is, they have the same value at $t=t_{0-}$ and $t=t_{0+}$, where $t=t_{0-}$ denotes the time just before a switching event, and $t=t_{0+}$ is the time just after the switching event, assuming that the switching event takes place at $t=0$.
电容电压和电感电流是连续的，即它们在 $t=t_{0-}$ 和 $t=t_{0+}$ 时刻具有相同的值。式中 $t=t_{0-}$ 表示开关动作之前的瞬间，$t=t_{0+}$ 表示开关动作之后的瞬间，并假设开关动作时刻为 $t=0$。

5. The natural response or transient response is the circuit's temporary response that will die out with time. The forced response or steady-state response is the behavior of the circuit a long time after an external excitation is applied. The total or complete response consists of the natural response and the forced response.
自然响应或暂态响应是电路的临时响应，它将随时间的延长而消失。强迫响应或稳态响应是加上外部激励后的电路长时间的行为特征。电路的完全响应由其自然响应和强迫响应组成。

6. The natural response is obtained when no independent source is present. It has the general form as

$$x(t)=x(0)e^{-t/\tau}$$

where x represents current through (or voltage across) a resistor, a capacitor, or an inductor, and $x(0)$ is the initial value of x.
对于没有独立电源的电路，其响应为自然响应(或暂态响应)，它的一般形式为：

$$x(t)=x(0)e^{-t/\tau}$$

这里 x 表示流过电阻、电容或电感的电流，或者表示电阻、电容或电感两端的电压。$x(0)$是 x 的初始值。

7. The step response is the response of the circuit to a sudden application of a DC current or voltage. Finding the step response of a first-order circuit requires the initial value $x(t_0^+)$, the final value $x(\infty)$, and the time constant τ. With these three items, we obtain the step response as

$$x(t)=x(\infty)+[x(t_0^+)-x(\infty)]e^{-t/\tau}$$

A more general form of this equation is

$$x(t)=x(\infty)+[x(t_0^+)-x(\infty)]e^{-(t-t_0)/\tau}$$

Or we may write it as

$$\text{Instantaneous value} = \text{Final} + [\text{Initial}-\text{Final}]\ e^{-(t-t_0)/\tau}$$

阶跃响应是电路突然加上一个直流电流或电压时的电路响应。要得到一阶电路的阶跃响应需要知道初始值 $x(t_0^+)$、终止值 $x(\infty)$和时间常数 τ。有了这三个值，则阶跃响应是：

$$x(t)=x(\infty)+[x(t_0^+)-x(\infty)]e^{-t/\tau}$$

更一般的表达式为：

$$x(t)=x(\infty)+[x(t_0^+)-x(\infty)]e^{-(t-t_0)/\tau}$$

或可写成：

$$\text{瞬时值}=\text{终值}+[\text{初值}-\text{终值}]e^{-(t-t_0)/\tau}$$

第七节　二阶电路

Section 7　Second-order Circuits

RLC 并联电路　parallel RLC circuit
RLC 串联电路　series RLC circuit
二阶电路的冲激响应　impulse response of second-order circuit
★ 二阶电路的阶跃响应　step response of second-order circuit

二阶微分方程　second-order differential equation
根　root
共轭复根　complex conjugate root
★ 过阻尼响应　overdamped response
★ 临界阻尼响应　critically damped response
临界阻尼情形　critically damped case
★ 欠阻尼响应　underdamped response
微分方程　differential equation
无源/零输入 RLC 并联电路　source-free RLC parallel circuit
★ 无源/零输入 RLC 串联电路　source-free RLC series circuit
振荡情形/欠阻尼情形　oscillatory case (underdamped case)
阻尼比　damping ratio

1 A second-order circuit is characterized by a second-order differential equation. It consists of resistors and the equivalent of two energy storage elements.
二阶电路可以由二阶微分方程来描述。它由电阻器和两个等效的储能元件组成。

2 The determination of the initial values $x(0)$ and $dx(0)/\mathrm{d}t$ and final value $x(\infty)$ is crucial to analyzing second-order circuits.
分析二阶电路的关键是确定初值 $x(0)$ 和 $dx(0)/dt$ 及终值 $x(\infty)$。

3 The RLC circuit is second-order because it is described by a second-order differential equation. Its characteristic equation is $s^2+2\alpha s+\omega_0^2=0$, where α is the damping factor and ω_0 is the undamped natural frequency, and for a series circuit, $\alpha=R/2L$, and for a parallel circuit, $\alpha=1/2RC$, and for both cases, $\omega_0=1\sqrt{LC}$.
RLC 电路是二阶电路是因为它可以由一个二阶微分方程描述，其特征方程为：$s^2+2\alpha s+\omega_0^2=0$，这里 α 是阻尼系数，ω_0 是无阻尼自然频率。对于串联电路 $\alpha=R/2L$，对于并联电路 $\alpha=1/2RC$，两种情况下均有 $\omega_0=1\sqrt{LC}$。

4 If there are no independent sources in the circuit after switching (or a sudden change), we regard the circuit as source-free. The complete response is the natural response.
如果在换路或突然改变后电路中没有独立电源，我们可以把电路看成是无源的，电路的全响应是自然响应。

5 The natural response of an RLC circuit is overdamped, underdamped, or critically damped, depending on the roots of the characteristic equation. The response is critically damped when the roots are equal ($s_1=s_2$ *or* $\alpha=\omega_0$), overdamped when the roots are real and unequal ($s_1\neq s_2$ *or* $\alpha>\omega_0$), or underdamped when the roots are complex conjugate ($s_1=s_2^*$ *or* $\alpha<\omega_0$).
一个 RLC 电路的自然响应是过阻尼、欠阻尼还是临界阻尼取决于特征方程的根。当根是两个相等根($s_1=s_2$ 或 $\alpha=\omega_0$)时是临界阻尼响应。当根是两个不相等的实根($s_1\neq s_2$ 或 $\alpha>\omega_0$)时是过阻尼响应。当根是一对共轭复根($s_1=s_2^*$ 或 $\alpha<\omega_0$)时是欠阻尼响应。

6 If independent sources are present in the circuit after switching, the complete response is the sum of the natural response and the forced or steady-state response.
如果换路后电路中有独立电源，电路的全响应是自然响应和受迫(稳态)响应之和。

第八节　相量法
Section 8　Phasor Method

★ 参考相量　reference phasor
初相　initial phase
★ 电流相量　current phasor
★ 电路元件方程的相量形式　phasor relations for circuit elements
★ 电压相量　voltage phasor
反相　opposite phase
幅值/振幅　amplitude
幅频特性　amplitude-frequency characteristic
幅值相量　amplitude phasor
复平面　complex-number plane
极坐标形式　polar form
角频率　angular frequency
欧拉公式　Euler's formula
频率　frequency
时域　time domain

实部　real part
同相　in-phase
相角　phase angle
★ 相量　phasor
相量法　phasor method
★ 相量图　phasor diagram
相频特性　phase-frequency characteristic
★ 相位差　phase difference
虚部　imaginary part
异相　out of phase
正弦函数　sinusoidal function
直角坐标形式　rectangular form
指数形式　exponential form

1 A sinusoid is a signal that has the form of the sine or cosine function.
正弦量是有正弦或余弦函数形式的信号。

2 A phasor is a complex number that represents the amplitude and phase of a sinusoid. Given the sinusoid $u(t)=U_m\cos(\omega t+\phi)$, its phasor $\dot{U}$ is

$$\dot{U}=U_m\angle\phi$$

相量是一个复数,能表示正弦量的幅值和相位。给定正弦量 $u(t)=U_m\cos(\omega t+\phi)$,其相量$\dot{U}$是:

$$\dot{U}=U_m\angle\phi$$

3 In AC circuits, voltage and current phasors always have a fixed relation to one another at any moment of time. If $u(t)=U_m\cos(\omega t+\phi_u)$ represents the voltage through an element and $i(t)=I_m\cos(\omega t+\phi_i)$ represents the current through an element, then $\phi_i=\phi_u$ if the element is a resistor, ϕ_i leads ϕ_u by 90° if the element is a capacitor, and ϕ_i lags ϕ_u by 90° if the element is an inductor.
在交流电路中,电压和电流的相量在任何时刻(瞬间)都有将它们联系起来的固定关系。若 $u(t)=U_m\cos(\omega t+\phi_u)$表示元件两端的电压,$i(t)=I_m\cos(\omega t+\phi_i)$表示流过该元件的电流,则:若该元件是电阻,那么 $\phi_i=\phi_u$;若是电容器,那么 ϕ_i超前于 ϕ_u90°;若是电感器,那么 ϕ_i滞后于 ϕ_u90°。

4 Basic circuit laws (Ohm's and Kirchhoff's) apply to AC circuits in the same manner as they do for DC circuits.
电路的基本定律(欧姆定律和基尔霍夫定律)也适用于交流电路,其形式与直流电路中的基本定律一样。

5 The differences between $u(t)$ and $\dot{U}$ should be emphasized:
(1) $u(t)$ is the instantaneous or time-domain representation, while $\dot{U}$ is the frequency or phasor-domain representation.
(2) $u(t)$ is time dependent, while $\dot{U}$ is not. (This fact is often forgotten by students.)
(3) $u(t)$ is always real with no complex term, while $\dot{U}$ is generally complex.
注意以下几点 $u(t)$与 $\dot{U}$的差别:
(1) $u(t)$是瞬时或时域的表示,而 $\dot{U}$是频率或相量域的表示。
(2) $u(t)$是与时间有关的,而 $\dot{U}$与时间无关(这一点学生常常不注意)。
(3) $u(t)$总是实数且没有复数项,而$\dot{U}$一般都为复数。

第九节　正弦稳态电路的分析
Section 9　Sinusoidal Steady-state Analysis

并联谐振　parallel resonance
并联谐振阻抗　parallel resonance impedance
波形　waveform
串联谐振　series resonance
串联谐振阻抗　series resonance impedance
代数形式　algebraic form
带宽,通频带　bandwidth
★ 导纳　admittance
★ 导纳三角形　admittance triangle
等效变换　equivalent transformation
★ 等效导纳　equivalent admittance
等效电抗　equivalent reactance

等效电纳　equivalent susceptance
★ 等效阻抗　equivalent impedance
电度表　watthour meter
电抗　reactance
电流方向　current direction
电路选择性　selectivity of the circuit
电纳　susceptance
电位计　potentiometer
电压符号　voltage symbol
电压极性　voltage polarity
电阻性阻抗　resistive impedance
动态电路　dynamic circuit
动态电阻　dynamic resistance
动态线路　dynamic route
动态元件　dynamic element
端点电压　terminal voltage
额定电流　rated current
额定电压　rated voltage
额定功率　rated power
额定容量　rated capacity
峰值　peak value
★ 复功率　complex power
★ 复阻抗　complex impedance
感抗　inductive reactance
感纳　inductive susceptance
感性　inductive
感性阻抗　inductive impedance
功率三角形　power triangle
★ 功率因数　power factor
★ 功率因数补偿/校正　power factor correction
功率因数角　power factor angle
共轭匹配　conjugate matching
固定电阻　fixed resistor
固有频率/自然频率　natural frequency
计算机辅助电路分析　computer-aided circuit analysis
可变电阻　variable resistor
模拟电压表　analog voltmeter
能量守恒定律　law of conservation of energy
逆时针方向　anti-clockwise
欧姆表　ohmer
品质因数　quality factor
平均功率　average power
平均值　average value
千瓦时　kilowatt hour(kWh)
容抗　capacitive reactance
容纳　capacitive susceptance
容性　capacitive
容性阻抗　capacitive impedance
实际直流电流源　practical DC current source
实际直流电压源　practical DC voltage source
★ 视在功率　apparent power
数字电压表　digital voltmeter
顺时针方向　clockwise
瞬时功率　instantaneous power
瓦特表　wattmeter
无功分量　reactive component
无功伏安/乏　reactive volt-ampere(var)
★ 无功功率　reactive power
无源线性电路　passive linear circuit
★ 谐振电路　resonance circuit
谐振电路阻抗　resonant circuit impedance
★ 谐振频率　resonant frequency
★ 谐振阻抗　resonance impedance
选频特性　frequency-selection characteristic
有功分量　active component
★ 有功功率　active power
正弦量　sinusoid variable
正弦稳态　sinusoidal steady state
★ 正弦稳态响应　sinusoidal steady-state response
直流电阻　DC resistance
★ 阻抗　impedance
阻抗的并联　impedance in parallel
阻抗的串联　impedance in series
阻抗模　impedance module
阻抗三角形　impedance triangle

1 The impedance Z of a circuit is the ratio of phasor voltage across it to the phasor current through it. The admittance Y is the reciprocal of impedance. Impedances are combined in series or in parallel the same way as resistances in parallel; that is, impedances in series add while admittances in parallel add.

电路的阻抗 Z 是电路两端的电压相量与流过它的电流相量之比，导纳 Y 是阻抗的倒数。阻抗的串联和并联与电阻的串并联方法相同，即串联时阻抗相加，并联时导纳相加。

2 We apply nodal and mesh analysis to AC circuits by applying KCL and KVL to the phasor form of the

circuits.
由于 KCL 和 KVL 适用于电路的相量形式，所以，可以用节点电压法和网孔电流法等方法来分析交流电路。

3 Steps to analyze AC circuits:
(1) Transform the circuit to the phasor or frequency domain;
(2) Solve the problem using circuit techniques (nodal analysis, mesh analysis, superposition, etc.);
(3) Transform the resulting phasor to the time domain.
分析交流电路的步骤：
(1) 将电路转换到频域或相量域；
(2) 用各种电路技术(节点分析、网孔分析、叠加原理等)求解电路；
(3) 将频域的结果转换到时域。

4 The average power is the average of the instantaneous power over one period. The apparent power (in VA) is the product of the rms values of voltage and current. A resistive load (R) absorbs power at all times, while a reactive load (L or C) absorbs zero average power.
平均功率是一个周期内瞬时功率的平均值。视在功率(以 VA 单位)是电压和电流有效值的乘积。电阻负载(R)任何时候都吸收功率，而电抗负载 L 或 C 吸收的平均功率为零。

5 For maximum average power transfer, the load impedance must be equal to the complex conjugate of the Thevenin impedance.
最大平均功率传输条件是负载阻抗必须等于戴维宁阻抗的共轭复数。

6 The principle of conservation of AC power states that the complex, real and reactive powers of the sources equal the respective sums of the complex, real and reactive powers of the individual loads.
交流功率的守恒定理：电源的复功率、有功功率、无功功率等于它在各个单独负载上的复功率、有功功率、无功功率之和。

7 The power factor is the cosine of the phase difference between voltage and current:
$$\lambda = \mathrm{pf} = \cos(\theta_v - \theta_i)$$
It is also the cosine of the angle of the load impedance or the ratio of active power to apparent power. The pf is lagging if the current lags voltage (inductive load) and is leading when the current leads voltage (capacitive load).
功率因数是电压和电流相位差的余弦函数：
$$\lambda = \mathrm{pf} = \cos(\theta_v - \theta_i)$$
功率因数也是负载阻抗角的余弦函数，或者是有功功率与视在功率之比。若电流滞后于电压(电感性负载)，则 pf 是滞后的；若电流超前于电压(电容性负载)，则 pf 是超前的。

8 The process of increasing the power factor without altering the voltage or current to the original load is known as power factor correction. Power factor correction is necessary for economic reasons. It is the process of improving the power factor of a load by reducing the overall reactive power.
不改变原始负载的电压、电流而提高功率因数的过程称为功率因数的改进。从经济原因考虑，功率因数的提高是必需的。改进负载功率因数也就是降低了总的无功功率。

9 Resonance is a condition in an RLC circuit in which the capacitive and inductive reactances are equal in magnitude, thereby resulting in a purely resistive impedance.
谐振是 RLC 电路的一种状态，该电路中电容和电感的电抗大小是相等的，结果呈现出纯电阻的阻抗性质。

第十节　含有磁耦合电感的电路
Section 10　Magnetically Coupled Circuits

T 形网络　T-connected network
变比　transformation ratio
★ 变压器　transformer
★ 初级电路/原边　primary circuit

初级线圈 primary winding
磁场 magnetic field
磁链 flux linkage
磁耦合 magnetically couple
磁通 magnetic flux
★ 次级电路/副边 secondary circuit
次级线圈 secondary winding
电感串并联 series-parallel combination of inductance
电容串并联 series-parallel combination of capacitance
二端口耦合电感元件 two-port coupled inductors
★ 反接/反向串联 inversed connection/connection in opposition
反映阻抗 reflected impedance
符号 notation
★ 互感 mutual inductance
互感电抗 mutual inductive reactance
空心变压器 air-core transformer
空心线圈 air-core coil
理想变压器 ideal transformer
耦合电感元件 coupled inductor
耦合系数 coefficient of coupling
★ 耦合线圈 coupled coil
★ 顺接/正向串联 connection in aiding
四端元件 four-terminal component
铁芯线圈 iron-core coil
★ 同名端 dotted terminals
韦伯 Weber (Wb)
线圈匝数 number of turns on the coil
匝数比 turns ratio
自感 self-inductance

1 The polarity of the mutually induced voltage is expressed in the schematic by the dot convention. The dot convention is stated as follows: If a current enters the dotted terminal of one coil, the reference polarity of the mutual voltage in the second coil is positive at the dotted terminal of the second coil. Alternatively, if a current leaves the dotted terminal of one coil, the reference polarity of the mutual voltage in the second coil is negative at the dotted terminal of the second coil.

互感电压的极性在电路中的表达要遵守同名端规则。同名端规则是:若电流进入一个线圈的同名端,则在第二个线圈的同名端处,其互感电压的参考极性是正的。若电流离开一个线圈的同名端,则在第二个线圈的同名端处,其互感电压的参考极性是负的。

2 An ideal transformer is a unity-coupled, lossless transformer in which the primary and secondary coils have infinite self-inductances. A step-down transformer is one whose secondary voltage is less than its primary voltage. A step-up transformer is one whose secondary voltage is greater than its primary voltage.

理想变压器是无损耗而且其初级和次级线圈有无穷大自感量的全耦合变压器。降压变压器的次级电压小于其初级电压,升压变压器的次级电压大于其初级电压。

第十一节 三相电路
Section 11 Three-phase Circuit

ABC/或正/相序 abc/or positive/sequence
ACB/或负/相序 acb/or negative/sequence
a 相电压 a-phase voltage
b 相电压 b-phase voltage
c 相电压 c-phase voltage
Y-Y 电路 wye-wye(Y-Y) circuit
不对称三相电路 unbalanced three-phase circuit
传输线阻抗 transmission-line impedance
单相等效电路 single-phase equivalent circuit
★ 对称三相电路 balanced three-phase circuit
★ 两表法 two-wattmeter method
★ 三表法 three-wattmeter method
★ 三相电路 three-phase circuit
三相电源 three-phase voltage source
三相三线制 three-phase three-wire system
★ 三相四线制 three-phase four-wire system

三相制　three-phase system
瞬时电压　instantaneous voltage
★ 线电流　line current
★ 线电压　line voltage
★ 相电流　phase current
★ 相电压　phase voltage
中性线端　neutral terminal
中线　neutral wire

1 The phase sequence is the order in which the phase voltage of a three-phase generator occurs with respect to time. In an *ABC* sequence of balanced source voltages, $\dot{U}_{an}$ leads $\dot{U}_{bn}$ by 120°, which in turn leads $\dot{U}_{cn}$ by 120°. In an *ACB* sequence of balanced voltages, $\dot{U}_{an}$ leads $\dot{U}_{cn}$ by 120°, which in turn leads $\dot{U}_{bn}$ by 120°.

相序是三相发电机相电压产生的时间顺序。对称电压源的 *ABC* 相序情况是$\dot{U}_{an}$超前于$\dot{U}_{bn}$ 120°，$\dot{U}_{bn}$又超前于$\dot{U}_{cn}$ 120°。对称电压的 *ACB* 相序是$\dot{U}_{an}$超前于$\dot{U}_{cn}$ 120°，$\dot{U}_{cn}$又超前于$\dot{U}_{bn}$ 120°。

2 The easiest way to analyze a balanced three-phase circuit is to transform both the source and the load to a Y-Y system and then analyze the single-phase equivalent circuit. An unbalanced three-phase system can be analyzed using nodal or mesh analysis.

分析对称三相电路的最方便的方法是将电源和负载都转换成 Y-Y 系统，然后，再分析其单相等效电路。对于不对称三相系统的分析可以用节点电压法或网孔分析法。

3 The total instantaneous power in a balanced three-phase system is constant and equals to the average power.

对称三相系统的总瞬时功率是个常数，且等于其平均功率。

4 The total real power in three-phase systems is measured using either the three-wattmeter method or the two-wattmeter method.

三相系统总有功功率的测量可以用三表法，也可以用两表法。

第十二节　拉普拉斯变换
Section 12　The Laplace Transform

★ s 域的等效电路　s-domain equivalent
部分分式法/分解定理　partial fraction/expansion method
初始电流　initial current
★ 初始条件　initial condition
初值定理　initial-value theorem
单极点　simple pole
动态电路　dynamic circuit
分部积分法　integration by part
★ 附加电流源　appended current source
★ 附加电压源　appended voltage source
傅里叶变换　Fourier transform
积分性质　integration property
极点　pole
假分式　improper rational function
★ 拉普拉斯变换　Laplace transform
拉普拉斯变换对　Laplace transform pairs
拉普拉斯反变换　inverse Laplace transform
零初始条件　zero initial condition
零点　zero
留数法　residue method
频域函数　phasor domain function
时域函数　time domain function
实数单根　real simple root/distinct real root
收敛因子　convergence factor
完全配方法　completing the square
微分性质　differentiation property
线性性质　linearity property
延迟性质　time-delay property/time-shift property
一阶极点　first-order pole
有理真分式　proper rational function
原函数　original function
★ 运算导纳　operation admittance
★ 运算电路　operation circuit

运算法 operation method

★ 运算阻抗 operation impedance

展开系数 expansion coefficient

指数函数 exponential function

终值定理 final-value theorem

重极点 repeated pole

Steps in applying the Laplace transform:

(1) Transform the equivalent circuit from the time domain to the s-domain.

(2) Solve the circuit using nodal analysis, mesh analysis, source transformation, superposition, or any circuit analysis technique with which we are familiar.

(3) Take the Laplace inverse transform of the solution and thus obtain the solution in the time domain.

用拉普拉斯变换法分析电路的步骤:

(1)将电路从时域转换为 s 域的等效电路;

(2)用节点电压法、网孔电流法、电源变换原理、叠加原理以及所学过的其他电路分析技术求解电路;

(3)对得到的电路解进行拉普拉斯逆变换,最后得到电路的时域解。

第十三节 二端口网络

Section 13 Two-port Network

导抗 immittance

导纳参数 admittance parameter

导纳参数矩阵 admittance parameter matrix

短路导纳参数矩阵 short-circuit admittance parameter matrix

短路输出导纳 short-circuit output admittance

短路输入导纳 short-circuit input admittance

短路输入阻抗 short-circuit input impedance

短路转移导纳 short-circuit transfer admittance

对称的 symmetrical

★ 二端口网络 two-port network

二端口元件 two-port element

开路输出导纳 open-circuit output admittance

开路输出阻抗 open-circuit output impedance

开路输入阻抗 open-circuit input impedance

开路转移阻抗 open-circuit transfer impedance

开路阻抗参数矩阵 open-circuit impedance parameter matrix

驱动点导纳 driving-point admittance

驱动点阻抗 driving-point impedance

线性网络 linear network

一端口网络 one-port network

★ 转移导纳 transfer admittance

转移函数 transfer function

★ 转移阻抗 transfer impedance

阻抗参数 impedance parameter

阻抗参数矩阵 impedance parameter matrix

A two-port network is an electrical network with two separate ports for input and output. The six parameters used to model a two-port network are the impedance [z], admittance[y], hybrid[h], inverse hybrid [g], transmission [T], and inverse transmission [t] parameters. The two-port parameters can be calculated or measured by short-circuiting or open-circuiting, the appropriate input or output port.

二端口网络是一个有两个分开端口作为输入和输出的电子网络。有六个参数可描述双端口的性质:阻抗[z]、导纳[y]、混合[h]、逆混合[g]、传输[T]和逆传输[t]。双端口参数可以由短路或开路相应的输入或输出端口来计算或测量。

第二部分　实验

Part Two: Experiment

第××章　电路原理实验

Section ×× Experiments on Principle of Electric Circuit

Lab1: Kirchhoffs Law and Superposition Theorem

Type: Confirmatory

The experiment date: ×× ×× ×××× Place: ××

Professional Class: ×× Name: ××

Student No.: ×× Instructed by: ×× Term: ××

1. Objectives

Better understanding of Kirchhoff's Law and understanding of the content and scope of Superposition Theorem.

2. Equipments and Components Needed

DG013T, DY031T, and DG054－1T

3. Tasks and Procedure (Including schematic diagram)

(1) Experimental principle

Kirchhoff's Law is the basic of lumped circuit. It includes circuit law and voltage law.

$$\Sigma I = 0$$

Kirchhoff's current Law (KCL) states that in the lumped circuit, at any time, at any node, the algebraic sum of currents entering a node (or a closed boundary) is zero, namely:

$$\Sigma I = 0$$

$$\Sigma U = 0$$

Kirchhoff's Voltage Law (KVL) states that in the lumped circuit, any time, the algebraic sum of all voltages around any closed path (or loop) in a circuit equals zero, namely:

$$\Sigma U = 0$$

Superposition Theorem is an important theorem of linear circuits.

The Superposition Theorem states that the voltage across (or current through) an element in a linear circuit is the algebraic sum of the voltages across (or currents through) that element due to each independent source acting alone.

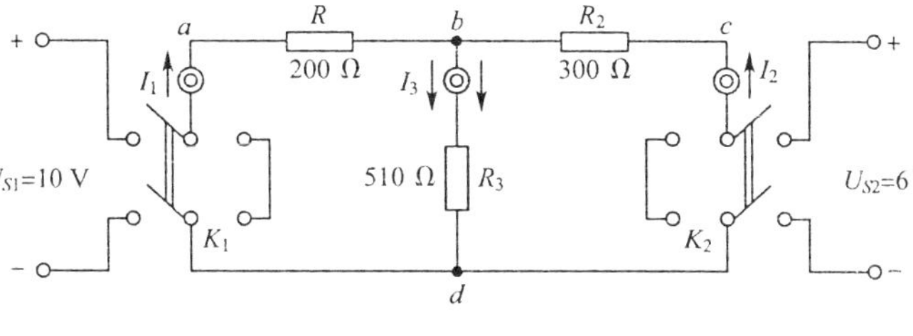

figure 1. Experimental Circuit

(2) Procedure

① Kirchhoff's Law

Connect the circuit as shown in Fig. 1. I_1, I_2, I_3 are circuit sockets, K_1, K_2 are double-pole-double-throw switches.

Turn K_1, K_2 to short circuit side, and regulate the regulated power supply, making $U_{S1}=10V$, $U_{S2}=6V$ (use 20v DC voltmeter of DG054－1T to measure the voltage output of DY031T respectively).

Turn K_1, K_2 to power supply side, measure and take notes with the parameters in Table 1 and Table 2 to verify Kirchhoff's Law.

Table 1. Kirchhoff Circuit Law

I1(mA)	I2(mA)	I3(mA)	Verifying node b: $\Sigma I=0$
15.7	－2.5	－13.2	$\Sigma I=0$

Table 2. Kirchhoff Voltage Law

Uab(V)	Ubc(V)	Ubd(V)	Uda(V)	Ucd(V)	Verifying $\Sigma U=0$	
					Loop abcda	Loop abda
3.18	0.81	6.82	－10.00	6.01	$\Sigma U=0$	$\Sigma U=0$

② Superposition Theorem

The experimental circuit is shown in Figure. 1.

Turn K_2 to short circuit side, K_1 to power supply side, and make U_{S1} function alone. The voltages across and currents through each of the elements were then measured and recorded in Table 3.

Turn K_1 to short circuit side, K_2 to power supply side, let the circuit be energized by U_{S2} only, then measure the circuits through and the voltages across each of the elements, and put them into Table 3.

The data of the two power suppliers functioning together can be taker from procedure 1.

Table 3. Superposition Theorem

	I_1(mA)	I_2(mA)	I_3(mA)	U_{ab}(V)	U_{bc}(V)	U_{bd}(V)
U_{S1} Functions alone	25.3	－16.1	－9.4	5.08	4.89	4.89
U_{S2} Functions alone	－9.7	13.4	－3.7	－1.96	－4.03	1.97
U_{S1}, U_{S2} Interaction	15.7	－2.5	－13.2	3.17	0.81	6.82
Verifying Superposition Priciple	25.3＋(－9.7) ＝15.6	－16.1＋13.4 ＝－2.7	－9.4＋(－3.7) ＝－13.1	3.12	0.86	6.86

4. Result Analysis

In Table 1, by the experimental data obtained: for node b, it met $\Sigma I = I_1 + I_2 + I_3 = 0$. The experimental KCL results verified KCL. That is, in the lumped circuit, at any time, the algebraic sum of all branches currents entering a node equals zero constantly.

In Table 2, for loop abcda $U_{ab}+U_{bc}+U_{cd}+U_{da}=3.18+0.81+6.01+(-10.00)=0$. Verifying Kirchhoff's voltage law was established. That is in the lumped circuit, at any time, the algebraic sum of all the voltages around any closed path (loop or mesh) is zero.

The experimental Superposition Theorem results shown in Table 3 did not meet the predicted values. All the equations produced values within 0.5 volt(or ampere) away from the measured values, but the errors were still small enough to conclude that Superposition Theorem is valid.

第二章　数字电子技术
Chapter 2　Digital Electronics Technology

课程简介

数字电子技术是所有电子工程和大部分理科专业的基础课之一。数字电子中的信号是模拟信号的离散带，而不是一个连续的范围。在一个离散带里，所有的值都代表同一个状态。在大多数情况下，只有两种状态，它们分别代表两个不同的电压带：一个是接近参考电压（通常称为“地”或0电位），另一个接近电源电压，在布尔域中分别对应着“假”(0)和“真”(1)。

“数字”这个术语来源于计算机通过计数完成的操作方式。多年以来数字电子技术仅限于计算机系统的应用。时至今日，数字技术已经在很多领域都得到了广泛的应用。例如，电视、通信系统、雷达、航空及导航系统、军事系统、医疗器械、工业过程控制以及日常电子产品。

Course Summary

Digital electronics is one of the fundamental courses found in all electrical engineering and most science programs. Signals in digital electronics represent the discrete bands of analog levels, rather than a continuous range, all levels within a discrete band represent the same signal state. In most cases, there are only two states, representing two voltage bands: one near a reference value (typically termed as “ground” or zero volts) and the other near the supply voltage, corresponding to the “false” (0) and “true” (1) values of the Boolean domain respectively.

The term digital is derived from the way computers perform operations, by counting digits. For many years, applications of digital electronics were confined to computer systems. Today, digital technology is applied in a wide range of areas. Such applications as television, communications systems, radar, navigation and guidance systems, military systems, medical instrumentation, industrial process control, and consumer electronics.

第一节　绪论
Section 1　Introduction

模拟信号　analog signal
★ 数字信号　digital signals
★ 逻辑电平　logic level
上升时间　rise time
下降时间　fall time
周期性的　seasonal
调幅　amplitude modulation
调频　frequency modulation
离散信号　discrete signal
连续信号　continuous signal
量化　quantification
★ 波形　waveform
脉冲重复频率　pulse repetition rate (PRR)
比特率　bit rate
二值数字逻辑　binary digital logic
时序图　timing diagram
★ 晶体管—晶体管逻辑
transistor-transistor logic (TTL)
★ 互补金属氧化物半导体
complementary metal-oxide-semiconductor (CMOS)
★ 占空比　duty ratio
权　weights
二进制编码的十进制数
binary-coded-decimals (BCD)
补码　complement code
反码　one's complement
余三码　excess three code
格雷码　Gray code
符号数　signed number
无符号数　unsigned number
负号　minus sign
正号　plus sign
溢出　overflow
最高位　most significant digit (MSD)
最低位　least significant digit (LSD)
基数　radix

Electronic circuits can be divided into two broad categories: digital and analog. Digital electronics involves quantities with discrete values, and analog electronics involves quantities with continuous values. Although you will be studying the fundamentals of digital quantity in this book, you should also know about analog because many applications require both.
电路可分为两大类:数字电路和模拟电路。数字电路包括以离散值表示的量,模拟电路则包括连续值表示的量。尽管在本书中我们将学习数字量的基本原理,也需要知道模拟量的知识,因为许多应用两者都会用得上。

Decimal to Binary Conversion: Divide the decimal number to be converted successively by 2, ignoring the remainders, until you have a quotient of 0. The remainders will be used later to determine the answer.
十进制转换成二进制的方法:将要转换的十进制数连续地被 2 除,每一步的余数先不考虑,直到商为 0,然后可以根据每一步得到的余数求出二进制数。

第二节 逻辑代数基础

Section 2 Logic Algebra Foundation

★ 布尔代数 Boolean algebra
★ 与 and
★ 或 or
★ 非 no
★ 与非 nand
★ 或非 nor
★ 与或非 and-or-invert
异或 exclusive-or
同或 exclusive-nor/nonexclusive or
★ 组合逻辑 combinational logic
逻辑函数 logic function
★ 逻辑变量 logic variable
逻辑常量 logic constant
★ 逻辑符号 logic symbol
★ 逻辑表达式 logic expression
★ 真值表 truth table
★ 最小项 miniterm
最大项 maxterm
相邻项 adjacency
特征方程 characteristic equation
反函数 inverse function
乘积项 product term
恒等式 identity
交换率 commutative rate
结合率 associative rate
分配率 distributive rate
摩根定理 de Morgan's theorem
对偶函数 dual function
反演规则 complementary operation theorem
★ 化简 simplification
★ 卡诺图 Karnaugh map
★ 无关项 don't care terms
奇偶发生/检验器 parity generation /checker
偶校验 even
奇校验 odd
竞争冒险 race and hazard

Boolean algebra: Boolean algebra which was formulated by George Boole, an English mathematician (1815-1864), described propositions whose outcome would be either true or false. In computer work it is used in addition to describe circuits whose state can be either 1 (true) or 0 (false).
布尔代数:布尔代数由英国数学家乔治·布尔(1815—1864)创立,用来描述结果只有真或假两种结果的命题。在计算机中,它还用来描述电路的两种状态 1(真)或 0(假)。

Miniterm: A product term in which all the variables show exactly once, either complemented or uncomplemented, is called a miniterm. Its characteristic property is that it represents exactly one combination of the binary variables in a truth table. It has the value 1 for that combination and 0 for all others.
最小项:在乘积项中,所有的变量都以原变量或反变量的形式出现一次,且只出现一次,则该乘积项称作最小项。最小项的特点是它只与真值表中二进制变量的一组取值组合相对应,只有该组合取值才使其为 1,其他的组合项取值都为 0。

第三节　逻辑门电路

Section 3　Logic Gate Circuit

★ 二极管　diode
三极管　bipolar junction transistor (BJT)
多级与非门电路　multilevel nand circuit
反向恢复时间　reverse recovery time
二输入与门　two-input and gate
门阵列　gate array
三极管—三极管电路
transistor-transistor logic(TTL)
动态特性　dynamic characteristics
图腾柱　totem pole
★ 三态门　three state gate
集电极开路　open collector
干扰信号　disturbance signal
工作点　operating point
上拉电阻　pull-up resister
开启电压　threshold voltage
开关时间　switching time
开关特性　switching characteristics
多发射极三极管　multiemitter transistor
拉电流　draw-off current
有源下拉电路　active pull-down circuit
扇出　fan out
扇入　fan in
射极耦合　emitter-coupled
功耗　power dissipation
延时—功耗积
time delay-power dissipation product
饱和电流　saturation current
★ 线与　wire-and
★ 噪声容限　noise margin
临界　critical
高阻态　high impedance state
传输延迟时间　propagation delay time
传输特性　transfer characteristics
片选　chip select
正逻辑　positive logic
负逻辑　negative logic
肖特基二极管　Schottky diode
★ 反相器　inverter
双列直插式封装　dual in-line package (DIP)
传输门　transmission gate (TG)
模拟开关　analog switch

注1 Three state gate: The three-state, tri-state, or 3-state logic allows output ports to assume a high impedance state in addition to the fundamental 0 level and 1 level, effectively "removing" the output from the circuit. This allows multiple circuits to share the same output line or lines (such as a bus).
三态门：三态或三态逻辑，允许输出端除了输出 0 状态和 1 状态之外，还可输出一个高阻态。这个高阻态可以有效地将输出从电路中"移除"。这就允许多个电路共享一条或多条输出线(类似总线)。

注2 Positive and Negative Logic: Except during transition, the binary signals at the inputs and outputs of any gate have one of two values: H or L. One value represents logic 1 and the other logic 0. Choosing the high level H to represent logic 1 defines a positive-logic-system. Choosing the low level L to represent logic 1 defines a negative-logic-system.
正逻辑和负逻辑：除了在传输的过程中，一个二进制信号在所有门电路的输入和输出端都只有两种取值：高电平或低电平，一个代表逻辑 1，另一个代表逻辑 0。如果用高电平代表逻辑 1，则是正逻辑系统，如果用低电平代表逻辑 1，则是负逻辑系统。

第四节　基础组合逻辑电路

Section 4　Combinational Logic Circuit

小规模集成电路　small-scale integrated circuit (SSI)
★ 中规模集成电路
medium-scale integrated circuit (MSI)
大规模集成电路　large-scale integrated circuit (LSI)
超大规模集成电路
very large-scale integrated circuit (VLSI)
专用集成电路
application specific integrated circuit
功能表　function table
管脚　pin
编码　coding
★ 编码器　encoder
★ 译码器　decoder

★ 二——十进制译码器 BCD decoder
★ 优先编码器 priority encoder
多路数据选择器 multiplexer
多路数据分配器 demultiplexer
数码比较器 magnitude comparator
码制转换器 code converter
数码显示器 digital display
★ 使能端 enable
约束 inhibit
★ 扩展 expansion
译码器 decoder
辉光数码管 glow discharge nixie tube
荧光数码管 fluorescent nixie tube
七段显示器 seven-segment display
液晶显示器 liquid crystal display (LCD)
加数 addend
被加数 augend
进位 carry
来自低位进位 carry-in
向高位进位 carry-out
★ 半加器 half adder
★ 全加器 full adder
串行进位加法器 ripple carry adder
并行加法器 parallel adder
减法器 subtracter
借位 borrow
被减数 minuend
减数 subtrahend
差 difference
超前进位加法器 look-ahead carry adder
超前进位产生器 look-ahead carry generator
算术逻辑单元 arithmetic logic unit (ALU)
函数产生器 function generator

1 Decoder: A decoder is a combinational circuit that covers binary information from the n coded inputs to a maximum of 2^n unique outputs. If the n-bit coded information has unused bit combinations, the decoder may have fewer than 2^n output.
译码器:译码器是能将 n 位二进制数表示的特定信息"翻译"出来的一种组合电路。全译码的译码器有 2^n个输出端,一个输出端对应一个最小项。如果 n 位二进制数有没用到的组合,则输出端的个数会小于 2^n。

2 Encoder: An encoder is a combinational logic circuit that essentially performs a "reverse" decoder function. An encoder accepts an active level on one of its inputs representing a digit, such as a decimal or octal digit, and converts it to a coded output, such as binary or BCD.
编码器:编码器基本上是与译码器函数相反的一个组合电路。当编码器的一个输入端输入有效电平时,它代表一个数字,可以是十进制数也可以是八进制数,然后编码器把它转换成二进制或十进制代码输出。

第五节 锁存器和触发器
Section 5 Latch and Flip-Flop

★ 时序电路 sequential circuit
★ D 锁存器 D latch
时钟触发器 clocked flip-flop
★ 时钟信号 clock signal
★ 脉冲 pulse
基本 RS 触发器 basic RS flip-flop
主从触发器 master-slave flip-flop
★ 边沿 edge
★ 触发 trigger
电平触发 level trigger
★ 上升沿 rise edge
★ 下降沿 fall edge
正边沿 positive edge
负边沿 negative edge
同步触发器 synchronous flip-flop
翻转 overturn
★ 复位 reset
★ 置位 set
★ 清零 clear
机械开关 mechanical on-off
抖动 dithering
未定义 undefined
图形符号 graphics symbol
延迟 postpone
★ 特性表 characteristic table
★ 驱动方程 driving equation
★ 初始状态 initial state
可能状态 potential state
保持时间 hold time

D-Latch: Latch is an electronic device that can be used to store one bit of information. The D latch is used to capture, or 'latch' the logic level which is present on the data line when the clock input is high. If the data on the D line changes state while the clock pulse is high, then the output changes following the input.

D锁存器：锁存器是一种能用来存储一位信息的电子设备。当时钟输入是高电平时，D锁存器用来捕捉或"锁存"数据线上的逻辑电平值。在时钟脉冲是高电平期间，如果数据线上的数据发生了变化，那么输出端也会随着输入的变化而变化。

Master-Slave Flip-Flop: The Master-Slave Flip-Flop consists of two grade Flip-Flop. One receive the input signals and its state is determined by input is called the Master, and the other, its input is linked up with Master's output and its state is determined by the Master's state is called the Slave.

主从触发器：主从触发器由两级触发器构成，其中一个接收输入信号，它的状态直接受输入的控制，称为主触发器。另一个的输入端与主触发器的输出端相连，它的状态受主触发器的控制，称为从触发器。

第六节　时序逻辑电路
Section 6　Sequential Logic Circuit

反馈　feedback
存储电路　memory circuit
异步时序电路　asynchronous sequential circuit
★ 同步时序电路　synchronous sequential circuit
★ 激励表　excitation table
串行输入　serial input
★ 现态　present state
★ 次态　next state
★ 状态表　state table
★ 状态图　state diagram
状态转换　state convert
闭合回路　closed circuit
状态化简　state simplification
等价状态　equivalence state
无效状态　invalid state
★ 模　module
翻转触发器　toggle flip-flop
保持、有效　hold
手册、指南　manuals
移位寄存器　shift register
★ 频率计　frequency counter
并入串出　parallel-in serial-out
字节　byte
总线　bus
★ 二进制计数器　binary counter
★ 递增-递减计数器　up-down counter
★ 分频　frequency division
★ 可逆计数器　reversible counter
启动　startup
计数模式　counter mode
环形计数器　orbicular counter
双向移位寄存器　bidirectional shift register

Sequential Logic Circuit: The behavior of a sequential logic circuit is determined by the input, output, and present state of the circuit. The output and the next state are a function of the inputs and the present state.

时序逻辑电路：时序逻辑电路的行为不仅仅受输入信号的影响，还受电路的输出信号和现态的影响。其输出信号和次态是输入信号和现态的函数。

Register: A register includes a set of flip-flops. Since each flip-flop is capable of storing one bit of information, an n-bit register, including n flip-flops, is capable of storing n bit of binary information. In a broader sense, a register consists of a set of flip-flops, together with gates that implement their state.

寄存器：寄存器包括一组触发器。因为一个触发器能存储一位二进制信息，所以n位寄存器包含n个触发器，能存储n位二进制信息。从广义上讲，寄存器由触发器和门电路组成，它们一起决定寄存器的状态。

第七节 脉冲波形的产生与整形

Section 7 Pulse Waveform Generation and Transform

滞后 hysteresis
★ 不稳多谐振荡器 astable multivibrator
振荡周期 oscillation
★ 阈值电平 threshold level
石英晶体振荡器 crystal oscillator
微分型 differential
★ 单稳态触发 monostable trigger
★ 双稳态 bistable
脉冲宽度 pulse width
可重复触发 retriggerable
不可重复触发 nonretriggerable
★ 555 定时器 555 timer
★ 施密特触发器 Schmitt trigger
★ 上限阈值电压 upper threshold voltage
★ 下限阈值电压 lower threshold voltage
★ 回差电压 backlash voltage
电压比较器 voltage comparator
充电 charge
放电 discharge

1 Monostable trigger: In a monostable trigger, one of the states is stable, but the other state is unstable. A trigger causes the circuit to enter the unstable state. After entering the unstable state, the circuit will return to the stable state after a set time. Such a circuit is useful for creating a timing period of fixed duration in response to some external events.

单稳态触发器:在单稳态触发器中,两个状态中一个状态是稳定的,而另一个状态是不稳定的。一个触发可引起电路进入不稳定状态。进入不稳定状态后,在设定的时间内,电路又会返回稳定状态。这种电路通常用来设定一段固定的时间用来响应外部事件。

2 Schmitt trigger: Schmitt trigger is a special trigger that has backlash voltage. As the input voltage rises, the output stays at a low or 0 value until the input voltage reaches upper threshold. At this upper threshold, the output snaps to a logic 1 value. When the input voltage drops, the output does not return to logic 0 until the input voltage drops below the lower threshold. The difference between the upper threshold and lower threshold is called backlash voltage.

施密特触发器:施密特触发器是一种具有回差电压的特殊触发器。输入电压在上升的过程中,触发器输出一直保持低电平或逻辑 0 不变,直到上升到高电平阈值电压,这时,输出从低电平跳到高电平。输入电压在下降的过程中,下降到低电平阈值电压时,触发器的输出由高电平下降到低电平。高电平阈值电压和低电平阈值电压之间的差值,称为回差电压。

第八节 半导体存储器

Section 8 Semiconductor Memory

★ 随机存储器 random access memory (RAM)
★ 只读存储器 read only memory (ROM)
读/写存储器 read-write memory (RWM)
静态存储器 static memory
动态存储器 dynamic memory
快闪存储器 flash memory
★ 存储矩阵 memory array
存储单元 memory cell
存储时间 storage time
★ 读周期 read cycle
再生(刷新) regenerate (refresh)
行选择线 row-select line
列选择线 column-select line
字 word
可编程 ROM programmable ROM (PROM)
可擦可编 ROM erasable programmable ROM (EPROM)
电可擦除的 PROM electricity EPROM (E^2PROM)
可编程阵列逻辑 programmable array logic (PAL)

1 ROM: Read-only memory (ROM) is a class of storage medium used in computers and other electronic devices. Data stored in ROM cannot be modified, or can be modified only slowly or with difficulty, so it is mainly used to distribute firmware (software that is very closely tied to specific hardware, and unlikely to be updated frequently).

ROM:只读存储器(ROM)是一类用在计算机或其他电子设备中的存储媒介。存储在ROM中的数据不能被修改,或者修改起来非常慢,或者非常困难,所以它主要用来放置固定程序(与硬件电路联系很紧密的一种程序软件,不需要频繁更新)。

2 RAM: Random access memory(RAM) is one of the typical memories that are used in various parts of a computer. RAM accepts new information for storage to be available later for use. The process of storing new information in memory is referred to as a memory write operation. The process of transferring the stored information out of memory is referred to as a memory read operation.

RAM:随机存储器(RAM)是组成计算机的基本存储单元之一。它接收新的信息并存储起来以备后用。存储器接收新信息的过程称为"写"操作,将存储的信息输出的过程称为"读"操作。

第九节 可编程逻辑器件
Section 9 Programmable Logic Device(PLD)

通用阵列逻辑
generic array logic (GAL)
复杂可编程逻辑器件
complex programmable logic device
硬链接 hard link
在系统可编程
in-system programmability (ISP)
集总布线区 global routing pool (GRP)
通用逻辑块 generic logic block (GLB)
缓冲 cushion
擦除 erase
现场可编程逻辑阵列
field programmable logic array (FPLA)
现场可编程门阵列
field programmable gate array (FPGA)
宏单元 macro cell
输出逻辑宏单元 output logic macro cell (OLMC)
知识产权 intellectual property (IP)
逻辑单元阵列 logic cell array (LCA)
可配置逻辑块 configurable logic block (CLB)
输出输入块 input output block (IOB)
内部连线 interconnect
布线 wiring

1 Programmable logic device(PLD): A programmable logic device or PLD is an electronic component used to build reconfigurable digital circuits. Unlike a logic gate, which has a fixed logic function, a PLD has an undefined function at the time of manufacture. Before the PLD can be used in a circuit it must be programmed, that is, reconfigured.

可编程逻辑器件(PLD):可编程逻辑器件是用来重构数字电路的电器组件。与逻辑门电路不一样,每个逻辑门电路都有它固定的逻辑功能,而PLD在生产的时候并没有固定的功能。想要在电路中使用PLD,之前必须要对它进行编程,这就是所谓的"重构"。

2 FPGA: A field-programmable gate array (FPGA) is an integrated circuit designed to be configured by a customer or a designer after manufacturing, hence "field-programmable". The FPGA configuration is generally specified using a hardware description language (HDL), similar to that used for an application-specific integrated circuit (ASIC)

现场可编程门阵列(FPGA):FPGA是一种集成电路,在生产出来之后可由用户或设计师自行配置使用,因此称为"现场可编程"。FPGA的配置一般使用硬件描述语言(HDL),这种语言类似于一种专为专用集成电路而设计的语言。

第十节 数模与模数转换器
Section 10 Digital-to-Analog and Analog-to-Digital Convertor

★ 权电阻 weighted resistor
★ 权电流 weighted current
倒置梯形 inverted ladder
双积分 dual slope
逐次逼近 successive approximation
取样—保持电路 sample-hold circuit
★ 分辨率 resolution
采样率 sampling rate
单调性 monotonicity
量化误差 quantization error
精度 precision

1 DAC and ADC: In electronics, a digital-to-analog converter (DAC or D-to-A) is a device that converts a digital (usually binary) code to an analog signal (current, voltage, or electric charge). An analog-to-digital converter (ADC) performs the reverse operation. Signals are easily stored and transmitted in digital form, but a DAC is needed for the signal to be recognized by human senses or other non-digital systems.

DAC 与 ADC:在电子学中,数模转换器(DAC)是一种可以将数字量(通常是二进制)转换成模拟量(电流、电压或电荷)的设备。模数转换器(ADC)执行的是相反的过程。信号以数字量的形式易于存储和传输,但是 DAC 对于那些人类感官或其他非数字系统要处理的信号来说就是必要的了。

2 Precision: Precision is the maximal windage of convertor's actual conversion characteristic curve and perfect conversion characteristic curve. Convertor's precision is determined by various errors. Three basic error sources are: maladjustment error, plus error and nonlinear error.

精度:精度是转换器实际转换特性曲线与理想转换特性曲线之间的最大偏差。转换器的转换精度由各项误差综合决定。转换器有三种基本误差源:失调误差、增益误差和非线性误差。

第三章　高级语言程序设计

Chapter 3　High-level Language Programming

课程简介

C＃语言是一种基于.NET的完全面向对象的编程语言，已先后被欧洲计算机制造商协会和国际标准化组织批准为高级语言开发标准(ECMA－334、ISOflEC23270)。随着.NET技术的普及，C＃语言已成为开发基于.NET的企业级应用程序的首选编程语言。

高级语言程序设计是信息与计算科学专业的重要必修课。课程详细介绍了C＃程序设计及其应用技术，讲授C＃程序设计基础、Windows应用程序设计和Web应用程序设计三部分。主要内容包括C＃语言基础知识、面向对象的编程技术、Windows窗体控件、目录与文件管理、图形图像处理、ADONET、报表设计、类库与控件库设计以及Web应用程序开发。以锻炼动手能力为手段，引导学生从初学者成为程序员，使其能熟练利用计算机解决实际问题。

Course Summary

The C＃ language is an object-oriented programming language completely based on. NET, and it has been approved to be the standard for advanced language development by the European Computer Manufacturers Association and the International Organization for Standardization (ECMA-334, ISOflEC23270). With the popularization of. NET technology, C＃ language has been the preferred programming language for the. NET-based enterprise applications.

The advanced programming language is an important compulsory subject for the major of information and computer science. The course introduces the C＃ programming and its application technologies, covering basic C＃ programming, Windows applications and Web applications. The main contents include the basis of C＃ language, object-oriented programming technology, Windows form controls, directory and file management, graphics and image processing, ADONET, report design, design of class and control libraries and development of Web application. It aims to enhance students' practical ability, and make the students to be able to develop programs and solve the problems proficiently.

第一节　概述

Section 1　Summary

★ 应用程序接口
Application Programming Interface (API)
中间语言　Intermediate Language (IL)
准时生产方式 Just In Time (JIT)
Java 运行环境
Java Runtime Environment (JRE)
★ 可扩展标记语
Extensible Markup Language (XML)
终止状态编码
termination status code
委托　delegate
★ 框架　framework
★ 应用程序　application
★ 主函数　main function

C＃ is just one of the languages available for. NET development, but in my opinion it is certainly the best. It has the advantage of being the only language designed from the ground up for the . NET Framework and may be the principal language used in versions of . NET that are ported to other operating systems. To keep languages such as the. NET version of Visual Basic as similar as possible to their predecessors yet compliant with the CLR, certain features of the . NET code library are not fully supported. By contrast, C＃ is able to make use of every feature that the . NET Framework code library has offered. The latest version of . NET includes several improvements to the C＃ language, partly in response to requests from developers, making it even more powerful.

C#是用于.NET开发的一种语言，但它是最好的一种语言。C#的优点是，它是唯一彻头彻尾为.NET Framework设计的语言，是在移植到其他操作系统上的.NET版本中使用的主要语言。要使诸如VB.NET的语言尽可能类似于其以前的语言，且仍遵循CLR，就不能完全支持.NET代码库的某些功能。但C#能使用.NET Framework代码库提供的每种功能。.NET的最新版本还对C#语言进行了几处改进，满足了开发人员的要求，使之更强大。

第二节 数据类型用法与流程控制
Section 2 Data Types Usage and Flow Control

值类型 value type
引用类型 reference type
★堆栈 stack
堆 heap
受管制的堆 managed heap
小数型 decimal
★有符号的 signed
★无符号的 unsigned
★变量 variable
★常量 constant
函数 function
★对象 object
装箱 boxing
拆箱 unboxing
★秩 rank
阵列 array
联接 join
分开 split
★枚举 enum
泛型 generic
哈希集合 HashSet
排序字典 sorted dictionary
后进先出 Last In First Out (LIFO)
布尔型 Bool
★循环 loop
★转到 goto
★跳出循环 break
★跳出当前循环 continue

Branching enables you to conditionally execute code, which, when combined with looping, allows you to create convoluted structures in your C# code. When you have loops inside loops inside if structures inside loops, you start to see why code indentation is so useful. If you shift all your code to the left of the screen, it instantly becomes difficult to parse by eye, and even more difficult to debug. It is well worth making sure you've got the hang of indentation at this stage - you'll appreciate it later on. VS does a lot of this for you, but it's a good idea to indent code as you type it anyway.

分支结构可以有条件地执行代码，当分支与循环一起使用时，可以在C#代码中创建出比较复杂的结构。把循环嵌套起来，再放在循环中的if结构中，就会发现为什么说代码的缩进是非常有用的。如果把所有代码都移到屏幕左端，就很难分析它们了，甚至难以调试。此时应确保代码的缩进——用户在以后使用时即可体会到它的种种优势。VS为此做了大量的工作，但最好在输入代码时进行缩进。

第三节 面向对象的编程
Section 3 Object-Oriented Programming

★重载 overload
★静态 static
结构 struct
方法 method
基类 base class
扩充类 derived class
★虚拟 virtual
非虚拟 non-virtual
★重写 override
隐藏 hide
抽象 abstract
★回调 callback
★初始化 initialize
★索引 index
★实体 entity
条件 condition
XML结构定义
XML Schemas Definition (XSD)

An object is a building block of an OOP application. This building block encapsulates part of the application, which may be a process, a chunk of data, or some more abstract entities.

In the simplest sense, an object may be very similar to a struct type such as those you saw earlier, containing members of variable and function types. The variables contained make up the data stored in the object, and the functions contained give access to the functionality of the object. Slightly more complex objects might not maintain any data; instead, they can represent a process by containing only functions. For example, an object representing a printer might be used, which would have functions enabling control over a printer (allowing you to print a document, a test page, and so on).

Objects in C# are created from types, just like the variables you've seen already. The type of an object is known by a special name in OOP, its class. You can use class definitions to instantiate objects, which means to create a real, named instance of a class. The phrases "instance of a class" and "object" mean the same thing here; be sure to note at this point that "class" and "object" mean fundamentally different things.

对象就是OOP应用程序的一个组成部件。这个组成部件封装了部分应用程序,这部分程序可以是一个过程、一些数据或一些更抽象的实体。

简单地说,对象非常类似于前面讨论的结构类型,包含变量成员和函数类型。它所包含的变量组成了存储在对象中的数据,其中包含的函数可以访问对象的功能。略为复杂的对象可能不包含任何数据,而只包含函数,表示一个过程。例如,可以使用表示打印机的对象,其中的函数可以控制打印机(允许打印文档、测试页等)。

C#中的对象是从类型中创建的,就像前面的变量一样。对象的类型在OOP中有一个特殊的名称:类。可以使用类的定义实例化对象,这表示创建该类的一个实例。"类的实例"和"对象"含义相同,注意"类"和"对象"是完全不同的概念。

第四节 窗体、控件、目录与文件
Section 4 Forms, Controls, Directory and Files

★ 组件对象模型
Component Object Model (COM)
按钮 button
★ 多文档窗体
Multi-Document Interface (MDI)
不显示图标 none
手形 hand
问号 question
感叹号 exclamation
星号 asterisk
★ 停止 stop
★ 错误 error
★ 警告 warning
信息 information
透明 transparent
锚定 anchor
停靠 dock
★ 分组控件 GroupBox
工具提示组件 ToolTip
错误提示组件 ErrorProvider
定时组件 Timer
★ 列表框 ListBox
★ 下拉框 ComboBox
★ 文本框 TextBox
★ 复选框 CheckBox
★ 复选框列表 CheckedListBox
单选按钮 RadioButton
时间日期选择 DateTimePicker
★ 图像列表 ImageList
快捷菜单 ContextMenuStrip
工具栏 ToolStrip
状态栏 StatusStrip
★ 列表视图 ListView
★ 树形视图 TreeView
选项卡控件 TabControl
任务栏图标 NotifyIcon
环境 environment
文件 file
路径 path
阴影 hatch
通用转换格式
Universal Transformation Format(UTF)

The TabControl works slightly differently from all other controls you've seen so far. The control itself is really little more than a container for the tab pages that is used to display the pages. When you double-click a TabControl in the Toolbox, you are presented with a control that already has two TabPages added to it.

When the mouse moves over the control, a small button with a triangle appears at the control's upper-right corner. When you click this button, a small window is unfolded. This is called the Actions Window and is designed to allow you to easily access selected properties and methods of the control. You may have noticed this earlier as many controls in Visual Studio include this feature, but the TabControl is the first of the controls in this chapter that actually allows you to do anything interesting in the Actions Window. The Actions Window of the TabControl allows you to easily add and remove TabPages at design time.

TabControl 的工作方式与前面的控件有一些区别。这个控件只不过是用于显示选项卡的选项卡页面的容器。在工具箱中双击 TabControl 时，就会显示一个已添加了两个 TabPages 的控件。

选择该控件时，在控件的右上角就会出现一个带三角形的小按钮。单击这个按钮，就会打开一个小窗口，即 Actions 窗口，用于访问控件的所选属性和方法。Visual Studio 中的许多控件都有这个特性，但 TabControl 是本章第一个允许在 Actions 窗口中执行某些操作的控件。使用 TabControl 的 Actions 窗口，可以方便地在设计期间添加和删除 TabPages。

第五节　图像处理与数据操作

Section 5　Image Processing and Data Manipulation

★ 图形设备接口
Graphics Device Interface (GDI)
高度　height
宽度　width
图形　graphics
★ 直线　line
★ 矩形　rectangle
★ 多边形　polygon
★ 曲线　curve
★ 椭圆　ellipse
★ 扇形　pie
填充　fill
位图　bitmap
矢量图　metafile
显示　show
智能提示　intellisence
可移植网络图形
Portable Network Graphic (PNG)
旋转　rotate
★ 开放式数据互连
Open Database Connectivity(ODBC)
★ 数据集　dataset
公共语言运行时
Common Language Runtime (CLR)
语言集成查询
Language INtegrated Query(LINQ)

Every table in a relational database is organized into rows, where each row represents a single record. The rows are organized into columns. All the rows in a table have the same column structure. For example, the Orders table has these columns: OrderID, CustomerID, EmployeeID, OrderDate, etc.

For any given order, you need to know the customer's name, address, contact name, and so forth. You could store that information with each order, but that would be very inefficient. Instead, we use a second table called Customers, in which each row represents a single customer. In the Customers table, there is a column for the CustomerID. Each customer has a unique ID, and that field is marked as the primary key for that table. A primary key is the column or combination of columns that uniquely identifies a record in a given table.

关系型数据库中所有表总是按行组织的，每一行代表一个记录。行再组成多个列。一个表中所有行都具有同样的列结构。例如 Orders 表有如下列：OrderID、CustomerID、EmployeeID 和 OrderDate 等。

对于任意一个订单，需要知道客户名称、地址、联系人姓名等等。可以让每个订单都存储这样的信息，但效率很不好。相反，我们使用另一个名为 Customers 的表，它的每一行都代表一个客户。该表中有一列叫 CustomerID。每个客户都有唯一的 ID，该字段被标记为这个表的主键。所谓主键就是在一个表中可以唯一标识一个记录的一列或多列的组合。

第六节 报表、类库与控件库设计

Section 6 Reporting, Class Libraries and Control Libraries Design

★ 报表数据库 Reporting Database
特性 attribute
★ 属性 property
Web 服务 Web Service
报表 reporting
摘要 abstract
水晶 crystal
★ 加载 load
★ 组件 component
★ 控件 control
描述 description
用户 user
种类 category
★ 客户机 Client
★ 服务器 Server
框架类库
Framework Class Library (FCL)

1 Server-side Support

The plumbing necessary to discover and invoke web services is integrated into the. NET Framework and provided by classes within the System. Web. Services namespace. Creating a web service requires no special programming on your part; you need only write the implementing code, add the [WebMethod] attribute, and let the server do the rest.

服务器端支持

创建 Web Services 需要的支持集成到了. NET 框架中，由名字空间 System. Web. Services 下的类提供。在你这一边不需要特殊的编程来创建网络服务。你只需要编写实现的代码，加上[WebMethod]属性，然后让服务器完成剩余的工作。

2 Client-side Support

You make use of a web service by writing client code that acts as though it were communicating directly with the host server by means of a URL. However, in reality, the client interacts with a proxy. The job of the proxy is to represent the server on the client machine, to bundle client requests into SOAP messages that are sent on to the server, and to retrieve the responses that contain the results.

用户端支持

客户端使用 Web Service 的代码编写就像直接跟一个本地服务器通过 VRL 进行通信，但实质上是通过一个代理跟宿主服务器进行通信。代理的工作是在用户的机器上代表了服务器，把用户的请求打包到 SOAP 消息，然后发送至服务器，并且接受带有运行结果的响应。

第七节 Web 应用程序设计基础与正则表达式

Section 7 Basic Web Applications and Regular Expressions

统一资源标志符
Uniform Resource Identifier (URI)
域名系统 Domain Name System (DNS)
Java 虚拟机 Java Virtual Machine (JVM)
导航 navigate
重新 refresh
★ 首部 head
★ 主体 body
★ 标题 title
★ 样式 style
层叠样式表 Cascading Style Sheets (CSS)
选择项目 SelectedItem
选择模式 SelectionMode
★ 超文本标记语言
Hypertext Markup Language (HTML)
★ 超文本传送协议
Hypertext Transport Protocol (HTTP)

A regular expression is applied to a string, that is, to a set of characters. Often that string is an entire text document.

The result of applying a regular expression to a string is either to return a substring, or to return a new string representing a modification of some part of the original string. Remember that strings are immutable and cannot be changed by the regular expression.

By applying a properly constructed regular expression to the following string:

One,Two,Three Liberty Associates, Inc.

正则表达式主要用于字符串,即一组字符。这往往意味着一整篇文本文档。

对应字符串应用正则表达式的结果,要么是返回子串,要么返回一个新字符串,表示原字符串某部分的修改。记住字符串是不可变的,因此用正则表达式也改变不了。

通过对以下字符串应用正确构造的正则表达式:

One、Two、Three Liberty Associates Inc。

第八节 ASP. NET Web 服务器控件

Section 8 ASP. NET Web Server Controls

单行 singleline
多行 multiline
密码 password
★ 用户自定义编码 User Encoded
深亚微米 deep-submicron
★ 水平的 horizontal
★ 垂直的 vertical
单元格 cell
★ 选择 select
★ 删除 delete
★ 插入 insert
★ 更新 update
存储过程 stored procedure
一般项模板 item template
交替项模板 alternating item template
选定项模板 selected item template
编辑项模板 edit item template
标题行模板 header template
脚注行模板 footer template
★ 相等 equal
★ 大于 greater than
★ 大于或等于 greater than equal
★ 小于 less than
★ 小于或等于 less than equal
类型比较 data type check

To implement a Web service, you can derive the Web service class from System. Web. Services. WebService. The WebService class provides access to ASP. NET Application and Session objects. Using this class is optional, and you have to derive from it only if you need easy access to the properties the class offers.

WebService Property	Description
Application	Returns an HttpApplicationState object for the current request.
Context	Returns an HttpContext object that encapsulates HTTP specific information. With this context the HTTP header information can be read.
Server	Returns an HttpServerUtility object. This class has some helper methods to do URL encoding and decoding.
Session	Returns an HttpSessionState object to store some state for the client.
User	Returns a user object implementing the IPrincipal interface. With this interface, you can get the name of the user and the authentication type.
SoapVersion	Returns the SOAP version that is used with the Web service. The SOAP version is encapsulated in the enumeration SoapProtocolVersion.

要实现 Web 服务，可以从 System. Web. Services. WebService 中派生 Web 服务类。Webservice 类提供了对 ASP. NET Application 和 Session 对象的访问，这个类是可选的，只有需要访问该类提供的属性时，才需要从这个类中派生。

属性	说明
Web Service Application	为当前请求返回一个 HttpApplicationState 对象。
Context	返回一个封装 HTTP 特定信息的 HttpContext 对象。在这里，可以读取 HTTP 标题信息。
Server	返回一个 HttpServerUtility 对象。这个类有一些帮助方法，可以进行 URL 编码和解码。
Session	返回一个 HttpSessionState 对象，以存储客户机的一些状态信息。
User	返回一个实现接口 IPrincipal 的用户对象，使用这个接口可以得到用户名和身份验证类型。
SoapVersion	返网 Web 服务使用的 SOAP 版本。SOAP 版本封装在 SoapProtocolVersion 枚举中。

第四章　模拟电子技术

Chapter 4　Analog Electronics Technology

课程简介

课程目标：使学生掌握模拟电子技术的基本工作原理、分析方法和基本技能，能够分析和设计简单的模拟电子系统，为深入学习后续课程和从事有关电子技术方面的实际工作打好基础。

课程内容：研究各种半导体器件的性能、电路及其应用的学科。模拟电子技术基础主要分析、研究和设计双极型、场效应管等分立元件组成的信号放大电路和集成运算放大电路、集成运放组成的信号运算电路、信号的处理电路、信号的产生和整形电路以及直流稳压电源。

预修课程：大学物理、电路原理、数字电子技术。

Course Summary

Goal: to understand the basic principle, method and technique of "Analog Electronics Technology"; analyse and design some simple "analog electronic systems", and lay the foundation for future study of related electronic technology.

Content: to study the properties and functions of various "semiconductor"; design and study bipolar, FET, and other discrete components of the signal amplification circuit and integrated operational amplifier circuit, the integrated operational amplifier composed of signal computing circuit, the signal processing circuit, the signal generation and shaping circuit and the DC power supply.

Prerequisites: Undergraduate Physics, Circuit Theory, Digital Electronics.

第一节　绪论

Section 1　Introduction

整体设计过程　the overall process
最大限度地提高性能　maximize performance
导航　navigation
波形整形　wave-shaping
子系统　subsystem
功能块　functional blocks
信号源　signal sources
电源　power supplies
峰值检波器　the peak detector
输入阻抗　input impedance
集成电路　integrated circuit
提取　extract
激励　stimulus
振幅　amplitude
传感器　transducer
采样　sample
操纵　manipulate
量化误差　quantization error
干扰　disturbance
附加噪声　the addition of noise
初始电平　the original levels
★电压放大模型　the voltage-amplifier model
电流放大模型　the current-amplifier model
互阻放大模型　the transresistance-amplifier model
复数增益　complex gain
电流增益　current gain
分立电路　discrete circuits
流程图　flowchart
波动　fluctuation
整流器　rectifier
临界　extreme
参数　parameter
组件　component
功率增益　power gain
负载效应　loading effects
级联放大器　cascaded amplifiers
电源效率　power efficiency
分贝表示法　decibel notation
★相移　phase shift

Amplifiers can be modeled as voltage amplifiers, current amplifiers, transresistance amplifiers, or transconductance amplifiers.

放大器可以看作电压放大器、电流放大器、互阻放大器或跨导放大器。

第二节　运算放大器
Section 2　Operating Amplifier

★ 虚短　virtual short
★ 虚断　virtual open
★ 虚地　virtual ground
运算电路　operational circuit
比例运算电路　scaling circuit
★ 电压跟随器　voltage follower
差分输入　differential input
反相输入　inverting input
同相输入　noninverting input
T 型反馈网络　T type feedback network
求和电路　summing circuit
微分电路　differential circuit
指数电路　exponential circuit
对数运算电路　logarithmic circuit
★ 外特性　external characteristic
巴特沃思滤波器　Butterworth filter
乘法运算电路　multiplication circuit
除法运算电路　division circuit
积分运算电路　integration circuit
中心频率　center frequency
状态变量　state variable

If a Gaussian process is stationary, then the process is also strictly stationary. If a Gaussian process $X(t)$ is applied to a stable linear filter, then the random process $Y(t)$ developed at the output of the filter is also Gaussian. Gaussian processes that are stationary in the narrow sense may be realized by way of certain dynamical systems.

如果高斯过程是平稳的,那么也一定是严格平稳的。如果高斯过程 $X(t)$ 通过一个稳定线性滤波器,那么,滤波器的输出 $Y(t)$也是高斯型的。平稳高斯过程从狭义上来说可以通过动态系统来实现。

第三节　二极管及其基本电路
Section 3　Diodes and Diode Circuits

半导体　semiconductor
本征　intrinsic
掺杂　doping
共价键　covalent bond
空穴　hole
N 型　N type
P 型　P type
自由电子　free electron
★ 载流子　carrier
半导体二极管　semiconductors diodes
点接触型　point contact type
等效电路　equivalent circuit
伏安特性　Volt Ampere characteristics
发光　light-emitting
符号　symbol
光电二极管　photodiode
结构　construction
★ 理想模型　ideal model
稳压二极管　zener diode
★ 截止区　cut off region
理想二极管模型　the ideal-diode model
小信号模型　small signal model
折线化模型　piecewise model
耗尽层　depletion region/depletion zone
整流器　rectifier
★ 稳压电路　voltage-regulator circuits
线性小信号等效电路
linear small-signal equivalent circuits
半导体基本概念　basic semiconductor concept
面结型二极管的物理机理
physics of the junction diode
开关高频二极管的性能
switching and high-frequency diode behavior
恒流区　constant current region
结型　junction type
电流方程　current equation
★ 开启电压　threshold voltage
★ 输出特性　output characteristics
★ 击穿电压　breakdown voltage
★ 等效电路　equivalent circuit
极间电容　interelectrode capacitance
扩散电容　diffusion capacitance

势垒电容 barrier capacitance	信噪比 signal-to-noise ratio
★放大区 active region	二极管 diode

1 u_D and i_D represent the total instantaneous diode voltage and current. At times, we may wish to emphasize the time-varying nature of these quantities and then we use $v\text{-}p(t)$ and $i\text{-}p(t)$.
u_D和i_D表示二极管的电压和电流总瞬时二值。有时，为了强调这些量随时间变化的性质，我们用$v\text{-}p(t)$和$i\text{-}p(t)$表示瞬时值。

2 V_Q and I_Q represent the DC diode current and voltage at the quiescent point.
V_Q和I_Q表示二极管在静态工作点处的直流电压和电流。

3 Diodes that are intended to operate in the breakdown region are called Zener diodes. Zener diodes are often used in applications for which a constant voltage in breakdown is desirable.
工作在击穿区域的二极管被称为齐纳二极管。齐纳二极管最可取的是它在反向击穿状态下的恒压特性。

4 The ideal-diode model is a short circuit for forward currents and an open circuit for reverse voltages.
理想二极管模型是加正向电压短路有正向电流，加反向电压开路。

5 In the forward direction, the ideal diode conducts any current forced by the external circuit while displaying a zero voltage drop. The ideal diode does not conduct in the reverse direction; any applied voltage appears as reverse bias across the diode.
理想二极管在正向偏置时导通，二极管两端的压降为零。理想二极管反向偏置时截止，二极管反向偏置电压为外加电压。

第四节　双极结型三极管及放大电路基础
Section 4　Bipolar Junction Transistors and Amplifier Base

★放大电路 amplifier	★反向偏置 reverse bias
旁路电容 by-pass capacitor	反向饱和电流 reverse saturation current
★静态工作点 quiescent point	特征频率 characteristic frequency
耦合电容 coupling capacitor	图解分析法 graphical analysis
★负载线 load line	★交流负载线 alternating current load line
输出电阻 output resistance	非线性失真 non-linear distortion
输入电阻 input resistance	h参数小信号模型 Hybrid small signal model
★工作点稳定 operating point stabilization	最大输出幅值 maximum output amplitude
光电耦合器 photocoupler	直流模型 DC model
★交流通路 alternating current path	射级偏置电路 emitter biasing circuit
静态工作点 quiescent point	偏置电流 bias current
射极跟随器 emitter follower	★通频带 pass band
放大概念 amplification concept	多级放大电路 multistage amplifier
h参数模型 h-parameter model	变跨导型乘法器 variable transconductance multiplier
图解法 graphical method	稳定判据 stability criterion
共射组态 common-emitter configuration	幅值裕度 gain margin
共基组态 common-base configuration	放大作用 amplification effect
共集组态 common-collector configuration	转移特性 transfer characteristics
特性曲线 characteristic curve	多发射结晶体管 multiple emitter transistor
截止区 cut off region	电流放大系数 current amplification factor
★饱和区 saturation region	有源元件 active component
★正向偏置 forward bias	

负载线分析　load-line analysis
相位裕度　phase margin
连接方式　configuration
变压器耦合　transformer coupled
变压器耦合放大电路　transformer coupling amplifier
U_{BE}倍增　U_{BE} multiplier
准互补电路　quasi complementary circuit
直接耦合放大电路　direct coupled amplifier
阻容耦合放大电路　RC coupled amplifier
★ 频率响应　frequency response
频率特性　frequency characteristic
幅频特性　amplitude frequency characteristic
发射结电容　emitter junction capacitor
集电结电容　collector junction capacitor
上限截止频率　upper cut-off frequency/high 3-dB frequency
high 3-dB frequency
相频特性　phase frequency characteristic
下限截止频率　lower cut-off frequency/low 3-dB frequency
中频　intermediate frequency
瞬态响应　transient response
带宽　bandwidth
波特图　Bode diagram/Bode plot
★ 零点漂移　zero drift
校正措施　compensation method
稳定裕度　stability margin
相位裕度　phase margin
超前校正　phase lead compensation
滞后校正　phase lag compensation
共射截止频率　common emitter cut-off frequency

1 Depending on the bias conditions on its two junctions, the BJT can operate in one of the three possible modes: cut-off (both junctions reverse-biased), active (the EBJ forward-biased and the CBJ reverse-biased), and saturation (both junctions forward-biased). For amplifier applications, the BJT is operated in the active mode. Switching applications make use of the cut-off and saturation modes.
根据两结的不同偏止状态，BJT 以三种状态之一工作：两结反偏—截止；发射结正偏，集电结反偏—放大；两结正偏—饱和。在放大电路中，BJT 在放大状态工作，在开关电路中，BJT 在截止和饱和状态工作。

2 Two amplifiers are cascaded by connecting the input of the second to the output of the first. The overall voltage, current, or power gains are the product of the respective individual gains, the load of the first stage depending on the input of the second.
两个放大器级联就是第二级的输入连接第一级的输出。总电压、电流或功率增益是各级增益的乘积，第一级的负载取决于第二级的输入。

第五节　场效应管放大电路
Section 5　Field-effect Amplifier

场效应管　field-effect transistor
衬底　substrate
恒流区　constant current region
CMOS 电路　CMOS circuit
夹断电压　pinch off voltage
增强型　enhancement
绝缘栅型　isolated gate type
漏极　drain
栅极　gate
源极　source
单极型晶体管　unipolar transistor
金属氧化物绝缘栅场效应管
metal oxide insulated gate FET
多晶硅　polysilicon
栅极偏置电路　gate bias circuits

1 Distortion occurs in FET amplifiers because of the non-uniform spacing of the drain characteristics. Distortion is less pronounced for small signal amplitudes.
FET 放大器发生失真的原因是漏极特性间距的不均匀。信号幅度小时不明显。

2 For use as amplifiers, FETs are usually biased in the saturation region.
作为放大器，场效应管通常工作于饱和区。

3 The amplifier gain remains almost constant over the mid frequency band. It falls off at high frequencies where transistor-model capacitors no longer have very high reactance. For AC amplifiers the gain falls off at low frequencies as well because the coupling and bypass capacitors no longer have very low reactance.
放大电路的放大倍数在中频段几乎保持不变。在高频段，由于晶体管的电容容抗降低，放大倍数会下降，在低频段，由于耦合电容容抗升高，放大倍数也会下降。

第六节 模拟集成电路
Section 6 Analog Integrated Circuits

★运算放大电路 operational amplifier
集成电路特点 features of integrated circuits
差模信号 difference-mode signal
共模信号 common-mode signal
恒流源 constant current source
差分放大电路 differential amplifier
差模放大倍数 differential-mode gain
共模放大倍数 common-mode gain
共模抑制比 common-mode rejection ratio
场效应管差分放大电路 FET differential amplifier
★有源负载 active load
等效电路 equivalent circuit
比例电流源 scaling current source
多路电流源 multiple current source
镜像电流源 current mirror
威尔逊电流源 Wilson current source
集成运算放大电路
integrated operational amplifier circuit
理想运放 ideal operational amplifier
开环增益 open-loop gain
失调电流 offset current
失调电压 offset voltage
通用型 popular type
专用型 special type
截止频率 cut-off frequency/3-dB frequency
同相输入端 noninverting input terminal
性能扩展 performance extension
单极型集成电路 unipolar integrated circuit
保护电路 protecting circuit

All signals can be considered to be composed of sine waves of various amplitudes, frequencies, and Phases. To amplify a signal without distortion, the amplifier must have constant gain for all of the frequencies contained in the signal.

所有的信号都可以看成是将各种振幅、频率和相位的正弦波组成。放大信号不失真，放大器必须对所有频率的信号有恒定增益。

第七节 放大电路中的反馈
Section 7 Feedback in Amplifier

反馈放大电路 feedback amplifier
反馈概念 feedback concept
反馈通路 feedback path
稳定判据 stability criterion
闭环增益 closed-loop gain
环路增益 loop gain
共模抑制比 common-mode rejection ratio
反馈极性判断 feedback polarity examination
正反馈 positive feedback
★负反馈 negative feedback
反馈组态 feedback configuration
电压串联 voltage-series
电流串联 current-series
反馈网络 feedback network
反馈信号 feedback signal
电流并联 current-parallel
电压并联 voltage-parallel
反馈系数 reverse transmission factor/feedback factor
深度负反馈电路
circuit with strong negative feedback
分析方法 method of analysis
深度负反馈电路的特点
properties of circuit with strong negative feedback
引入负反馈的一般原则
general rules for introducing negative feedback

★ 自激振荡 self-excited oscillation
★ 干扰 interference
自举电路 bootstrapping circuit
基本方程 basic equation
负反馈电路的自激振荡
self-excited oscillation of negative feedback circuit

Negative feedback amplifier is employed to make the amplifier gain less sensitive to component variations, in order to control input and output impedances, extend bandwidth, reduce nonlinear distortion, and enhance signal-to-noise (and signal-to-interference) ratio.

负反馈放大电路能够稳定放大倍数、改变输入和输出电阻、扩展频带、减小非线性失真和提高信噪比。

第八节 功率放大电路
Section 8 Power Amplifier

功率放大电路 power amplifier
甲类放大 class A amplification
丙类 class C
达林顿复合管 Darlington transistor
散热 heat dissipation
★ 互补电路 complementary pair
★ 交越失真 crossover distortion
推挽 push-pull
BTL 电路 balanced transformerless circuit
倍压整流电路 voltage doubler circuit
最大输出功率 maximum output power
低频功率放大电路
low frequency power amplifier
集成功放 integrated circuit power amplifier

Output stages are classified according to the transistor conduction angle: class A (360°), class AB (slightly greater than 180°), class B(180°), and class C(smaller than 180°).

功率放大电路的输出级根据晶体管的导通角分类：甲类(导通角 360°)、甲乙类(导通角稍大于 180°)、乙类(导通角 180°)和丙类(导通角小于 180°)。

第九节 信号的处理与信号的产生电路
Section 9 Signal Processing and Signal Generation Circuit

限幅 clipping
波形发生电路 waveform generator
函数发生器 function generator
★ 正弦波振荡电路 sinusoidal oscillator
串并联(文氏桥)式振荡器
Wien bridge oscillator
选频 frequency selective amplifier
变压器反馈式 transformer feedback
电感反馈式(电感三点式) Hartley feedback
电容反馈式(电容三点式) Colpitts feedback
石英晶体 crystal oscillator
分频 frequency division
占空比 duty ratio
品质因数 quality factor
振荡条件 criterion of oscillation
限幅电路 clipping circuits
变压器反馈式正弦波振荡电路
transformer feedback sinusoidal oscillator
电感反馈式正弦波振荡电路
Hartley feedback sinusoidal oscillator
倍频 frequency multiplication
倍频器 frequency multiplier
波形变换电路 wave form converter
三角波变锯齿波
triangular wave-sinusoidal wave converter
方波发生器 square wave generator
三角波发生器 triangular wave generator
★ 正弦波振荡器 sinusoidal oscillator
锯齿波发生器 sawtooth wave generator
低通滤波器 low-pass filter
带通滤波器 band-pass filter
电压比较器 voltage comparator
阈值电压 threshold voltage
滞回比较器 regenerative comparator
带阻滤波器 band-reject filter
高通滤波器 high-pass filter
集成电压比较器 integrated voltage comparator
简单比较器 simple comparator
压控电压源 voltage-controlled voltage-source
通带电压放大倍数 pass-band voltage gain
通带截止频率 cut-off frequency of pass-band
特征频率 characteristic frequency

晶片 wafer
矩形波发生器 rectangular ware generator
分频器 frequency divider
混频器 mixer
信号转换电路 signal transfer circuit
★ 选频网络 frequency-selective network

1 Filters perform a frequency-selection function: passing signals whose frequency spectrum lies within a specified range, and stopping signals whose frequency spectrum falls outside this range.
滤波电路具有选频的功能:通过通带内的信号,滤除掉阻带的信号。

2 The basic structure of a sinusoidal oscillator consists of an amplifier and a frequency-selective network connected in a positive-feedback loop.
正弦波振荡电路由放大电路、选频网络和正反馈电路组成。

第十节 直流电路
Section 10 DC Circuit

★ 串联型稳压器 series voltage regulator
安全区保护 safety operating area protection
过热保护 thermal overload protection
半波整流 half wave rectifier
★ 桥式整流电路 bridge rectifier circuit
滤波电容 filtering capacitance
电容滤波器 capacitance filter
脉动系数 ripple factor
外特性 external characteristic
稳压管稳压电路 zener voltage regulator
★ 稳压电源 regulated power supply
过流保护 current overload protection
基准源 reference
单片集成稳压器
monolithic integrated regulator
开关型直流电源
switching mode direct power supply
并联型 parallel type
串联型 serial type

1 The regulated power supply consists of depressor, rectifier circuit and filter circuit and voltage regulator.
稳压电源由变压器、整流电路、滤波电路和稳压器组成。

2 Rectifier circuits are often useful in battery-charging circuits and for converting AC into nearly constant DC to power electronic circuits such as amplifier.
整流电路通常用于电池充电和把交流电转换成几乎恒定不变的直流电的电路中,如放大器中的电子电源。

第五章　单片机原理与接口技术

Chapter 5　Single-chip Computer Principles and Interface

第一部分　单片机原理与接口技术

Part One: Single-chip Computer Principles and Interface

课程简介

课程目标:单片机原理与接口技术是电子信息工程专业一门专业必修课。通过该课程的学习,使学生具备单片机应用系统的设计开发能力。课程内容:本课程介绍 AT89S51 单片机的原理及应用。内容包括以下四部分:

(1)AT89S51 单片机的片内硬件结构及片内各功能部件的工作原理及应用,包括时钟电路、复位电路、中断系统、定时器/计数器、串行口。

(2)AT89S51 的汇编语言指令系统、AT89S51 汇编程序设计。

(3)各种扩展接口设计,包括:存储器、I/O、键盘、显示器、A/D、D/A 接口电路设计以及驱动程序设计。

(4)单片机应用系统的软硬件设计。

Course Summary

Course Objectives: Single-chip Microcomputer Principles and Interface is a compulsory course of Electronic and Information Engineering. By the study of this course, the students can acquire the ability to design and develop SCM application system. Course Content: This course is an introduction to the principles and application of AT89S51 single-chip microcontroller unit. The course consists of four parts:

(1) The inner hardware structure and the working principles and application of the inner functional unit of AT89S51 single-chip microcontroller unit, including the clock circuit, the reset circuit, the interrupt system, the timer/counter and the serial COM port.

(2) The AT89S51 assemble language instruction repertoire, the AT89S51 assemble language programming.

(3) Extended interface circuit design, including memorizer, I/O extending, keyboard, display, A/D & D/A interface circuit design and various driver programming for above different interface circuits.

(4) The software and hardware design of the application system of the single-chip computer.

第一节　微型计算机基础

Section 1　Basis of Microcomputer

★ 微型计算机　microcomputer
微处理器　microprocessor
单片机　single-chip microcomputer/Micro Control Unit(MCU)/single-chip microcontroller
个人计算机　personal computer
数　number
集成电路　integrate circuit
★ 二进制　binary system
★ 八进制　octal system
★ 十进制　decimal system
★ 原码　original code
★ 反码　one's complement
补码　base complement
★ ASCII 码
American Standard Code for Information Interchange
BCD 码　Binary Code Decimal
★ 十六进制　hexadecimal system
字符　character
整数　integer
尾码　mantissa
阶码　exponent
★ 浮点数　floating-point data
实数　real data
★ 硬件　hardware

★ 软件　software
正　positive
负　negative
符号　sign
溢出　overflow
奇偶　parity

In the past few years, enormous advances have been made in the cost, power and ease of use of microcomputers. It is now possible, with a relatively small expenditure, to purchase a microcomputer system that will take data, quickly analyze them and display the results or control a process. This has been made possible by the development of technology that can fabricate millions of transistors, diodes, resistors, capacitors, and conductors on a single silicon integrated circuit chip.

在过去的几年中，微型计算机在其价格、性能和使用方面，有了长足的进步。现在，我们花少量的费用就可以购买一个计算机系统来完成数据的收集和快速分析并显示结果或者控制一个过程。这完全仰仗于可将成百万个晶体管、二极管、电阻、电容以及导体制作在一块单一的硅集成电路芯片上的技术。

第二节　51 系列单片机硬件结构
Section 2　The Hardware Architecture of 51 Series MCU

★ 中央处理器　central processing unit (CPU)
8 位机　8-bit computer
位　bit
字节　byte
字　word
双字　double word
时钟　clock
指令周期　instruction cycle
★ 进位标志　carry flag
辅助进位标志　auxiliary carry flag
★ 溢出标志　overflow flag
符号标志　sign flag
★ 零标志　zero flag
★ 中断标志　interrupt flag
寄存器　register
控制单元　controlling unit
累加器　accumulator
存储　store
控制器　controller
译码器　decoder
缓冲器　buffer
时序　sequence
复位　reset
置位　set
掉电　power down
堆栈　stack
PC　Personal Computer
输入输出　I/O, Input/Output
随机存取存储器
Random Access Memory (RAM)
专用寄存器　Special Function Register
程序计数器　Program Counter (PC)
程序状态字　Program Status Word (PSW)
堆栈指针　Stack Pointer (SP)
时钟电路　clock circuit
复位电路　reset circuit
数据总线　data bus
地址总线　address bus
控制总线　control bus

The 8051 series of single-chip microcontrollers are highly integrated microcomputers with an 8-bit CPU, memory, interrupt controller, timers, serial I/O and digital I/O on a single piece of silicon.

8051 系列单片机是一个高集成度的微处理器，在其硅片上有八位 CPU、存储器、中断控制器、定时器及串行和并行接口。

第三节　51 系列单片机指令系统
Section 3　Instruction System of 51 Series MCU

寻址方式　addressing mode
寄存器寻址　register addressing
立即寻址　immediate addressing
直接寻址　direct addressing
寄存器间接寻址　register indirect addressing
基址加变址寻址　base plus index addressing
寄存器相对寻址　register relative addressing
相对基址加变址寻址
base relative plus index addressing
操作数　operand

操作码 opcode
源操作数 source operand
目的操作数 destination operand
汇编 assembling
机器语言 machine language
汇编语言 assembly language
汇编程序 assembly program
位移量 displacement
字符串 character string
顺序 sequential
随机 random
指令系统 instruction system
数据传送指令 data move instruction
算术运算指令
arithmetic operation instruction
逻辑运算指令 logic operation instruction
控制转移指令 control transfer instruction
位操作指令 bit operation instruction
数据传送 MOV (Move)
读取程序存储器数据 MOVC (Move Code)
外部 RAM 的数据传送
MOVX (Move External RAM)
字节交换 XCH (Exchange)
低半字节交换
XCHD (Exchange low-order Digit)
入栈 PUSH (Push onto Stack)
出栈 POP (Pop from Stack)
加法 ADD (Addition)
带进位加法 ADDC (Add with Carry)
带借位减法 SUBB (Subtract with Borrow)
十进制调整 DA (Decimal Adjust)
加 1 INC (Increment)
减 1 DEC (Decrement)
乘法 MUL (Multiplication, Multiply)
除法 DIV (Division, Divide)
逻辑与 ANL (AND Logic)
逻辑或 ORL (OR Logic)
逻辑异或 XRL (Exclusive-OR Logic)
清零 CLR (Clear)
取反 CPL (Complement)
循环左移 RL (Rotate Left)
带进位循环左移
RLC (Rotate Left through the Carry flag)
循环右移 RR (Rotate Right)
带进位循环右移
RRC (Rotate Right through the Carry flag)
低 4 位与高 4 位交换 SWAP (Swap)
子程序绝对调用
ACALL (Absolute subroutine Call)
子程序长调用 LCALL (Long subroutine Call)
子程序返回 RET (Return from Subroutine)
中断返回 RETI (Return from Interruption)
短转移 SJMP (Short Jump)
绝对转移 AJMP (Absolute Jump)
长转移 LJMP (Long Jump)
比较不相等则转移
CJNE (Compare Jump if Not Equal)
减 1 后不为 0 则转移
DJNZ (Decrement Jump if Not Zero)
结果为 0 则转移 JZ (Jump if Zero)
结果不为 0 则转移 JNZ (Jump if Not Zero)
有进位则转移
JC (Jump if the Carry flag is set)
无进位则转移 JNC (Jump if Not Carry)
位为 1 则转移 JB (Jump if the Bit is set)
位为 0 则转移 JNB (Jump if the Bit is Not set)
位为 1 则转移,并清除该位
JBC(Jump if the Bit is set and Clear the bit)
空操作 NOP (No Operation)

Efficient software development for the microprocessor requires a complete familiarity with the addressing modes employed by each instruction. The data-addressing mode of 51 series MCU includes immediate addressing, direct addressing, register indirect addressing, base plus index addressing, register relative addressing, base relative addressing and base relative plus index addressing.

微处理器的高效软件开发,需要对其寻址方式十分熟悉。51 系列单片机的数据的寻址方式包括立即寻址、直接寻址、寄存器间接寻址、基址加变址寻址、寄存器相对寻址、相对基址寻址、相对基址加变址寻址。

第四节 51 系列单片机程序设计
Section 4 Program Design of 51 Series MCU

汇编语言的格式 assembly language format
指示性语句 indicative sentence

指令语句　instruction sentence
分支　branch
循环　cyclic
代码转换　code-switching
算术运算　arithmetic operation
逻辑运算　logical calculus
控制转移　control transfer
布尔运算　boolean operation
等于　EQ，＝，Relational equal
不等于　NE，<>，Relational not equal
大于　GT，>，Relational greater than
大于等于
GE，>=，Relational greater than or equal
小于　LT，<，Relational less than
小于等于　LE，<=，Relational less than or equal
位存储器地址　bit memory address
★ 无符号数　unsigned number
★ 有符号数　signed number
无符号数加法　unsigned number addition
无符号数减法　unsigned number subtraction
无符号数乘法　unsigned number multiplication
无符号数除法　unsigned number division
循环体　loop body
循环结束　loop end
循环结束条件　loop end condition
循环初态　loop initial state
常数　constant
变量　variable
缓冲器　buffer
起始地址　beginning address
常数表　constant table
变量表　variable table

The assembly program converts a symbolic source module (file) into a hexadecimal object file. The linker program reads object files that are created by the assembly program and links them together into a single execution file.

汇编程序将符号源程序（文件）变为十六进制码的目标文件。链接程序读入（多个）由汇编程序产生的目标文件并将其链接成一个单一的可执行文件。

第五节　中断系统
Section 5　Interrupt System

优先级　priority level
★ 中断　interrupt
★ 中断源　interrupt source
★ 中断请求　interrupt request
中断链　interrupt chain
中断请求标志　interrupt request flag
中断允许　interrupt enable
外部中断　external interrupt
内部中断　internal interrupt
控制位　control bit
溢出中断　overflow interrupt
中断响应　interrupt respond
禁止　disable
禁止中断　disabled interrupt
复位状态　reset state
入口地址　entry address
中断入口地址　interrupt entry address
中断返回　return from interruption
中断服务程序　interrupt service routine
★ 保护现场　protecting locality
★ 恢复现场　resuming locality
中断条件　interrupt condition
定时器中断　timer interrupt
计数器中断　counter interrupt
串行口中断　serial port interrupt

The IP register sets one of two main priority levels for the various interrupt sources. Set the corresponding bit to "1" to configure interrupt as high priority and to "0" to configure interrupt as low priority.

寄存器 IP 为各个中断源设置两个中断优先级，把相应的位置设置为"1"，可以把对应中断源的优先级设置为高优先级；反之设置为"0"，则把该中断源的优先级设置为低优先级。

第六节　定时器与计数器
Section 6　Timer and Counter

定时器　timer
计数器　counter

工作方式　operation mode
机器周期　machine cycle
★ 晶振　crystal oscillator
晶振频率　crystal oscillator frequency
定时器方式　timing mode
计数器方式　counting mode
运行控制位　executive control bit
方式选择位　mode select bit
中断标志位　interrupt flag bit
计数长度　count length
启动计数　start counting
停止计数　stop counting
中断溢出　interrupt overflow
分频　frequency division
倍频　frequency doubling
外部输入脉冲　external input pulse
方波　square wave
开中断　enable interrupt
关中断　disenable interrupt
初始值　initial value
查询　enquiry
查询方式　enquiry mode
振荡频率　oscillation frequency

The 8051 has two 16-bit timer/counters, namely: timer 0 and timer 1. Each timer/counter consists of two 8-bit registers THx and TLx (x = 0 and 1). Both can be configured to operate either as timers or event counters. In "timer" function, the TLx register is incremented in every machine cycle. Thus one can think of it as counting machine cycles. Since a machine cycle consists of 12 oscillator periods the maximum count rate is 12 times of the oscillator frequency.

8051 有两个 16 位定时/计数器，分别为定时器 0 和定时器 1，每一个定时/计数器包含两个 8 位寄存器，即 THx 和 TLx。每一个定时/计数器都可以构成一个十六位的定时或计数。在定时器功能时，每一个机器周期使 TLx 增加，因此可以把机器周期看作计数周期。由于一个机器周期由 12 个振荡周期构成，因此最大计数时间是振荡周期的 12 倍。

第七节　串行接口
Section 7　Serial Interface

串行接口　serial interface
通讯　communication
通讯方式　communication mode
★ 串行通讯　serial communication
★ 并行通讯　parallel communication
异步通讯　asynchronous communication
同步通讯　synchronic communication
帧　frame
帧格式　frame format
起始位　start bit
停止位　stop bit
接收端　receiving terminal
发送端　sending terminal
空闲位　vacancy bit
检测　testing
数据位　data bit
奇偶校验位　parity bit
波特　baud
波特率　baud rate
半双工　semi duplex
全双工　full duplex
接收控制器　receiving controller
发送控制器　sending controller
接收缓冲器　receiving buffer
发送缓冲器　sending buffer
波特率发生器　baud rate generator
发送数据　send data
接收数据　receive data
数据发送位　data transmission bit
发送中断标志　transmission interrupt flag
接收中断标志　reception interrupt flag
方式选择位　mode select bit
分布式　distributivity
分布式系统　distributivity system
多机通讯　multimachine communication
地址帧　address frame
数据帧　data frame
主机　host computer

The serial port of 8051 is full duplex, meaning it can simultaneously transmit and receive. It is also receive-buffer, meaning it can commence reception of a second byte before a previously received byte has been read from the receive register.

8051 的串行口是全双工的，可以同时发送和接收数据。它具有接收缓存器，在接收寄存器读出已经接收到的一个字节之前，可以接收第二个字节。

第八节 存储器扩展设计

Section 8 Memory Expending Design

程序存储器扩展 program memory expending
数据存储器扩展 data memory expending
只读存储器 read-only memory
★ 随机存储器 random access memory
★ 静态存储器 static memory
扩展能力 extended capability
外部数据总线 external data bus
外部地址总线 external address bus
外部控制总线 external control bus
内部数据总线 internal data bus
内部地址总线 internal address bus
内部控制总线 internal control bus
总线方式 bus mode
地址锁存 address latching
地址锁存器 address latching unit
地址锁存信号 address latching signal
数据锁存信号 data latching signal
★ 锁存器 latch unit
存储器写信号 memory writing signal
存储器读信号 memory reading signal
高电平触发 high level trigging
低电平触发 low level trigging
反向器 reviser
存储器容量 memory capacity
片选 chip selection
片选信号 chip selection signal
编址 addressing
译码器 decoder

The five memory spaces of the 8051 are: Program Memory, External Data Memory, Internal Data Memory, Special Function Registers and Bit Memory.

8051 的五类存储器分别是程序存储器、外部数据存储器、内部数据存储器、特殊功能寄存器和位存储器。

第九节 输入输出电路设计

Section 9 Input and Output Circuit Design

输入 input
输出 output
接口 interface
接口电路 interface circuit
可编程接口 programmable interface
双向数据线 bi-directional data wire
接口芯片 interface chip
封装 capsulation
封装形式 capsulation form
双列直插式 dual in line type
输入锁存器 input latching unit
输出锁存器 output latching unit
输入缓冲器 input buffer
输出缓冲器 output buffer
输入工作方式 input operation mode
输出工作方式 output operation mode
双向工作方式 bi-directional operation mode
★ 选通 strobe
选通方式 strobe mode
位控方式 bit control mode
三态 tristate
三态门 tristate gate
选通输入 strobed input
选通输出 strobed output

The parallel input/output port allows the microcomputer to communicate directly with logic voltages in the external digital world and handles most of the problems of control and synchronization with the microprocessor address and data buses.

并行输入/输出端口允许微型计算机以逻辑电压的形式直接与外部的数字设备进行通信，以处理控制和微处理器的数据总线和地址总线的同步问题。

第二部分　实验

Part Two: Experiment

课程简介

课程目标:本课程是电子信息工程专业的一门必修课程。通过实验,使学生掌握 8051 单片机上机调试过程,了解并掌握简单的 8051 单片机外围接口技术。锻炼学生的理论联系实际的能力,并培养学生的实践动手能力。课程内容:(1)汇编语言的使用与 Keil C 调试;(2)键盘扩展及数码管显示;(3)单片机定时器和中断系统的使用;(4)单片机的串行口的工作原理及使用;(5)单片机扩展模数与数模转换。

Course Summary

Course objectives: Single-chip Computer Principles and Interfaces Experiment is a compulsory course of Electronic and Information Engineering. By the study of this course, students can master the debugging process of 8051 MCU, understand and master the simple 8051 MCU peripheral interface technology. And the students can integrate theory with practical abilities, and the students' practical ability can be developed. Course Content: (1) using assembly language and debugging program by Keil C. (2) extension of the keyboard and digital display. (3) the use of the timer and interrupt system in MCU. (4) MCU serial port works and the using of serial port. (5) digital-analog and analog-digital conversion.

第××章　单片机原理与接口技术实验

Section ×× Single-chip Computer Principles and Interfaces Experiment

Lab1: Finding Extremum

Type: verification

The experiment date: ××　××　××××　Place: ××

Professional Class: ××　Name: ××

Student No.: ××　Instructed by: ××　Term: ××

1. Objectives

①to be familiar with instruction system of 51 series MCU

②to be familiar with debugging environment of software Keil C

③to master the basic method of finding extremum

④to master the method of program design on assembly language and the method of program debugging

2. Equipments and Components Needed

Computer, simulation software

3. Experimental Requirement

According to the experimental content, you should program, and complete the debugging process to get the correct results.

4. The Program of Experimental Procedure

```
        ORG 0000H
        AJMP MAIN
        ORG 0100H
MAIN :  MOV SP,#60H
        MOV R0,#30H
        MOV R1,#10
```

```
         MOV A, #0
         MOV DPTR, #TAB
LOOP :   MOVC A,@A+DPTR
         MOV @R0,A
         INC R0
         INC DPTR
         MOV A, #0
         DJNZ R1,LOOP
         MOV R0, #30H
         MOV R1, #10
         MOV 60H, #0
LOOP1:   MOV A,@R0
         CJNE A,60H,XX
         SJMP XX1
  XX :   JC XX1
         MOV 61H,A
         MOV @R0,60H
         MOV 60H,61H
  XX1 :  INC R0
         DJNZ R1,LOOP1
         SJMP $
  TAB :  DB 01H, 02H, 03H, 04H, 05H
         DB 06H, 07H, 08H, 09H, 0AH
         END
```

5. Experiment Result

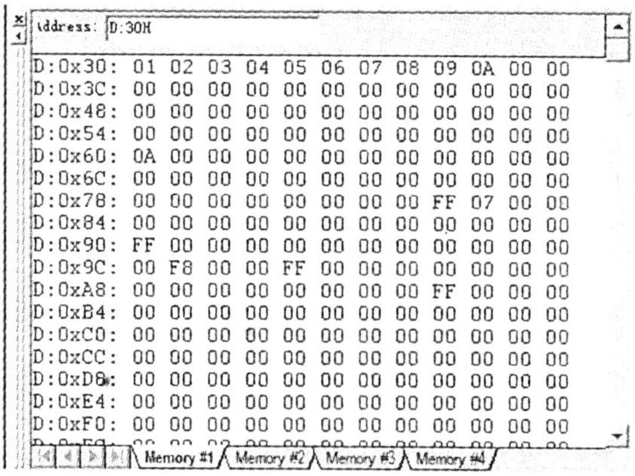

第六章　信号与系统

Chapter 6　Signals and Systems

第一部分　信号与系统

Part One: Signals and Systems

课程简介

《信号与系统》是电气信息类专业本科生的一门必修学科基础课。课程基本内容概括为：一个信号、二种系统、三大变换和四个域分析。“一个信号”是确定性信号；“二种系统”即连续时间系统和离散时间系统；“三大变换”是傅里叶变换、拉普拉斯变换和Z变换；“四个域分析”即时域分析、频域分析、复频域分析和Z域分析。

通过本门课的学习，使学生能够熟练掌握信号的表示、运算；了解系统的性质及表示；掌握系统的时域分析；熟练掌握卷积、卷积和；掌握信号的傅里叶分析方法和频谱的分析、抽样定理；掌握连续系统拉普拉斯变换分析；掌握离散信号的Z变换及离散系统的Z变换分析。为后续《数字信号处理》《通信原理》《自动控制原理》《随机信号分析》等课程的学习奠定理论基础。

Course Summary

Signals and Systems is one of the basic compulsory courses for the electrical information engineering majors. The basic content of this course can be summed up as one signal, two systems, three transforms and four-domain analysis. "One signal" refers to the deterministic signal; "two systems" refer to continuous time system and discrete time system; "three transforms" refer to Fourier transform, Laplace transform and Z transform; "Four-domain analysis" refer to the time-domain, frequency-domain, complex frequency and Z-domain analysis.

This course will enable the students to acquire theory and practical skills on the following aspects: the expression and calculation of signals, properties and expressions of systems, time-domain analysis of systems, convolution and convolution sum, Fourier analysis, frequency analysis and sampling thermo, continuous system Laplace transformation analysis and the discrete signal Z transformation and its analysis. This course is the basis of the following *Digital Signal Processing*, *Communication Principle*, *Automatic Control Principle* and *Random Signal Analysis*.

第一节　绪论

Section 1　Introduction

信息网络　information network
消息　message
信息　information
电路　circuit
物理系统　physical system
非物理系统　nonphysical system
函数　function
周期　period
★周期信号　periodic signal
非周期信号　nonperiodic signal
确定性信号　deterministic signal
随机信号　random signal
混沌　chaos
★连续(时间)信号　continuous (time) signal
★离散(时间)信号　discrete (time) signal
数字信号　digital signal
模拟信号　analog signal
指数信号　exponential signal
正弦信号　sine signal
余弦信号　cosine signal
时间常数　time constant
角频率　angular frequency
复指数信号　complex exponential signal
欧拉公式　Euler's formula

抽样函数 sampling function
高斯(钟形脉冲)函数 Gaussian function
能量信号 energy signal
功率信号 power signal
奇异函数 singularity function
斜变信号 ramp signal
阶跃信号 step signal
★ 单位阶跃信号 unit step signal
阶跃函数 step function
单位阶跃函数 unit step function
符号(正负号)函数 signum function
脉冲 pulse
矩形脉冲信号 rectangular pulse signal
冲激函数 impulse function
单位冲激函数 unit impulse function
★ 单位冲激信号 unit impulse signal
δ 函数 delta function
狄拉克函数 Dirac's function
电子偶 doublet
冲激偶 impulse doublet
对偶性 duality
分解 decomposition
分量 component
直流分量 direct component
交流分量 alternating component
偶分量 even component
奇分量 odd component
脉冲分量 pulse component
实分量 real component
虚分量 imaginary component
实部 real part
虚部 imaginary part
分形 fractal
阶(次) order
方程 equation
代数方程 algebraic equation
★ 微分方程 differential equation
偏微分方程 partial differential equation
★ 差分方程 difference equation
★ 线性系统 linear system
非线性系统 nonlinear system
★ 时不变系统 time-invariant system
时变系统 time-varying system
★ 连续时间系统 continuous-time system
★ 离散时间系统 discrete-time system
集总的 lumped
参数 parameter
集总参数系统 lumped-parameter system
分布参数系统 distributed-parameter system
即时系统 instantaneous system
动态系统 dynamic system
可逆系统 invertible system
齐次性(均匀性) homogeneity
叠加性 superposition property
★ 因果系统 causal system
状态变量方法 state variable method
变换域方法 transform domain method

1 Signals are represented mathematically as functions of one or more independent variables. For example, a picture can be represented by brightness as a function of two spatial variables, and a speech signal can be represented mathematically by acoustic pressure as a function of time.

信号可以表示成一个或者多个独立变量的函数。例如,一幅图片可以表示成二维空间变量的亮度函数,语音信号可以表示成声压随时间变化的数学函数。

2 To understand the material in this text, the reader is assumed to have a basic knowledge of calculus, along with some knowledge of differential equations and the first circuit course in electrical engineering.

为了理解本文内容,应假设读者已经掌握积分以及微分基本知识,并已经学习过电子工程的第一门电路课程。

3 In this section and the next, we introduce several basic continuous-time and discrete-time signals. Not only do these signals occur frequently, but they also serve as basic building blocks from which we can construct many other signals.

本节及下节,我们将介绍几种基本连续时间与离散时间信号。不仅因为这些信号出现频率高,而且它们还是构建很多其他信号的基本分量。

第二节 连续时间系统的时域分析

Section 2 Time-domain Analysis of Continuous-time Systems

时域 time domain
特解 particular solution
特征方程 characteristic equation
特征根 characteristic root
齐次解 homogeneous solution
★ 自由响应 natural response
★ 强迫响应 forced response
★ 完全响应 total response
激励函数 activation function
响应函数 response function
★ 矩阵 matrix
范德蒙特矩阵 Vandermonde matrix
固有(自然)频率 natural frequency
★ 初始状态 initial state
起始状态 original state
线性时不变系统 linear time-invariant system
状态方程 state equation
初始条件 initial condition
★ 零输入响应 zero-input response
★ 零状态响应 zero-state response
★ 稳态响应 steady-state response
★ 瞬态响应 transient response
零输入线性 zero-input linearity
零状态线性 zero-state linearity
★ 冲激响应 impulse response
卷积 convolution
★ 卷积积分 convolution integral
★ 阶跃响应 step response
卷积的性质 properties of convolution
算子符号 operational notation

例1 Consider a system whose input $x(t)$ and output $y(t)$ satisfy the first order differential equation $\frac{dy(t)}{dt}+3y(t)=x(t)$. Now let $x_1(t)$ and $x_2(t)$ be arbitrary signals so that $x_1(t)=0$ for $t<t_1$, $x_2(t)=0$, for $t<t_2$. Let $y_1(t)$ be the system output for input $x_1(t)$, $y_2(t)$ be the system output for input $x_2(t)$, and $y_3(t)$ be the system output for $x_3(t)=ax_1(t)+\beta x_2(t)$. If it shows that $y_3(t)=ay_1(t)+\beta y_2(t)$, we may therefore conclude that the system under consideration is linear.

假设系统的输入 $x(t)$与输出 $y(t)$满足一阶微分方程$\frac{dy(t)}{dt}+3y(t)=x(t)$。使 $x_1(t)$与 $x_2(t)$是任意信号,且 $t<t_1$ 时,$x_1(t)=0$,$t<t_2$ 时,$x_2(t)=0$,且 $y_1(t)$是输入为 $x_1(t)$时系统输出,$y_2(t)$是输入为 $x_2(t)$时的系统输出。$y_3(t)$是输入 $x_3(t)=ax_1(t)+\beta x_2(t)$的系统输出。如果 $y_3(t)=ay_1(t)+\beta y_2(t)$,我们就可以得出结论:该系统是线性的。

例2 More generally, to solve a differential equation, we must specify one or more auxiliary conditions, and once these are specified, we can then, in principle, obtain an explicit expression for the output in terms of the input.

更一般的情况是,为了解微分方程,我们必须指定一个或者更多个辅助条件,一旦这些条件被指定,在原则上就可以得到给定输入情况下的精确输出表达式。

第三节 傅里叶变换

Section 3 Fourier Transform

傅里叶变换 Fourier transform
傅里叶分析 Fourier analysis
频域 frequency domain
★ 频域分析 frequency domain analysis
正弦分量 sine component
余弦分量 cosine component
★ 傅里叶级数 Fourier series
三角傅里叶级数 trigonometric Fourier series
★ 频谱 frequency spectrum/spectrum
基波分量 fundamental component
谐波分量 harmonic component
狄利克雷条件 Dirichlet condition

离散频谱　discrete spectrum
包络线　envelope
指数傅里叶级数　exponential Fourier series
幅度频谱　amplitude spectrum
相位频谱　phase spectrum
复数频谱　complex frequency spectrum
★ 傅里叶系数　Fourier coefficient
奇函数　odd function
偶函数　even function
奇谐函数　odd harmonic function
脉冲宽度　width of pulse
最小均方误差　minimum mean square error
周期矩形信号　periodic rectangle signal
频谱密度　spectrum density
频谱函数　spectrum function
频谱密度函数　spectrum density function
连续频谱　continuous spectrum
傅里叶变换的性质　properties of Fourier transform
对称性　symmetry
实函数　real function
虚函数　imaginary function
尺度(变换)特性　scaling property
时移特性　time-shifting property
频移特性　frequency-shifting property
卷积定理　convolution theorem
时域卷积定理　time domain convolution theorem
频域卷积定理　frequency domain convolution theorem
相关　correlation
自相关　autocorrelation
时域抽样　time domain sampling
冲激抽样　impulse sampling
频域抽样　frequency domain sampling
★ 抽样定理　sampling theorem
时域抽样定理　time domain sampling theorem
★ 抽样频率　sampling rate
★ 抽样间隔　sampling interval
混叠　aliasing
频域抽样定理　frequency domain sampling theorem
★ 奈奎斯特频率　Nyquist frequency
★ 奈奎斯特间隔　Nyquist interval
雷达信号　radar signal
升余弦滚降信号　raised cosine roll-off signal
幅度失真　amplitude distortion
相位失真　phase distortion
线性失真　linear distortion
佩利—维纳准则　Paley-Wiener criterion
群时延　group delay
量化　quantization
调制　modulation
振幅调制(调幅)　amplitude modulation
载波　carrier wave/carrier
记忆系统　memory system

1 This example illustrates the basic idea behind Fourier's development as a representation for aperiodic signals. Specifically, we think of an aperiodic signal as the limit of a periodic signal as the period becomes arbitrarily large, and we examine the limiting behavior of the Fourier series representation for this signal.

本例展示了傅里叶作为非周期信号表示方法的演变历程。特殊情况下,可以把非周期信号看成周期趋近于任意大的周期信号的极限情况,即该信号的傅里叶级数表示的极限情况。

2 Just as with periodic signals, there is an alternative set of conditions which are sufficient to ensure that $\hat{x}(t)$ is equal to $x(t)$ for any t except at a discontinuity, where it is equal to the average of the values on either side of the discontinuity.

正像周期信号,有一系列的条件足以保证对除了在不连续点外的所有 t,$\hat{x}(t)$ 等于 $x(t)$,在不连续点处,函数值等于不连续点两侧函数值的平均。

3 If a signal $x(t)$ is not bandlimited, it is said to have infinite bandwidth or an infinite spectrum. Since bandlimited signals cannot be time limited, time-limited signals cannot be bandlimited, and thus all time-limited signals have infinite bandwidth.

如果信号 $x(t)$ 不是带限的,我们就说它有无限带宽或无限频谱。由于带限信号不能是时限的,时限信号不能是带限的，所以，所有的时限信号都有无限的带宽。

When computing or displaying the Fourier transform of a real-valued signal, the real and imaginary parts or magnitude and phase of the transform only need to be specified for positive frequencies, as the values for negative frequencies can be determined directly from the values for $\omega>0$ using the relationships just derived.
当计算或显示实信号傅里叶变换时，变换的实部与虚部或幅度与相位仅需要随着正频率变化即可，因为负频率处的函数值可以直接根据刚得到的关系及 $\omega>0$ 时的函数值直接求得。

第四节 拉普拉斯变换、连续时间系统的 S 域分析

Section 4 The Laplace Transform and the S-domain Analysis of Continuous-time Systems

★拉普拉斯变换 Laplace transform
复频率 complex frequency
复频域 complex frequency domain
收敛 convergence
★收敛域 region of convergence (ROC)
收敛轴 axis of convergence
原函数 original function
传递函数 transform function
单边拉普拉斯变换 single-sided Laplace transform
双边拉普拉斯变换 two-sided Laplace transform
横坐标 abscissa
收敛横坐标 abscissa of convergence
指数阶函数 function of exponential order
拉普拉斯变换的性质
properties of Laplace transform
初值定理 initial value theorem
终值定理 final value theorem
★拉普拉斯逆变换 inverse Laplace transform
部分分式展开 partial fraction expansion
有理函数 rational function
有理分式 rational fraction
共轭 conjugate
留数 residue
留数定理 residue theorem
围线 contour
围线积分 contour integral
诺顿定理 Norton's theorem
★系统函数 system function
网络函数 network function
转移函数 transfer function
传输算子 transfer operator
实轴 real axis
虚轴 imaginary axis
★零极点图 zero-pole plot/zero-pole diagram
★频率响应 frequency response
截止频率 cut-off frequency
★滤波网络 filter network
理想低通滤波器 ideal low-pass filter
通带 pass-band
通带宽度 width of pass-band
★全通网络 all-pass network
全通函数 all-pass function
★最小相移网络 minimum-phase network
最小相移函数 minimum-phase function
★稳定系统 stable system
不稳定系统 nonstable system
临界稳定系统 marginally stable system
稳定 stabilization
元件模型 component model
一阶极点 first order pole
频响特性 frequency response characteristics
相位检波器 phase detector

As with their continuous-time counterparts, discrete-time filters described by linear constant-coefficient difference equations are of considerable importance in practice. Indeed, since they can be efficiently implemented in special- or general-purpose digital systems, filters described by difference equations are widely used in practice. As in almost all aspects of signal and system analysis, when we examine discrete-time filters described by difference equations, we find both strong similarities and important differences with the continuous-time case. In particular, discrete-time LTI systems described by difference equations can either be recursive and have impulse responses of infinite length or be nonrecursive and have finite-length impulse responses.

正像它们的连续时间相对应的部分那样，用线性常系数差分方程描述的离散时间滤波器在实践中起着非常重要的作用。的确，因为它们可以通过专用或通用数字系统实现，使用差分方程描述的滤波器在实际中广泛应用。正像几乎所有的信号与系统分析中那样，当我们考虑使用差分方程描述的离散时间系统时，既寻找和连续时间系统的高度相似性，也寻找重要的差异性。尤其是使用差分方程描述离散时间线性时，不变系统可以是递归的，具有无限长冲激响应，也可以是非递归的，具有有限长冲激响应。

2 Let $h(n)$ denote the output response of the system when the input $x(n)$ is equal to the unit sample signal $\delta(n)$ with no initial energy in the system at time $n=0$. The response $h(n)$ is referred to as the unit sample response of the system. The output response $y(n)$ resulting from input $x(n)$ with no initial energy at time $n=0$ equals to the convolution of the unit-sample response $h(n)$ with the input $x(n)$.

在时间 $n=0$ 时，输入 $x(n)$为单位样值信号 $\delta(n)$，且系统是零状态的，系统的输出响应 $h(n)$称为系统的单位样值响应。在零状态时，输入 $x(n)$的输出响应 $y(n)$等于单位样值响应 $h(n)$和输入 $x(n)$的卷积。

3 An important property of the system described by the linear constant-coefficient difference and differential equations is that they can be represented in very simple and natural ways in terms of block diagram interconnections of elementary operations. This is significant for a number of reasons. One is that it provides a pictorial representation which can deepen our understanding of the behavior and properties of these systems. In addition, such representations can be of considerable value for the simulation or implementation of the systems. The corresponding representation for discrete-time difference equations suggests simple and efficient ways in which the systems that the equations describe can be implemented in digital hardware.

由线性常系数差分和微分方程描述的系统一个重要的特点是：它们可以以很简单而且很自然的方式用若干基本运算的方框图互联来表示。这样做是很有意义的。其一是它给出一种形象化的表示，这有助于加深对这些系统的特性和性质的理解。另外，这种表示对于系统的仿真或实现有很大的价值。离散时间差分方程方框图的表示还能对由差分方程描述的系统以数字硬件方式来实现提供一些简便而有效的方式。

4 As an application of the difference equation framework, a linear constant-coefficient input/output differential equation can be discretized in time, resulting in a difference equation that can then be solved by recursion. This discretization in time actually yields a discrete-time representation of the continuous-time system defined by the given input/output differential equation.

在差分方程的应用中，线性常系数输入/输出微分方程可以在时间上离散化，使得差分方程可以利用递归求解。时间上的离散化将产生一个离散时间表达式，这个表达式是由给定的连续时间系统的输入/输出微分方程所定义的。

第五节　Z 变换、离散时间系统的 Z 域分析

Section 5　The Z Transform and the Z-domain Analysis of Discrete-time Systems

★ 双边 Z 变换　bilateral Z transform

★ 单边 Z 变换　single-sided Z transform

洛朗级数　Laurent series

围线积分法　contour integral method

幂级数　power series

帕塞瓦尔定理　Parseval theorem

幂级数展开法 power series expansion method
部分分式展开法 partial fraction expansion method
离散时间傅里叶变换(序列的傅里叶变换) discrete time Fourier transform (DTFT)
相位检波器 phase detector

1 The relationship between the Z-transform and Fourier transform for discrete-time signals parallels closely the corresponding discussion in Section 9. 1 for continuous-time signals, but with some important differences. In the continuous-time case, the Laplace transform reduces to the Fourier transform when the real part of the transform variable is zero. Interpreted in terms of the s-plane, this means that the Laplace transform reduces to the Fourier transform on the imaginary axis. In contrast, the Z-transform reduces to the Fourier transform when the magnitude of the transform variable Z is unity. Thus, the Z-transform reduces to the Fourier transform on the contour in the complex Z-plane corresponding to a circle with a radius of unity, as indicated in Figure 10. 3. This circle in the Z-plane is referred to as the unit circle and plays a role in the discussion of the Z-transform similar to the role of the imaginary axis in the s-plane for the Laplace transform.

离散时间信号变换与傅里叶变换之间的关系和 9.1 节中连续时间信号的相关讨论非常类似,但有一些很重要的不同点。在连续时间情况下,当变换变量的实部为 0 时,拉普拉斯变换就简化为傅里叶变换。使用 s 平面的术语解释意味着虚轴上的拉普拉斯变换就是傅里叶变换。相对比情况下,当 Z 变换的变换变量 Z 的幅度为 1 时,Z 变换简化为傅里叶变换。因此,复数 Z 平面上半径为 1 的单位圆上的 Z 变换简化为傅里叶变换,如图 10.3 所示。Z 平面上的该圆被称为单位圆,在 Z 变换中扮演的角色与拉普拉斯变换中 s 平面的虚轴类似。

2 If the Z-transform $X(z)$ of $x(n)$ is rational, and if $x(n)$ is left sided, then the ROC is the region in the Z-plane inside the innermost nonzero pole, i. e. , inside the circle of radius equal to the smallest magnitude of the poles of $X(z)$ other than any at $z=0$ and extending inward to and possibly including $z=0$. In particular, if $x(n)$ is anticausal, then the ROC also includes $z=0$.

如果 $x(n)$ 的 z 变换 $X(z)$ 是有理的,且 $x(n)$ 是左边序列,那么收敛域是 Z 平面内最里边非零极点内区域,即半径等于除了 $z=0$ 外的其余 $X(z)$ 极点最小幅度,并继续向内延伸可能包含 $z=0$。尤其,如果 $x(n)$ 是非因果的,那么收敛域也包括 $z=0$。

3 Let $X(z)$ be given in the rational form $X(z)=B(z)/A(z)$ with the polynomials $B(z)$ and $A(z)$ written in descending powers of z. To compute the inverse Z-transform $x(n)$ for a finite range of values of n, $X(z)$ can be expanded into a power series in z^{-1} by dividing $A(z)$ into $B(z)$ using long division. The values of the signal $x(n)$ are then "read off" from the coefficients of the power-series expansion.

令 $X(z)$ 以有理函数 $X(z)=B(z)/A(z)$ 的形式给出,$B(z)$ 与 $A(z)$ 都写成 z 的降幂形式。为计算出在 n 的有限范围内的 Z 反变换 $x(n)$,可应用长除法即 $A(z)$ 队以 $B(z)$ 将 $X(z)$ 展开成 z^{-1} 的幂级数形式。则信号 $x(n)$ 的值可通过幂级数展开的系数直接"读出"。

4 Using long division as described above, the inverse Z-transform $x(n)$ of $X(z)$ can be computed for any finite range of integer values of n. However, if an analytical expression for $x(n)$ is desired that is valid for all $n \geqslant 0$, it is necessary to use partial fraction expansion as was done in the Laplace transform theory.

上面应用长除法计算 Z 反变换,对于任何整数值 n 都可以由 $X(z)$ 计算出 Z 反变换 $x(n)$。然而如果要求得到对于所有 $n \geqslant 0$ 都成立的 $x(n)$ 解析表达式,与拉普拉斯变换原理一样需要应用部分分式展开。

5 Because there exists a close connection between bilateral and unilateral Z-transforms, the calculation of unilateral transforms proceeds much as for bilateral transforms, with the caveat that we must take

care to limit the range of summation in the transform to $n \geqslant 0$. Similarly, the calculation of inverse unilateral transforms is basically the same as for bilateral transforms, once we consider of the fact that the ROC for a unilateral transform is always the exterior of a circle.
由于双边和单边Z变换之间的紧密联系,因此单边变换的计算和双边变换也相差不多,只是要预先注意考虑在变换求和中的极限是对 $n \geqslant 0$ 进行的。同理,单边Z反变换的计算基本上与双边变换相同,只要考虑到对单边变换而言,其ROC总是位于某一个圆的外边。

第六节 系统的状态变量分析

Section 6 State Representation of Systems

积分器 integrator
系统的仿真 simulation of system
★ 信号流图 signal-flow graph
节点 node
支路 branch
输入节点(源点) source node
输出节点(阱点) sink node
通路 path
开通路 open path
闭通路 closed path
前向通路 forward path
流图转置 transposition of flow graph
★ 梅森公式 Mason formula
可观测性 observability
可控制性 controllability
★ 状态变量 state variable
状态矢量 state vector
状态空间 state space
轨迹 trajectory
状态轨迹 state trajectory
★ 状态方程 state equation
★ 输出方程 output equation
对角线矩阵 diagonal matrix
约当矩阵 Jordan matrix
矢量微分方程 vector differential equation
矢量差分方程 vector difference equation
矩阵指数 matrix exponential
状态转移矩阵 state transition matrix
特征矩阵 characteristic matrix
矢量差分方程 vector difference equation
传输算子 transfer operator
相位检波器 phase detector

第二部分 实验

Part Two: Experiment

第××章 信号与系统实验

Section ×× Experiments of Signals and Systems

Lab 4: Frequency Spectrum Analysis of ECG Signal
Type: verification
The experiment date: ×× ×× ×××× Place: ××
Professional Class: ×× Name: ××
Student No.: ×× Instructed by: ×× Term: ××

1. Objectives

(1)To know the physical meaning of the Fourier transform and understand the connotation of the Fourier transform deeply.

(2) To better understand signal analysis engineering application; develop the comprehensive application ability in the field of signal analysis.

(3)To practice the operation instructions of ECG signal based on MATLAB.

(4)To understand the MIT-BIH database of ECG signal's storage-way and its characteristics.

(5)To embolden the understanding of sampling theorem.

2. Equipments and Components Needed

Personal computer.

3. Tasks and Procedure (Including schematic diagram)

(1)Read a period of ECG signal in the MIT-BIH ECG database.

(2)Use Fourier transform to change ECG signal, and draw the time domain and frequency domain waveform, the requirement of the horizontal axis of the time domain waveform for time (in second), frequency domain of the horizontal axis of the waveform for frequency(Hz).

Cut out QRS and T waves and analyze their spectrums. They are showed in Fig. 1.

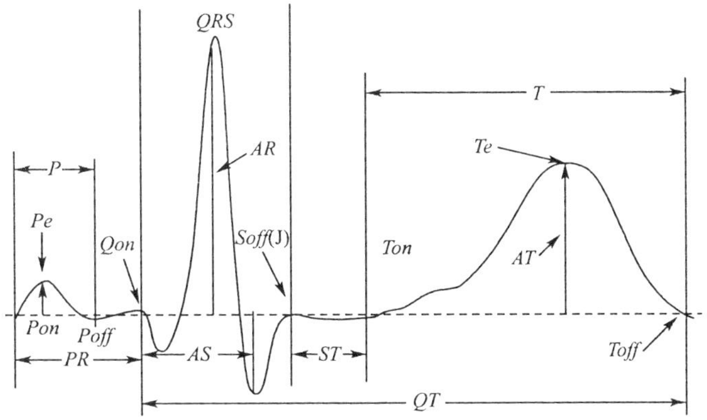

Fig. 1 Normal ECG Waveform and Characteristic Parameters

(3)Analyze the spectrums of ECG signals

Fourier transform builds up the concept of signal spectrum. The Fourier analysis is to analyze the signal spectrum, bandwidth and so on. The analysis is no exception either; it needs to adopt Fourier transform.

For continuous time signal $f(t)$, its Fourier transform $F(\omega)$ is $F(\omega)=\int_{-\infty}^{\infty} f(t)e^{-j\omega t}dt$.

The continuous time Fourier transform especially fits for the theory analysis of the continuous time signal. But as $f(t)$ and $F(\omega)$ are both continuous functions, it does not fit for computer processing.

So we use the Fourier transform of the numerical method to solve this problem.

If $f(t)$ catches the value interval $[t_1, t_2]$, define $T=t_2-t_1$ as the length and sample N numbers. Let $\Delta t=\frac{T}{N}$, then

$$F(\omega) = \sum_{n=0}^{N-1} f(t_1+n\Delta t)e^{-j\omega(t_1+n\Delta t)}\Delta t = \Delta t \cdot \sum_{n=0}^{N-1} f(t_1+n\Delta t)e^{-j\omega(t_1+n\Delta t)}$$

Assume $F(\omega)$ can catch the value interval $[\omega_1, \omega_2]$, if we give homogeneous sampling for k, then

$$F(\omega_1+k\Delta\omega) = \sum_{n=0}^{N-1} f(t_1+n\Delta t)e^{-j(\omega_1+k\Delta\omega)\cdot(t_1+n\Delta t)}$$

And, $\Delta\omega=\frac{\omega_2-\omega_1}{k}$ is the frequency sampling interval.

4. The record of the experiment form:

ECG signal spectrum:

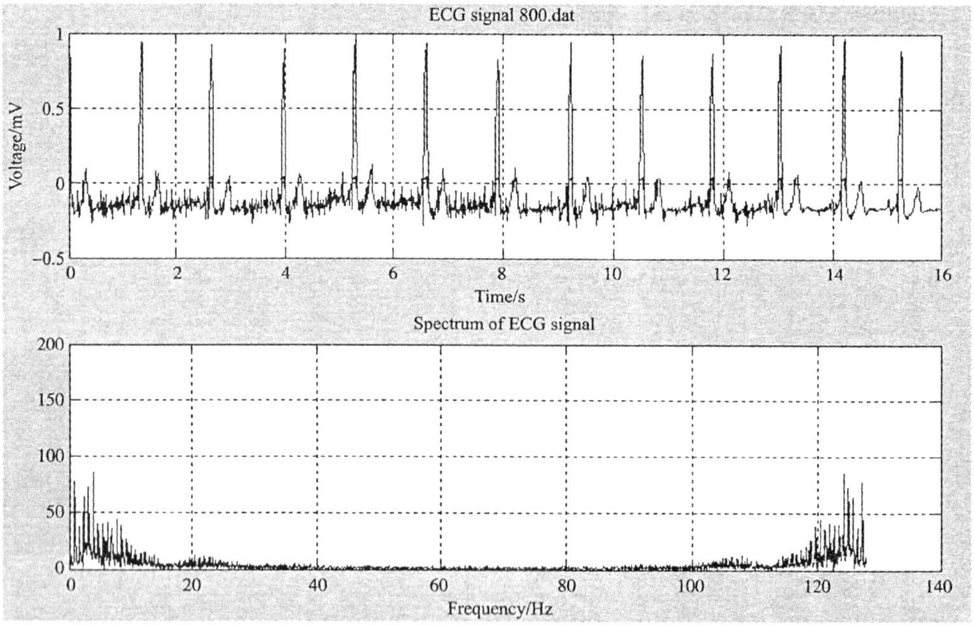

Fig. 2 The Wave and Spectrum of ECG Signal

The sub-waves and their spectrums:

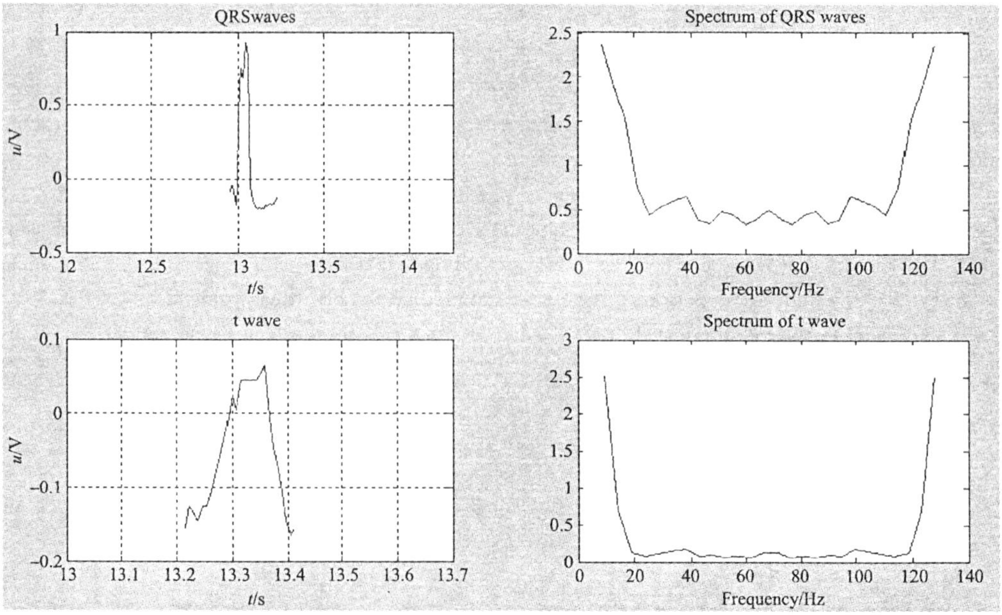

Fig. 3 The Wave and Spectrum of QRS and T

5. Data analysis

Continuous time Fourier transform is particularly suitable for time continuous signal, while engineering applications often require sampling data to Fourier analysis, in which case we often can't get the analytical expression of the signal, so we should use Fourier transform of the numerical calculation method, and then deal with problems with the help of MATLAB.

6. Answer the questions

(1) If the sampling rate is changed, what condition must be met to recover the original ECG signal?

Answer: According to the sampling theorem, we can conclude that when the minimum sampling frequency is $2f(m)$ (while $f(m)=2\pi/\omega_m$), we can learn the original ECG signal by the discrete digital signal.

(2) Talk about what you learn about "Fourier transform" after doing this experiment.

Answer: The essence of the Fourier transform is to separate a signal to many sine/complex index signals and then plus them. That is, transform the signal into the sum of a series of sign signals. It actually expands the discrete Fourier series of spectrum to a continuous spectrum.

第七章　电磁场理论
Chapter 7　Electromagnetic Field Theory

课程简介

《电磁场理论》这门课是电子信息工程专业的一门专业基础课。本课程介绍了麦克斯韦方程的电磁准静态形式在介质、导体中的应用，以及边值问题。本课程的主要内容有：电磁力，力密度，力张量，包括磁化、极化，电磁场的热动力学，动态方程和能量守恒，电磁波的传播和稳定性，以及电荷传输的现象。

通过本课程的学习，学生能够说出麦克斯韦方程并解释它们与两个粒子之间的力的关系，可以对场进行微观和宏观描述，能够用向量分析法求解电磁场问题，能够用向量分析法分析麦克斯韦方程并解决一般问题，能够根据电磁学理论定义场，并说出该场遵循的定律。

Course Summary

Electromagnetic Field Theory is a basic course of Electronic Information Engineering. This course examines electric and magnetic quasi-static forms of Maxwell's equations applied to dielectric, conduction, and magnetization boundary value problems. Topics covered include: electromagnetic forces; force densities; stress tensors, including magnetization and polarization; thermodynamics of electromagnetic fields; equations of motion, and energy conservation; propagation and stability of electromechanical waves; charge transport phenomena.

Through this course, students will be able to state Maxwell's equations and explain how they can be related to the force between two particles, give a semiclassical description of the microscopic origin and interpretation of macroscopic fields (D and H) in matter, apply vector analysis to the solution of problems in electromagnetism, use vector analysis to apply Maxwell's equations and solve standard problems, define the fields commonly used in electromagnetism, and state the laws these fields obey.

第一节　矢量分析
Section 1　Vector Analysis

★ 矢量　vector
★ 标量　scalar
矢量场　vector field
标量场　scalar field
★ 矢量积　product of vector
★ 标量积　product of scalar
点积　dot product
叉积　cross product
右螺旋法则　right-hand principle
★ 哈密顿算符　Hamiltonian factor
单位矢量　unit vector
投影　projection
斯托克斯定理　Stokes' theorem
★ 静态场　static field
★ 动态场　dynamic field
★ 时不变场　time-invariant field
★ 时变场　time-varying field
等值面　equivalence
通量　flux
★ 散度　divergence
★ 旋度　curl
有旋的　rotational
无旋的　irrotational
★ 环量　circulation
★ 梯度　gradient
直角坐标系　Cartesian co-ordinate system
柱面坐标系　cylindrical co-ordinate system
球面坐标系　spherical co-ordinate system

1 Vector field:

If a quantity which is specified in a region to define a field is a vector then the corresponding field is called a vector field. For example, the gravitational force on a mass in a space is vector field. This force has a value at various points in a space and always has a specific direction. The other examples of vector field are the velocity of particles in a moving fluid, wind velocity of atmosphere, voltage gradient in a cable, displacement of a flying bird in a space, magnetic field existing from north to south field, etc.

矢量场:如果在一个区域中定义一个场的量是矢量,那么这个相应的场就叫做矢量场。例如空间中物体的万有引力场就是矢量场。这个力在空间的每一点都有一个值,而且有一个确定的方向。矢量场的其他例子还有:在流体中粒子的速度、大气中的风速、电缆中电压的梯度、空间中飞鸟的位移、从北方到南方都存在的磁场等。

2 Stokes' theorem:

The Stokes' theorem relates the line integral to a surface integral. It states that the line integral of $\vec{F}$ around a closed path L is equal to the integral of curl of $\vec{F}$ over the open surface S enclosed by the closed path L.

Mathematically it is expressed as $\oint_L \vec{F} \cdot d\vec{L} = \int_S (\nabla \times \vec{F}) \cdot d\vec{S}$

斯托克斯定理:

斯托克斯定理把线积分与面积分联系起来。它说的是:

$\vec{F}$ 沿闭合路径 L 的线积分等于 $\vec{F}$ 的旋度对由闭合路径 L 所包围的开放平面 S 的积分。

它的数学表达式是:$\oint_L \vec{F} \cdot d\vec{L} = \int_S (\nabla \times \vec{F}) \cdot d\vec{S}$。

第二节 电磁场的基本规律
Section 2 Basic Laws in Electromagnetic Field

★ 电荷 charge
正电荷 positive charge
负电荷 negative charge
★ 静电场 electrostatic field
连续性方程 equation of continuity
★ 点电荷 point charge
★ 线电荷 line charge
★ 面电荷 surface charge
★ 体电荷 volume charge
无限长线电荷 infinite line charge
无限大带电平面 infinite sheet of charge
电荷线密度 line charge density
电荷面密度 surface charge density
电荷体密度 volume charge density
★ 电流密度 current density
★ 恒定电流 steady current
体电流 volume current
面电流 surface current
线电流 line current
★ 电场强度 electric field intensity
库仑定律 Coulomb's law
闭合回路 closed path
★ 源变量 source variable
★ 场变量 field variable
★ 电通(量)密度 electric flux density
★ 介电常数 dielectric constant
★ 磁场 magnetic field
★ 恒定磁场 steady magnetic field
★ 磁通量 magnetic flux
★ 磁通密度 magnetic flux density
电磁感应定律
law of electromagnetic induction
★ 磁场强度 magnetic field intensity
★ 磁感应强度 magnetic induced intensity
★ 磁导率 permeability
★ 位移电流 displacement current
★ 传导电流 conduction current
运流电流 convection current
均匀的 homogenous
极化 polarization
电极化强度 electric polarization intensity
★ 束缚电荷 bound charge
★ 极化系数 polarization coefficient
相对介电常数 relative dielectric constant
非线性电介质 nonlinear dielectric
★ 电导率 conductivity
电偶极子 electric dipole
★ 磁偶极子 magnetic dipole
★ 磁矩 magnetic moment
★ 磁化强度 magnetization intensity vector
★ 磁介质 magnetic medium
自由电子 free electron

磁化电流 magnetic current
磁化率 magnetic susceptibility
顺磁性 paramagnetism
抗磁性 diamagnetism
★ 磁化面电流 magnetic surface current
★ 磁化体电流 magnetic volume current
★ 磁阻 reluctance
非线性磁路 nonlinear magnetic circuit
磁化特性曲线 magnetization characteristic curve
★ 导体 conductor
★ 电介质 dielectric
★ 理想导体 ideal conductor
★ 理想的电介质材料 ideal dielectric material
★ 麦克斯韦方程 Maxwell's equation
边界 boundary
★ 边界条件 boundary condition
★ 边界值问题 boundary value problem
★ 法向分量 normal component
★ 切向分量 tangential component
自由空间 free space
本构关系 constitutive relationship

1 Magnetic flux density:

The total magnetic lines of force, i. e. , magnetic flux crossing a unit area in a plane at right angles to the direction of flux is called magnetic flux density. It is denoted as $\vec{B}$ and is a vector quantity. It is measured in weber per square meter (Wb/m^2), which is also called Tesla (T). This is similar to the electric field intensity $\vec{E}$ in electrostatics.

磁通密度：

垂直穿过单位面积平面的所有磁力线(即磁通)，叫做磁通密度。它用 $\vec{B}$ 来表示，是一个矢量。它的单位是韦伯每平方米(Wb/m^2)，也叫做特斯拉(T)。它与静电学中的电场强度 $\vec{E}$ 相似。

2 Current density:

The current density is a vector quantity associated with the current and denoted as $\vec{J}$. The current density is defined as the current passing through the unit surface area, when the surface is held normal to the direction of the current. The current density is measured in amperes per square meter (A/m^2).

电流密度：

电流密度是一个与电流有关的矢量，用 $\vec{J}$ 表示。电流密度定义为垂直穿过单位面积平面的电流。电流密度的单位是安培每平方米(A/m^2)。

第三节 静态电磁场及其边值问题的解

Section 3 Static Electromagnetic Field and Solutions of Boundary Problems

积分方程 integral equation
微分方程 differential equation
高斯定律 Gauss's Law
★ 电位函数 electric potential function
★ 负梯度 negative gradient
导数 derivative
泊松方程 Poisson's equation
等电位体 equipotential volume
恒定电场 steady electric field
★ 对称性 symmetry property
诺伊曼边界条件 Neumann boundary condition
混合边界条件 mixed boundary condition
唯一性定理 uniqueness theorem
★ 等位面 equipotential surface
★ 电势 electric potential
电势差 electric potential difference
电容 capacitance
电容系数 capacitance coefficient
感应系数 induction coefficient
★ 自电导 self-conductance
★ 互电导 mutual conductance
电场能量 electric field energy
电动势 electromotive force
静电力 electrostatic force
能量体密度 energy volume density
磁特性方程 magnetic characteristic equation
基本变量 basic variable
★ 磁感线 magnetic induced line
偏微分方程 partial differential equation

重叠区域　overlap area
★ 矢量磁位　magnetic vector potential
标量磁位　magnetic scalar potential
库仑规范　Coulomb's gauge
★ 自电感　self-inductance
★ 互电感　mutual inductance
耦合系数　coefficient of coupling
磁链　magnetic flux linkage
磁场能量　magnetic field energy
互感系数　mutual inductance coefficient
自感系数　self-inductance coefficient
★ 磁力　magnetic force
★ 磁能密度　magnetic energy density
★ 安培环路定律　Ampere's circuital law
分离变量法　dissociative variable method
分离常数　dissociative constant
双曲函数　hyperbolic function
指数函数　indicial function
密度函数　density function
正弦函数　sinusoidal function
衰减的　attenuated
★ 欧拉方程　Euler equation
待定常数　indeterminate constant
正交性　orthogonality
★ 镜像法　method of images
★ 镜像电荷　the image charge
有限差分法　finite-difference method
解析解　analytical solution
数值解　numerical solutions
精度　accuracy
简单迭代法　simply iterative method

Vector magnetic potential:

The magnetic flux density is always solenoid (continuous) because its divergence is zero. A vector whose divergence is zero can be expressed in terms of the curl of another vector quantity as

$$\vec{B} = \nabla \times \vec{A}$$

where $\vec{A}$ is called the magnetic vector potential and is expressed in Weber's per meter (Wb/m).

矢量磁位：

磁通密度是无散的(连续的)，因为它的散度为零。一个散度为零的矢量可用另一个矢量的旋度表示

$$\vec{B} = \nabla \times \vec{A}$$

此处 $\vec{A}$ 就是矢量磁位，以韦伯每米表示。

Method of images:

In the method of images, a conducting plane is temporarily ignored, and an imaginary charge is placed behind the plane. The imaginary charge is equal in magnitude and opposite in polarity to the real charge. The distance between the real and the imaginary charges is twice the distance between the real charge and the plane.

镜像法：

所谓镜像法，就是暂时忽略导电平面的存在，并在平面后面放置虚拟电荷。虚拟电荷与真实电荷大小相等，极性相反，它们之间的距离是真实电荷与平面距离的两倍。

第四节　时变电磁场

Section 4　Time-varying Electromagnetic Field

★ 感应电动势　induced electromotive force
★ 感应电场　induced electric field
★ 保守场　conservative field
★ 非保守场　nonconservative field
电磁能量守恒定律
law of conservative of energy in electromagnetism
★ 坡印廷定理　Poynting's theorem
★ 坡印廷矢量　Poynting vector
能流矢量　energy flow vector
瞬时值　instantaneous value
★ 波动方程　wave equation
动态矢量位　dynamic vector potential
动态标量位　dynamic scalar potential
洛伦兹条件　Lorentz condition
★ 亥姆霍兹方程　Helmholtz equation
★ 时谐场　time-harmonic field
功率流密度　power flow density
★ 平均坡印廷矢量　average Poynting vector

复数的 complex | 复矢量 complex vector

1 Electromagnetic induction:

The process of inducing an emf in a coil (also called a loop) by placing it in a time-varying magnetic field is now commonly called as an electromagnetic induction. In fact, the electromagnetic induction will take place if one of the following conditions holds:

1) The coil continuously changes its shape or position when the magnetic flux distribution in the region is uniform. The shape can be changed by squeezing or stretching the coil.

2) The magnetic flux linking the coil changes with time and the coil is in motion and/or changes its shape.

3) The magnetic flux passing through (linking) a stationary coil varies as a function of time.

电磁感应:

将线圈(亦称环路)放在时变磁场内感应一个电动势的过程称为电磁感应。事实上,当下列条件之一存在时,即有电磁感应:

1)线圈在均匀磁场中连续改变它的形状或位置。线圈的形状可用挤压或拉伸来改变。

2)交链线圈的磁通量随时间变化,并且线圈会运动和(或)改变它们的形状。

3)随时间变化的磁通穿过(交链)静止线圈。

2 Poynting vector:

As power flows in certain direction, it is a vector quantity. To illustrate this, consider that the field is transmitted in the form of electromagnetic waves from an antenna. Both the fields are sinusoidal in nature. The power radiated from antenna has a particular direction. Hence to calculate a power density, we must carry out a cross product of $\vec{E}$ and $\vec{H}$. The power density is given by,

$$\vec{S} = \vec{E} \times \vec{H}$$

where $\vec{S}$ is called Poynting Vector, named after an English Physicist John N. Poynting. $\vec{S}$ is the instantaneous power density vector associated with the electromagnetic field at a given point. The direction of $\vec{S}$ indicates instantaneous power flow at the point.

坡印廷矢量:

当能量沿一个方向流动时,它就成为一个矢量。为了说明这个现象,我们假设这个场是以电磁波的形式从天线发出。这两个场都是正弦的,从天线辐射出的能量有一个确定的方向。因此,要计算能量密度,我们必须采用 $\vec{E}$ 和 $\vec{H}$ 的叉积。能量密度表示为

$$\vec{S} = \vec{E} \times \vec{H}$$

其中 $\vec{S}$ 是坡印廷矢量,是根据英国物理学家约翰·N·坡印廷的名字命名的。$\vec{S}$ 是与给定点的电磁场相关的瞬时能量密度矢量。$\vec{S}$ 的方向表示该点瞬时能量流的方向。

第五节 均匀平面波在无界空间中的传播

Section 5 Propagation of Uniform Plane Waves in Free Space

★ 均匀平面波 uniform plane wave
★ 周期函数 cycle/period function
角频率 angular frequency
★ 波长 wavelength
★ 波数 number of wave
★ 相速 phase speed
波源 source of wave
★ 本征阻抗 intrinsic impedance
波的极化特性 polarized characteristic of wave
★ 直线极化 linear polarization
★ 圆极化 circular polarization
★ 椭圆极化 elliptical polarization
衰减系数 attenuation coefficient
★ 相位系数 phase coefficient
集肤深度 skin depth
损耗介质 lossy dielectric
色散 dispersion
★ 色散效应 dispersive effect

★ 驻波　standing wave
★ 行波　traveling wave
波腹　loop
波节　node
★ 横电磁波　transverse electromagnetic wave
★ 群速　group velocity
包络波　enveloped wave
传播　propagation
传播系数　propagation coefficient

1 Skin depth:

The distance through which the amplitude of the traveling wave decreases to 37% of the original amplitude is called skin depth or depth of penetration. It is inversely proportional to the square root of frequency. So for the frequencies in the microwave range, the skin depth or depth of penetration is very small for good conductors. And all the fields and currents may be considered as confined to a very thin layer near the surface of the conductor. This thin layer is nothing but the skin of the conductor, hence this is called skin effect.

集肤深度:行波的振幅减小到原来的 37%时所传播的距离就叫做集肤深度或穿透深度。它与频率的平方根成反比。所以,对于在微波范围内的频率来说,良导体的集肤深度或穿透深度非常小。所有的场和电流都被限制在了导体表面非常薄的一层里。这个薄层就是导体的皮肤,因此它也叫做集肤效应。

2 Polarization:

Consider a uniform plane wave traveling in positive z-direction. Then the field vectors $\vec{E}$ and $\vec{H}$ lie in x-y plane, which is perpendicular to the direction of propagation of a uniform plane wave. Being an electromagnetic wave, as wave travels in a space, both the fields undergo same variations with respect to time.

There are different types of polarization of uniform plane wave as given below.

1) Linear polarization
2) Elliptical polarization
3) Circular polarization

极化:一个均匀平面波沿+z 方向传播。场矢量 $\vec{E}$ 和 $\vec{H}$ 位于 x-y 平面,并与均匀平面波的传播方向垂直。一个电磁波在空间中传播,电场和磁场随时间做同样变化。

均匀平面波的极化类型如下所示:

1) 直线极化
2) 椭圆极化
3) 圆极化

第六节　均匀平面波的反射与透射

Section 6　Reflection and Transmission of Uniform Plane Waves

分界面　interface
★ 反射波　reflected wave
★ 透射波　transmitted wave
★ 入射波　incident wave
反射系数　reflection coefficient
透射系数　transmission coefficient
电抗　reactance
电阻　resistance
电抗分量　reactance component
电阻分量　resistance component
表面电阻率　surface resistivity
表面电抗　surface reactance
表面阻抗　surface impedance
垂直的　perpendicular
★ 垂直入射　perpendicular incidence
★ 斜入射　oblique incidence
★ 平行极化　parallel polarization
★ 垂直极化　perpendicular polarization
入射　incidence
反射　reflection
折射　refraction
入射角　angle of incidence
反射角　angle of reflection
折射角　angle of refraction

1 Oblique incidence:

When a uniform plane wave strikes obliquely on the surface (either conductor or dielectric), the behavior of the reflected wave is decided by the polarization of the incident wave. There are two cases for the oblique incidence as given below.

Case (i): The electric field vector is perpendicular to the plane of incidence. In other words, the electric field vector is aligned parallel to the boundary surface. This is called horizontal polarization.

Case (ii): The magnetic field vector is aligned parallel to the boundary surface. In other words, the magnetic field vector is perpendicular to the plane of incidence while the electric field vector is aligned parallel to the plane of incidence. This is called vertical polarization.

斜入射:当一个均匀平面波斜入射到媒质表面(导体或介质)上时,反射波的性质由入射波的极化决定。斜入射有两种情况,如下所示。

情况1:电场矢量与入射平面垂直。换句话说,电场矢量与分界面平行,这叫做水平极化。

情况2:磁场矢量与分界面平行。换句话说,磁场矢量与入射平面垂直,而电场矢量与入射平面平行,这叫做垂直极化。

2 Plane of incidence:

A plane of incidence is a plane containing the vector in the direction of propagation of the incident wave and the normal to the boundary surface.

入射平面:入射平面是入射波传播方向上的矢量与分界面法线构成的平面。

第八章　通信电子线路

Chapter 8　Electronic Circuits on Communications

第一部分　通信电子线路

Part One: Electronic Circuits on Communications

课程简介

通信电子线路是电子信息类专业一门重要的专业基础课程，具有较强的理论性、工程性以及实践应用背景。这门课程涉及无线通信系统中许多基本技术和基本通信电路模块，主要包括谐振选频电路、高频小信号放大器电路、高频功率放大器电路、高频振荡器、频谱搬移电路、调制解调电路模块、反馈自动控制电路等。通过这门课程的学习，学生能够掌握和理解以上无线通信系统中各种线路的组成原理、设计方法以及基本分析方法。同时，学生应具有系统设计和工程应用能力。

Course Summary

Electronic Circuits on Communications is a primary, basic course for electronic information majors, with substantial theories, engineering property and frequent application as its characteristics. The course is concerned with many basic technologies and basic modules of wireless communication circuit, complete with resonant circuit, high frequency small signal amplifier circuit, HF power amplifier circuit, HF oscillator, spectrum shifting circuit, modulation circuit and feedback control circuit, etc. By learning the course, students can understand the important composition principles, design methods and basic analysis approaches of the above circuits in wireless communication system. Meanwhile, students should be able to develop the capability of the system design and engineering application.

第一节　绪论

Section 1　Introduction

★ 基带信号　base band signal
★ 载波信号　carrier signal
★ 已调信号　modulated signal
广播　radio broadcast
★ 无线电　radio
接收机　radio receiver
发射机　radio transmitter
天线　antenna
天线开关　antenna switch
★ 无线电波　radio wave
★ 传输信道　transmission channel
★ 频谱　frequency spectrum
3G 通信网　3-Generation network
★ 频率　frequency
频谱分配　spectrum assignment
★ 无线电中继系统　radio-relay system
无线电中继站　radio-relay station
无线通信系统　wireless communication system
★ 中波　medium wave (MW)
★ 长波　long wave (LW)
★ 短波　short wave (SW)
超短波　ultra-short wave
超长波　ultra-long wave
★ 低频　low frequency (LF)
★ 中频　medium frequency (MF)
★ 高频　high frequency (HF)
甚高频　very high frequency (VHF)
特高频　ultra high frequency (UHF)
超高频　super high frequency (SHF)
极高频　extremely high frequency (EHF)
电离层　ionosphere
对流层　troposphere
对流层反射　troposphere reflection
对流层散射　troposphere scatter
★ 调制特性　modulation characteristics
时分同步码分多址　Time Division-Synchronous

Code Division Multiple Access (TD-SCDMA)
宽带码分多址 Wideband Code Division Multiple Access (WCDMA)
码分多址 2000 Code Division Multiple Access 2000 (CDMA2000)
卫星通信 satellite communication

1 Electronic Circuit on Communications is the important basis of all kinds of wireless communication systems and wireless communication devices. A wireless communication system mainly composes of radio transmitter, receiver, antenna, antenna switch, etc.
通信电子线路是无线通信系统的基础，是各种通信设备的重要组成部分。一个无线通信系统主要由无线电发射机、接收机、天线以及天线开关等部分构成。

2 According to working frequency band, a wireless communication system can be divided into medium wave communication system, short wave communication system, ultra-short wave communication system and satellite communication system, etc.
无线通信系统根据工作频段主要有中波通信系统、短波通信系统、超短波通信系统、微波通信系统以及卫星通信系统等。

第二节 高频电路基础
Section 2 Basis of High-frequency Electronic Circuit

★ 高频电子线路 HF electronic circuit
★ 有源器件 active component
★ 二极管 diode
★ 元件(器件) component
★ 组件 module / package
★ 无源元件 passive element
★ 无源网络 passive network
★ 电阻 resistance
电阻特性 resistance characteristic
★ 电容 capacitance
★ 电感 inductance
★ 电抗 reactance
电抗特性 reactance characteristic
★ 阻抗 impedance
★ 三极管 triode
肖特基势垒二极管 Schottky barrier diode
砷化镓二极管 gallium arsenide diode
变容二极管 varactor
晶体管 transistor
场效应管 field effect transistor (FET)
谐振特性 resonant characteristic
通频带 pass band
肖特基势垒场效应管 Schottky barrier FET
砷化镓场效应管 gallium arsenide FET
★ 集成电路 integrated circuit (IC)
★ 专用集成电路
application-specific integrated circuit
★ 谐振 resonance
★ 串联谐振电路 series resonant circuit
★ 串联谐振频率 series resonant frequency
★ 串联谐振阻抗 series resonant impedance
★ 并联谐振电路 parallel resonant circuit
★ 并联谐振频率 parallel resonant frequency
★ 并联谐振阻抗 parallel resonant impedance
★ 品质因数 quality factor (Q)
有载品质因数 loaded Q/external Q
线圈品质因数 coil Q
★ 失谐 detuning
★ 接入系数 access coefficient
耦合 coupling
耦合谐振电路 coupled resonant circuit
★ 耦合线圈 coupling coil / coupling induction
★ 耦合系数 coupling coefficient
临界耦合系数 critical coupling coefficient
耦合阻抗 coupling impedance
耦合因子 coupling divisor / coupling factor
矩形系数 rectangular coefficient
参差调谐 staggering
★ 参差调谐电路 stagger-tuned circuit
★ 参差调谐放大器 stagger-tuned amplifier
变压 transformation
变压器 transformer
变压比 transformer ratio
变压器损耗 transformer loss

励磁电阻 excitation resistance
励磁电流 excitation current
励磁损耗 excitation loss
★ 传输 transfer / transmission
传输线 transmission line
石英 quartz
石英晶体 quartz crystal
石英晶体谐振器 quartz crystal resonator
石英晶体振荡器 quartz crystal oscillator
★ 滤波器 filter
陶瓷滤波器 ceramic filter
声表面波 surface acoustic wave
声表面波滤波器
surface acoustic wave filter
★ 衰减器 attenuator
匹配器 matching box
匹配负载 matching load
★ 匹配负载阻抗 matching load impedance
匹配用电阻网络 matching resistance network
★ 干扰 disturbance / interference
干扰电平 interference level
干扰电流 disturbing current
干扰抑制 interference suppression
★ 噪声 noise
噪声干扰 noise trouble
噪声分布 noise distribution
噪声电平 noise level
噪声电流 noise current
噪声抑制 noise suppression / noise limiting
热噪声 thermal noise
白噪声 white noise

例1 High frequency components and module are significant elements in communication electric circuit, such as resistance, inductance, capacitance, diode, triode and series resonant circuit unit, parallel resonant circuit unit, quartz crystal resonator and so on.
高频元件和模块是通信电子线路的重要元素，比如电阻、电感、电容、二极管、三极管和串联谐振回路、并联谐振回路以及石英晶体谐振器等。

例2 When resonant state happens in series resonant circuit unit, capacitive reactance value of resonant circuit is equal to inductance reactance value. Meanwhile, impedance of series resonant circuit is the smallest and current is the biggest when voltage signal added to the two ends of circuit is constant.
在串联谐振回路中发生谐振时，感抗与容抗相等。谐振回路的两端加一个恒压信号，阻抗会最小，流过电流最大。而在并联谐振回路中，回路两端流入的电流恒定，在谐振时阻抗最大。

第三节 高频谐振放大器

Section 3 High-frequency Resonant Amplifier

★ 高频小信号放大器 HF small signal amplifier
窄频带 narrow band
宽频带 wide band
★ 增益 gain / amplification
★ 增益系数 gain factor
增益带宽积 gain bandwidth product
★ 等效电导 equivalent conductance
★ 等效电抗 equivalent reactance
★ 等效电阻 equivalent resistance
★ 等效电感 equivalent inductance
★ 等效电路 equivalent circuit
等效变换 equivalent transformation
★ 稳定性 stability / steadiness
稳定性判据 stability criterion
★ 放大器性能 amplifier performance
★ 中和法 neutralization process
★ 失配法 mismatch process
★ 归一化 normalization
★ 集成放大器 integrated amplifier
★ 功率放大器 power amplifier
电流导通角 angle of current conduction
★ 波形系数 waveform factor
★ 效率 efficiency
★ 集电极 collector / collecting electrode
集电极反向电流 collector backward current
集电极区域 collector region
集电极击穿电压 collector break down voltage
集电极电阻 collector resistance

集电极电容　collector capacity
集电极电路　collector circuit
集电极负载　collector load
集电极饱和电压　collector saturation voltage
集电极放大系数　collector multiplication factor
集电极波形　collector waveform
集电极效率　collector efficiency
集电极消耗功率　collector consumed power
集电极-基极结　collector-base junction
集电极最大电流　collector maximum current
★ 发射极　emitter electrode
★ 基极　base electrode
基极反向电流　base reverse current
基极分压电阻　base bleeder resistance
基极电压　base voltage
基极电阻　base resistance
基极电流　base current
基极电路　base circuit
基极接地放大电路
grounded-base amplification circuit
基极接地等效电路
grounded-base equivalent circuit
基极偏置电路　base bias circuit
基极-集电极结　base-collector junction
★ 基极耦合　base coupling
★ 基极注入　base injection
★ 动特性　dynamic characteristic
振幅特性　amplitude characteristic
调制特性　modulation characteristic
负载特性　load characteristic
负载电压　load voltage
负载电流　load current
负载电路　load circuit
负载电阻　load resistance
负载功率　bearing power / load power
欠压状态　undervoltage state
过压状态　overvoltage state
★ 临界状态　critical state
★ 失真　distortion / anamorphose
★ 失真波形　distorted waveform
★ 载流子　conduction electron
★ 馈电　feed
馈电电路　feed circuit
★ 栅极　grid electrode
★ 漏极　drain electrode
★ 源极　source electrode
合成　composition / synthesis/ complexity
★ 合成器　synthesizer
★ 功率合成器　power synthesizer
模块放大器　module amplifier

1 HF small signal amplifier is an important circuit unit in communication electric circuit, which can amplify the amplitude of the input high frequency signal. The performance metrics of the amplifier are the gain, selectivity and stability, etc.
高频小信号放大器是通信电子线路重要电路,主要实现高频信号幅值的放大,性能主要由增益、选择性、稳定性等方面体现。

2 HF power amplifier is generally located at the end of a wireless communication system, which mainly accomplishes energy enhancement, and makes emission signal transmit farther away. Power amplifier can not amplify the energy but convert the energy of DC power supply into the power of high frequency output signal under the control of input signal.
高频功率放大器通常位于无线通信系统的末端,完成发射信号的能量增强,从而使发射信号传输得更远。功率放大器不是能量的放大,而是在输入信号的控制下,将电源直流功率转换成高频输出信号的高频功率。

第四节　正弦波振荡器
Section 4　Sine Wave Oscillator

能量转换器　energy converter
★ 正反馈　positive feedback
正弦波振荡器　sine wave oscillator
正弦波　sine wave
★ 三角波　triangular wave
★ 锯齿波　sawtooth wave

★ 矩形脉冲 rectangular pulse
矩形波 rectangular wave
★ 反馈 feedback / retraction
★ 反馈元件 feedback element
★ 反馈比 feedback ratio
★ 反馈系统 feedback system
反馈电阻 feedback resistance
反馈导纳 feedback admittance
反馈电容 feedback capacitance
反馈电流 feedback current
反馈电路 feedback circuit
★ 反馈系数 feedback coefficient
反馈环路 feedback loop
★ 反馈谐振电路 feedback type resonant circuit
★ 反馈振荡 feedback oscillation
反馈振荡电路 feedback oscillating circuit
★ 反馈振荡器 feedback oscillator
反馈耦合振荡器 feedback coupling oscillator
互感耦合振荡器
coupling oscillator of mutual induction
★ 正反馈 positive feedback
★ 负反馈 negative feedback
负阻振荡器 negative-resistance oscillator
★ 平衡条件 balanced condition
★ 起振条件 oscillatory condition
稳定条件 stability condition
★ 三点式振荡器 three-point oscillator
★ 电容三点式振荡
three-point capacitance oscillator
★ 电容反馈 capacitive feedback
电容反馈振荡器 capacitive feedback oscillator
电感三点式振荡器
three-point inductance oscillator
电感反馈 inductive feedback
电感反馈振荡器 inductive feedback oscillator
改进型电容振荡器 capacitive feedback oscillator
振荡 oscillation
★ 振荡电路 oscillation circuit /oscillatory circuit
★ 振荡条件 oscillating condition
★ 振荡波形 oscillating wave
★ 振荡频率 oscillation frequency
★ 振荡器 oscillator
★ 频率 frequency
★ 压控振荡器 voltage controlled oscillator (VCO)
频率失真 frequency distortion
★ 频率特性 frequency characteristic
★ 频率稳定性 frequency stability
石英晶体振荡器 quartz crystal oscillator
并联振荡电路 parallel oscillatory circuit
串联振荡电路 series oscillatory circuit
并联晶体振荡器 parallel crystal oscillator
串联晶体振荡器 series crystal oscillator
间歇振荡 chopping oscillation
频率占据 frequency pulling
寄生振荡 parasitic oscillation

1 Sine wave oscillator is a positive feedback oscillator and mainly consists of amplifier unit and feedback network. Sine wave oscillator must meet the balanced condition, oscillatory condition and stability condition.
正弦波振荡器是一个正反馈型振荡器,主要由放大器部分和反馈网络两部分构成。正弦波振荡器必须满足平衡条件、起振条件和稳定条件下才能工作。

2 Capacitance and inductance constitute selection frequency network and feedback network in LC oscillator. Three-point LC oscillator has two basic circuits: three-point capacitance oscillator and three-point inductance oscillator.
在 LC 振荡器中,电容、电感两个电抗元件组成了回路的选频网络和反馈网络。三点式振荡器有两种基本电路,分别是电容三点式振荡器和电感三点式振荡器。

第五节 线性频谱搬移电路
Section 5 Linear Spectrum Shifting Circuit

★ 频谱搬移 spectrum shifting
★ 线性频谱搬移 linear spectrum shifting
★ 非线性频谱搬移 nonlinear spectrum shifting
★ 线性电路 linear circuit

线性搬移电路 linear shifting circuit
线性时变系统 linear time-varying system
线性时变电路 linear time-varying circuit
★ 非线性 nonlinear
★ 非线性元件 nonlinear element
★ 非线性电路 nonlinear circuit
非线性搬移电路 nonlinear shifting circuit
伏安 volt-ampere
★ 伏安特性 volt-ampere characteristic
★ 幂 power
泰勒级数 Taylor series
★ 傅里叶级数 Fourier series
★ 傅里叶变换 Fourier transformation
★ 傅里叶反变换 Fourier inverse transformation
超越函数 transcendental function
★ 基波 fundamental wave
★ 谐波 harmonic wave
幂级数 power series
高次谐波 higher harmonic wave
谐波成分 harmonic component
谐波电流 harmonic current
差分对电路 differential pair circuit
模拟乘法器 analog multiplier
二极管电路 diode circuit
平衡二极管电路 diode balanced circuit
环形二极管电路 diode ring circuit
双差分对电路 double differential pair circuit
晶体频谱搬移电路 transistor spectrum shifting circuit

例1 Spectrum shifting circuit is the most basic circuit unit of wireless communication system, which is divided into linear spectrum shifting circuit and nonlinear spectrum shifting circuit according to the variation of frequency spectrum. Amplitude modulation and demodulation and frequency mixing circuit are the range of linear spectrum shifting circuit, and frequency modulation and demodulation and phase modulation and demodulation belong to nonlinear spectrum shifting circuit.
频谱搬移电路是无线通信系统中最基本的单元电路,根据频谱结构是否发生变化,又分为线性频谱搬移电路和非线性频谱搬移电路。振幅调制与解调、混频电路属于线性频谱搬移电路,而频率调制与解调、相位调制与解调属于非线性频谱搬移电路。

例2 Diode circuit is widely applied to communication devices, which are linear time-varying circuits. According to the difference of structure and function, a diode circuit could be single diode circuit, diode balanced circuit and diode ring circuit.
二极管电路广泛用于通信设备中,属于线性时变电路。根据结构和功能不同,二极管电路分为单二极管电路、平衡二极管电路以及环形二极管电路。

第六节 振幅调制、解调及混频
Section 6 Amplitude Modulation, Demodulation and Frequency Mixing

★ 振幅调制 amplitude modulation
调制解调器 modem
★ 调制器 modulator
解调器 demodulator
调制方式 modulation system
调制失真 modulation distortion
调制系数 modulation factor
调制灵敏度 modulation sensitivity
调制范围 modulation range
调制法 modulation method
调制指数 modulation index
调制度 modulation degree
调制深度 modulation depth
调制稳定度 modulation stability
★ 解调 demodulation
★ 解调器电路 demodulator circuit
解调方式 demodulation method
★ 载波 carrier wave / carrier
载波功率 carrier power
载波振幅 carrier amplitude
载波频谱 carrier spectrum
载波频率 carrier frequency
已调波 modulated wave
模拟调制 analog modulation

数字调制　digital modulation
振幅调制　amplitude modulation (AM)
普通调幅　conventional amplitude modulation
双边带调幅
double side band amplitude modulation
单边带调幅　single side band amplitude modulation
高电平调制　high-level modulation
低电平调制　low-level modulation
二极管调制电路　diode modulation circuit
二极管调制器　diode modulator
★ 二极管检波　diode detection
★ 二极管检波器　diode detector
二极管混频器　diode mixer
二极管峰值检波器　diode peak detector
差分对调制器　differential pair modulator
集电极调制　collector modulation
集电极调制电路　collector modulation circuit
集电极调幅　collector amplitude modulation
基极调制　base modulation
基极调制电路　base modulation circuit
基极调幅　base amplitude modulation
★ 滤波法　filter method
★ 移相法　phase-shifting method
★ 移相定理　phase-shifting theorem
★ 移相电路　phase-shifting circuit
移相电容器　phase-shifting capacitor
包络检波器　envelope detector
包络解调电路　envelope demodulation circuit
包络线　envelope line
同步检波　synchronous detection
同步检波器　synchronous detector
同步解调　synchronous demodulation
倒易混频　reciprocal frequency mixing
二极管峰值包络检波器
diode peak envelope detector
★ 传输系数　transmission coefficient
★ 输入阻抗　input impedance
惰性失真　inert distortion
底部切削失真　bottom cutting distortion
乘积型　product model
乘积检波　product detection
乘积检波电路　product detector circuit
乘积解调　product demodulation
乘积解调电路　product demodulator circuit
叠加型　superposition model
★ 变频　frequency conversion
★ 变频器　converter / frequency transformer
★ 混频　frequency mixing
★ 混频电路　mixer circuit
★ 混频器　mixer
混频管　mixer tube
混频二极管　mixer diode
中频信号　intermediate frequency signal
变频增益　frequency conversion gain
★ 互调　intermodulation
互调干扰　intermodulation interference
互调失真　intermodulation distortion
交调干扰　beat interference
★ 交调失真　crosstalk
叠加型同步检波
superposition model synchronous detection
乘积型同步检波　product model synchronous detection

例1 Modem is an important component of communication devices. Based on different modulation principles, modulation method includes amplitude modulation, frequency modulation and phase modulation.
调制解调器是通信设备中重要部件。根据模拟调制原理的不同，主要有振幅调制、频率调制以及相位调制。

例2 Amplitude modulation method is simple and easily implemented but inefficiently, which is mainly used in wireless broadcast system. Single sideband modulation (SSB) has better energy efficiency, but the modulation process is too complicated to be easily implemented.
在振幅调制电路中，AM 法调制简单、容易实现，但效率低，主要应用于无线电广播系统中。单边带调制(SSB)效率较高，但是调制过程相对复杂，不容易实现。

第七节 频率调制与解调

Section 7 Frequency Modulation and Demodulation

★ 角度调制 angular modulation
★ 相位调制 phase modulation
频偏 frequency offset
相偏 phase offset
调频指数 frequency modulated index
★ 频率调制 frequency modulation
★ 频率解调 frequency demodulation
★ 频率解调电路 frequency demodulation circuit
★ 鉴频 frequency discrimination
频率检波 frequency detection
★ 鉴相 phase discrimination
★ 鉴相电路 phase discriminating circuit
★ 鉴相器 phase discriminator
★ 相位检波 phase detection
★ 调频指数 frequency modulation index
★ 调频灵敏度 frequency modulation sensitivity
调频波 frequency modulation wave
★ 贝塞尔函数 Bessel function
★ 调相波 phase modulation wave
★ 调频器 frequency modulator
★ 调频方法 frequency modulation method
直接调频法
immediate frequency modulation method
间接调频法
indirect frequency modulation method
变容二极管 variable capacitance diode/varicap
直接调频电路
immediate frequency modulation circuit
间接调频电路
indirect frequency modulation circuit
鉴频器 frequency discriminator
鉴频方法 frequency discrimination method
振幅鉴频法
amplitude frequency discrimination method
相位鉴频法 phase frequency discrimination method
直接鉴频法
immediate frequency discrimination method
间接鉴频法
indirect frequency discrimination method
★ 鉴频电路 frequency discrimination circuit
比例鉴频器 ratio frequency discriminator
正交鉴频器 quadrature frequency discriminator
★ 限幅电路 clipper circuit
★ 调频发射机 frequency modulated transmitter
调频接收机 frequency modulated receiver
调频立体声广播 FM stereo broadcasting
调频指数 frequency modulated index
调相指数 phase modulated index
限幅电路 limiter circuit

1 Angular modulation is an important modulation mode in wireless communication system, which let base band signal linearly change the angular of carrier signal. With different modulation methods, angular modulation is divided into frequency modulation and phase modulation.
角度调制是无线通信中一种重要的调制方式,是用调制信号去改变载波信号的角度。根据调制方法的不同,角度调制分为频率调制和相位调制。

2 Frequency modulation makes base band signal control the frequency of high frequency carrier, which can make carrier signal frequency linearly change with the base band signal.
频率调制就是让调制信号控制高频载波信号的频率,使高频载波信号的频率随着调制信号的变化成线性变化。

第八节 反馈控制电路

Section 8 Feedback Control Circuit

反馈控制 feedback control
参考信号 reference signal
★ 自动增益控制 automatic gain control (AGC)
★ 自动频率控制 automatic frequency control (AFC)
自动相位控制 automatic phase control (APC)
★ 锁相环 phase locked loop (PLL)

★ 比较器 comparator
控制信号发生器 controlled signal generator
★ 反馈网络 feedback network
★ 反馈信号 feedback signal
★ 误差信号 error signal
电平检测器 level detector
★ 电压比较器 voltage comparator
★ 频率比较器 frequency comparator
★ 相位比较器 phase comparator
★ 动态范围 dynamic range
响应时间 response time
反馈控制电路 feedback control circuit
★ 鉴相器 phase detector (PD)
环路滤波器 loop filter (LF)
环路方程 loop equation
★ 压控振荡器 voltage controlled oscillator (VCO)
★ 频域 frequency domain
★ 时域 time domain
★ 积分滤波器 integral filter
比例积分滤波器 ratio integral filter
有源积分滤波器 active integral filter
锁定 lock on
★ 跟踪 follow-up / tracing / tracking
★ 跟踪电路 tracking circuit
★ 捕获 trap / acquisition / capture
★ 开环传递函数 open loop transfer function
★ 闭环传递函数 closed loop transfer function
★ 误差传递函数 error transfer function
★ 频率合成器 frequency synthesizer
锁相环解调器 phase locked loop demodulator
锁相振荡器 phase locked oscillator
★ 锁相式频率合成器
phase locked frequency synthesizer
暂态特性 transient characteristics
稳态特性 steady characteristics
跟踪特性 tracking characteristic
环路滤波器 loop filter

1 According to the diversity of the control object, feedback control circuit is divided into three classes: automatic gain control (AGC), automatic phase control (APC) and automatic frequency control (AFC).
反馈控制电路根据控制对象参量的不同分为三类,分别是自动增益控制、自动相位控制以及自动频率控制。

2 Phase-locked loop is an important circuit of wireless communication system and a phase negative feedback control system, which composes of phase detector (PD), loop filter (LF) and voltage controlled oscillator (VCO).
锁相环是无线通信系统中的重要电路,是一个相位负反馈控制系统,主要由鉴相器 PD、环路滤波器 LF 和压控振荡器 VCO 组成。

第二部分 实验
Part Two: Experiment

第××章 通信电子线路实验

Section ××of Electronic Circuits on Communications

Lab 1: Tuned Amplifier
Type: verification
The experiment date: ×× ×× ×××× Place: ××
Professional Class: ×× Name: ××
Student No.: ×× Instructed by: ×× Term: ××

1. Objectives

(1)To make students be familiar with electronic components and HF circuit experimental box.
(2)To be familiar with resonant property, pass band and selectivity of resonant circuit.
(3)To learn the principles, amplified capacity and analysis methods of tuned amplifier.

2. Experiment Instruments

- dual tracer oscilloscope
- sweep frequency instrument
- high frequency signal generator
- millivolt meter
- multi-function meter
- experimental circuit board

3. Experiment Data

Tab. 1 static measurement

Practical measure value		Calculated value		According to Vce, whether the circuit is working in amplified region		Reason
V_B	V_E	I_C	V_{CE}	Yes	No	The value of Vce is larger
3.21V	2.48V	2.48mA	9.52V	Y	N	

* V_B and V_E is the static voltage of the base and emitter of the transistor respectively.

Tab. 2 experiment data of dynamic measure

V_i(V)		20	40	50	60	70	80	100	110	120	140
V_o(V)	R_e=1kΩ	0.8	1.4	1.8	2.0	2.2	2.3	2.5	2.6	2.7	2.8
	R_e=500Ω	0.9	1.7	2.1	2.5	2.8	3.2	3.7	3.8	4.0	4.2
	R_e=2kΩ	0.6	1.0	1.2	1.3	1.4	1.5	1.6	1.7	1.7	1.7

Tab. 3 measured results of V_o under different f_o

f_o(MHz)		9.5	10.0	10.3	10.5	10.7	10.9	11.1	11.4	11.9
V_o(V)	R=10kΩ	2.6	3.4	4.2	3.6	3.1	2.8	2.5	2.1	1.8
	R=2kΩ	2.3	3.0	3.2	3.0	2.6	2.4	2.1	1.8	1.5
	R=470Ω	1.2	1.4	1.5	1.4	1.3	1.2	1.1	1.0	1.0

4. Experiment Analysis

(1) According to $I_C=I_E$, that is $I_E=\frac{V_E}{R_e}=\frac{2.48\text{V}}{1000}$, $V_{CE}=V_{CC}-V_E=9.52\text{V}$. Because $V_{CC}/2<9.52<V_{CC}$, we can confirm the result that the circuit is working in linear amplified region.

(2) According to dynamic measure data, it is shown that we can get different dynamic range of the circuit. The reason is that the circuit works in different static working point when R_e is changed. Through the experiment data, we can observe that the circuit is working in the linear amplified region when $R_e=500$ and 1k. However, the output is basically unchanged with the V_i increasing when $R_e=2$k. The phenomena show that the circuit is working in saturated zone.

5. Experiment Questions

(1) Why do we conduct the static measurement of the experiment circuit?

When a high frequency signal needs to be amplified linearly in the amplitude, the amplifier shall work in linear amplified region. Therefore, we need to judge whether the circuit works in the linear region, which can be implemented based on the static measurement of the circuit.

(2) How do we determine the resonant state of the loop? Why?

In the parallel resonant circuit, the equivalent impedance of the loop is the largest. So the amplitude of the output signal of tuned amplified is the largest when the circuit is resonant circuit. Therefore, we confirm the resonant circuit if the output signal wave is the largest in the dual tracer oscilloscope.

第九章 数据通信与网络技术

Chapter 9 Data Communication and Network Technology

第一部分 数据通信与网络技术

Part One: Data Communication and Network Technology

课程简介

本课程是电子信息工程专业的专业必修课。通过本课程的学习，学生将了解数据通信与网络技术的基本概念和基本原理，掌握网络实践的基本技术和方法。

这门课程系统地讲授了数据编码技术、数据传输技术以及计算机网络的体系结构，详细介绍了局域网和城域网、网络互连与 Internet、网络操作系统以及网络安全技术。配合该课程的实验教学，设置了物理层、数据链路层、网络层以及应用层的实验。

Course Summary

This course is a professional course of Electronic and Information Engineering. Through the study of this course, students will learn the basic concept and basic principle of data communication and network technology, and master the basic techniques and methods of network practice.

The data coding technology, the data transmission technology, as well as the architecture of computer network are introduced systematically in this course. Local area network and metropolitan area network, network internetworking and Internet, network operating system and network security technology are expounded. To accord with the experiment teaching of this course, experiments on physical layer, data link layer, network layer, and application layer are carried out.

第一节 数据通信基础

Section 1 Data Communication Basis

幅移键控 amplitude-shift keying (ASK)

★ 自动请求重发
automatic request for repeat (ARQ)

同轴电缆 coaxial cable

数据电路端接设备
data circuit-terminating equipment (DCE)

数据终端设备 data terminal equipment (DTE)

★ 前向纠错 forward error correction (FEC)

频分复用 frequency-division multiplexing

频移键控 frequency-shift keying (FSK)

曼彻斯特码 Manchester encoding

★ 多模光纤 multimode optical fiber

不归零制 nonreturn to zero

相移键控 phase-shift keying (PSK)

★ 屏蔽双绞线 shielded twisted pair (STP)

★ 单模光纤 single mode optical fiber

时分复用 time-division multiplexing

★ 非屏蔽双绞线 unshielded twisted pair (UTP)

波分复用 wave-division multiplexing (WDM)

Data rate depends on three factors: the bandwidth available, the level of the signals used and the quality of the channel. Nyquist's theorem defines the relationship between hardware bandwidth and the theoretical maximum rate at which data can be sent. Shannon's theorem gives a limit on the rate at which data can be sent in the presence of noise.

数据速率取决于三种因素：有效带宽、使用的信号电平数、通道的质量。奈奎斯特定理定义了硬件带宽与数据传送的理论最大速率之间的关系。香农定理给出了在噪声环境下数据传送的速率限制。

Although a CRC is mathematically complex, it can be implemented with simple, inexpensive hardware. CRC detects the following errors: all burst errors of length r less than degree G(x); all burst errors affecting an odd number of bits; all burst errors of length equal to r+1 with probability $(2^{r-1}-1)/2^{r-1}$; all burst errors of length are greater than r+1 with probability $(2^r-1)/2^r$.

尽管循环冗余校验在数学上是复杂的，但可以通过简单的、并不昂贵的硬件实现。循环冗余码可以完全检测以下错误：所有长度 $r<G(x)$ 的次数的突发错误；所有影响奇数个比特位的任意长度的突发错误；以 $(2^{r-1}-1)/2^{r-1}$ 的概率检测出所有长度为 $r+1$ 的突发错误；以 $(2^{r}-1)/2^{r}$ 的概率检测出所有长度 $>r+1$ 的突发错误。

第二节 计算机网络简介

Section 2 Introduction to Computer Network

接入网 access network
★ 应用层 application layer
通信子网 communication subnet
★ 数据链路层 data link layer
接口数据单元 interface data unit (IDU)
因特网服务提供商 Internet service provider (ISP)
★ 网络层 network layer
★ 物理层 physical layer
★ 表示层 presentation layer
专用网 private network
★ 协议数据单元 protocol data unit (PDU)
公用网 public network
请求评注 request for comments (RFC)
资源子网 resource subnet
服务数据单元 service data unit (SDU)
★ 会话层 session layer
服务访问点 service access point (SAP)
★ 运输层 transport layer

1 The physical layer coordinates the functions required to carry a bit stream over a physical medium. It deals with the mechanical and electrical specifications of the interface and transmission medium. It also defines the procedures and functions that physical devices and interfaces have to perform for transmission to occur. The data link layer provides for the reliable transfer of information across the physical link, and sends blocks with the necessary synchronization, error control, and flow control. The network layer is responsible for the source to destination delivery of a packet, possibly across multiple networks. The transport layer is responsible for process to process delivery of the entire message. A process is an application program running on a host. The session layer is the network dialog controller. It establishes, maintains and synchronizes the interaction among communicating systems. The presentation layer provides independence to the application processes from differences in data representation. The application layer provides access to the OSI environment for users and also provides distributed information services.

物理层包含那些在物理介质上传输比特流所必需的功能，定义了接口与传输介质的机械和电气特性，也定义了物理设备和接口为了传输而必须执行的过程和功能；数据链路层提供跨越物理层链路的可靠信息传递，携带必要的同步、差错控制、流控制等信息发送数据块；网络层负责将分组从源地址传递到目的地址，可能会通过多个网络；传输层负责整个报文的进程到进程传递，进程是主机上运行的应用程序；会话层是网络的对话控制器，建立、维护和同步通信系统间的交互操作；表示层提供数据表示方式之间的差异与应用进程之间的独立性；应用层为用户提供到 OSI 环境的接入手段，同时提供分布式信息服务。

2 In theory, outgoing data passes down through the layers of the stack on the sending machine and up through the layers of the stack on the receiving machine.

理论上，在发送机上流出数据向下通过堆栈各层，在接收机上流入数据向上通过堆栈各层。

第三节 局域网和城域网

Section 3 LAN and MAN

基本服务集 basic service set (BSS)
★ 广播域 broadcast domain
总线拓扑 bus topology
★ 校园网 campus area network (CAN)
载波监听多路访问/冲突检测 carrier sense multiple access with collision detection (CSMA /CD)
★ 冲突域 collision domain
扩展服务集 extended service set (ESS)
★ 全球网 global area network (GAN)

★ 局域网　local area network (LAN)
★ 逻辑链路控制　logical link control (LLC)
★ 媒体访问控制　medium access control (MAC)
★ 城域网　metropolitan area network (MAN)
★ 个域网　personal area network (PAN)
环型拓扑　ring topology
星型拓扑　star topology
令牌总线　token bus
★ 广域网　wide area network (WAN)

1 The essential technology underlying all forms of LANs comprises topology, transmission medium and medium access control technique. Each LAN can be classified into one of a few basic categories, depending on its topology. Four topologies are in common use: bus, tree, ring, and star. The most common transmission media for local networking are twisted pair (unshielded and shielded), coaxial cable (baseband and broadband), optical fiber, and wireless (microwave and infrared).

所有形式局域网的底层核心技术都是由拓扑结构、传输媒体和媒体接入控制技术组成的。每个局域网根据它的拓扑结构可以被归到几个基本类型中的一类。常用的四种拓扑结构是:总线、树形、环形和星形。局域网最常用的传输媒体是双绞线(非屏蔽的和屏蔽的)、同轴电缆(基带和宽带)、光纤和无线(微波和红外线)。

2 The IEEE 802.3 standard, known as Ethernet, now encompasses data rates of 10 Mbps, 100 Mbps, 1Gbps and 10Gbps. For the lower data rates, the CSMA/CD MAC protocol is used. For the 1Gbps and 10Gbps options, a switched technique is used. Fiber channel is a switched network of nodes designed to provide high speed linkages for such applications as storage area networks.

以"以太网"闻名的 IEEE802.3 标准现在已经包含了 10Mbps、100Mbps、1Gbps 和 10Gbps 的数据率。较低的数据率使用的是 CSMA/CD MAC 协议,1Gbps 和 10Gbps 两项则需要使用交换技术。光纤通道是一种交换式的节点网络,可以为某些应用提供高速的连接,如存储网络。

3 An individual cell of an IR LAN is limited to a single room, because infrared light does not penetrate opaque walls. Spread spectrum LAN makes use of spread spectrum transmission technology. In most cases, these LANs operate in the ISM (industrial, scientific, and medical) bands. Narrowband microwave LANs operate at microwave frequencies but do not use spread spectrum. Some of these products operate at frequencies that require FCC licensing, while others use one of the unlicensed ISM bands.

红外线局域网的一个蜂窝只能限制在一个房间里,因为红外线无法穿过不透明的墙。扩频局域网利用了扩频传输技术,运行在 ISM(工业、科学和医学)波段内。窄带微波局域网运行在微波频率上,但没有使用扩频技术。有些产品运行的频率需要 FCC 的许可证,有些则使用了不需要许可的 ISM 波段。

第四节　网络互连与 Internet
Section 4　Internetworking and Internet

自治系统　autonomous system
边界网关协议　border gateway protocol (BGP)
网桥　bridge
域间无类别路由
classless inter-domain routing (CIDR)
外部网关协议　exterior gateway protocol (EGP)
网关　gateway
★ 文件传送协议　file transfer protocol (FTP)
★ 超文本传输协议
hypertext transmission protocol (HTTP)
因特网控制报文协议
internet control message protocol (ICMP)
★ 网际互连协议　internet protocol (IP)
内部网关协议　interior gateway protocol (IGP)
★ 网络地址转换　network address translation (NAT)
网络服务访问点　network service access point
★ 开放最短路径优先
open shortest path first (OSPF)
★ 服务质量　quality of service (QOS)
中继器　repeater
路由器　router
源路由网桥　source bridge
★ 路由信息协议　routing information protocol (RIP)
★ 简单报文传送协议
simple message transfer protocol (SMTP)
子网掩码　subnet mask

交换机　switch
★ 传输控制协议　transmission control protocol (TCP)
透明网桥　transparent bridge
★ 服务类型　type of service (TOS)
★ 用户数据报协议　user datagram protocol (UDP)

1 The transport protocol provides an end-to-end data transfer service that shields upper layer protocols from the details of the intervening network or networks. TCP provides application programs with a reliable, flow-controlled, full-duplex, and stream transport service. All messages from one TCP to another use the TCP segment format, including messages that carry data, acknowledgements and window advertisements, or messages used to establish and terminate a connection. UDP provides a connectionless service for application level procedures. UDP is basically an unreliable service; delivery and duplicate protection are not guaranteed.

运输协议提供了端到端的数据传送服务，为上层协议屏蔽了中介网络或网络群的细节。TCP 为应用程序提供可靠的、具有流量控制的、全双工的流传输服务。从一个 TCP 到另一个 TCP 的所有消息采用 TCP 段格式，包括承载数据的消息、确认消息和窗口消息，或者用来建立连接和终止连接的消息。UDP 为应用层的过程提供无连接服务。从本质上说，UDP 是不可靠的服务，无法许诺不会出现交付和重复的差错。

2 Distance vector routing requires that each node exchange information with its neighboring nodes. Each node maintains a vector of link costs for each directly attached network and distance and next hop vectors for each destination. Link state routing is designed to overcome the drawbacks of distance vector routing. When a router is initialized, it determines the link cost on each of its network interfaces.

距离向量路由选择要求每个节点与它们的相邻节点相互交换信息。每个节点必须为每个直接相连的网络维护它的链路代价向量，并为每个目的系统维护它的距离和下一跳向量。链路状态路由选择的设计克服了距离向量路由的缺点。路由器在初始化时就确定了自己的每个网络接口的链路代价。

第五节　网络操作系统

Section 5　Network Operating System

★ 活动目录　active directory
备份域控制器　backup domain controller
域　domain
★ 内核　kernel
★ 多任务　multi-task
★ 多线程　multi-thread
主域控制器　primary domain controller
工作组　workgroup

1 A program is a prepared sequence of instructions to accomplish a defined task. A process is an instance of a program that is executing. Each instance has its own address space and execution state. When a program executes, the value of the program counter determines which process instruction is executed next. The resulting stream of instructions, called a thread of execution, can be represented by the sequence of instruction addresses assigned to the program counter during the execution of the program's code.

程序是为了完成特定的任务而准备好的一个指令序列。进程是一个正在执行的程序实例，每个实例都有自己的地址空间和执行状态。程序执行时，由进程程序计数器的值来决定下面该执行哪一条指令。得到的指令流被称为执行线程，它可以用程序代码执行期间为程序计数器指定的指令地址序列来表示。

2 Operating systems organize physical disks into file systems to provide high level logical access to the actual bytes of a file. A file system is a collection of files and attributes such as location and name. Instead of specifying the physical location of a file on disk, an application specifies a filename and an offset. The operating system makes a translation to the location of the physical file through its file systems.

操作系统将物理磁盘组织成文件系统的形式，以提供对文件中实际字节的高级逻辑访问。文件系统是文件和属性的集合，属性包括位置和名称等。应用程序不用指定文件在磁盘上的物理位置，只需指定文件名和偏移量。操作系统通过它的文件系统将其翻译为物理文件的位置。

第六节 交换技术
Section 6 Switching Technology

接入链路 access link
★ 直通转发 cut-through
混合链路 hybrid link
生成树协议 spanning tree protocol
★ 存储转发 store and forward
中继链路 trunk link
虚拟局域网 virtual local area network (VLAN)

1 Store and forward switch accepts a frame on an input line, buffers it briefly, and then routes it to the appropriate output line. Cut through switch takes advantage of the fact that the destination address appears at the beginning of the MAC frame. Cut through switch begins repeating the incoming frame onto the appropriate output line as soon as it recognizes the destination address.
存储转发交换机从输入线路上接收帧，先缓存一下，然后再通过路由选择将其发到适当的输出线路上。直通式交换机利用了这样一个事实，目的地址总是出现在 MAC 帧的最前面。一旦直通式交换机识别出目的地址，就将收到的帧转发到适当的输出线路上。

2 The packet by packet switch operates in the identical fashion as a traditional router. Because the forwarding logic is in hardware, the packet by packet switch can achieve an order of magnitude increase in performance compared to the software based router. A flow-based switch tries to enhance performance by identifying flows of IP packets that have the same source and destination. Once a flow is identified, a predefined route can be established through the network to speed up the forwarding process.
分组式交换机与传统路由器的操作方式相同。由于转发逻辑在硬件上，与基于软件的路由器相比，分组式交换机在性能上呈数量级的增长。基于流交换机试图通过识别具有相同源点和终点的 IP 分组流来提高性能。一旦流被识别出来，就可以建立一条网络预先定义的路由，加快转发速度。

第七节 网络安全
Section 7 Network Security

访问控制表 access control lists
★ 认证中心 certification authority (CA)
计算机病毒 computer virus
计算机蠕虫 computer worm
数据加密标准 data encryption standard (DES)
数字签名 digital signatures
★ 动态主机配置协议
dynamic host configuration protocol (DHCP)
★ 防火墙 firewall
★ 代理服务器 proxy service
报文鉴别 message authentication
报文摘要 message digest
★ 私有密钥 private key
★ 公共密钥 public key
安全管理 security management
★ 安全插口层 secure socket layer (SSL)
特洛伊木马 Trojan horse
★ 拒绝服务 denial of service (DoS)
★ 入侵检测 intrusion detection

1 Passive threats, sometimes referred to as eavesdropping, involve attempts by an attacker to obtain information relating to a communication. Active threats involve some modification of the transmitted data or the creation of false transmissions.
被动威胁有时也称为窃听，攻击者试图获取某次通信的相关信息。主动威胁涉及对传输数据的某些修改，或制造一些假传输。

2 With symmetric encryption, two parties share a single encryption/decryption key. The principal challenge with symmetric encryption is the distribution and protection of the keys. A public key encryption scheme involves two keys, one for encryption and a paired key for decryption. The party

that generated the key pair keeps one of the keys private and makes the other key public.
使用对称加密时，参与双方共享一个加密/解密的密钥。对称加密所面临的主要挑战是密钥的分发与保管。公共密钥加密机制涉及两个密钥，一个用于加密，另一个配对的密钥用于解密。其中一个密钥由生成密钥对的一方秘密保存，另一个密钥公开。

3 Message confidentiality means that the sender and the receiver expect confidentiality. The transmitted message must make sense to only the intended receiver. To all others, the message must be garbage. Message integrity means that the data must arrive at the receiver exactly as they were sent. There must be no changes during the transmission, neither accidentally nor maliciously. Message nonrepudiation means that a sender must not be able to deny sending a message that he or she did send.
报文保密性是指发送方和接收方期望保持机密。传输的报文只对预定的接收方有意义，对其他人，报文毫无意义。信息完整性是指数据到达接收方时必须和它发送时保持一致。在传输过程中不能发生意外的或恶意的改变。不可否认性是指发送方无法否认已经发送过的报文。

第二部分 实验

Part Two: Experiment

第××章 数据通信与网络技术实验

Section ×× Data Communication and Network Technology Experiment

Lab4: Router Configuration

Type: Operation

The experiment date: ×× ×× ×××× Place: ××

Professional Class: ×× Name: ××

Student No.: ×× Instructed by: ×× Term: ××

1. Objectives

(1)To understand the basic principle of router;

(2)To master the basic configuration method of router;

(3)To master the configuration method for static route Algorithm;

(4)To master the configuration method for RIP protocol.

2. Equipments and Components Needed

- Router R2600
- Computer
- Straight Cable

3. Tasks and Procedure (Including schematic diagram)

(1)Experimental principle

The routers in an internet are responsible for receiving and forwarding packets through the interconnected set of networks. Each router makes routing decision based on knowledge of the topology and traffic/delay conditions of the internet. In a simple internet, a fixed routing scheme is possible. In more complex internets, a degree of dynamic cooperation is needed among the routers.

Static Routing Table:

A static routing table contains information entered manually. The administrator enters the route for each destination into the table. When a table is created, it can not update automatically when there is a change in the internet. The table must be manually altered by the administrator.

A static routing table can be used on a small internet that does not change very often, or on an experimental internet for troubleshooting. It is a poor strategy to use a static routing table in a big internet such as the Internet.

Dynamic Routing Table:

A dynamic routing table is updated periodically by using one of the dynamic routing protocols such as RIP, OSPF, or BGP. Whenever there is a change in the internet, such as a shutdown of a router or breaking of a link, the dynamic routing protocols update all the tables in the routers automatically.

The routers on a big internet such as the Internet need to be updated dynamically for efficient delivery of the IP packets.

(2)Procedure

①Connect computers and routers as figure 1.

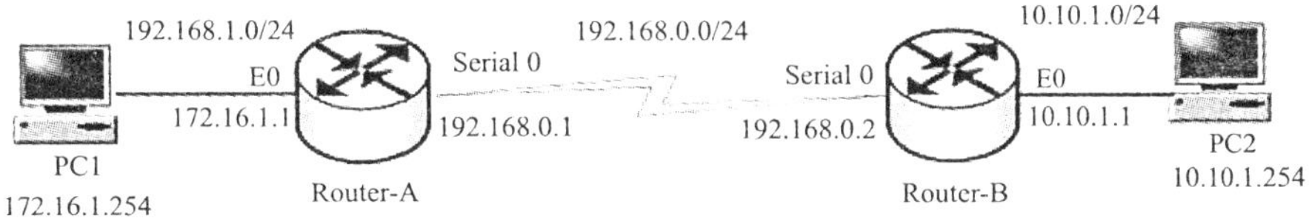

Figure 1. topology

②Change command among operation models.

router>enable

router#

router#configure terminal

router(config)#

router(config)#interface fastethernet0

router(config-if)#

router(config-if)#exit

router(config)#

router(config-if)#end

router(config-if)#

③Plan IP address of host as table 1, and IP address of router as table 2.

Table 1. host configuration

host	IP address	subnet mask	gateway
PC1	172.16.1.254	255.255.0.0	172.16.1.1
PC2	10.10.1.254	255.0.0.0	10.10.1.1

Table 2. router configuration

interface	IP address	subnet mask
Router_A/E0	172.16.1.1	255.255.0.0
Router_A/S0	192.168.0.1	255.255.255.0
Router_B/E0	10.10.1.1	255.0.0.0
Router_B/S0	192.168.0.2	255.255.255.0

④Configure router name.

router(config)#hostname *Router_AAA*

Router_AAA(config)#

router(config)#hostname *Router_BBB*

Router_BBB(config)#
⑤Configure interface parameter of router.
Router_A(config-if)#ip address 172.16.1.1 255.255.0.0
Router_A(config-if)#no shutdown
Router_A (config-if)#ip address 192.168.0.1 255.255.255.0
Router_A (config-if)#clock rate 64000
Router_A (config-if)#no shutdown
Router_B (config-if)#ip address 10.10.1.1 255.0.0.0
Router_B (config-if)#no shutdown
Router_B (config-if)#ip address 192.168.0.2 255.255.255.0
Router_B (config-if)#clock rate 64000
Router_B (config-if)#no shutdown
⑥Configure static routing.
Router_A (config)#ip route 10.0.0.0 255.0.0.0 192.168.0.2
Router_B (config)#ip route 172.16.0.0 255.0.0.0 192.168.0.1
⑦Configure RIP routing.
Router_A (config)#ip routing
Router_A (config)#router rip
Router_A (config-router)#network 10.0.0.0
Router_A (config-router)#version 2
Router_B (config)#ip routing
Router_B (config)#router rip
Router_B (config-router)#network 172.16.0.0
Router_B (config-router)#version 2
⑧Configure PC1 and PC2 as table 1.

4. The record of the experiment form

(1)Test connectivity from PC1
c:\>ping 10.10.1.254

Disply:

Pinging 10.10.1.254 with 32 bytes of data:
Reply from 10.10.1.254: bytes=32 time<1ms TTL=62
Reply from 10.10.1.254: bytes=32 time<1ms TTL=62
Reply from 10.10.1.254: bytes=32 time<1ms TTL=62
Reply from 10.10.1.254: bytes=32 time<1ms TTL=62
Ping statistics for 10.10.1.254:
    Packets: Sent=4, Received=4, Lost=0(0% loss),
Approximate round trip times in milli-seconds:
    Minimum=0ms, Maximum=0ms, Average=0ms

Result:

PC1 is connected with PC2.
(2)Test connectivity from PC2
c:\>ping 172.16.1.254

Disply:

Pinging 172.16.1.254 with 32 bytes of data:
Reply from 172.16.1.254: bytes=32 time<1ms TTL=62
Reply from 172.16.1.254: bytes=32 time<1ms TTL=62

Reply from 172. 16. 1. 254: bytes=32 time<1ms TTL=62

Reply from 172. 16. 1. 254: bytes=32 time<1ms TTL=62

Ping statistics for 172. 16. 1. 254:

Packets: Sent=4, Received=4, Lost=0(0% loss),

Approximate round trip times in milli-seconds:

Minimum=0ms, Maximum=0ms, Average=0ms

Result:

PC2 is connected with PC1.

5. Result Analysis

From the experiment results, we know our configurations are right. The computer is connective when there is a route item, and the computer is not connective when there is not any route item.

6. Answer the Questions

What should you pay attention to when planning IP address?

Answer: The network id should be the same as whose interface is connected directly. The host id should be different from whose interface is not connected directly. The network id should be different from whose interface is not connected directly.

第十章　EDA 技术

Chapter 10　EDA Technology

第一部分　EDA 技术

Part One: EDA Technology

课程简介

EDA 是电子设计自动化的缩写，在 20 世纪 90 年代初从计算机辅助设计(CAD)、计算机辅助制造(CAM)、计算机辅助测试(CAT)和计算机辅助工程(CAE)发展而来。EDA 技术就是以计算机为工具，设计者在 EDA 软件平台上，用硬件描述语言 HDL 完成文件设计，然后由计算机自动地完成逻辑编译、化简、分割、综合、优化、布局、布线和仿真，直至对于特定目标芯片的适配编译、逻辑映射和编程下载。EDA 在教学、科研、产品设计与制造等各方面都发挥着巨大的作用。在教学方面，几乎所有理工科(特别是电子信息)类的高校都开设了 EDA 课程。主要是让学生了解 EDA 的基本概念和基本原理，掌握用 HDL 语言编写规范，掌握逻辑综合的理论和算法，使用 EDA 工具从事简单系统的设计，为今后工作打下基础。

Course Summary

EDA is the abbreviation of Electronic Design Automation, which was developed from computer aided design (CAD), computer aided manufacturing (CAM), computer aided testing (CAT) and computer aided engineering (CAE) in the early 1990s. EDA technology uses computer as the tool, the designer uses HDL to finish files' design on the EDA software platform, then the computer automatically completes logic compilation, reduction, division, synthesis, optimization, layout and simulation, until the adapter compilation, logic mapping and programming downloading for a particular goal chips. EDA plays a tremendous role in teaching, scientific research, product design, manufacturing and other aspects. In teaching, almost all the science and engineering (especially electronic information) universities teach EDA class. The main purpose of this course is to let students understand the basic concepts and principles of EDA, grasp the basic specification with HDL language, grasp the logic synthesis theory and algorithm, engage in the simply system design using EDA tools, so as to lay a solid foundation for the future work.

第一节　概论

Section 1　Summarize

★ 电子设计自动化
electronic design automation (EDA)
★ 专用集成电路
application specific integrated circuit (ASIC)
单片电子系统　system on a chip (SOC)
★ 硬件描述语言
hardware description language (HDL)
计算机辅助设计
computer aided design (CAD)
计算机辅助制造
computer aided manufacture (CAM)
计算机辅助测试
computer aided testing (CAT)
计算机辅助工程
computer aided engineering (CAE)
自顶向下　top-down
自下而上　bottom-up
集成的，综合的　integrated
★ 集成电路　integrated circuit (IC)
基于单元的集成电路
cell-based integrated circuit (CBIC)
电气与电子工程师协会
Institute of Electrical and Electronic Engineers (IEEE)
硬件调试　hardware debugging
★ 半定制　semi-custom

★ 全定制 full-custom
★ 知识产权 intellectual property (IP)
★ 门阵列 gate array
母片 master slice
★ 标准单元 standard cell
走线道 feed-through
走线道单元 feed-through cell
空单元 empty cell
设计重用 design reuse
系统规格说明 system specification
系统划分 system division
逻辑设计与综合 logic design and synthesis
版图设计 layout design
版图规划 layout floor planning
版图验证 layout verification
布局 placement
布线 routing
设计规则检查
design rule checking (DRC)
电气规则检查
electric rule checking(ERC)
封装和测试 package and test
参数反注 parameter back-annotate
EDA 网表文件生成器 EDA Netlist Writer
深亚微米 deep-submicron
可编程片上系统
system on programmable chip (SOPC)
编辑数据接口
compiler database interface
核 core

To keep pace with this rapid change, electronics products have to be designed extremely quickly. Analogue design is still a specialized profession. Digital design has become very dependent on computer aided design (CAD)——also known as design automatic (DA) or electronic design automation (EDA). The EDA tools allow two tasks to be performed: synthesis, in other words, the translation of a specification into an actual implementation of the design; and simulation, in which the specification or the detailed implementation can be exercised in order to verify correct operation.

为了跟上快速变化的步伐,电子产品的设计也非常地快。模拟设计仍是一个特殊行业。数字设计则主要依靠计算机辅助设计(CAD)——也称为设计自动化(DA)或电子设计自动化(EDA)。EDA 工具可以实现两个任务:综合和仿真。综合,换句话说是将设计描述转换成实际实现;仿真用于检验详细描述或具体实现,以验证设计的正确性。

In top-down design, a design moves from the top to the bottom in the abstraction hierarchy. First we create an executable model from a written natural language specification, iteratively decompose the top-level model into components until the leaf nodes are RTL-level models, and finally use a synthesis tool to translate the RTL models into gate-level models..

自顶向下是从抽象层次的顶部出发,逐步地到达底部。首先从自然语言定义里产生一个可执行模型,不断自顶向下对模型进行分解,直到每个叶节点都是寄存器传输级模型,最后使用综合工具将 RTL 模型转换为门级模型。

There are two ways to describe a design for simulation: structural and behavioral modeling. A structural model for a component is built from smaller components. The structural model specifies the external connections, the internal components and the nets that connect them. The behavior of the model is determined by the behavior of the components and their connections. A behavioral model is more like a program——it uses functions, assignments, etc. to describe how to compute the component's outputs from its input. However, the behavioral model deals with events, not with variables as in a sequential programming language. Simulation languages define special constructs for recognizing events and for generating them.

有两种方法来描述设计的模拟:结构化建模和行为建模。对元件结构化模型,是以更小的子元件来组成的。结构化的建模规范了外部连接、内部元件以及连接它们的网络。而建模的行为则是由元件的行为和它们相互的连接来决定的。行为建模类似于一个程序,它使用函数、赋值等等描述如何从一个元件的输入来计算它的输出。然而,用行为建模来处理事件时,不像串行程序设计语言要使用变量。模拟语言定义了特殊的结构来记录事件并且产生事件。

IC design requires refining an idea through many levels of detail. Starting from a specification of what

the chip must do, the designer must create an architecture which performs the required function, expand the architecture into a logic design, and further expand the logic design into a layout.
IC设计需要从各个设计层次来考察其设计思想。从规定芯片功能规范开始,设计人员就必须建立一个实现一定功能的体系结构,然后,将体系结构延伸到逻辑设计,再进一步将逻辑设计具体到电路版图设计。

5 Hierarchical design is commonly used in programming: a procedure is written not as a huge list of primitive statements but as calls to simpler procedures. Each procedure breaks down the task into smaller operations until each step is refined into a procedure simple enough to be written directly.
层次设计的思想常常用在编程上:不是采用大量的最原始的语句来编写一个程序,而是通过对一些更简单的子程序的调用来实现某个程序。每个程序都被分解为一些更小的功能模块,这种分解一直进行到实现某种功能的每一步操作可以直接写入芯片。

第二节 FPGA/CPLD 结构原理
Section 2 FPGA/CPLD Structure Principle

★ 现场可编程门阵列
field programmable gate array (FPGA)
★ 复杂可编程逻辑器件
complex programmable logic device (CPLD)
电子设计交换格式
electronic design interchange format (EDIF)
可编程门阵列 programmable gate array
可编程只读存储器
programmable read only memory (PROM)
可编程逻辑阵列
programmable logic array (PLA)
可编程阵列逻辑
programmable array logic (PAL)
通用阵列逻辑 generic array logic (GAL)
熔丝 fuse
反熔丝 antifuse
一次性可编程器件
one time programming (OTP)
★ 逻辑阵列块 logic array block (LAB)
可编程连线阵
programmable interconnect array (PIA)
工程 project
设计环境 design environment
清零 clear
置位 preset
时钟 clock
时钟使能 clock enable
时钟到输出 clock to output
逻辑单元 logic cell
时钟频率 clock frequency
行频 line frequency
场频 field frequency
输入/输出单元 I/O element (IOE)
嵌入式阵列块 embedded array block (EAB)
可配置逻辑块 configurable logic block (CLB)
输入/输出接口块 I/O port block (IOB)
静态存储器
static random access memory (SRAM)
只读存储器 read only memory (ROM)
熔丝图 fuse map
输出逻辑宏单元 output macro cell (OLMC)
查找表 look up table (LUT)
逻辑单元 logic element (LE)
进位链 carry-in
级联链 cascade-in
粗粒度 coarse-grained
快速通道 fast track
嵌入式存储器 embedded memory
嵌入式乘法器 embedded multiplier
数控频率合成
numerically controlled oscillators (NCO)
SRAM 目标文件 SRAM object file (SOF)
编程目标文件 programmer object file (POF)
仿真网表文件 simulation netlist file (SNF)
可测性设计 design for test (DFT)
联合测试行动组 joint test action group (JTAG)
边界扫描测试 board scan test (BST)
测试数据输入 test data input (TDI)
测试数据输出 test data output (TDO)
测试模式选择 test mode select (TMS)
测试时钟输入 test clock input (TCK)
测试复位输入 test reset input (TRST)

用户电子标签 user electronic signature (UES)
边界扫描描述语言
the boundary scan description language (BSDL)
主动串行 active serial (AS)
被动并行同步 passive parallel synchronous (PPS)
被动并行异步 passive parallel asynchronous (PPA)
被动串行异步 passive serial asynchronous (PSA)
在电路可重配置 in-circuit reconfigurability (ICR)
多阵列矩阵 multiple array matrix (MAX)
灵活逻辑单元矩阵
flexible logic element matrix (FLEX)
高级逻辑单元矩阵
advanced logic element matrix (APEX)

1 A field-programmable gate array (FPGA) is a block of programmable logic that can implement multi-level logic functions. FPGAs are most commonly used as separate commodity chips that can be programmed to implement larger functions than can be fit into a programmable logic device (PLD). However, small blocks of FPGA logic can be useful components on-chip to allow the user of the chip to customize part of the chip's logical function.
现场可编程门阵列(FPGA)是能实现多级逻辑功能的可编程逻辑模块。大多数 FPGA 作为独立的商品芯片来使用,跟可编程逻辑器件(PLD)相比,它能通过编程来实现更大的逻辑功能。然而,FPGA 中的较小模块逻辑是有用的在片部件,允许用户定制芯片的部分逻辑功能。

2 Application specific integrated circuit (ASIC) is an integrated circuit produced for a specific application and generally produced in relatively small volumes. A range of design technologies can be used to implement an ASIC: PLDs, Gate Arrays, FPGAs, Standard Cell, and Custom. However, like other generic definitions in the computer field, for example, RAM, the name ASIC has taken on a more specialized meaning. PLDs and FPGAs are referred to as Programmable Logic, while the term ASIC is reserved for Standard Cell and Gate Arrays where a chip is actually fabricated as opposed to being programmed at the customer's site.
专用集成电路(ASIC)是为某个专门应用制造的集成电路,一般生产量较小。实现 ASIC 可使用一系列技术:PLD、门阵列、FPGA、标准单元和定制。然而,与计算机领域的其他类属定义相似,如 RAM 一样,ASIC 所代表的是一个更为专业化的意思。PLD 和 FPGA 被称为可编程逻辑,而 ASIC 则指标准单元和门阵列,其芯片实际上是制造而不是在用户端进行编程。

3 The most common placement-and-routing systems use standard cells, which are logic gates, latches, flip-flops, or occasionally slightly larger functions like full adders.
最常用的布局、布线系统是标准单元库,它包括逻辑门、寄存器、触发器,或偶尔稍微多一点功能的如全加器。

第三节 VHDL 设计初步
Section 3 Introduction to VHDL Design

★超高速集成电路硬件描述语言
very high speed integrated circuit hardware description language (VHDL)
文本编辑器 test editor
★实体 entity
结构体 architecture
端口 port
★进程 process
库 library
工作库 work library
标识符 identifier
★信号 signal
★综合 synthesis
★仿真 simulate
★编译 compiler
元件 component
D 触发器 D-flip flop
上升沿 rising edge
标准逻辑矢量
standard logic vector
网表提取 netlist extraction
信息处理器 message processor

底层编辑　floorplan editor
印刷电路板　printed circuit board (PCB)
配置　configure
在系统编程　in system program (ISP)
闪速存储器　flash union

1 In VHDL, a given logic circuit is represented as a *design entity*. The logic circuit represented can be as complicated as a microprocessor or as simple as an AND gate. A design entity, in turn, consists of two different types of descriptions: the *interface description* and one or more *architectural bodies*. The interface description defines the inputs and outputs of the design entity. An architectural body specifies either the behavior of the entity or specifies a structural decomposition of the entity using more primitive components.

在 VHDL 中，特定的逻辑电路用设计实体来表示，被表示的逻辑电路可以像微处理器一样复杂，也可以像与门一样简单。设计实体按照如下顺序包括两种不同类型的描述：接口描述和一个或多个结构体。接口描述定义设计实体的输入和输出，结构体则定义了实体的行为或采用更加初级的组件来构成实体的结构化模型。

2 VHDL is a general-purpose programming language as well as a hardware description language, so it is possible to create VHDL simulation programs ranging in abstraction from gate-level to system. VHDL has a rich and verbose syntax that makes its models appear to be long and verbose. However, VHDL models are relatively easy to understand once you are used to the syntax.

VHDL 既是一种通用编程语言，也是一种硬件描述语言，所以，它可以编写从门级到系统各个抽象级别的 VHDL 模拟程序。VHDL 具有丰富和冗长的语法而使其编写的模块显得较冗长。然而，一旦你对其语法熟悉后，VHDL 模块理解起来就相对容易一些。

3 Hardware description languages (HDLs) are the most important modern tools used to describe hardware. HDLs become increasingly important as we move to higher levels of abstraction. While schematics can convey some information very clearly, they are generally less dense than textual descriptions of languages. Furthermore, a textual HDL description is much easier for a program to generate than is a schematic with pictorial information such as placement of components and wires.

硬件描述语言是被用于描述硬件的最重要的现代设计工具。越到高层抽象，硬件描述语言就变得越重要。当用原理图方式能非常清楚地表达某些信息时，它通常比语言的文本描述更简洁。然而，HDL 的文本描述却比用原理图方式更容易说明诸如元件及连线的位置这类信息。

第四节　Quartus II 应用向导

Section 4　Quartus II Application Wizard

可擦除可编程逻辑器件
erasable programmable logic device (EPLD)
新工程向导　new project wizard
包　package
EDA 工具设置　EDA tool settings
EDA 设计输入　EDA design entry
综合工具　synthesis tool
仿真工具　simulation tool
设备　device
说明　description
时序分析工具　timing analysis tool
全屏幕　full screen
警告　warning
仿真模式　simulation mode
仿真设置　simulator settings
先入先出　first-in first-out(FIFO)
编译报告　compilation report
被动串行模式　passive serial mode
★ 原理图编辑器　schematic editor
★ 波形编辑器　waveform editor
原理图文件　schematic file
元件　symbol
功能设计　function design
综合后仿真　simulate after synthesis
信号探针　signal probe
混合电压　mix voltage (MV)
分配编辑器　assignment editor
输入引脚　input pin

输出引脚　output pin
布线倍增器　router effort Multiplier
内埋节点　buried node
JTAG 间接配置文件
JTAG indirect configuration file
硬件设置　hardware setup
配置器件　configuration device
添加器件　add device
选择器件　select device
编译器网表文件提取器
compiler netlist extractor
集成综合器　integrated synthesis
逻辑综合器　logic synthesizer
逻辑分割器　partitioner
适配器　fitter
★ 时序分析　timing analyzer
装配器　assembler
总线值　bus value
工程更改记录　engineering change order
资源属性编辑器　resource property editor
资源属性检查　check resource property
超大规模集成
★ very large scale integration (VLSI)
大规模集成
large scale integration (LSI)
中规模集成
medium scale integration (MSI)
小规模集成
small scale integration (SSI)
旁路　bypass
节点名称　node name
更改类型　change type
旧值　old value
目标值　target value
当前值　current value

1 Quartus II software provides comprehensive online documentation that answers many of the questions that may arise when using the software. The documentation is accessed from the Help menu. To get some idea of the extent of documentation provided, it is worthwhile for the reader to browse through the Help menu. For instance, selecting Help > How to Use Help gives an indication of what type of help is provided. The user can quickly search through the Help topics by selecting Help > Search, which opens a dialog box into which keywords can be entered. Another method, context-sensitive help, is provided for quickly finding documentation for specific topics. While using most applications, pressing the F1 function key on the keyboard opens a Help display that shows the commands available for the application.

Quartus II 软件提供了综合在线文档，以查询应用该软件时出现的问题。文档从帮助菜单进入，读者通过浏览帮助菜单可以得到多种文档形式。例如，选择帮助>如何获得帮助，能够看到提供的所有帮助。应用者也可通过选择帮助>搜索，在弹出的对话框中填上关键词而得到快速搜索主题。另一个方法，上下文相关帮助，可以为某一特定主题快速地找到文档说明。使用这些功能时，按下键盘上的 F1 功能键，打开帮助显示，显示出应用中的可用指令。

2 The full design and each module are synthesized in logic, then are simulated in function and timing on QUARTUS II EDA tool-desk of ALTERA Corp.

整个设计及其各个模块都在 ALTERA 公司的 EDA 工具 QUARTUSⅡ 平台上进行了逻辑综合及功能和时序仿真。

3 We have to specify the type of device in which the designed circuit will be implemented. Choose CycloneTM II as the target device family. We can let Quartus II software select a specific device in the family, or we can choose the device explicitly. We will take the latter approach.

想要实现设计电路必须指定器件，选择 CycloneTM II 作为目标器件家族。可以让 Quartus II 软件自动从器件家族内选择一个芯片，或者自己选择特定芯片。这里采用后一种方法。

4 Schematic editors: An editor which can be used to create and display an interconnected set of graphic tokens. The graphic tokens correspond to structural primitives, and thus, the interconnected net corresponds to a structural model.

原理图编辑器：用来创建和显示一系列互连的图形标记的编辑器。图形标记和结构基本单元一一对应，因而互连的电路则对应一个结构模型。

第五节 VHDL 设计进阶
Section 5 Advancement VHDL Design

数据对象 data object
★ 变量 variable
★ 常量 constant
位矢量 bit-vector
★ 流水线 pipelining
信号赋值语句 signal evaluate
系统划分 system division
逻辑设计与综合 logic design and synthesis
循环 loop
三态门 triple gate
三态总线 tristate bus line
移位寄存器 shift register
高阻态数据 high impedance function data
双向端口 bidirectional port
代码 code
顺序语句 sequential statement
并行赋值 parallel assignment
占空比 duty ratio
物理设计 physical design
版图级 layout level
描述级 descriptive level
固有延时 inertial delay
传输延时 transport delay
仿真延时 simulation delay
行为描述 behavior description
★ 寄存器传输级
register transport level (RTL)
★ 系统容量 system capacity
★ 溢出 overflow
★ 寻呼 page
呼叫传递 call delivery

1 A data object is a container in which values of a stated type may be stored. There are three classes of data object.

Constant: an object whose value is specified at compile time and cannot be changed by VHDL statements.

Variable: a data object whose current value can be changed by VHDL statements.

Signal: a data object that has a time dimension. VHDL statement may assign future values to the data object without affecting the current value. Using waveforms, a series of future values may be assigned. The current value cannot be changed.

数据对象是可以保存所声明类型的值的容器。有三类数据对象。

常量:值在编译时被指定,不可由 VHDL 语句改变的数据对象。

变量:当前值可以由 VHDL 语句改变的数据对象。

信号:具有时间量纲的数据对象。VHDL 语句可以把将来的值赋给信号而不影响当前值。使用波形,可以赋一串将来的值。当前的值不可改变。

2 The basic unit of modeling in VHDL is the process. A process defines the actions that are taken whenever any input to the process is activated by an event. A process starts with the name of the process and a sensitivity list. The sensitivity list declares all the signals to which the process is sensitive: if any of these signals changes, the process should be evaluated to update its outputs.

VHDL 语言中建模的基本单元是进程。进程定义了当它被任何输入到进程的事件所激活时,它应该执行的行为。一个进程开始应具有进程名和敏感量表。敏感信号量表说明了对该进程敏感的所有信号。如果其中任何一个信号改变,进程就开始执行计算并更新它的输出。

3 The sequential process is written in a particular style that is recognized by synthesis and works properly during simulation. The sequential process is activated by activity on the clock or reset lines. A reset causes the machine's state to be reset. A clock edge is tested for by the condition, which checks for an event on CLOCK and a '1' value for CLOCK after the event takes place.

时序进程用综合工具能够识别的特殊风格而写成,并在仿真过程中能够正确地运行。时序进程由时钟或复位信号来激活。复位可使状态机的状态复位。检测条件是用来检测时钟的上升沿,对于事件 CLOCK 和 CLOCK='1'值发生时,该时钟的上升沿就被认为有效。

第六节 宏功能模块与 IP 应用
Section 6 Megafunction and IP Application

★ 参数可设置模块库
library of parameterized modules (LPM)
数字信号处理器
digital signal processor (DSP)
直接数字合成器
direct digital synthesizer (DDS)
起始位 start bit
数据位 data bits
校验位 parity bit
存储器初始化文件
memory initialization file
十六进制文件 hexadecimal file
字长 word size
枚举类型 enumeration types
整数类型 integer types
数组类型 array types
记录类型 record types
时间类型 time types
实数类型 real types
布尔型 Boolean types
时钟使能 enable clock (EC)
多核 multicore
元件库 symbol libraries
消去网格 snap to grid
自然数类型 natural type
正整数类型 positive type
波形设计 waveform design
在系统存储器读写编辑器
in-system memory content editor
路径延时 path delay
导出数据到文件
export data to file
从文件输入数据
import data from file
建立时间 clock setup time
有限脉冲响应 finite impulse response (FIR)
授权文件 license file
文件 documentation
时钟最大频率
maximum clock frequency (Fmax)
数控振荡器
numerically controlled oscillators (NCO)
保持时间 clock hold time
只读存储器 read only memory (ROM)
随机存储器
random access memory (RAM)
恢复时间 overlay time
寄存器配平 register balancing

1 After synthesis is complete, one simulates the generated structural model to verify that it is correct (ASIC sell-off). This is done for two reasons. First, one cannot completely trust the transformations performed by the synthesis tool. Their correctness is partially established by customer feedback. Second, one must verify the timing of the synthesized circuit.
在综合结束之后,可对得到的结构模型进行仿真,以验证其正确性。这样做有两个原因,首先,不可完全信任综合工具进行的转化。它们的正确性部分由用户反馈来建立。第二,必须验证综合后电路的时序。

2 High-level synthesis allows designers to concentrate on the architectural design, rather than spend a great deal of time mapping the architecture to logic or layout. High-level synthesis can produce useful productivity gains when used to automate the transformation of the architecture to register-transfer form, but high-level synthesis can aid productivity in other ways.
高级综合允许设计者将注意力集中于体系结构的设计上,而不是在将体系结构映射到逻辑或是在版图上花费大量的时间。当使用体系结构到寄存器传输级结构的自动转换时,高级综合通过这种方式常常会导致有益的生产效率,但高级综合也可用其他方式来使得效率提高。

3 In RTL synthesis, the design is specified in terms of register operations and transformed automatically into gates and flip-flops. Behavioural synthesis takes the process one stage further. The hardware to be synthesized is described in terms of an algorithm, from which the registers and logic are derived. In principle, it is not necessary to use a hardware description language for behavioural synthesis; indeed subsets of conventional programming languages such as C have been used.
在 RTL 综合中,根据寄存器操作指定设计,并且自动转换成门和触发器。行为则更深一层。综合的硬件用算法描述,寄存器和逻辑门都从这个算法中派生而来。原则上,行为综合没有必要适用硬件描述语言,真正用到的是传统编程语言(如 C)的子集。

第七节 有限状态机设计

Section 7 FSM Design

有限状态机
finite state machine (FSM)
★状态图 state diagram
状态表 state table
当前状态 current state
下一状态 next state
互斥 mutual exclusion
聚合 aggregates
字符 character
提取 extract
一位热码编码 one-hot encoding
状态机查看器 state machine viewer
基于单元的集成电路
cell-based integrated circuits (CBIC)
状态机文件 state machine file
系统级可编程芯片
system on programmable chip (SOPC)
数字信号处理
digital signal processing (DSP)
异步 asynchronous
高电平有效 active-high
兆采样数/秒
million samples per second (MSPS)
约翰逊码 Johnson encoded
兆条指令/秒
million instructions per second (MIPS)
用户自定义编码 user encoded
深亚微米 deep-submicron
硬件调试 hardware debugging
默认型编码 default encoded
安全状态机 safe state machine
命令行模式 shell mode
专用时钟 dedicated clock
有限状态机编译器 FSM compiler
优化 optimize
仿真器通道文件 lator channel file (SCF)
管脚到管脚 pin-to-pin
时钟分配网络 clock distribute net (CDN)
在系统可重构 in-system configuration
快闪 fastflash
逻辑核 logic core

1 The first step in the design of a finite state machine(FSM) is to decide whether a Moore or a Mealy circuit should be designed. In a Moore machine, the outputs settle to their final values a few gate delays after the active edge of the clock. The outputs are constant for the remainder of the clock period, even if the inputs happen to change during the clock period. In a Mealy machine, since the outputs are a function of the inputs, an output may change in the middle of a clock period if an input changes. A Moore machine may require more states than the corresponding Mealy machine.

设计有限状态机的第一步是决定是设计 Moore 型还是 Mealy 型电路。在 Moore 机中,输出在时钟的活动沿到达后的几个门延迟之后即得到输出值,并且在该时钟周期的剩余时间内保持不变,即使输入在该时钟周期内发生改变,输出值也保持不变。在 Mealy 机中,因为输出是输入的函数,如果输入改变,输出可以在一个时钟周期的中间发生改变。Moore 机比对应的 Mealy 机可能需要更多的状态。

2 A one-hot code uses n bits to encode n states; the i bit is 1 when the machine is in the i state. We can use such a code to easily compute state subset membership, by simply computing the OR of the state bits in the subset. But this solution has two problems. First, it requires a lot of memory elements for the present state: a machine with 64 states requires at least six memory elements for arbitrary codes, but 64 states for a one-hot encoding. Second, one-hot encoding doesn't help if an output depends on more than one state. It's best to examine the machine for time-critical outputs which depend on the present state and to construct codes which efficiently represent the time-critical state combinations, then use area-minimizing coding for the rest of the states.

一位热码编码采用 n 比特来对 n 个状态进行编码。当状态机处在第 i 个状态时,第 i 个比特位是 1。

通过简单的计算状态子集中比特的“或”运算，我们可以使用这样的编码来计算状态子集的数目。但是这种方案存在两个问题。首先，当前状态的存储需要许多存储元件：具有 64 种状态的一个状态机，任意一个编码都需要最少六个存储元件来实现，而 64 种状态只是一个一位热码编码。第二，如果一个输出依赖于更多一位热码状态，一位热码编码就没有什么帮助。最好由关键时间的输出来检查状态机，这样依赖于当前状态和通过有效替代关键时间的状态组合构建其代码，然后，由状态的其他部分使用面积最小化来进行编码。

The two-process model, registers and next state and output logic, are very common way to model state machines in VHDL. It is also possible to have a three-process model. The register process is the same as before, but the next state and output logic blocks are separated, as in the Moore and Mealy models.

两进程模型，寄存器一个进程、下一状态和输出逻辑一个进程，是用 VHDL 语言建立状态机的常用方法。也可以建立三进程模型。寄存器像以前一样占用一个进程，但是下一状态和输出逻辑模块就如同 Moore 或者 Mealy 状态机模型中所示，是分开的，各占一个进程。

第二部分　实验

Part Two: Experiment

第××章　EDA 技术实验

Section ×× EDA Technology Experiment

Lab1: Multiplex Data selector

Type: designing experiment

The experiment date: ××　××　××××　Place: ××

Professional Class: ××　Name: ××

Student No.: ××　Instructed by: ××　Term: ××

1. Objectives

(1) To master the use of Max_PlusII software platform.

(2) To master the design method of the multiplex.

2. Equipments and Components Needed

EDA experiment equipment, wire, etc.

3. Tasks and Procedure (Including schematic diagram)

(1) Tasks

(a) Design a 4-to-1 Multiplexer that can select one from the four input frequencies with VHDL.

(b) Simulate the program.

(c) Download the program to a specified chip and verify the correctness of the design.

(2) Experimental principle

Table 1 4-to-1 Multiplexer true value table

input / output / selector		a, b, c, d
S1	S0	y
0	0	a
0	1	b
1	0	c
1	1	d

According to table 1, the principle of the 4-to-1 Multiplexer is simple, when S1=0 and S0=0, y=a, when S1=0 and S0=1, y=b, when S1=1 and S0=0, then y=c, else y=d.

(3)Procedure

(a)Debug the program. If compile successfully, then simulate it.

(b)Observe the simulation waveform.

(c)Download the program to a chip. Connect circuit and observe the experimental result.

(4)Programs

```
library ieee;
use ieee. std_logic_1164. all;
entity mux4 is
port (s1,s2: in std_logic;
        a,b,c,d  : in std_logic;
        y          : out std_logic);
end entity mux4;
architecture behav of mux4 is
signal s : std_logic_vector (1 downto 0);
begin
  s<=s1&s2;
  process(s,a,b,c,d)
    begin
      case s is
        when "00"=>y<=a;
        when "01"=>y<=b;
        when "10"=>y<=c;
        when "11"=>y<=d;
        when others=>null;
      end case;
    end process;
  end behav;
```

4. The Record of the Experiment Form:

Fig. 1 shows the simulation result for 4 to 1 multiplex.

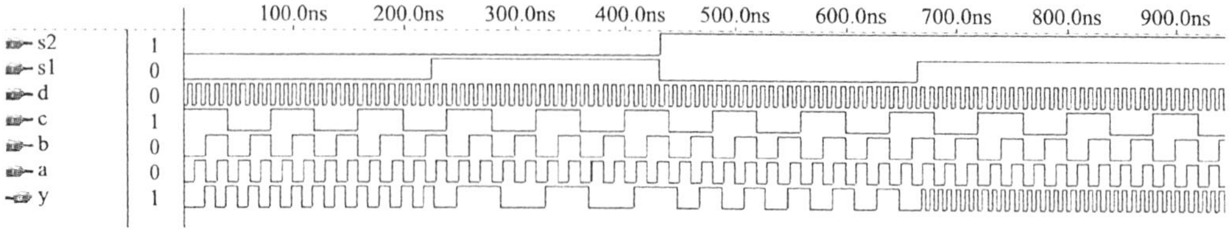

Figure 1　the simulation result for 4 to 1 multiplex

By observing the hardware phenomenon, we can find the hardware result corresponds with the true value table.

5. Result Analysis

From the simulator results and hardware results, we know our program is right. When S1=0 and S0=0, y=a. When S1=0 and S0=1, y=b. When S1=1 and S0=0, y=c, else y=d.

6. Answer the Questions

(1)What kind of statement is the simplest in all the multiplexer realizations?

Answer: "Case" statement is the simplest.

(2)After compiled, it appeared "... VHDL syntax error:..." in the too window. What types of errors have appeared in the program?

Answer: It means there is a "语法错误".

第十一章　短距离无线通信技术

Chapter 11　Short-range Wireless Communications Technology

第××章 短距离无线通信技术

Section ××Short-range Wireless Communications Technology

Lab1：Wireless temperature sensor experiment

Type：comprehensive

The experiment date：××　××　××××　Place：××

Professional Class：××　Name：××

Student No.：××　Instructed by：××　Term：××

1. Objectives

(1) To understand the basic principle of the Z-stack protocol stack.

(2) To master the programming method of wireless sensor networks.

(3) To design a wireless temperature sensor network.

2. Equipments and Components Needed

C51RF-3 emulator，CC2430 module，PK LCD panels，2.4G antenna，etc.

3. Experimental Requirements

Sensor nodes collect temperature and send these data to a central collection node for processing. Only one central node in the system collects this information and then sends it to the computer through the serial port after processing. This information can be seen in the serial debugging tools or HyperTerminal by the user. In order to improve the network load，we can increase the center for the collection node.

System Requirements：

(1) Automatically form a network.

(2) The sensor device can automatically join the network and automatically complete the binding.

(3) If the sensor device does not receive a response from the central node，it will automatically remove the binding with the central node. Then，find the new center node again，and bind with the new center node.

4. Key Points

Network formation

- Initialization
  - ★ ZigBee system reset (zb_SystemReset)
  - ★ ZigBee start request (zb_StartRequest)
- Configuration
  - ★ ZigBee read configuration (zb_ReadConfiguration)
  - ★ ZigBee write configuration (zb_ WriteConfiguration)
  - ★ ZigBee access to device information (zb_GetDeviceInfo)

• Equipment, network and service discovery

★ ZigBee device discovery request (zb_FindDeviceRequest)

★ ZigBee device binding requests (zb_BindDeviceRequest)

★ ZigBee allowed to bind requests (zb_AllowBindRequert)

★ ZigBee allowed the request to join (zb_PermitJoinRequest)

Data transmission

★ ZigBee sends a data request (zb_SendDataRequest)

5. Experimental Procedures

(1) Hardware connection

• 2.4G antennas are connected respectively with CC2430 modules.

• Two CC2430 modules are correctly connected withed the PK LCD panels.

• C51RF-3 emulator is properly connected with a PK LCD panel.

• C51RF-3 emulator and a PC use a USB cable connect.

(2) Program

Use "IAR7.30B" to open Z-Stack protocol stack, port the code, and write applications.

(3) Compile, download

• In the IAR window "Workspace", select "SimpleCollectorEB" (collection device) module program to compile, if compiled correctly, download the program to one of the CC2430 module to debug. This module is a collecting device (coordinator).

• In the IAR window "Workspace", select "SimpleSensorEB" (temperature collection device) module program to compile, if compiled correctly, download the program to another CC2430 module to debug. This module is the temperature collection module (terminal equipment).

Figure1. Compiler interface

(4) View the phenomenon

• Open the serial debugging aides, the baud rate set to 38400, 8 data bits, 1 stop bit, no parity bit.

• Remove the emulator USB cable, use another USB cable for the module supply.

• Toggle the PK LCD panel switch "S2" to "ON" side, operating each module according to the procedural requirements, viewing the experimental results.

6. Important Process and Methods

(1) Network formation

The coordinator scan all the channel which the parameters specified by ZCD_NV_CHANLIST, select the minimum energy channel for use. If the system have two or more minimum energy channels, coordinator will select the smallest serial number in the ZB network channel for use. At the same time, coordinator will select the network ID specified by ZCD_NV_PANID. Routers and terminal equipment will scan the channels which established by the configuration parameters (ZCD_NV_CHANLIST) and try to find the specified network ID by parameters (ZCD_NV_PANID).

ZDO_StartDevice() function in the network is responsible for start device, coordinator, routers, terminal equipment can be started by this function, then equipment accords to its type to create or discover the network and joins it.

Function prototype:

```
ZDO_StartDevice (
                 byte logicalType,
                 devStartModes_t startMode,
                 byte beaconOrder,
                 byte superframeOrder
                 )
```

(2) Binding

• Establish binding

Use function zb_BindDeviceRequest () to initiate a binding request.

```
zb_BindDevice (
              uint8 create,            // Whether to create a binding,
                                       //TRUE created FALSH removed.
              uint16 commandId,        // Command ID, binding based on a //command
              uint8 * pDestination     // Point to expand address pointer
              )
```

• Remove binding

Remove binding and establish the bind request function are both zb_ BindDeviceRequest (), but parameters not the same (the first parameter is FALSH).

7. Experimental Phenomena

First, reset the collection equipment module (coordinator). Press the "UP" key on the LCD module, then the LED1 (green light) on CC2430 module was lighted. The properties of this module was defined as the network coordinator. This module was responsible for building the network.

Secondly, reset the collection node module. Press the "OK" button on the LCD module, wait for a while. Then, press "UP" key on PK LCD panel three times, wait for about 1 minute, collecting node module will automatically restart as the terminal node. If one network exists, the module will be automatically added to the existing network and LED1 (green light) on this module will flash.

Finally, the terminal module will be automatically bound to the coordinator. If terminal module and coordination module binding are successful, the terminal module will send its own temperature to coordination on a regular.

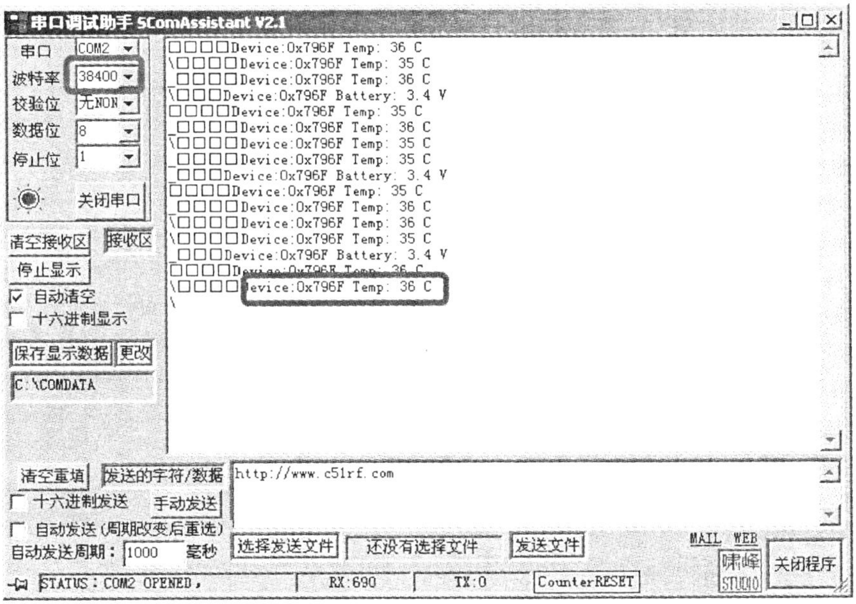

Figure2.　The data transfer interface

8. Answer the Questions

(1) How many different binding forms that ZigBee2006 protocol stack provides?

Answer: There are four different binding forms. They are automatic binding, assisted binding, centralized binding and application binding.

第十二章　数据结构与算法

Chapter 12　Data Structure and Algorithm

课程简介

《数据结构与算法》是计算学科的一门核心课程，它对提高学生的程序设计和算法设计与分析能力具有十分重要的作用。通过本门课程的学习，培养和训练学生能够根据实际问题的要求选择和设计合适的数据结构，编写质量高、风格好的应用程序。

课程内容主要包括：数据结构的基本概念、线性表、栈、队列、字符串、数组、广义表、树、图、查找和排序等。

Course Summary

Data Structure and Algorithm is a core curriculum in the computing discipline. It plays an important role in improving the ability of programming and algorithm design and analysis. By learning it, students can be trained to select and design suitable data structures and write programs with high quality and good style practically.

This course mainly includes the basic concepts of the data structures, linear list, stack and queue, string, array, generalized list, tree, graph, searching and sorting, etc..

第一节　概述

Section 1　Summary

数据元素　data element
数据对象　data object
数据类型　data type
抽象　abstract
★数据结构　data structure
★逻辑结构　logical structure
★物理结构　physical structure
★存储结构　storage structure
★顺序(存储结构)　sequential (storage structure)
★链式(存储结构)　linked (storage structure)
算法分析　algorithm analysis
★渐进分析　asymptotic analysis
渐进复杂度　asymptotic complexity
问题规模　problem scope
基本语句　basic statement
★大O记法　Big-O notation
正确性　correctness
可读性　readability
鲁棒性　robustness
频度　frequency count
计算理论　computability theory
计算复杂性理论　computational complexity theory

1. Abstract data type (ADT): Abstract Data Type (ADT) defines the domain and structure of the data, along with a collection of operations that access the data. It creates a user-defined data type whose operations specify how a client may manipulate the data.
抽象数据类型定义了数据取值范围和结构，以及对数据的操作。它给出了一种用户定义的数据类型，其运算符指明了用户如何操作数据。

2. Time complexity: Time complexity analysis aims to examine the internal structure of an algorithm by analyzing its design, including the number of comparison tests, the number of iterations, and the number of assignment statements used by the algorithm. Time complexity analysis is independent from any particular computer system. The criteria used to measure the computational complexity of the algorithm relative to n, the number of data items in the collection.
时间复杂度分析旨在检查算法的内部结构，所使用的方法是分析算法的设计，包括算法中使用的比较、赋值等各种语句的次数。时间复杂度分析独立于特定的计算机系统，它用算法处理的数据元素的个数 n 来衡量算法的计算复杂度。

3 Space complexity: Space complexity is used to measure the relative amount of internal memory used by an algorithm. It indicates what kind of computer is capable of running the algorithm and the overall system efficiency of the algorithm.
空间复杂度用来测定算法需要的内存空间大小，它可以用来说明算法适合在何种计算机上运行及算法的总体系统性能。

第二节 线性表

Section 2 Linear Lists

直接前驱 immediate predecessor
直接后继 immediate successor
随机存取 random access
顺序存取 sequential access
节点 node
尾标志 tail mark
★ 线性链表 linear linked lists
链表 linked lists
单链表 singly linked lists
双链表 doubly linked lists
头指针 head pointer
尾指针 rear pointer
存储密度 storage density
★ 循环链表 circular linked lists
指示器 cursor
静态链表 implementing linked lists using array
间接寻址 indirect address
双向链表
doubly linked lists 或 bi-directional linked lists

1 Linear lists: A linear list is the collection of objects that are sequentially accessed. It has a unique first and last element and each interior item has a unique successor. A linear list is a general description for structures that include arrays, stacks, queues, and linked lists.
线性表是顺序访问的对象集合。它只有唯一一个头元素和一个尾元素，中间各项都有唯一一个后继。线性表是数组、堆栈、队列和链表等结构的统称。

2 Sequential list: A sequential list is a kind of storage structure of linear list that stores elements in a sequential order. The structure holds an arbitrary number of items. The size of the list is modified by adding or deleting an item from the list, and the items in the list are accessed by their positions.
In a linear list, the first element occurs at the head of the list, and the last element occurs at the rear of the list. Each element except the first and the last has a unique predecessor and a unique successor.
顺序表是线性表的一种存储结构，这种线性表的结构存放着任意个数的元素。表的大小通过增加或删除表中的元素来改变，表中元素通过其位置来访问。
在线性表中，第一个元素位于表头，最后一个元素是表尾，除第一个元素和最后一个元素外，每一个元素都有唯一的前驱和唯一的后继。

3 Head node or header: An empty linked list contains a node, which has an uninitialized data field. This node is called the header and initially points to itself. The role of the header is to point the first "real" node in the list and hence the header is often referred to as a sentinel node.
一个空链表中包含一个节点，它有一个未经初始化的数据域。该节点叫头节点，初始化时它指向自己。头节点的作用是指向表中第一个"真正的"节点，因此它常被称为"哨位"节点。

4 Ordered list: An ordered list is a special type of list that maintains the elements in ascending order.
有序表是一种特殊的表，其元素按升序排列。

5 In cases where we need to access nodes in either direction, a doubly linked list is helpful. A node in a doubly linked list contains two pointers and one data field.
当我们需要双向访问节点时，双向链表是很有用的。双向链表中的节点含有两个指针域、一个数据域。

第三节　栈和队列

Section 3　Stacks and Queues

顺序栈　sequential stack
链栈　linked stack
栈顶　top
栈底　bottom
★ 后进先出　Last In First Out (LIFO)
上溢　overflow
表达式求值　expression evaluation
后缀表达式　postfix expression
汉诺塔算法　Tower of Hanoi algorithm
递归　recursion
队头(元素)　front (element)
队尾(元素)　rear (element)
★ 先进先出　First In First Out (FIFO)
双向队列　double-ended queue
★ 循环队列　circular queue
链队列　linked queue
共享　share
离散事件模拟　discrete event simulation

1 Stack: A stack is a list of items that are accessible at only one end of the list. Items are added or deleted from the list only at the top of the stack. A stack is said to have LIFO (last-in/first-out) ordering. A stack structure features operations that add and delete items. A Push operation adds an item to the top of the stack. The operation of removing an element from the stack is said to pop the stack.

栈是一种只能在表的一端访问元素的表,其元素只能从栈顶端增加或删除。出入栈的顺序为后进先出(LIFO, last-in/first-out)。栈结构的特殊性就在于其增加和删除元素的操作。压入(push)操作往栈顶增加一个元素。从栈顶删除一个元素的操作称为弹出(pop)。

2 Recursive procedure: An algorithm is defined recursively if its definition consists of: (1)One or more stopping conditions which can be evaluated for certain parameters. (2) A recursive step in which a current value in the algorithm can be defined in terms of a previous value. Eventually, the recursive step must lead to stopping conditions.

如果一种算法满足如下条件:(1)对应于某些参数可以求值的一个或多个终止条件;(2)一个递归步骤,其中,当前值可以根据先前某次值来定义。最后,递归步骤必须导致终止条件。则它就是递归的。

3 Queue: A queue is a data structure that stores elements in a list and permits data access only at the two ends of the list. An element is inserted only at the rear of the list and is deleted from the front of the list.

Elements are removed from the queue in the same order in which they are stored and hence a queue provides FIFO (first-in/first-out) or FCFS (first-come /first-served) ordering.

队列是以表形式存放元素,但只允许在表的两端访问元素的数据结构,其元素只能在表尾插入(入队),在表头删除(出队)。

队列删除元素的顺序和元素到达队列的顺序相同,可称为先进先出(FIFO, first-in/first-out)或先到先服务(FCFS,first-come/first-served)。

4 Priority queue: A queue is a data structure that provides a FIFO ordering of elements. The queue removes the "oldest" item from the list. Applications often require a modified version of queue storage in which the item of highest priority is removed from the list. This structure is called a priority queue.

一个队列是以 FIFO 顺序访问元素的数据结构,它从中删除"最老"的元素。实际应用中常需要另外一种队列,它删除优先级最高的元素,这种结构我们称为优先级队列。

第四节　串和数组

Section 4　Strings and Arrays

★ 子串　substring
主串　primary string
空串　null string
空格串　blank string

文本编辑　text editting
模式　pattern
存储密度　storage density
★ 三元组表　list of 3-tuples
三元组顺序表　sequential list of 3-tuples
十字链表　orthogonal list
★ 特殊矩阵　special matrix
★ 稀疏矩阵　sparse matrix

1 String: A string is a special form of an array that holds character data that identify names, words, sentences, and so forth. It treats the characters as a single entity and provides operations to access character sequences within the string.
串是一种特殊形式的数组,它存放着组成名字、单词、句子等的字符数据。它将字符视为单元实体,并提供操作以访问串中字符序列。

2 Pattern matching: A common pattern matching problem involves searching for one or more occurrences of a string in a text.
一个最普通的模式匹配问题就是在文本文件中查找串。

3 Array: An array is an example of a data collection. It defines a structured data type that holds a homogeneous list of items. A one-dimensional array is a finite, sequential list of elements of the same data type (homogeneous array). A two-dimensional array, often called a matrix, is a structured data type that is created by nesting one-dimensional arrays. Items are accessed by row and column indices. The element type of an array can include not only the built-in data type such as int or char but also the user-defined class type.
数组是一个数据集的例子。它定义了一个可以存放多个相同类型元素的结构化数据类型。一维数组是一个具有有限个相同数据类型元素的顺序表(同构数组)。二维数组通常称为矩阵,是一种由多个一维数组合成的结构化数据类型。其元素通过行和列下标存取。
数组元素的类型不但可以是原始类型如整型或字符型,也可以是用户定义的类类型。

4 Storage of one-dimensional array: A C++ one-dimensional array A is logically stored as a consecutive sequence of items in memory. Each item is of the same data type.
一维数组的存储:C++的一维数组 A 逻辑上在内存中连续存放,其每个元素的类型都相同。

5 Storage of two-dimensional arrays: A two-dimensional array can be initialized by assigning the items a row at a time.
二维数组的存储:二维数组可以通过一次赋值一行元素来初始化。

第五节　树和二叉树

Section 5　Trees and Binary Trees

根　root
(节点的)度　degree
叶子节点　leaf node
孩子节点　children node
分支节点　branch node
双亲　parents
兄弟　sibling
祖先　ancestors
子孙　descendants
★ 深度　depth
★ 层、层次　level
有序树　ordered tree
无序树　unordered tree
★ 森林　forest
(表达式的)中缀表示　infix notation
(表达式的)后缀表示　postfix notation
同构　isomorphic
遍历　traverse
双亲表示法　parent expression
孩子表示法　children expression
双亲孩子表示法　parent-children expression
孩子兄弟表示法　children-brother expression
★ 先序遍历　preorder traversal
★ 后序遍历　postorder traversal
★ 完全二叉树　complete binary tree
★ 满二叉树　full binary tree
二叉链表　binary linked list
三叉链表　trident linked list
判定树　decision tree
线索　thread

★ 线索二叉树　threaded binary trees
线索链表　threaded lists
等价关系　equivalence relation
等价类　equivalence class
★ 哈夫曼树　Huffman tree
★ 最优树　optimal tree
前缀编码　prefix code
哈夫曼编码　Huffman code
★ 路径　path
路径长度　path length
带权路径长度　weighted path length
(表达式的)前缀表示　prefix notation
★ 树的遍历　tree traversal
树的计数　enumeration of tree

1 Tree: A tree is a hierarchical structure that consists of nodes emanating from a root. A tree structure is characterized as a set of nodes that originate from a unique starting node called the root. Each node in a tree is the root of a subtree, which is defined by the node and all descendants of the node.
树是一种由根发散的节点所组成的层次结构。它的特点是它是由唯一的起始点"根(root)"开始的"节点"集合。树中的每个结点都是一棵"子树"的根,这个子树是由节点和节点的后代定义的。

2 Binary tree: A binary tree is a restricted class of tree in which each parent has no more than two children. A binary tree is a recursive structure. Each node is the root of its own subtree and has children, which are roots of the tree called the left and right subtrees of the node, respectively.
二叉树是一种特定的树,在这类树中,每个双亲的孩子数不超过两个。二叉树是一种递归结构,每个结点都是其子树的根并有孩子,这些孩子分别是被称为节点的左子树和右子树的根。

第六节　图和广义表
Section 6　Graphs and Generalized Lists

入度　in-degree
出度　out-degree
连通图　connected graph
连通分量　connected component
强连通图　strongly connected graph
强连通分量　strongly connected component
★ 邻接矩阵　adjacency matrix
★ 邻接表　adjacency lists
顶点　vertex
边　edge
弧　arc
弧尾　tail
弧头　head
★ 无向图　undirected graph
★ 有向图　directed graph or digraph
简单图　simple graph
完全图　completed graph
★ 邻接多重表　adjacency multi-lists
★ 图的遍历　traversing graph
稀疏图　sparse graph
稠密图　dense graph
子图　subgraph
★ 生成树　spanning tree
★ 生成森林　spanning forest
★ 最小生成树　minimal spanning tree
普里姆算法　Prim algorithm
克鲁斯卡尔算法　Kruskal algorithm
关节点　articulation point
重连通图　bi-connected graph
★ 有向无环图　directed acyclic graph
★ 拓扑排序　topological sort
拓扑序列　topological order
AOV-网　Activity On Vertex network
AOE-网　Activity On Edge network
★ 关键路径　critical path
始点　beginning
源点　source
终点　end
汇点　convergency
关键活动　critical activity
★ 最短路径　shortest path
二部图　bipartite graph
最大匹配　maximal matching
完全匹配　complete matching
增广路径　augmenting path
★ 广义表　generalized lists
头尾表示法　head-tail expression
★ 逆邻接表　inverse adjacency lists
★ 十字链表　orthogonal lists

1 Graph: A graph is a generalized hierarchical structure that is composed of a set of data items called

vertices and a set of edges that connect pairs of vertices. Graphs find applications in job scheduling, transportation, and so forth.
图是一种一般化的层次结构。它由一组叫做"顶点(vertex)"的数据项和一组连接各对顶点的"边(edge)"所组成。它在作业调度、运输等方面有着应用。

2 Depth-First Search(DFS): The search algorithm uses a list to maintain visited vertices and a stack to store adjacent vertices. After placing the initial vertex on the stack, we begin an iterative process that pops a vertex from the stack and then visits the vertex. We terminate when the stack is empty and return the list of visited vertices.
深度优先搜索:该搜索算法用一个表来维护被访问的顶点,用一个堆栈存储邻接顶点。在将初始顶点放入堆栈以后,开始迭代过程,从堆栈中弹出一个顶点并访问它。当堆栈为空时过程终止并返回被访问过的顶点表。

3 Breadth-First Search(BFS): The breadth-first search uses a queue. The algorithm uses the techniques developed for the depth-first search. Vertices are placed in a queue instead of a stack. An iterative process removes vertices from the queue until it is empty.
宽度优先搜索:宽度优先搜索使用队列。该算法使用与深度优先搜索相同的技术。顶点是放到队列中而非堆栈中。迭代过程从队列中删除顶点直到队列变空为止。

第七节 查找
Section 7 Searching

★ 静态查找表 static search table
★ 动态查找表 dynamic search table
主关键字 primary key
次关键字 second key
★ 查找 searching
★ 平均查找长度 Average Search Length (ASL)
斐波那契查找 Fibonacci search
斐波那契序列 Fibonacci numbers
★ 索引顺序查找 indexed sequential search
★ 分块查找 blocking search
★ 二叉排序树 binary sort tree
平衡因子 balance factor
平衡旋转 balance rotation
数字查找树 digital search tree
双链树 doubly linked tree
同义词 synonym
★ 冲突 collision
冲突的解决 collision resolution
★ 开放定址 open addressing
★ 线性探测 linear probing
★ 二次探测 quadratic probing
★ 伪随机探测 pseudo-random probing
★ 链地址法 chaining-address method
★ 直接定址 immediately allocate
随机数法 random number method
折叠法 folding method
移位叠加 shift folding
数字分析法 digit analysis method
间界叠加 folding at the boundaries
平方取中 mid-square method
估值函数 evaluation function
★ 再哈希 rehash
★ 装填因子 load factor

1 Search tables: Search tables are a series of list structures that allow the client to search for and retrieve data. In each structure, a Find method takes a key and traverses the list looking for a matching data item.
查找表:查找表是一系列允许客户程序搜索和取出数据的表结构。每种结构都有一个Find(查找)方法,它以关键字为参数,遍历表以找到匹配的数据项。

2 Sequential search: A sequential search looks for an item in a list using a target value called the Key. The algorithm begins at a user-supplied index, called start, and traverses the remaining items in the list, comparing each item with the Key. The scan continues until the Key is found or the list is exhausted. If the Key is found, the function returns the index of the matched element in the list; otherwise, the value -1 is returned.

顺序查找:顺序查找用一个称为 Key(关键字)的目标值来查找表中的元素。该算法从用户给出的起点开始,遍历表中的后续元素,并将元素值与 Key 比较,直到元素值与 Key 值相等或到表尾。如果找到 Key 值,函数返回该元素在表中的位置;否则,返回-1。

3 Binary search: The sequential search applies to any list. If the list is ordered, an algorithm, called the binary search, provides an improved search technique.

折半查找:顺序查找可适用于任意表。若被查找的表有序,则可用折半查找算法来查找,它是一种改进的查找算法。

4 Binary search tree: In a binary search tree, for each node, the data values in the left subtree are less than the value of the node and the data values in the right subtree are greater than or equal to the value of the node.

二叉查找树:在二叉查找树中,对每个节点,其左子树中的数据值都小于节点本身的值,而右子树中的数据值都大于或等于节点的值。

5 Balanced binary tree or height-balanced tree: Binary search tree is designed for rapid access to data. Ideally, the tree is reasonably balanced and has height approximately O(log2n). With some data, however, a binary search tree can be degenerate. In that case, the height is O(n) and access to the data is significantly slowed. We develop AVL tree in which every node is height-balanced. By this we mean that for each node in an AVL tree, the difference in height of its two subtree is at most 1.

平衡二叉树或平衡高度树:二叉搜索树是为快速访问数据而设计的。理想情况下,树是平衡分布的,其高度约为 O(log2n)。但对有些数据来说,二叉搜索树也可能是退化的。那时树高将是 O(n),访问数据的速度将明显变慢。我们要设计的是各节点具有平衡高度的 AVL 树。也就是说,在 AVL 树中任一节点的两个子树的高度差最多为 1。

6 Hash function : In most applications, a key is used to provide an indirect reference to the data. A function, called a hash function, maps the key into a range of integers and then uses the integer value to access the data.

A hash function must map a key to a integer value in the range 0 to n－1. Its design should limit collisions and guarantee efficient execution.

哈希函数:在多数应用中,关键字用来提供对数据的间接引用。哈希函数是将关键字映射到一定范围的整数内,然后用整数值来访问数据。

哈希函数必须将关键字映射为 0 到 n－1 范围内的整数值。其设计必须考虑减少冲突并保证执行效率。

7 Division method: The division method is the most commonly used hashing technique, requiring two steps. First the key must be transformed into an integer and then the value must be telescoped into the range 0 to n－1 using the remainder operator. In practice, the division method is used in most hashing applications.

除留取余法:除留取余法是最常用的哈希技术,它分为两个步骤。首先必须将关键字转换成整数值,然后再用求余数运算符将这一值缩到 0～n－1 的范围内。在实际的哈希应用中,除留取余法用得最多。

第八节 排序
Section 8 Sorting

正序 exact order
逆序 inverse order
反序 anti-order
稳定 stable
不稳定 unstable
单键排序 single-key sort
多键排序 multiple-key sort
★ 内部排序 internal sorting
★ 外部排序 external sorting
★ 稳定的排序法 stable sorting method
插入查找 insertion search
★ 插入排序 insertion sort

★ 直接插入排序 straight insertion sort
折半插入排序 binary insertion sort
2一路插入排序 2-way insertion sort
表插入排序 list insertion sort
★ 希尔排序 Shell's method
★ 缩小增量排序 diminishing increment sort
归并插入排序 merge insertion sort
★ 起泡排序 bubble sort
★ 快速排序 quick sort
简单(选择排序) simple (selection sort)
树形(选择排序) tree (selection sort)
锦标赛排序 tournament sort
★ 堆 heap
★ 堆排序 heap sort
★ 基数排序 radix sort
★ 最高位优先 most significant digit first (MSD)
★ 最低位优先 least significant digit first (LSD)
★ 链式基数排序 linked radix sort
磁带排序 sorting with tapes
间隙 gap
寻查时间 seek time
等待时间 latency time
传输时间 transmission time
段 segment
归并段 merging segment
有序段 sorted segment
延迟时间 delay time
字符组间的间隙 inter record gap (IRC)
块间的间隙 inter block gap (IBG)
多路归并 multi-way merge
败者树 tree of loser
置换-选择排序 replacement selection sort
并行操作处理 handling for parallel operation
最佳归并树 optimal merge tree
平衡归并 balanced merge
多步归并 polyphase merge
广义斐波那契序列 generalized Fibonacci numbers

1 Sorting: Sorting is the process of arranging a group of data elements into some desired order according to rules dependent upon a key or several keys contained in each data element.
排序:排序是根据每个数据元素中所含关键字所确定的规则,将一组数据元素排列成某种所需次序的过程。

2 Selection sort: Given a group of data items in random order, the selection sort repeatedly selects the smallest item from the group and moves it to a list that is forming in ascending order.
选择排序:对以随机顺序排列的一组数据项,选择排序将反复地从组中挑选出最小的数据项并将它移到正在形成的按升序排列的表中。

第十三章　检测技术与智能仪表设计

Chapter 13　Detection Technology and Intelligent Instrumentation Design

课程简介

课程目标：检测技术与智能仪表设计是电子信息工程专业的一门专业教育必修课，培养学生密切联系工程实际综合运用知识的能力。课程内容：信号制、抗干扰技术、测量误差与数据管理、电容式传感器、电感式传感器、应变式传感器、热电式传感器、仪表硬件电路设计、软件基础、系统监控程序的设计、容错设计。

Course Summary

Course objectives: detection technology and intelligent instrumentation design is a professional education course of electronic and information engineering. The course helps students to have a close contact with the engineering practice, and improve the ability to use knowledge comprehensively. Course Content: Signal system, anti-interference technology, measurement error and data management, capacitance sensor, inductance sensor, strain sensor, pyroelectric transducer, hardware circuit design of instrument, software base, design of the monitoring system and fault tolerant design.

第一节　概述

Section 1　Summary

★ 传感器　sensor/ transducer
★ 敏感元件　sensing element
★ 转换元件　switch element
★ 测量电路　measuring circuit
★ 检测技术　detection technique
★ 仪表　gauge/ meter
★ 智能仪器　intelligent instruments
静态特性　static characteristic
线性化　linearization
非线性误差　non-linearity error
最小二乘法　least square method
★ 灵敏度　sensitivity
★ 精确度　accuracy
★ 分辨率　resolution
迟滞　hysteresis
重复性　repeatability
★ 零点漂移　zero drift
温漂　temperature drift
动态特性　dynamic characteristic
传递函数　transfer function
★ 偏差　excursion
脉冲　impulse
校正　remedy
★ 精度　precision
物理量检测仪表
measuring instrument for physical quantity
★ 非电量检测仪
measuring instrument for non-electric quantity

The widespread development of sensors is transforming the physical world into a computing platform. Modern sensors not only respond to physical signals to produce data, but also embed computing and communication capabilities. They are thus able to store, process locally and transfer the data they produce.

通常情况下，传感器是把模拟的物理量转换为可测的数值量。随着现代技术的发展，传感器不仅可以转换模拟信号，而且还具有计算和通信的功能。因而，现代传感器可以在本地储存、处理数据，并能够远距离传送采集到的数据。

第二节　应力传感器

Section 2　Strain Pressure Sensor

应变片　strain gauge/ foil gauge
★ 应力传感器　strain sensor

★ 压力传感器
pressure pick-up/pressure transducer
★ 压敏二极管　pressure-sensitive diode
电极栅　electrode grid
横向效应　transverse effect
应变极限　strain limitation
温度误差　temperature error
★ 温度补偿　temperature compensation
★ 电桥　bridge
★ 应力传感器　strain pressure sensor
★ 智能压力变送器　smart pressure transmitter
★ 压敏电阻　voltage dependent resistor
压敏电桥　voltage-sensitive bridge
★ 压电传感器　piezoelectric transducer
★ 压阻式传感器　compressive resistance sensor
★ 压阻效应　compressive resistance effect
★ 压阻系数　compressive resistance coefficient
★ 电容式传感器　capacitance sensor
寄生电容　parasitic capacitance
差动电容传感器　differential capacitance sensor
等效电路　equivalent electric circuit
等臂电桥　equal-arm bridge
不平衡电容　unbalance capacitance
二极管检波电路　diode wave detector
★ 边缘效应　contour effects
★ 分布电容　distribution capacity
电流互感器　current transformer
★ 自感式传感器　self-induction sensor
★ 互感式传感器　mutual sensor
★ 电流互感器　current transformer
★ 电容式压力变送器
capacitance pressure transmitter
电容式液位探头　capacitance level probe
气隙　air gap
特性分析　characteristic analysis
电感线圈　induction coil
差动变压器　differential transformer
变换特性　changing characteristic
误差因数　error factor
激励电压　energizing voltage
零点残余电压　zero residual voltage
差压指示器　different pressure indicator
整流电路　rectification circuit
★ 加速度传感器　acceleration sensor
电涡流式传感器　electric swirl sensor
调幅　amplitude modulation
调频　frequency regulation
★ 电感元件　induction element
★ 谐振曲线　resonant curve
★ 位移测量　displace measure
转换测量　conversion measure
振幅测量　vibration amplitude measure
★ 位置变送器　position transmitter
★ 有源滤波器　active filter
无源元件　passive component
力敏元件　mechanical sensor
临界压力　critical pressure
★ 压电效应　piezoelectric effect
★ 差压变送器　differential pressure transmitter
★ 石英传感器　quartz sensor
★ 压电陶瓷　piezoelectric ceramic
★ 电压放大器　voltage amplifier
★ 阻抗变换器　impedance transformer
运算放大器　operation amplifier
动态响应　dynamic response
★ 压电式压力传感器
piezoelectric pressure sensor
★ 压电式流量计　piezoelectric flow meter
★ 差压传感器　differential pressure transducer
半导体应变式压力传感
semiconductor strain pressure sensor
★ 压电式加速度计　piezoelectric accelerometer
★ 电动测微仪　electronic gage

Compared with competing optical, inductive, and piezoresistive transducers, capacitive sensors have many advantages, among which are low cost and power usage, good sensitivity and speed. Capacitive sensors can detect motion, acceleration, flow and many other variables, therefore, they are used in a wide range of applications.

相对于光电传感器、感应传感器以及压电式传感器而言，电容式传感器有许多优点：价格低、耗电小以及灵敏度高、速度快。电容式传感器能够检测运动、加速度、流量以及很多其他变量，因此获得了广泛的应用。

第三节　数字传感器
Section 3　Digital Sensor

模数转换器　analog-to-digital converter
脉冲式数字传感器　impulse digital sensor
★ 光栅传感器　raster sensor
★ 位移传感器　displacement sensor
★ 位置变送器　position transmitter
★ 感应同步式　induction synchronous
★ 磁栅传感器　magnetic grid sensor
★ 感应同步器　inductosyn
★ 振簧式频率传感器
vibrating-reed frequency sensor
★ 二进制码　binary-code
循环码　cyclic code
固有频率　free running frequency
电磁法　electromagnetic method
★ 码盘　encoder

One major issue with a mobile robot acting as a gateway is the communication between the robot and the sensor network. Sensor networks typically communicate using 900 MHz radio waves. Mobile robots use laptops that communicate via 802.11, in the range of 2.4- to 2.483-GHz. Intel hopes to prove that a sensor net can be equipped with 802.11 capabilities to bridge the gap between robotics and wireless networks.

移动机器人装置能够起关键作用的一个问题是机器人装置与传感器网络的通讯问题。通常情况下传感器网络使用900 MHz的无线电波进行通讯。移动机器人使用膝上型电脑通讯，经过802.11协议，也就是在2.4GHz到2.483GHz的范围内。英特尔公司希望能生产一种传感器，具有802.11协议需要的能力，在机器人系统和无线网络间提供通讯。

第四节　热敏传感器
Section 4　Thermo-electric Sensor

★ 热电效应　thermo-electric effect
★ 热磁效应　thermo-magnetic effect
★ 热电偶　thermocouple
★ 热电阻　thermal resistance
★ 热敏开关　thermoswitch
接触电势　contact potential
温差电流　thermocurrent
环境温度　ambient temperature
热电极　hot electrode
★ 热电桥　thermal bridge
★ 热敏电阻器　thermal resistor
热敏元件传感器　thermistor element sensor
★ 冷端温度　cold end temperature
冷端补偿器　cold junction compensatory
铂电阻　platinum resistance
铜电阻　copper resistance
集成温度传感器　integrated temperature sensor
NFF型温度传感器　NFF temperature sensor
遮光路式温度传感器　hide temperature sensor
★ 红外线式温度传感器
temperature sensor through infrared ray
荧光辐射式温度传感器
temperature sensor through fluorescent radiation
★ 电阻—温度特性
electric resistance-temperature characteristic
伏安特性　current-voltage characteristic
★ 标称电阻　standard resistance
温度传感器　temperature sensor
干涉式温度传感器
disconcerting temperature sensor
★ 测温电路　temperature measuring circuit
★ 多谐振荡器　astable multivibrator
★ 温度系数　temperature coefficient
★ 继电效应　relay effect

A thermistor is a temperature sensor, made of semiconductor materials, that has been developed on the principle that semiconductor resistance changes with temperature. The particular semiconductor material used varies widely to accommodate temperature ranges, sensitivity, resistance ranges, and other factors.

热敏电阻是一种用半导体材料制成的温度传感器，它所利用的原理是当周围温度改变时，半导体材料的电阻也随之改变。为了满足测量温度时要求的测量范围、灵敏度、电阻范围以及其他测量要求，往往采用一些特殊的半导体材料。

第五节 固态传感器
Section 5 Solid State Sensor

★ 固态传感器 solid state sensor
力敏效应 mechanical effect
★ 磁敏传感器 magneto sensor
★ 磁阻传感器 magnetic resistance sensor
★ 霍尔元件 Hall element
★ 霍尔效应 Hall effect
★ 霍尔系数 Hall coefficient
霍尔压力变送器 Hall pressure transmitter
寄生直流电势 parasitic direct voltage
感应电势 induced electromotive force
磁电特性 magnetoelectric characteristic
法拉第效应式传感器 Faraday's effect-sensor
磁致伸缩式传感器 magnetostrictive sensor
★ 光电效应 electric-optical effect
★ 电磁效应 electro magnetic effect
★ 光电元件 photoelectric unit
温度补偿电路
temperature compensation circuit
★ 光敏传感器 light sensitive sensor
光敏元件 light sensitive element
★ 光电导探测器 photoconductive detector
光谱特性 light spectrum characteristic
稳定性 stability
光电池 photo battery
★ 光敏二极管 light sensitive diode
光敏三极管 light sensitive bipolar junction transistor
★ 光电传感器 photoelectric sensor
★ 光电转速计 photoelectric speed recorder
★ 转速传感器 rata sensor/speed sensor
★ CCD 图像传感器 CCD image sensor
★ 固态图像传感器 solid-state image sensor
固态温度传感器 solid-state temperature sensor
线形固态图像传感器
linear solid-state image sensor
集成红外 CCD 固态图像传感器 integrated infrared CCD solid-state image sensor
光敏区 light sensitive zone
行传输 line transmission
帧传输 frame transmission
★ 半导体气体传感器 semiconductor gas sensor
★ 气敏元件 gas sensitive sensor
气动量仪 air gage
相对湿度 relative humidity
绝对湿度 absolute humidity
★ 陶瓷温度传感器
ceramic temperature sensor
★ 流量变送器 flow transducer
电液型 electrohydromatic type
★ 液位变送器 level transducer
★ 数字式电液控制系统
digital electro-hydromatic control system
★ 涡流传感器 eddy sensor

Integrated circuit technology has led to the development of solid-state (SS) pressure sensors that find extensive application in the pressure ranges of 0 to 100 kPa. These small units often require no more than three connections, DC power, ground, and the sensor output. Pressure connection is via a metal tube.

随着集成电路技术的发展，固态压力传感器也得到极大的发展。固态压力传感器主要用于测量压力值为 0 到 100 千帕的场合。固态压力传感器体积一般都很小，而且只有电源端、接地端和传感器输出端。压力连接是通过一个金属管实现的。

第六节 光纤传感器
Section 6 Optical Fiber Sensor

★ 光纤传感器 optical fiber sensor
光导纤维 FF 型传感器 light guide fiber FF sensor
光纤转速传感器
optical fiber sensor for turn speed
光纤水声传感器
optical fiber sensor for water sound
光纤磁场电流传感器 optical fiber sensor for magnetic field and electric current

共振式光导纤维振动传感器 optical fiber vibration sensor
激光扫描测量装置 laser scanner
光导纤维 optical fiber
强度调制 strength modulation
偏振调制 polarization modulation
相位调制 phase modulation
光源 light source
固体激光器 solid energizer
气体激光器 gas energizer
半导体激光 semiconductor energizer
★ 光电检测器 photoelectric detector
★ 光电脉冲发生器 optoelectronic pulse generator
标定 calibrate
★ 静态标定 static calibrate
标定量程 calibrate span
动态标定 dynamic calibrate

The photodiode effect refers to the fact that photons impinge on the PN junction also alter the reverse current-verse-voltage characteristic of the diode. In particular, the reverse current will be increased almost linearly with light intensity. Thus, the photodiode is operated in the reverse-bias mode.

光敏二极管效应指的是当光敏二极管受到光照时,PN 结附近受到光子轰击,二极管的反向电流随电压变化而变化。也就是说,随着光照强度的增加,反向电流也随之增加,变化趋势呈线性。因此,光敏二极管工作在反向偏置。

第十四章 数字信号处理
Chapter 14 Digital Signal Processing

课程简介

本课程主要是使学生学习数字信号处理的基本理论、基本分析方法、基本算法和基本实现方法。要求学生通过本课程的学习，能掌握数字信号处理的基本概念和基本方法，并在理解相关基本概念和基本方法的基础上，切实掌握一些常用的数字信号处理算法，为实际应用打下基础。

Course Summary

This course is to enable students to learn the basic theory of digital signal processing, the basic analysis methods, the basic algorithms and the basic implementation methods. By learning this course, students can understand the basic concepts and acquire some basic methods of digital signal processing. Furthermore, students can effectively learn some common digital signal processing algorithms, which will lay a foundation for practical application.

第一节 时域离散信号和时域离散系统
Section 1 Time Domain Discrete Signal and Time Domain Discrete System

★ 模拟信号 analog signal
★ 数字信号 digital signal
★ 时域离散信号 time domain discrete signal
时域离散系统 time domain discrete system
★ 单位脉冲函数 unit impulse function
时域 time domain
频域 frequency domain
实时 real time
★ 线性系统 linear system
★ 因果系统 causal system
★ 线性时不变系统 linear time-invariant system
因果性 causality
实指数序列 real exponential sequence
周期序列 periodic sequence
复指数序列 complex exponential sequence
模拟角频率 analog angular frequency
数字频率 digital frequency
序列移位 sequence shift
序列翻转 sequence flip
尺度变换 scale transformation
线性常系数差分方程 linear constant coefficient difference equation
频谱混叠 spectrum aliasing
截止频率 cut-off frequency
折叠频率 folding frequency
周期延拓 period extension
解码器 decoder
零阶保持器 zero order holder
平滑滤波器 smoothing filter
内插函数 interpolating function
模数转换 analog-to-digital conversion
数模转换 digital-to-analog conversion
稳定性 stability
采样定理 sampling theorem
★ 欠采样 undersampling
★ 过采样 oversampling
★ 采样间隔 sampling interval
采样周期 sampling period
奈奎斯特采样速率 Nyquist sampling rate
奈奎斯特采样频率 Nyquist sampling frequency
抗混叠滤波器 antialiasing filter
抗镜像滤波器 anti-imaging filter
采集时间 acquisition time
量化电平 quantization level
★ 脉冲响应 impulse response
★ 阶跃响应 step response
二维数字信号 two-dimensional digital signals
数字矩阵 digital matrix

例 The Nyquist sampling rate is twice the highest frequency in the signal being sampled. Oversampling refers to sampling at a rate greater than the Nyquist rate. It eases the design of the antialiasing filter. Undersampling, on the other hand, refers to sampling at a rate that is slower than the Nyquist rate. It results in aliasing, which alters the spectrum of the signal.

奈奎斯特采样速率是被采样信号最高频率的二倍。大于奈奎斯特速率的采样称为过采样，能使抗混的滤波器的设计更容易。小于奈奎斯特速率的采样称为欠采样，能改变信号的频谱，导致混叠。

2 Analog-to-digital conversion occurs in two steps. The first step is sampling. Sampling instants normally occur at regular intervals called sampling periods. At each sampling point, the analog signal is sampled, and the value of the signal is held steady until the next sampling point. This process is called sample and hold. Sampling must be fast enough to capture the most rapid changes in the signal being sampled. If sampling is too slow, important signal characteristics can be lost, a problem called aliasing. Note that the act of sampling takes a finite amount of time, called the acquisition time of the sampler.

The second step in the conversion between an analog signal and a digital signal, which can begin at the completion of sample acquisition, is to quantize and digitize the analog values. The hold interval normally gives ample time for this. As soon as possible after each sampling instant, the converter selects the quantization level that approximates the sample-and-hold value as closely as possible and then assigns a binary digital code that identifies the quantization level. This completes the analog-to-digital conversion process.

模/数转换分两个步骤进行。第一步是采样。采样时刻通常处在固定的间隔点上，这个间隔称为采样周期。在每一个采样点对模拟信号进行采样，且将该采样值保持到下一个采样点的过程称为采样保持。采样要足够快，以捕捉被采样信号中的最快变化；如果采样太慢，将丢失重要的信号特征，出现混叠。值得注意的是采样也要占用有限的时间，称为采样器的采集时间。

模/数转换的第二步是对模拟值进行量化和数字化，这在采样完成后即可进行。采样保持期间有足够的时间完成这一步。每个采样结束后，转换器尽快选择与采样保持电平最接近的量化电平，然后分配一个二进制数字代码来标识这个量化电平。这样就完成了模/数转换过程。

第二节　时域离散信号和系统的频域分析

Section 2　Time Domain Discrete Signal and Frequency Domain Analysis of System

★ 傅里叶变换　Fourier transform

傅里叶系数　Fourier coefficient

★ 离散时间傅里叶变换

discrete time fourier transform (DTFT)

★ 共轭对称　conjugate symmetry

共轭反对称　conjugate dissymmetry

奇函数　odd function

偶函数　even function

实序列　real sequences

时移特性　time-shifting property

频移特性　frequency-shifting property

对称序列　symmetric sequences

频率响应　frequency response

幅度响应　magnitude response

相位响应　phase response

★ 离散傅里叶级数　discrete fourier series (DFS)

基频　fundamental frequency

★ 谐波频率　harmonic frequency

z 变换　z transform

z 平面　z plane

变换表　table of transform

逆 z 变换　inverse z transform

★ 收敛域　region of convergence

极点　pole

零点　zero

单位圆　unit circle

零极点图　pole-zero plot

临界稳定　marginal stabilization

复卷积定理　complex convolution theorem

★ 帕斯维尔定理　Parseval's theorem

★ 差分方程　difference equation

传输函数　transfer function

系统函数　system function

部分分式展开　partial fraction expansion

暂态特性　transient behavior

★ 暂态解　transient solution

稳态特性　steady state behavior

★ 稳态解　steady state solution

全通滤波器　all-pass filter

梳状滤波器　comb filter

镜像滤波器　imaging filter

1 The Fourier transform gives spectral characteristic about an analog signal. Because an unadulterated analog signal, rather than a digital signal, is used to compute the Fourier transform, this transform is unaffected by sampling or quantization.
傅里叶变换给出了模拟信号的频谱特性。由于傅里叶变换是针对纯粹的模拟信号的变换,而不是数字信号的变换,因此它不受采样或量化的影响。

2 Definition of the z transform :
The z transform of a sequence $x(n)$ is defined as

$$X(z) = Z\{x(n)\} = \sum_{n=-\infty}^{\infty} x(n)z^{-n}$$

where z is a complex variable. Note that $X(z)$ is only defined for the regions of the complex plane in which the summation on the right converges.
Z 变换定义:
序列 $x(n)$ 的 z 变换定义为

$$X(z) = Z\{x(n)\} = \sum_{n=-\infty}^{\infty} x(n)z^{-n}$$

这里 z 是复变量。注意 $X(z)$ 仅定义在绝对可和的收敛复平面上。

3 The unit circle is a circle with radius one centered at the origin of the z plane. A filter is stable if all its ples are inside the unit circle. A filter with poles on the unit circle is said to be marginally stable. A filter with poles outside the unit circle is unstable. Mathematically, the region of stability can be described as

$$|z| < 1$$

where the double bars refer to the magnitude of the complex number. Recall that the magnitude of a complex number $|z| = \mathrm{Re}z + j\mathrm{Im}z$ is calculated from the real and imaginary parts of the number by the equation

$$|z| = \sqrt{(\mathrm{Re}z)^2 + (\mathrm{Im}z)^2}$$

If the magnitude of each pole is less than one, and the poles are less than one unit's distance from the center of the unit circle, the filter is stable.
单位圆是以 z 平面的原点为圆心、半径为 1 的圆。如果滤波器的所有极点都在单位圆内,则滤波器是稳定的;若单位圆上有极点,则滤波器是临界稳定的;如果单位圆外有极点,则滤波器是不稳定的。数学上,稳定区域可表示为

$$|z| < 1$$

记号| |表示复变量的模值。复变量 $|z| = \mathrm{Re}z + j\mathrm{Im}z$ 的模值由实部和虚部按下式得到:

$$|z| = \sqrt{(\mathrm{Re}z)^2 + (\mathrm{Im}z)^2}$$

如果每个极点的模值都小于 1,也就是极点到单位圆中心的距离小于 1,则滤波器是稳定的。

第三节 离散傅里叶变换
Section 3 Discrete Fourier Transform

★ 离散傅里叶变换 discrete Fourier transform (DFT)
★ 离散傅里叶逆变换
inverse discrete Fourier transform (IDFT)
隐含周期性 implied periodicity
循环移位 circular shift
★ 循环卷积 circular convolution
卷积定理 convolution theorem
★ 频域采样定理
frequency domain sampling theorem
★ 线性卷积 linear convolution
数字卷积 digital convolution
共轭对称序列 conjugate symmetry sequence
共轭反对称序列 conjugate dissymmetry sequence
偶对称序列 even symmetry sequence
奇对称序列 odd dissymmetry sequence

频域采样　frequency domain sampling
频谱分析　spectrum analyzing
频谱图　spectrogram
预滤波器　prefilter
带限信号　band-limited signal
幅度频谱　magnitude spectrum
相位频谱　phase spectrum
频谱泄漏　spectral leakage
栅栏效应　shutter effect
截断效应　cut-off effect
★ 谱间干扰　disturbance between spectrum
★ 边界效应　boundary effect
频谱分量　spectrum component
谱分辨率　spectral resolution
频率分辨率　frequency resolution
补零　zero padding
线性调频 Z 变换　chirp-z transform
最小记录时间　minimum recording time
最大采样间隔　maximum sampling interval
最少采样点数　minimum sampling points

1 Equation for the DFT has a similar form to that of the DTFT. In fact, when the DFT and the DTFT operate on the same set of time samples, the DFT matches the DTFT exactly, but in terms of a finite number of points only. The DTFT produces magnitude and phase spectra that are smooth functions of frequency, and the DFT produces sampled version of the same spectra.
DFT 定义式和 DTFT 定义式的形式相似。实际上,仅对于有限个点而言,当对同一组时域采样信号进行 DFT 和 DTFT 时,DFT 与 DTFT 完全相符。DTFT 得到的幅度频谱与相位频谱图是频率的光滑函数,而 DFT 得到的是幅度频谱和相位频谱图的采样形式。

2 In DFT computation, the more computational and storage requirements are needed, the larger the amount of zero-padding is. So the arithmetic complexity allowed by a particular application decides the amount of zero-padding.
在 DFT 计算中,补零越多,其计算和存储量要求就越多。所以,某一应用所允许的算术复杂程度决定了补零的数目。

第四节　快速傅里叶变换(FFT)
Section 4　Fast Fourier Transform

★ 快速傅里叶变换　fast Fourier transform (FFT)
★ 旋转因子　twiddle factor
短序列　short sequence
子序列　subsequence
★ 时域抽取法 FFT
decimation-in-time FFT (DIT-FFT)
★ 频域抽取法 FFT
decimation-in-frequency FFT (DIF-FFT)
★ 基 2 时域抽取法 FFT
radix-2 decimation-in-time FFT
★ 蝶形运算　butterfly operation
分解　disassemble
运算流图　algorithm diagram
复数乘法　complex multiplication
复数加法　complex additions
倒序　reverse order
查表法　lookup table
原位运算　in situ computing
★ 蝶形单元运算　butterfly unit operation
★ 分裂基 FFT 算法　divide radix FFT algorithm
★ 离散哈特莱变换　discrete Hartley transform (DHT)
★ 离散哈特莱逆变换
inverse discrete Hartley transform (IDHT)
分裂基　split base
混合基　mixed base
核函数　kernel function
分辨率　resolution
叠加　superposition

1 One needs about N^2 complex multiplications in order to compute the DFT and IDFT of a length-N sequence. The complexity of the DFT grows with the square of the signal length. This severely limits its practical use for over lengthy signals.
为计算长为 N 的序列的 DFT 和 IDFT 需要 N^2 个复数乘法运算。DFT 的复杂性随着信号长度的平方而增长,这严重限制了过长信号的实际应用。

2 FFT algorithms may represent a tremendous decrease in complexity, which requires a number of

complex multiplications of the order of $N\log_2 N$.

FFT 算法要求复数乘法运算数为 $N\log_2 N$ 的阶数，这大大降低了复杂性。

第五节 时域离散系统的基本网络结构与状态变量分析法

Section 5 Aralytical Method of Basic Network Structure and State Variable in Time Domain Discrete System

无限长限单位脉冲响应网络 infinite unit impulse response network
流图 flow graph
实现结构 realization structure
★ 直接型滤波器 direct filter
★ 级联型滤波器 cascaded filter
并联型滤波器 parallel filter
频率采样结构 frequency sampling structure
线性相位结构 linear phase structure
延时单元 delay unit
窄带滤波器 narrowband filter
格型网络结构 lattice network structure

Several structures used to realize a given transfer function are introduced in this chapter. The structures associate with a specific difference equation through the use of the z transform. The transfer functions considered here will be of the polynomial form (nonrecursive filters) and of the rational-polynomial form (recursive filters). The properties of the given generic digital filter structures are also analyzed, which are related to the practical discrete-time systems.

这章介绍了几种常用于实现给定传输函数的结构。该结构与通过利用 Z 变换的特定差分方程有关。这里考虑的传输函数是多项式形式(非递归滤波器)和有理多项式形式(递归滤波器)。还分析了与实际离散时间系统相关联的一般滤波器的结构特性。

第六节 无限脉冲响应数字滤波器的设计

Section 6 Design of Infinite Impulse Response Digital Filter

★ 数字滤波器 digital filter
★ 模拟滤波器 analog filter
匹配转换 matching conversion
★ 无限脉冲响应 infinite impulse response (IIR)
经典滤波器 classical filter
频带 frequency band
干扰 disturbance
重叠 overlap
★ 现代滤波器 modern filter
★ 维纳滤波器 Winner filter
★ 卡尔曼滤波器 Kalman filter
★ 自适应滤波器 self-adapting filter
随机信号 stochastic signal
低通滤波器 lowpass filter
高通滤波器 highpass filter
带通滤波器 bandpass filter
带阻滤波器 bandstop filter
设计步骤 design step
非递归滤波器 non-recursive filter
相位延迟 phase delay
相位失真 phase distortion
消除 elimination
通带 pass band
★ 通带波纹 pass band ripple
过渡带 transition zone
阻带 stop band
★ 阻带波纹 stop band ripple
过渡带宽度 transition width
幅频特性 amplitude frequency characteristics
相频特性 phase frequency characteristics
信噪比 signal-to-noise ratio (SNR)
★ 衰减 attenuation
技术指标 technical indicator
通带边界频率 pass band boundary frequency
阻带截止频率 stop band cut-off frequency
分贝 decibel
抽取 decimation
损耗函数 loss function
衰减函数 attenuation function
相位校正 phase correction
非线性相位 nonlinear phase
频率变换法 frequency transform method
★ 巴特沃斯滤波器 Butterworth filter
★ 切比雪夫滤波器 Chebyshev filter
★ 椭圆滤波器 elliptic filter
★ 贝塞尔滤波器 Bessel filter

选择性 selectivity
抖动 dithering
★ 归一化 normalization
复变量 complex variable
一阶滤波器 first order filter
二阶滤波器 second order filter
滤波器阶数 filter order
滤波器形状 filter shape
通带宽度 passband width
中心频率 center frequency
脉冲响应不变法 impulse invariance
双线性变换法 bilinear transformation
比特率 bit rate
非线性映射 nonlinear image
平方误差 square error
误差函数 error function
幅度平方误差最小设计法
magnitude square error minimum designing
逼近理想 approximating ideal
波纹 ripple
滚降 roll-off

1 There are several other important differences between recursive and non-recursive filters. With recursive filters, it is not easy to achieve the linear phase that was guaranteed for non-recursive filters. However, recursive filters do have the advantage that they require far fewer coefficients than non-recursive filters to achieve similar performance specifications. The design approach that will be used for recursive filters is to choose a prototype analog filter that has the desired characteristics and then convert it to a digital filter.

递归滤波器和非递归滤波器之间还有很多其他重要的区别。递归滤波器很难实现非递归滤波器所具有的线性相位。然而，递归滤波器也有其优势，在实现类似的性能要求时，它比非递归滤波器所需的系数要少得多。设计递归滤波器的方法是选择具有待求特性的原型模拟滤波器，然后将其转换为数字滤波器。

2 Common analog filter types include Butterworth, Chebyshev Type I, Chebyshev Type II, and elliptic filters. They differ mainly in their general shapes. Butterworth filters are monotonic through the pass band and stop band, meaning they change smoothly in a single direction. Chebyshev Type I filters are monotonic through the stop band, but ripple in the pass band. Chebyshev Type II filters are monotonic in the pass band, but ripple in the stop band. Finally, elliptic filters are ripple in both the pass and stop bands.

通常模拟滤波器类型包括巴特沃斯、切比雪夫 I 型、切比雪夫 II 型和椭圆滤波器等。它们的主要区别在于特性的不同。巴特沃斯滤波器在通带和阻带都是单调的，意味着它们在一个方向上平滑变化；切比雪夫 I 型滤波器在阻带内是单调的，但在通带内是有波纹的；切比雪夫 II 型滤波器在通带内是单调的，但在阻带内是有波纹的；最后，椭圆滤波器在通带和阻带内都有波纹。

第七节 有限脉冲响应数字滤波器的设计

Section 7 Design of Finite Pulse Response Digital Filter

★ 有限脉冲响应 finite impulse response (FIR)
窗函数法 window function method
傅氏级数法 Fourier series method
★ 频率采样法 frequency sampling method
★ 切比雪夫等波纹逼近法
Chebyshev equiripple approximating method
等波纹 FIR 滤波器设计 equiripple FIR filter design
吉布斯效应 Gibbs effect
主瓣 main lobe
旁瓣 side lobe
峰值 peak
基本参数 basic parameter
最小衰减 minimum attenuation
★ 逼近函数 approximating function
插值 interpolation
逼近误差 approximating error
平滑 smoothing
群延时 group delay
时域约束条件 time domain constraints
第一类线性相位 the first class of linear phase
第二类线性相位 the second class of linear phase
间断点 discontinuous spot
误差加权函数 error weighting function
逼近精度 approximating precision

线性相位 linear-phase
★ 窗效应 window effect
窗长度 window length
有限字长效应 finite word length effect
★ 递归滤波器 recursive filter
★ 矩形窗 rectangle window
★ 三角形窗 Bartlett window
★ 汉宁窗 Hanning window
★ 哈明窗 Hamming window
★ 布莱克曼窗 Blackman window
★ 凯塞-贝塞尔窗 Kaiser-Basel window
插值算法 interpolation algorithm

1 Advantages of a linear-phase response:

- Design problem contains only *real* arithmetic and not *complex* arithmetic;
- Linear-phase filters provide no *delaydistortion* and only a fixed amount of delay;
- For the filter of length M (or order M-1) the number of operations is of the order of M/2 as we discussed in the linear phase implementation.

线性相位频率响应的优势:

- 设计只考虑实域运算而不考虑复域运算;
- 线性相位滤波器只带来固定的延时量而无延时失真;
- 在线性相位实现中,对于长度为 M 的滤波器(或阶数为 M-1)的计算量是我们已经论证过的阶数的 M/2。

2 One of the FIR filter design methods is to window the pulse response for an ideal low pass filter. After windowing, the filter shape is no longer ideal, but has a finite transition width and ripples in its pass and stop bands. The larger the number of terms in the window, the closer to ideal the filter shape will be. Choices of window functions include rectangular, Hanning, Hamming, Blackman, and Kaiser. Each offers a characteristic stop band attenuation. Band pass and high pass filters are produced by shifting a low pass filter prototype to the desired location in the frequency domain.

FIR 滤波器的一种设计方法是对理想低通滤波器的脉冲响应加窗函数,加窗之后,滤波器形状不再是理想的,但具有有限的过渡带宽度,并且在它的通带和阻带内有波纹。窗函数的项数越多,滤波器的形状越接近理想情况。供选择的窗函数有:矩形窗、汉宁窗、哈明窗、布莱克曼窗和凯塞窗。每种窗函数都提供了典型的阻带衰减。带通和高通滤波器可通过在频域中将低通滤波器原型移到所要求的位置上来实现。

第十五章　LabVIEW 技术
Chapter 15　LabVIEW Technology

课程简介

课程目标:通过该课程的学习学生应能够掌握虚拟仪器的基本原理及其软件设计方法,掌握虚拟仪器的测试分析和调试工具,并能够根据具体的环境完成测控及虚拟仪器系统的设计。

课程内容:介绍虚拟仪器的基本原理以及软件开发技术,以图形化编程 LabVIEW 作为虚拟仪器软件开发平台,讲述虚拟仪器软件设计的方法以及数据采集、仪器控制和应用实例。

Course Summary

Course Objectives: Through this course, students should master the following contents: the fundamental and software design method of virtual instrument, the testing analysis and debugging tools of virtual instrument, the design, measurement and control of virtual instrument system according to the specific environment.

Course Content: The fundamental and software development technology of virtual instrument, the software development platform with graphical programming LabVIEW, the software design method of virtual instrument, and the data acquisition, instrument control and application example.

第一节　绪论
Section 1　Introduction

★ 实验室虚拟仪器工程平台　Laboratory Virtual Instrument Engineering Workbench (LabVIEW)
NI 公司提供的图形编程语言开发工具　LabVIEW
用于虚拟仪器的 C 语言
C for Virtual Instrument (CVI)
安捷伦可视化工程环境　Agilent Visual Engineering Evironment (Agilent VEE)
NI 示例查找工具　NI Example Finder
LabVIEW 图形编程语言　G
★ 虚拟仪器　virtual instrument (VI)
数据流　dataflow
图形化语言　graphical language
★ 数据采集　data acquisition (DAQ)
通用功能接口总线
General Purpose Interface Bus (GPIB)
IEEE 488 标准
Institute of Electrical and Electronic Engineers (IEEE) 488 standard
串行端口　serial port
外围设备互联
Peripheral Component Interconnect (PCI)
CompactPCI 总线在仪器领域的扩展
CompactPCI eXtension for Instrumentation (PXI)
VME 总线在仪器领域的扩展
VME bus eXtension for Instrumentation (VXI)
VXI 即插即用联盟　VXI Plus & Play (VPP)
可互换的虚拟仪器
Interchangeable Virtual Instruments (IVI)
虚拟仪器软件体系结构
Virtual Instrument Software Architecture (VISA)
图形用户界面　Graphical User Interface (GUI)
互联网特性　Internet capabilities
联网　networking
共享库　shared library
★ 动态链接库　Dynamic Link Library (DLL)
软面板　soft front panel
代码接口节点　Code Interface Node (CIN)
工具包　toolkit
前面板　front panel
框图　block diagram
图标　icon
连接器　connector
工具条　toolbar
选项卡　palette
子选项卡　subpalette
层次　hierarchy
★ 控件　control
指示器　indicator
连线　wire
子 VI　subVI

用于辅助通用测量任务的子 VI express VI
端子 terminal
节点 node
弹出菜单 pop-up menu
帮助窗口 help window
★ 函数 functions
★ 结构 structures
选项 options
★ 数值型 numeric
★ 字符串型 string
★ 布尔型 boolean

LabVIEW is a highly productive graphical programming language for building data acquisition and instrumentation systems. With LabVIEW, you quickly create user interfaces that give you interactive control of your software system. To specify your system functionality, you simply assemble block diagrams - a natural design notation for scientists and engineers. This tight integration with measurement hardware facilitates rapid development of data acquisition, analysis, and presentation solutions.

LabVIEW 是一种高效的用于构建数据采集与仪器系统的图形化编程语言。使用虚拟仪器，您快速创建用户界面，让您交互控制您的软件系统。要指定您系统的功能，您只需装配块程序框图——一种针对科学家和工程师的自然设计注释。与测量硬件的紧密结合促进了数据采集、分析与演示解决方案的快速发展。

第二节 VI 编辑与调试技术

Section 2 VI Edit and Debugging Technology

复合按钮控件 ring control
格式和精度 format and precision
数值类型 numeric type
错误连线 bad wires
快捷键 shortcuts
标签 label
标题 caption
保存为前期版 save as earlier stage edition
还原 revert
项目 project
VI 属性 VI properties
错误列表 errors list
LabVIEW 类层次结构 LabVIEW class hierarchy
浏览关系 browse relations
类浏览器 class explorer
ActiveX 属性浏览器 ActiveX property explorer
启动窗口 start window
导航窗口 navigation window
当前值设置为默认值 make current values default
重新初始化为默认值 reinitialize all to default
自定义控件 customize control
导入图片至剪切板 import picture from
设置 Tap 键顺序 set tapping order
删除断线 remove broken wires
从层次结构中删除断点
remove breakpoint from hierarchy
创建子 VI create sub VI
禁止前面板网格对齐
prohibit the front panel grid alignment
对齐所选项 align the options
分布所选项 distribute the options
VI 修订历史 VI reference history
运行时菜单 run-time menu
添加至项目 add to project
生成 generate
生成全部 generate all
运行 run
筛选视图 select views
文件信息 file information
属性 properties
单步步入 single-step into
单步步过 single-step over
单步步出 single-step out
断点 breakpoint
调用时挂起 suspend when called
结束时打印 print at completion
结束时记录 log at completion
数据记录 data logging
切换至运行模式 change to run mode
连接远程前面板 connect to remote front panel
调试应用程序或共享库
debug application or share library
仪器 instrumentation
MathScript 窗口 MathScript window
比较 compare
性能分析 performance analysis

安全 safety
用户名 user name
生成可执行文件 generate executable documents
转换程序生成脚本
convert project and generate script
源代码控制 source code control
LLB 管理器 LLB manager
导入 import
共享变量 shared variable
在磁盘上查找 VI find VIs on disk
NI 范例管理器
NI example manager
远程前面板连接管理器
remote front panel connection manager
Web 发布工具 Web publishing tool
高级 advanced
显示程序框图 show block diagram
左右两栏显示 the left and right
上下两栏显示 the up and down
最大化窗口 full size
显示即时帮助 show context help
锁定即时帮助 lock context help
搜索 LabVIEW 帮助 search the LabVIEW help
解释错误 explain error
本 VI 帮助 help for this VI
查找范例 find example
查找仪器驱动器 find instrument driver
网络资源 web resources
连续运行 run continuously
终止执行 abort execution
暂停 pause
文本设置 text settings
调整 justify
对齐对象 align objects
分布对象 distribute objects
调整对象大小 resize objects
数值范围 data range
添加指示针 add the indicating needle
刻度 scale
操作值 operate value
定位/调整大小/选择 position/size/select
编辑文本 edit text
进行连线 connect wire
对象快捷菜单 object shortcut menu
滚动窗口 scroll window
设置/清除断点 set/clear breakpoint
探针数据 probe data
获取颜色 get color
设置颜色 set color
加 add
减 subtract
乘 multiply
除 divide
商与余数 quotient & remainder
转换 conversion
加 1 increment
减 1 decrement
数组元素相加 add array elements
数组元素相乘 multiply array elements
复合运算 compound arithmetic
数据操作 data operation
绝对值 absolute value
最近数取整 round to nearest
向下取整 round to－infinite
向上取整 round to＋infinite
按 2 的幂缩放 scale by power of 2
复数 complex
平方根 square root
平方 square
取负数 negate
倒数 reciprocal
符号 sign
缩放 scale
数值常量 numeric constant
枚举常量 enum constant
下拉列表常量 ring constant
随机数(0－1) random number(0－1)
表达式节点 expression node
正无穷大 ＋infinite
负无穷大 －infinite
数学与科学常量 additional numeric constants
提示条 tip strip

If the Run button appears as a broken arrow, this indicates that the LabVIEW program or VI cannot compile because of programming errors. When all of the errors are fixed, the broken Run button will be substituted by the regular Run button.

如果运行按钮显示为一个断箭，这表明由于编程错误，LabVIEW 的程序或 VI 不能编译。一旦确定错误，被损坏的运行按钮将被正常的运行按钮取代。

第三节 程序结构、数据类型及图形显示
Section 3 Program Structure, Data Type and Graphic Display

For 循环 for loop
★ While 循环 while loop
★ 定时结构 timed structure
★ 条件结构 case structure
★ 事件结构 event structure
MathScript 节点 MathScript node
平铺式顺序结构 flat sequence structure
层叠式顺序结构 stacked sequence structure
公式节点 formula node
程序框图禁用结构 block diagram banned structure
条件禁用结构 case banned structure
反馈节点 feedback node
迭代端子 iteration terminal
条件端子 conditional terminal
计数端子 count terminal
隧道 tunnel
强制点 coercion dot
移位寄存器 shift register
选择函数 select function
选择器端子 selector terminal
对话框 dialog box
表达式节点 expression node
共享变量 shared variable
局部变量 local variable
全局变量 global variable
修饰 decorations
★ 数组 array
自动索引 auto-indexing
多态性 polymorphism
数组大小 array size
索引数组 index array
替换数组子集 replace array subset
插入数组元素 insert into array
删除数组元素 delete from array
初始化数组 initialize array
创建数组 build array
数组子集 array subset
数组最大值与最小值 array max & min
重排数组维数 reshape array
一维数组排序 sort 1D array
搜索一维数组 search 1D array
拆分一维数组 split 1D array
反转一维数组 reverse 1D array
一维数组移位 rotate 1D array
一维数组插值 interpolate 1D array
阈值一维数组 threshold 1D array
交织一维数组 interleave 1D array
抽取一维数组 decimate 1D array
★ 二维数组转置 transpose 2D array
数组常量 array constant
簇 cluster
错误簇 error cluster
数组至簇转换 array to cluster
簇至数组转换 cluster to array
数组至矩阵转换 array to matrix
矩阵至数组转换 matrix to array
解除捆绑 unbundle
捆绑 bundle
按名称解除捆绑 unbundle by name
按名称捆绑 bundle by name
创建簇数组 build cluster array
索引与捆绑簇数组 index & bundle cluster array
簇常量 cluster constant
转换为变体 changed into variant
平化字符串至变体转换 ping-string to variant
变体至数据转换 variant to data
变体至平化字符串转换 variant to ping-string
变体属性 variant properties
字符串长度 string length
连接字符串 concatenate strings
★ 部分字符串 string subset
附加字符串函数 additional string functions
替换子字符串 replace substring
搜索替换字符串 search and replace string
匹配模式 match pattern
匹配正则表达式 regular expression match
格式化日期/时间字符串 format date/time string
字符串/数值转换 string/number conversion
扫描字符串 scan from string
格式化写入字符串 format into string
电子表格字符串至数组转换
spreadsheet string to array
数组至电子表格字符串转换
array to spreadsheet string
字符串/数组/路径转换
string/array/path conversion

★ 字符串输入控件　string control
★ 字符串显示控件　string indicator
组合框　combo box
文件路径输入控件　file path control
文件路径显示控件　file path indicator
创建文本　build text
删除空白　trim white space
转换为大写字母　to upper case
转换为小写字母　to lower case
空格常量　blank space constant
字符串常量　string constant
空字符串常量　empty string constant
回车符常量　carriage return constant
换行符常量　line feed constant
行结束常量　end of line constant
制表符常量　tab constant
写入电子表格文件　write to spreadsheets file
读取电子表格文件　read from spreadsheets file
★ 写入测量文件　write to measurement file
★ 读取测量文件　read measurement file
打开/创建/替换文件　open/create/replace file
关闭文件　close file
★ 格式化写入文件　format into file
扫描文件　scan from file
写入文本文件　write characters to file
读取文本文件　read characters from file
写入二进制文件　write to binary file
读取二进制文件　read from binary file
创建路径　build path
拆分路径　strip path
★ 文件常量　file constant
配置文件 VI　configuration VIs
存储　storage
高级文件函数　advanced file functions
★ 曲线　plot
曲线图例　plot legend
★ 坐标图例　scale legend
图形选项卡　graph palette
条形图模式　strip mode
示波器模式　scope mode
扫描图模式　sweep mode
★ 光标　cursor
机械动作　mechanical action
★ 坐标图　XY graph
3D 图形　3D graph
波形数据类型　waveform data type
混合信号图形　mixed signal graph
多种光标形状　multi-plot cursor
★ 动态数据　dynamic data
★ 波形图表　waveform chart
波形图　waveform graph
XY 图　XY graph
Express XY 图　Express XY graph
强度图表　intensity chart
强度图　intensity graph
数字波形图　digital waveform graph
混合信号图　mixed-signal graph
★ 三维曲面图　3D surface graph
★ 三维参数图　3D parametric graph
★ 三维曲线图　3D curve graph
★ 三维图片控件　3D picture controls
获取波形成分　get waveform component
★ 创建波形　build waveform
设置波形属性　set waveform attribute
获取波形属性　get waveform attribute
模数转换　analog to digital waveform
数模转换　digital to analog waveform
索引波形数组　index waveform array
复制波形 Δt　copy waveform delta t
对齐波形时间标识　align waveform timestamps
获取波形子集　get waveform subset
获取终止时间值　get final time value
波形持续时间　waveform duration
按 Δt 缩放　scale by delta t
获取 XY 值　get XY value
获取波形时间标识数组
get waveform timestamps array
模拟波形　analog waveform
数字波形　digital waveform
波形文件 I/O　waveform file I/O
三维图形属性　3D graph properties
图片绘制　picture plots
图片函数　picture functions
★ 图形格式　graphics formulates
三维图片控件　3D picture controls

Similar to most programming languages, LabVIEW supports all common data types such as integers, floats, strings, and clusters (structures) and can readily interface with external libraries, ActiveX components, and .NET framework. Each data type is graphically represented by wires of different colors and thickness.

类似于大多数编程语言，LabVIEW 支持所有常用的数据类型，如整数、浮点数、字符串，簇(结构)，还可随时与外部图书馆、ActiveX 组件和“. NET”框架连接。每个数据类型通过不同颜色和粗细的电线图形代表。

第四节 数据处理与信号分析
Section 4 Data Processing and Signal Analysis

数据处理 data processing
信号分析 signal analysis
波形生成 waveform generation
★ 波形调理 waveform conditioning
数据采集 data acquisition (DAQ)
★ 数据采集系统
Data Acquisition System (DAS)
信号 signals
模拟 analog
数字 digital
频率 frequency
幅度 amplitude
周期 period
★ 脉冲宽度 pulse duration
★ 占空比 duty cycle
预冲 preshoot
过冲 overshoot
上升速度 slew rate
总谐波失真 Total Harmonic Distortion (THD)
信号与噪声失真比
Signal to Noise And Distortion(SINAD)
接地信号 grounded signal
浮地信号 floating signal
接地基准 grounded reference
采样频率 sampling rate
奈奎斯特频率 Nyquist frequency
信号调理 signal conditioning
差分测量 differential measurement
信号端测量 signal-ended measurement
仿真设备 simulated device
标定 scale
任务 task
波形测量 waveform measurement
信号生成 signal generation
信号运算 signal processing
窗口 window
滤波器 filter
谱分析 spectrum analysis
变换 transform
★ 逐点 point by point
失真 distortion
错误处理 error handling
均方根 Root Mean Square (RMS)
★ 最大峰值 maximum peak
★ 最小峰值 minimum peak
★ 峰—峰值 peak to peak
一个周期的平均值 cycle average
一个周期的均方根值 cycle RMS

Whether you are taking measurements from thermocouples, strain gauges, IEPE accelerometers, bridge-based sensors or quadrature encoders, LabVIEW offers you a reliable and easy platform to gather data. With LabVIEW, you can quickly acquire and generate signals from plug-in boards, USB devices, and Ethernet-based systems.

无论您在使用热电偶、张力测量装置、IEPE 加速计、桥接传感器还是正交编码装置进行测量，LabVIEW 都为您提供了一个可靠且易于使用的数据收集平台。利用 LabVIEW，您可以快速采集和生成来自插入式板卡、USB 设备和基于以太网的系统的信号。

第五节 应用实例
Section 5 Application Example

数据通信 data communication
★ DAQ 助手 DAQ assistant
模拟输入 analog input
★ 模拟输出 analog output
★ 缓冲区 buffer
★ 采样 sample
★ 通道 channel
★ 虚拟通道 virtual channel
触发 triggering
NI-DAQmx 任务 NI-DAQmx task

★ 端口　port
线路　line
流动　streaming
连续采集　continuous uisition
向导　wizard
计数器　counter
★ 脉冲　pulse
共享变量　shared variable
队列操作　queue operation
同步　synchronize
协议　agreement
互联接口　interconnection interface
库与可执行　libraries and execution
源代码控制　source code control
Multisim 工具包　Multisim Kit.
输入设备控制　input device control
控制设计与仿真　control design and simulate
采集信号　acquire signals
生成信号　generate signals
创建信号　create signals
加载/保存信号　load/save signals
处理　processing
信号操作　signal operation
执行过程控制　execution control
★ 仪器驱动程序　instrument driver
仪器 I/O 助手　instrument I/O assistant
串行　serial
★ 采样点数　number of samples
★ 采集速率　scan rate
应用程序接口　application program interface
自动测试设备　auto test equipment
自动测试系统　auto test system
中央资源板　central resource board
数据采集控制　data acquisition control
直接存储器存取　Direct Memory Access (DMA)
数字万用表　data multimeter
数字测试仪器　digital test instrument
功能接口板　functional interface board
量化器满量程　full scale range
在线设备编程　in-line device programming
工业标准结构　industry standard architecture
智能虚拟仪器　intelligent virtual instrument
被测单元　unit under test
万用背板总线　versatile backplane bus
应用软件开发接口
Application Program Interface (API)
资源管理器通信通道　resource manager session
器件通信通道　device session

The driver software is a lower level driver that interfaces LabVIEW software with the DAQ boards. As a user of LabVIEW, one does not have to worry about configuration and control of components within DAQ boards. LabVIEW identifies each board by a device number and therefore one can have devices as many as the computer can accept on their expansion slots. LabVIEW can also combine and display inputs from various sources like inputs from serial and parallel port.

该驱动程序软件是一个较低水平的把 LabVIEW 软件与数据采集板连接到一起的驱动程序。作为 LabVIEW 的一个用户，大可不必担心数据采集板内配置和组件的控制。LabVIEW 用设备标号定义每个板，因此人们可以用很多的设备犹如计算机可以有很多的扩充槽。LabVIEW 还可以合并与显示从不同端口比如串行端口和并行端口输入的信号。

第十六章 DSP 技术

Chapter 16 DSP Technology

课程简介

数字信号处理器是专门用来处理数字信号处理任务的微处理器。本课程从介绍基本原理、硬件结构、软件资源入手，结合外围接口的一些基本实验如：FIR 滤波器实验、无限脉冲响应滤波器，以及数理分析方法快速傅立叶变换（FFT）在 DSP 中的应用。本课程是 TMS320C54xDSP 的基础课程，重点介绍 C54xDSP 芯片的硬件架构、汇编和 C 语言编程、CCS 集成开发环境使用，以及在工程领域的应用，比如，FFT，FIR，IIR 等滤波器的应用等内容。

学生学完该课程后应该了解常用的数字信号处理器的基本知识；熟悉数字信号处理器工作原理；掌握利用数字信号处理器完成数字信号处理的过程和方法，并能够完成系统设计。

Course Summary

Digital Signal Processors are microprocessors specifically designed to handle Digital Signal Processing tasks. This course introduces the basic principle, hardware structure, software resources and some basic experiments of the combination of peripheral interfaces, which include FIR filter experiments, infinite pulse response filter, and mathematical analysis method of Fast Fourier Transform (FFT) in the DSP application. This course is a basic course of TMS320C54xDSP, emphasizing on C54xDSP chip architecture, assembler and C language programming, CCS integrated development environment, as well as application in the field of engineering, such as FFT, FIR, IIR filter.

Upon completion of this course, students can understand the common basic knowledge of digital signal processors, be familiar with the works of digital signal processors, master digital signal processor to complete the process and methods of digital signal processing, and be able to complete the system design.

第一节 绪论

Section 1 Introduction

★ 数字信号处理器 digital signal processor
★ 微控制器 microcontroller
冯·诺依曼结构 Von Neumann architecture
★ 哈佛结构 Harvard architecture
改进的哈佛结构 modified Harvard architecture
★ 多总线结构 multi-bus architecture
流水线技术 pipelining technique
多处理单元 multi-processing unit
软仿真器 simulator
硬仿真器 emulator
★ 集成开发环境 Code Composer Studio (CCS)
DSP 入门套件 DSP starter kit
评估模块 evaluation module
数据处理 data manipulation
数学计算 mathematical calculation
★ 循环缓冲 circular buffering
脱机处理 off-line processing
★ 实时处理 real-time processing
★ 每秒执行百万条指令
Millions of Instruction Per Second (MIPS)
★ 每秒执行百万条操作
Millions of Operation Per Second (MOPS)

1 One of the biggest bottlenecks in executing DSP algorithms is transferring information to and from memory and data. This includes data, such as samples from the input signal and the filter coefficients, as well as program instructions, the binary codes that go into the program sequencer.
执行 DSP 算法的最大瓶颈之一是信息传输和存储。这包括输入信号的样本数据和滤波器系数，以及程序指令和程序的二进制码。

2 The simplest Von Neumann processors contain a single, shared memory for programs and data, with only a single bus for memory access. Because only one instruction or one piece of data can be retrieved

at once, most parts of the computer are inactive at any given time. Programs for these processors proceed in a very serial fashion: an instruction is fetched from memory, the instruction is decoded, and the instruction is executed. When execution requires data to be written to or read from memory, the fetch of the next instruction must wait for execution completion of the previous instruction. The only way to speed things up is to increase the speed of the bus, the memory, or the computational units.

最简单的冯·诺依曼处理器包括一个由程序和数据共享的存储器以及用于存储器访问的单一总线。因为一次只能处理一条指令或一个数据，所以在任何指定时间，计算机的大部分资源都是闲置的。这些处理器的程序按照一种极为串行的方式进行：从存储器里取出一条指令，解释这条指令，执行这条指令。当执行过程中需要把数据从存储器中读出或写入的时候，取下一条指令就必须等到前一条指令执行完毕才能进行。系统瓶颈就在于这个单一的指令和数据共享的存储器。提高速度的唯一方法是提高总线、存储器或者计算单元的速度。

3 Most DSP processors are based on a Harvard architecture design. This architecture features separate program and data memories. The program memory is designed to contain instructions, while the data memory is designed to hold data. The separation of these two memories means that program code and data items can be fetched simultaneously, one from each memory. Naturally, additional buses are needed in order to realize the advantages of the separate memories. In a modified Harvard architecture, also in very common DSP devices, separate memories are maintained, but program memory may contain a mixture of program instructions and data.

绝大多数 DSP 处理器都是基于哈佛结构设计的。这种结构的特点是分离了程序和数据存储器。程序存储器被设计用来装载指令，而数据存储器被设计用来保存数据。这两个存储器的分离意味着程序代码和数据项可同时从不同的存储器中取出。当然，为了实现分离存储器的优点需要一些附加的总线。在一种改进的哈佛结构中同时也是 DSP 器件常用结构，保留了分离的存储器，但程序存储器可能含有混合的程序指令和数据。

第二节 TMS320C54x 的硬件结构

Section 2 Hardware Architecture of TMS320C54x

★ 算术逻辑单元 Arithmetic Logic Unit (ALU)
★ 乘法器 multiplier
★ 累加器 accumulator
★ 移位寄存器 shift register
★ 地址发生器 address generator
★ 程序总线 program bus
★ 数据总线 data bus
★ 地址总线 address bus
★ 辅助寄存器 auxiliary register
★ 中央处理单元 Central Processing Unit (CPU)
状态寄存器 status register
算术移位 arithmetic shift
逻辑移位 logical shift
条件移位 condition shift
桶形移位器 barrel shifter
上溢 overflow
下溢 underflow
时钟周期 clock cycle
数据宽度 data width
符号扩展 sign-extend
环形缓冲器 circular buffer
随机存储器 Random Access Memory (RAM)
只读存储器 Read-Only Memory (ROM)
单寻址 single address
双寻址 dual address
中断标志寄存器 interrupt flag register
中断屏蔽寄存器 interrupt mask register

1 All DSPs have specialized hardware units that allow them to carry out the operations most common in DSP algorithms rapidly and efficiently. One such unit is the MAC, or multiplier/accumulator. This unit, as its name suggests, is optimized to perform rapid, repetitive multiplication and addition, operations that are central to DSP filtering. On ordinary processors, multiplications are time-consuming operations that may require multiple clock cycles to complete. On a DSP, multiplications

occur within a single clock cycle or better.
所有DSP都有专门的硬件单元以便迅速而有效地执行DSP算法中最常用的运算。MAC或者乘法器/累加器就是这样一个单元。正如它的名字所暗示的那样,这个单元被优化用于执行快速的、重复性的乘法和加法,而这些运算是DSP滤波的核心。对于一般的处理器来讲,乘法是一个耗时的运算,可能需要多个时钟周期才能完成。而对于DSP来说,乘法在单个时钟周期或者更少的时间内就可以实现。

2 All processors have shifting capability. What makes DSP shifters special is that they can shift an input as much as the full width of the shift register left or right, in a single instruction cycle. Data used in DSP calculations sometimes need to be scaled to maintain a consistent number format. Scaling requires dividing all incoming data by some scaling factor and then multiplying by the same scaling factor after processing is complete. Fast arithmetic shifting is a convenient way to implement this scaling. When a binary number is shifted one position to the right, it is divided by 2; when a binary number is shifted one position to the left, it is multiplied by 2. Arithmetic left shifts zero-fill the result, which means the new bits at the right are zeros. Arithmetic right shifts sign-extend the result, which means the sign bit, or the most significant bit, is repeated at the left for each shift position to the right.
所有处理器都有移位功能。DSP移位器的特殊之处在于,它可以在一个指令周期内把输入左移或右移达到移位寄存器的最大宽度。DSP计算中所用的数据有时候需要进行缩放处理,以保持相同的数据格式。缩放需要把所有输入数据除以某个比例因子,并在处理结束之后,再乘以相同的比例因子。快速算术移位是实现比例缩放的一种简便方法。当把二进制数右移一位时,相当于除以2;当把二进制数左移一位时,相当于乘以2。算术左移零填充,意味着右边新的比特是0。算术右移符号扩展,意味着每向右移动一位,符号比特即最高有效位都要在左边重复出现一次。

3 DSPs are equipped with address generators whose job is to provide fast access to memory locations from an address stored in a register. These special hardware units perform the address generation tasks that would otherwise occupy other parts of a busy microprocessor. In fact, address generators contain own ALUs (arithmetic logic units), which makes them powerful processors. They support address wraparound, which enables them to support circular buffers. Since so many DSP algorithms rely on the use of a fixed number of past data values, a sliding window in the form of a circular buffer is a natural choice for access.
DSP配备有地址发生器,它的作用是由存储于寄存器中的地址对存储器单元提供快速存取。这个特殊的硬件单元执行地址发生的任务,否则该任务将占据繁忙的微处理器的其他部分。实际上,地址发生器有自己的ALU(算术逻辑单元),这就使它们成为强大的处理器。它们支持地址盘绕,从而使它们也支持环形缓冲器。因为许多DSP算法都依赖于使用一个固定数目的以前的数值,所以环形缓冲器形式的滑动窗口对于存取是一种自然的选择。

第三节 TMS320C54x的指令系统
Section 3 Instruction System of TMS320C54x

★ DSP汇编语言 DSP assembly language
文本编辑器 text editor
指令代码 instruction code
★ 指令集 instruction set
汇编源代码 assembly source code
重定位码 relocatable code
寻址方式 addressing mode
立即寻址 immediate addressing
绝对寻址 absolute addressing
直接寻址 direct addressing
间接寻址 indirect addressing
累加器寻址 accumulator addressing
★ 存储器映射寄存器寻址
memory-mapped register addressing
堆栈寻址 stack addressing
数据存储器寻址 data memory addressing
程序存储器寻址 program memory addressing
★ 端口寻址 port addressing

数据指针 data pointer
★堆栈指针 stack pointer
单操作数指令 single operand instruction
双操作数指令 dual operand instruction

1 Assembly language is the command language for DSPs. Beyond the basic computing and control capabilities that assembly languages must offer for all microprocessors, assembly languages for DSPs exploit instructions that can speed up repetitive DSP tasks. Naturally, increasing speed of execution must be a part of this effort. Most DSP instructions now execute within one clock cycle or less. The faster the processor, therefore, the smaller the time to execute a singe instruction.

汇编语言是 DSP 的指令语言。除了汇编语言为所有微处理器必须提供的计算和控制功能外，汇编语言还为 DSP 开发出了加速重复性 DSP 任务的指令。提高执行速度必然是努力的一个方面。现在大多数 DSP 指令只在一个或更少的时钟周期内执行。处理器的速度越快，执行一条指令的时间就越少。

2 Another way to reduce execution time for repetitive tasks is to offer efficient looping constructs. Most DSPs provide what is called zero overhead looping. All processors offer some form of a do-until loop, which executes a group of instructions until an end condition is reached. DSPs speed the looping process with a counter register whose status is automatically checked and whose value is automatically decremented at the end of each loop. No additional statements are required to test whether the count has expired, nor to decrement the count value.

另一种减少重复性任务执行时间的方法是提供有效的循环结构。大部分 DSP 提供所谓的零字头循环。所用的处理器都提供某种形式的 do-until 循环，它执行一组指令直到达到结束条件为止。DSP 通过一个计数寄存器来加速该循环过程，这个计数器的状态是被自动检测的，而且在每个循环的末尾，其值自动减小。不需要另外的语句去检测计数是否终止，或减小计数值。

3 Because of the high degree of hardware parallelism present in most DSPs, multifunction instructions are also common. When multiple buses are available, one read from each memory can occur simultaneously. Similarly, a memory read or memory write can occur together with a computation. Even reads from two memories and a MAC(multiply/accumulate) operation can occur at the same time.

由于大多数 DSP 都具有高度的硬件并行结构，多功能指令是另一个常见的特点。当使用多总线时，可以同时进行每个存储器的读操作。类似的，一个存储器读或存储器写可以与一个计算同时进行。甚至从两个存储器的读操作与一个 MAC(乘法/累加)操作也可以同时进行。

4 Some DSPs offer a repeat instruction that repeats the next instruction the number of times specified. It can be used, for example, with a single move instruction to move a group of data values to memory, or with a single MAC instruction to perform the repeated multiplications and additions required to implement an FIR filter.

某些 DSP 提供重复指令，它按照指定次数重复一条指令。例如，用单个移动指令使一组数据值移进存储器，或者用单个 MAC 指令执行重复的乘法和加法运算以实现 FIR 滤波。

第四节 TMS320C54x 的软件开发

Section 4 Software Development of TMS320C54x

★汇编器 assembler
链接器 linker
编译器 compiler
★仿真器 simulator
归档器 archiver
★调试器 debugger
代数式指令翻译器
mnemonic to algebraic translator utility
建库工具 library-build utility
十六进制转换工具 hex conversion utility
绝对地址列表器 absolute lister
交叉引用列表器 cross-reference lister
浮点数常量 fractional point constant
字符常数 symbolic constant
字符串 character string
汇编语言指令 assemble language instruction

汇编伪指令 assembler directive
宏 macro
★ 宏指令 macro directive
段寄存器 section register
公共目标文件格式 common object file format
未初始化段 uninitialized section
★ 初始化段 initialized section
装入存储器分配 load allocation
输入段 input section
段的类型 section type
填充值 fill value
零字头循环 zero overhead looping
动态范围 dynamic range
满刻度范围 full scale range
★ 分辨率 resolution
小数比特 fractional bit

On the software side, DSPs offer specialized instructions that their unique hardware structures make possible. For instance, zero overhead looping is handled by a program sequencer that is independent of the computational units. Because counting and comparing are managed by this program sequencer, extra cycles don't need to be stolen from calculation time. Further speed and efficiency advantage are gained through multifunction instructions. These instructions permit multiple memory reads and writes to occur in the same instruction cycle as a multiplication and addition. They are made possible through the use of multiple memories, accessed by multiple buses.

软件方面,DSP 提供被其独特硬件所支持的专门指令。例如,零字头循环由独立于计算单元的程序序列器处理。由于计数和比较工作由该程序序列器管理。所以不需要从计算时间中取得额外的周期。通过多功能指令可以进一步获得速度和效率上的优点。这些指令允许多个存储器的读和写在于加法和乘法相同的指令周期中出现。通过采用以多条总线访问多个存储器使之成为可能。

The number formats used by DSPs to represent real numbers fall into two major categories: fixed point and floating point. Each of these formats allows a DSP to store and combine real numbers, but each has important advantages and disadvantages. While DSPs operate exclusively on binary data, DSP programs most often rely on binary or hexadecimal formats to represent numbers.

DSP 表示实数所用的数字格式主要分成两类:定点和浮点。每种格式都允许 DSP 对实数进行存储和组合,但也都具有重要的优点和缺点。当 DSP 只对二进制数据操作时,DSP 程序通常借助二进制或十六进制格式表示数字。

To compare fixed point and floating point formats, the concepts of dynamic range and resolution are required. Dynamic range, reported in dB, refers to the ratio of the maximum possible range of the signal, called the full scale range, to the smallest signal difference that can be resolved, the quantization step size.

Dynamic range=20log Full scale range/Smallest resolvable difference

An alternative form of this definition, which gives a slightly larger result, is:

Dynamic range=20log(Number of possible signal levels)

Resolution refers to the size of the step between two adjacent numbers in a number system. The smaller the step size, the better the resolution of the system and the more closely a real number can be approximated. For a given full scale range, the better the resolution, the greater the dynamic range of the system. Resolution may be increased by increasing the number of fractional bits in a number format. In a binary number, fractional bits are the bits to the right of the binary point. Since a limited number of bits is available, quantization errors affect all numbers represented in fixed or floating point formats, no matter how many fractional bits are used. Except for the very largest signals in range, these errors can never be greater than half of the step size between adjacent quantization levels.

为了比较定点和浮点格式,需要动态范围和分辨率的概念。动态范围以 dB 为单位,指的是信号的最大可能范围,也称为满刻度范围,其与可解析的最小信号差值即量化步长之比为:

动态范围=20log 满刻度范围/最小可解析差值

它的另一种给出稍微大一些结果的定义形式是:

动态范围＝20log(可能的信号级数目)

分辨率指的是在一个数字系统中,两个相邻数字之间的步长。步长越小,系统的分辨率越高,一个实数就能更精确地得到近似。对于一个给定的满刻度范围,分辨率越高,系统的动态范围就越大。可以通过增加数字格式中的小数的比特数来提高分辨率。在一个二进制数中,小数比特是指在二进制小数点右边的比特。由于只可利用有限的比特数,因此不管用多少小数比特,以定点或浮点格式表示的所有数字都会受到量化误差的影响。除非对于幅度非常大的信号,这些误差不会比相邻量化级之间步长的一半大。

第五节 DSP 集成开发环境

Section 5 Code Composer Studio of DSP

CCS 安装 setup of CCS
系统配置 system configuration
窗口 window
菜单 menu
工具条 toolbar
★ 光标 cursor
工程 project
★ 存储器映射 memory map
标准工具栏 standard toolbar
调试窗口工具 debug window toolbar
★ 断点 breakpoint
探测点 probe point
剖切点 profiler point
使能剖析时钟 enable clock
时钟设置 clock setup
★ 参数 argument
下载程序 load program
图形标题 graph title
起始地址 start address
采集缓冲区大小 acquisition buffer size
自动伸缩 autoscale

1 Code Composer Studio™ (CCStudio) is an integrated development environment (IDE) for Texas Instruments (TI) embedded processor families. CCStudio comprises a suite of tools used to develop and debug embedded applications. It includes compilers for each of TI's device families, source code editor, project build environment, debugger, profiler, simulators, real-time operating system and many other features. The intuitive IDE provides a single user interface taking you through each step of the application development flow. Familiar tools and interfaces allow users to get started faster than ever before and add functionality to their application thanks to sophisticated productivity tools.

Code Composer Studio™(CCStudio)是用于德州仪器(TI)嵌入式处理器系列的集成开发环境(IDE)。CCStudio 包含一整套用于开发和调试嵌入式应用的工具。它包含适用于每个 TI 器件系列的编译器、源码编辑器、项目构建环境、调试器、描述器、仿真器、实时操作系统以及多种其他功能。直观的 IDE 提供了单个用户界面,可帮助您完成应用开发流程的每个步骤。借助于精密的高效工具,用户能够利用熟悉的工具和界面快速上手并将功能添加至他们的应用。

2 Code Composer Studio is based on the Eclipse open source software framework. The Eclipse software framework was originally developed as an open framework for creating development tools. Eclipse offers an excellent software framework for building software development environments and it is becoming a standard framework used by many embedded software vendors. CCStudio combines the advantages of the Eclipse software framework with advanced embedded debug capabilities from TI resulting in a compelling feature-rich development environment for embedded developers.

Code Composer Studio 以 Eclipse 开源软件框架为基础。Eclipse 软件框架最初作为创建开发工具的开放框架而被开发。Eclipse 为构建软件开发环境提供了出色的软件框架,并且逐渐成为备受众多嵌入式软件供应商青睐的标准框架。CCStudio 将 Eclipse 软件框架的优点和 TI 先进的嵌入式调试功能相结合,为嵌入式开发人员提供了一个引人注目、功能丰富的开发环境。

3 Code Composer Studio supports running on both Windows and Linux PCs. Not all features or devices are supported on Linux see Linux Host Support for details.

Code Composer Studio 可在 Windows 和 Linux PC 上运行。并非所有功能或器件都与 Linux 兼容,

详细信息请参见 Linux 主机支持。

4. SYS/BIOS is an advanced, real-time operating system for use in a wide range of TI digital signal processors (DSP), ARM microprocessors and microcontrollers. It is designed for use in embedded applications that need real-time scheduling, synchronization and instrumentation. It provides preemptive multitasking, hardware abstraction and memory management. SYS/BIOS is royalty free and is included within Code Composer Studio.
SYS/BIOS 是一款用于广泛 TI 数字信号处理器（DSP）、ARM 微处理器和微控制器的高级实时操作系统。其专为用于需要实时调度、同步和仪表的嵌入式应用而设计。其提供超前多任务、硬件抽象和内存管理。SYS/BIOS 不含版税且随附于 Code Composer Studio。

5. Code Composer Studio includes C/C++ compilers tailored for TI's embedded device architectures. Compilers for C6000™ and C5000™ digital signal processor devices get the most out of the powerful performance potential of those architectures. Compilers for TI ARM® and MSP430 microcontrollers, while not sacrificing performance altogether, are more attuned to the code size needs of those application domains. The compiler for TI's real-time C2000™ microcontrollers takes the best advantage of the many performance and code size features available in this architecture.
Code Composer Studio 包括专为 TI 嵌入式器件架构而设计的 C/C++ 编译器。用于 C6000™ 和 C5000™ 数字信号处理器器件的编译器能最大限度地发挥这些架构性能潜力。TI ARM® 和 MSP430 微控制器的编译器，在无损性能的前提下，更能满足那些应用域的代码大小需要。TI 的实时 C2000™ 微控制器的编译器充分利用了此架构中提供的诸多性能和代码大小特点。

6. Support for C++ could not be any better, especially now that EABI is rolling out. EABI (Extended Application Binary Interface) is a modern set of standards for organizing compiler generated code. EABI standards include the ELF object file format, the same format used in Linux. Higher levels of programming available only in C++, through templates and function in-lining, see much improvement due to EABI. EABI support is presently available for ARM, C6000 DSP and MSP430 compilers, and will soon be available on the other TI compilers.
针对 C++ 的支持登峰造极，尤其在 EABI 推出的现在。EABI（扩展应用程序二进制接口）是一套组织编译器生成代码的现行标准。EABI 标准包括 ELF 对象文件格式，此格式同样用于 Linux 中。通过模板和函数内联实现的仅在 C++ 提供的更高层次的编程，在 EABI 支持下，获得了卓越改进。EABI 支持目前适用于 ARM、C6000 DSP 和 MSP430 编译器，并且很快将在其他 TI 编译器上提供。

7. Optimization supplied in TI compilers is world class. The software pipelining optimization of the C6000 DSP compiler is the cornerstone upon which is built most of the performance success of that architecture. Numerous other optimizations, both generic and target specific, boost performance for all TI compilers. Such optimizations can be applied at multiple levels: within statements and blocks of statements, throughout functions, entire files, and even across files.
TI 编译器的优化能力达到世界领先水平。C6000 DSP 编译器的软件流水化优化能力为这一架构性能的大部分成功奠定了基础。其他大量优化，无论是通用的还是针对于特定目标的，都提高了所有 TI 编译器的性能。上述优化可应用于多个层次：语句或语句块中，贯穿于函数、整个文件中，甚至跨文件。

8. System Analyzer is a suite of tools that provide real-time visibility into the performance and behavior of application code, and allow for analysis of information that is collected from software and hardware instrumentation. System Analyzer enables benchmarking, CPU & task load monitoring, operating system execution monitoring and multi-core event correlation.
System Analyzer 是一款为应用代码性能和行为提供实时直观视图的工具套件，能够对软硬件仪器上收集的信息进行信息分析。System Analyzer 实现了基准设定、CPU 与任务负载监控、操作系统执行监控以及多核事件关联等。

第六节 DSP 片内外设

Section 6 On-chip Peripherals of DSP

★ 片内存储器 on-chip memory
★ 片外存储器 off-chip memory
串行端口 serial port
主机接口 Host Port Interface (HPI)
可编程定时器 programmable timer
通用 I/O 口 general I/O port
多通道缓冲串口
Multi-channel Buffered Serial Ports (McBSPs)
等待状态发生器 wait-state generator
外部存储器 external memory
时钟发生器 clock generator
周期寄存器 period register
控制寄存器 control register
定时器中断 timer interrupt
发送数据寄存器 sending data register
接收数据寄存器 receiving data register
同步串口 synchronous serial port
缓冲串行接口 buffered serial port
★ 时分复用串口
time-division multiplexing serial port
★ 复位串行接口 reset serial port
程序空间 program space
数据空间 data space
分区转换 partition conversion
★ 串行外设接口 Serial Peripheral Interface (SPI)
★ 直接存储器访问 Direct Memory Access (DMA)

1 This code configures the derail ports on the DSP. The serial ports are configured by writing to memory mapped control registers. SPORT0 is configured to use autobuffering and multi-channel mode with an external serial clock and external frame sync. Autobuffering can be thought of as serial DMA. The serial port uses the address generators to access data memory automatically. Multi-channel mode is enabled and configured for 32 channels. In multi-channel mode each channel is a word and associated with a time slot. In each of the 32 time slots the serial port can transmit and receive data or do nothing, tristating the data for that time slot. One frame consists of all 32 channels. One frame sync will start a frame transfer.

这段代码用来配置 DSP 的串行端口。串行端口通过写存储器映射控制寄存器实现配置。SPORT0 被配置成使用自动缓冲和多通道模式,具有外部时钟和外部帧同步。自动缓冲装置可以看做串行端口 DMA。串行端口用地址发生器自动访问数据寄存器。允许多通道模式,并且配置成 32 通道。在多通道模式中,每一个通道是一个字,并且对应于一个时间段。在 32 个时间段的每一段,串行端口可以发送和接收数据或者什么也不做,使这个时间段的数据处于三种状态。一帧包括所有 32 个通道。帧同步将启动一个帧传送。

2 Most DSPs offer a combination of on-and off-chip memory options. On-chip memory can be accessed much more quickly than off-chip memory. For this reason, most DSPs offer some quantity of on-chip Random Access Memory (RAM) or Read Only Memory (ROM). A portion of this memory is marked as program memory, and the rest is designated as data memory. Not infrequently, memories are capable of holding both program instructions and data, as specified by the programmer.

大部分 DSP 提供了在片和离片存储器的联合选择。在片内存储器的存取比片外存储器快得多。因此,大部分 DSP 提供一定量的在片内随机存取存储器(RAM)或只读存储器(ROM)。一部分这样的存储器用作程序存储器,剩下的被设计成数据存储器。存储器经常由编程员指定,既能装卸指令又能装卸数据。

3 Often, external memory can also be connected to a DSP, through an input/output port. Naturally, access to external memories is very slow compared to on-chip accesses. The DSP may need to wait additional clock cycles while items are retrieved from off-chip memories. For this reason, internal memories are now much larger than those in the past, so that little or no external memory will be

required.

通常，外部存储器通过输入/输出端口也可以连接到DSP。当然，存取外部存储器比在片内存取要慢许多。DSP需要等待额外的时钟周期以从片外存储器中取回数据。因此，现在的内部存储器都比过去的大很多，以至于只需很少或不需要外部存储器。

第七节 TMS320C54x 基本系统设计
Section 7 Basic System Design of TMS320C54x

DSP基本系统 DSP basic system
★ 数据地址发生器 Data Address Generator (DAG)
★ 索引寄存器 index register
修正寄存器 modify register
长度寄存器 length register
程序流程控制 program flow control
混杂 miscellaneous
★ 循环 loop
★ 跳转 jump
子程序调用 subroutine call
条件转移 conditional statement
存储器单元 memory location
模拟器件公司 analog devices
★ 锁存器 latch
双缓冲锁存器 double buffer latch
JTAG接口 Joint Test Action Group interface
启动模式 boot mode
启动表 boot table

1 Computational units of TMS320C54x include an arithmetic logic unit, a multiplier/accumulator, and shifter unit. The arithmetic logic unit contains two independent 40-bit accumulators, allowing 40-bit addition. The 40-bit shifter permits all shifts for scaling and fractional mathematics to occur in parallel with arithmetic operations. In addition to the computational units, two address generators, one for data and one for program addresses, facilitate rapid memory access.

TMS320C54x的计算单元包括一个算术逻辑单元、一个乘法器/累加器以及一个移位器单元。算术逻辑单元包括两个独立的40比特的累加器，可以进行40比特的加法运算。40比特的移位器允许所有为实现缩放和小数数学的移位操作以并行的算术运算进行。除了计算单元，还有两个用于产生数据和程序地址的地址发生器，便于快速的存储器存取。

2 TMS320C50 DSPs perform between 20 and 40 MIPS. The TMS320C54x group provides 40 MIPS. The newest fixed point DSPs, the TMS320C64x family, can provide a staggering 8800 MIPS. This DSP offers advanced VLIW architecture bearing Texas Instruments' velocity trademark. With this architecture, up to eight instructions can be performed in each clock cycle; so while the DSP runs at 1100 MHz, its instruction rate is much higher. Two subtractions, two additions, two multiplications and two loads all execute in a single clock cycle. In addition, the 'C64x offers instruction set extensions that simplify programming for digital communication and image processing applications.

TMS320C50 DSP的执行能力在20和40 MIPS之间。TMS320C54x系列提供40 MIPS。最新的定点DSP TMS320C64x系列，可惊人地达到8800 MIPS。这种DSP具有先进的VLIW结构。该结构配有德州仪器公司的velocity商标。基于这种结构，每个时钟周期可以执行8条指令。因此当DSP工作在1100 MHz时，它的指令速率是非常高的。两次减法、两次加法、两次乘法和两次取数都在一个时钟周期内完成。此外'C64x提供指令集扩展，以简化数字通信和图像处理应用中的编程。

第八节 TMS320C54x 应用系统设计举例
Section 8 Application Design Example of TMS320C54x

超标量结构 superscalar architecture
★ 多指令多数据
Multiple Instructions on Multiple Data (MIMD)
甚长指令字 Very Long Instruction Word (VLIW)
符号比特 sign bit
★ 2的补码 two's complement

重复指令　repeat instruction
幂级数展开　power series expansion
查找表　lookup table
★ 主处理器　host processor
数据转换器　data converter
全局数据总线　global data bus
★ 正弦波发生器　sine wave generator
布尔操作符　boolean operator
特殊寄存器　particular register
滤波器系数　filter coefficient
输入数据缓冲器　input data buffer
扬声器　speaker
直接 2 型方程　direct form 2 equation

1 A simple but important task for a DSP is to produce a sine wave of a specified frequency. Unlike in high level languages, sine functions are not available as assembly language instructions, so they must be approximated using numerical tricks.

DSP 一个简单而又重要的任务是产生一个特定频率的正弦波。与其他高级语言不同，汇编语言指令不能用正弦函数，因此它们必须用数值计算近似。

2 Like FIR filters, IIR filters are used in many DSP tasks. The algorithm is very similar for both filters, but because IIR filters rely on both inputs and outputs, two loops are required instead of just one.

与 FIR 滤波器一样，IIR 滤波器也在许多 DSP 任务中使用。两个滤波器的算法非常相似，但由于 IIR 滤波器既依赖输入也依赖输出，因此不仅需要一个而是需要两个循环。

第十七章　可编程控制器原理与应用

Chapter 17　Programmable Controllers-Theory and Implementation

课程简介

本课程是电子信息工程专业的限选课程，该课程在教学计划中占有一定的重要地位。本课程介绍可编程控制器 PLC 的组成与结构特点，详细介绍 S7-200 系列 PLC 指令系统与编程方法，使学生从实际出发，掌握 PLC 用于工业生产过程的原理与方法。培养学生利用 PLC 技术、计算机技术、通信技术解决工程实际问题的能力。

Course Summary

Programmable Controllers-Theory and Implementation is one of the basic compulsory courses for electrical information engineering majors. It gives introduction to the composition and structure characteristics of programmable controllers (PLC) and elaborates on the PLC instruction set and programming methods of S7-200 series. The course is aimed at helping students have a good command of the theory and methods of PLC used in industrial production process so as to develop students' ability to solve practical engineering problems with PLC technology, computer technology and communication technology.

第一节　可编程控制器介绍

Section 1　Introduction to Programmable Controller

★ 可编程控制器　programmable controller
固体的　solid-state
集成电路　integrated circuit
机电设备　electromechanical device
控制功能　control function
★ 存储指令　storing instruction
数据操作　data manipulation
概念图　conceptual diagram
★ 接口电路　interfacing circuitry
现场设备　field device
逻辑控制器　logic controller
实际应用　practical application
顺序　sequencing
算术、计算　arithmetic
模形式　modular form
组件　subassemblies
★ 继电器逻辑　relay logic
★ 梯形图格式　ladder diagram format
自动操作　automation
制造业　manufacturing
★ 重复操作　repetitive operation
★ 诊断指标　diagnostic indicator
前任　predecessor
哲学方法　philosophical approach
增强　enhancement
微处理机　microprocessor
终端　terminal
★ 积分单元　integral unit
热(电)偶　thermocouple
应变计　strain gauges
快速输入　fast-response input
外部设备　peripheral equipment
系统文件　system documentation
先进的 PLC　sophisticated PLCs
编程设备　programming peripheral
压力传感器　pressure transducer
执行程序　executing the program
电源　power supply
不凝结湿度　noncondensing humidity
转矩　torque
吸气流量　suction flow
预定值　predetermined value
配料比　batching ratio
温度曲线　temperature sensor

可逆皮带输送机　reversible belt conveyor
磁性分离器　magnetic separator
配置输入　configuration of input
安装方便　ease of installation
预接线端子排　prewired terminal strip

例1 PLCs monitor and control the dye processing in the textile industry.
纺织工业中,PLC监视和控制生产加工过程。

例2 A set of thumb wheel switches and a push button can be easily configured to input new preset values to any number of software timers.
一套拇指轮开关和按钮可以轻松为任何数量的软件定时器配置新的预设值。

第二节　进制和编码
Section 2　Number Systems and Codes

★ 十进制系统　decimal system
十进制数字系统　decimal number system
★ 二进制数字系统　binary number system
八进制计数系统　octal numbering system
★ 十六进制系统　hexadecimal system
十进制数　decimal equivalent
最低位数字　the least significant digit
最高位数字　the most significant digit
乘法　multiplication
补充方法　complement method
解释形式　interpretable form
检测　detect
负数　negative number
算术运算　arithmetic operation
理解和使用　understand and employ
十六进制数字　hex digit
内存地址　memory address
计算十进制值　calculate the decimal value
字母数字代码　alphanumeric codes
二进制编码　binary coded
★ 绝对编码器　absolute encoder
寄存器　register
数据操作　data manipulation
段显示器　segment display
断面扫描　section of the scan
字节　byte

例1 The BCD format uses four bits to represent a single decimal digit.
二进制编码的十进制格式使用四位表示一个十进制数字。

例2 Data stored in binary format can be directly converted to its decimal equivalent without any special restrictions.
在没有任何限制的情况下,二进制格式存储的数据可以直接转换为十进制数。

第三节　逻辑概念
Section 3　Logic Concepts

★ 逻辑触点符号　logic contact symbology
预定状态　predetermined states
★ 二电平等级　two distinct voltage levels
绝对地　arbitrarily
★ 正逻辑　positive logic
★ 负逻辑　negative logic
非当前状态　nonoccurrence of the event
★ 真值表　truth table
★ 按钮　push button
报警喇叭　alarm horn
变流器　inverter
传统的梯形图　conventional ladder diagram
希望逻辑组合　desired logic combination
接点符号　contact symbology
传达命令　convey command
输出装置　output device
垂直线　vertical line
输入设备　input device
电流　current flow
外壳安装　enclosure placement
常开　normally open
机电继电器　electromechanical relay

内部输出　internal output

重复使用的触点　repeated use of contacts

结合律　associative law

分配律　distributive law

闪烁小灯　pilot light

1. The programmed rung concept is a direct carryover from the hardwired relay ladder diagram.
编程思想是直接利用继电器逻辑的梯形图思路。

2. The logic implemented in PLCs is based on the three basic logic functions that we discussed in the previous sections.
PLC 中的逻辑是基于三个基本逻辑功能,我们在前面的章节讨论过。

第四节　处理器、电源、编程装置

Section 4　Processor, the Power Supply, and Programming Devices

★ 三元件　three-component organization

必需元素　necessary elements

积分关系　integral relationship

巨大的计算和控制能力
tremendous computing and control capability

监控程序　supervisory program

管理功能　housekeeping functions

★ 操作员接口　an operator interface

智能模块　intelligent module

独立控制任务　independent control tasks

复杂度控制器
degree of sophistication of the controller

执行控制程序　execute the control program

图形反复扫描　graphic representation of the scan

为简单起见　for the sake of simplicity

★ 程序扫描　program scan

★ 更新扫描　update scan

★ 扫描时间　scan time

内部信号处理器　internal signal processor

工艺故障　process malfunction

扫描评价　scan evaluation

脉冲展宽　pulse stretcher

恢复程序　resume program

子系统配置　subsystem configuration

由…组成　be composed of

确认有效性　confirm the validity

纠正行动　corrective action

错误的类型　type of errors

同等;类似;相同　parity

★ 错误检查　error-checking

★ 帧冗余校验　vertical redundancy

★ 奇偶校验位　check parity bit

★ 检查和　check sum

块检查字符　block check character

循环冗余检查　cyclic redundancy check

纵向冗余校验　longitudinal redundancy check

无效数据　invalid data

汉明码　hamming code

诊断法　diagnostics

工业设施　industrial facilities

恒压变压器　constant voltage transformer

隔离变压器　isolation transformer

电源负载　power supply loading

1. In this case, there are several power supply options.
在这个例子中,有几个电源供应方法。

2. Undoubtedly, the best solution to a problem is anticipation of the problem.
毫无疑问,最佳的解决问题方法是问题的防范。

第五节　存储系统和输入/输出接口

Section 5　The Memory System and Input/Output Interaction

探讨关系　explore the relationship

★ 启动要求　start-up requirement

★ 执行记忆　executive memory

★ 周边设备　peripheral devices

应用程序的内存　application memory

★ 挥发性记忆体　volatile memory

★ 非易失性存储器　nonvolatile memory

磁盘拷贝　disk copy

保留内容　retain content
备用电池　battery backup
计数器预置值　counter preset value
本性地　by nature
存储区域　storage area
数据输入　data entry
可擦除的　erasable
电可改写的　electrically alterable
额外的　additional
内存图　memory map
内存地址　memory address
执行区　executive area
暂存区　scratch pad area
数据表区域　data table area
★ 用户程序区　user program area
★ 数据表部分　data table section
输入表　input table
输出表　output table
用户程序段　user program section
机架内　inside the rack
参考地址　reference address
所有的指令　all instruction
执行　the execution
由于　due to
更新输入表　update the input table
相应的　corresponding to

1 This will be useful when assigning register addresser in the program.
当分配寄存器地址时，这将是有用的。

2 With this in mind, let's set the table boundaries.
记住这一点，我们来设置表格的边界。

第六节　离散输入/输出系统
Section 6　The Discrete Input/Output System

★ 离散的　discrete
物理连接　physical connection
功能特点　functional charateristics
★ 模拟　analog
★ 操纵　manipulation
机架外壳　rack enclosure
规划阶段　programming stage
主架　master rack
当地的机架　local rack
★ 容纳能力　housing capability
★ 远程机架　remote rack
诊断数据　diagnostic data
强调　emphasize
终端点　terminal point
通用的例子　generic example
★ 槽的位置　slot location
数字地址　digit address
★ 远程子系统　remote subsystem
模拟　accommodate analog
功能接口　function interface
同轴电缆　coaxial cable
噪声电阻　noise resistance
在不同的　at various
远程定位　distant location
离散输入接口　discrete input interfaces
映射方案　mapping scheme
主要部分　primary part
漏极和源极　sinking and sourcing
配置　configuration
邻近　proximity
隔离输入接口　isolated input interface
标准计数元件　standard counterparts
模块化　modularity
离散输出接口　discrete output interface
触点输出接口　contact output interface
旁路站　bypass station
额定输入电压　input voltage rating
输入阈值电压　input threshold voltage
输入延迟　input delay
输入阈值电压　input threshold voltage
浪涌电流　surge current
数字分辨率　digital resolution
保险丝额定输出　output fuse rating
线径　wire size
环境温度　ambient temperature rating
湿度　humidity rating

1 The number input or output circuits are on a single module.

数据输入或输出电路，是在一个单一的模块。

The type and rating of fuses should be used in the interface.
熔断器的类型和等级，应在接口中采用。

第七节 模拟输入输出系统

Section 7 The Analog Input/Output System

有效工具 invaluable tool
★ 连续信号 continuous signal
配料及温度控制
batching and temperature control
完成任务 accomplish task
无限状态 infinite state
分度 fraction of a degree
多位装置 multibit device
算术运算 arithmetic calculation
计算目的 computational purpose
★ 传感器 transducer
发射机 transmitter
★ 单极的 unipolar
★ 双极 bipolar
电压 voltage
★ 分辨率 resolution
★ 通道操作 channel operating
条件 condition
★ 十进制值 decimal value
温度传感器 temperature transducer
多通道 multiple channel
计数值 count value
单端 single-ended
差动输入 differential input
电力线频率 power line frequencies
电源选择 power supply selection
无效范围 non-valid range
缩放 scaling
明显的延迟 noticeable delay
外壳 enclosure

Differential is the most common configuration when individually isolated outputs are required.
当需要单独隔离输出时，微分是最常见的配置。

Data transfers to analog modules with multiple output channels are updated one channel per scan.
在每个扫描周期，多个输出通道传输到模拟模块的数据都要被更新。

第十八章　综合电子系统设计
Chapter 18　Design on Synthetical Electronic Systems

课程简介

综合电子系统设计是一门理论和实践相结合的课程。它融入了现代电子设计的新思想和新方法，架起一座利用单元模块实现电子系统设计的桥梁，帮助学生进一步提高电子设计能力，引导、培养大学生理论联系实际的学风，加强学生工程实践能力的训练和培养，促进广大学生踊跃参加课外科技活动。

Course Summary

Design on synthetical electronic systems is a course which integrates theory with practice. It employs the modern methods and ideas of electronic design to find out a strategy for electronic system using unit module. It will improve students' ability to design electronic systems. Moreover, the course will guide and train students' style of study integrating theory with practice, improve their ability of engineering training, and motivate them to take part in extracurricular technological activities.

第一节　微机化电子系统的设计
Section 1　Design of Microcomputerization Electronic System

★ 随机存取存储器　random access memory (RAM)
动态随机存取存储器
dynamic random access memory (DRAM)
★ 静态随机存取存储器　static random access memory
可擦可编程只读存储器
erasable programmable read-only memory(EPROM)
电可擦可编程只读存储器
electrically EPROM (EEPROM)
★ 中断请求　interrupt request
大规模集成电路　large scale integration (LSI)
★ 集成电路　integrated circuit (IC)
集成电路特点　features of integrated circuits
★ 通用型　popular type
专用型　special type
性能扩展　performance extension
单极型集成电路　unipolar integrated circuit
参数　parameters
点接触型　point contact type
符号　symbol
结构　construction
★ 并行输入/输出　parallel input / output
射频　radio frequency
复位信号　reset signal
★ 串行外围接口　serial peripheral interface
中断器开关选择器　switching select repeater
同步开关　synchro-switch
片上系统　system on a chip (SOC)
★ 地址总线　address bus
★ 数据总线　data bus
I/O 空间　I/O space
★ 指令指针　instruction pointer
中断　interrupt
中断延迟　interrupt latency
中断服务程序　interrupt service routine (ISR)
中断类型　interrupt type
★ 中断向量　interrupt vector
内存映射　memory map
★ 内存空间　memory space
★ 微控制器　microcontroller
多处理　multiprocessing
多任务　multitasking
目标代码　object code
目标文件　object file
★ 操作系统　operating system
外设　peripheral
物理地址　physical address
优先　priority
★ 进程　process
★ 处理器　processor
处理器族　processor family

With the development of Micro-Electronics and Computer technology, more and more electronics products are becoming smaller and more complex. The innovation of computer design technology makes design of electronics easier.

微电子技术、计算机技术的飞速发展不但使电子产品的小型化、微型化进程加快，系统越来越复杂，同时计算机应用的变革也使电子产品的设计更加容易。

第二节　模拟系统的设计
Section 2　Design of Analog System

中央处理单元　central processing unit (CPU)
控制信号　control signal
蜂鸣器　buzzer
★ 模拟/数字转换　analog to digital (A/D)
★ 模拟/数字转换器
analog to digital convertor (ADC)
电荷耦合器件　charge-coupled device
二极管　diode
直接模拟存储技术
direct analog store technology
直流　direct current (DC)
交流　alternating current (AC)
双列直插封装　dual in-line package
二极管晶体管逻辑　diode-transistor logic
被测器件　device under test
数字电压表　digital voltmeter
射极耦合逻辑　emitter coupled logic
电子数据交换　electronic data interchange
转换结束　end of conversion
静电放电　electro-static discharge
场效应晶体管　field-effect transistor
运放　operational amplifier
集成运算放大电路
integrated operational amplifier circuit
★ 理想运放　ideal operational amplifier
★ 开环增益　open-loop gain
★ 有源负载　active load
截止频率　3-dB-frequency
同相输入端　non-inverting input terminal
固定时间　fixed time
接地　ground (GND)
★ 输入/输出　input/output (I/O)
反馈放大电路　feedback amplifier
★ 频率特性　frequency characteristic
幅频特性　amplitude frequency characteristic
光电二极管　photodiode
放大电路　amplifier
旁路电容　by-pass capacitor
耦合电容　coupling capacitor
★ 输出电阻　output resistance
★ 输入电阻　input resistance
工作点稳定　operating point stabilization
光电耦合器　photocoupler
放大概念　amplification concept
最大输出幅值　maximum output amplitude
直流模型　DC model
多级放大电路　multistage amplifier
稳压二极管　zener diode
转移特性　transfer characteristics
电流放大系数　current amplification factor
放大区　active region
变压器耦合　transformer coupled
CMOS 电路　CMOS circuit
电流方程　current equation
★ 放大作用　amplification effect
输出特性　output characteristics
转移特性　transfer characteristics
直接耦合放大电路　direct coupled amplifier
阻容耦合放大电路　RC coupling amplifier
上限截止频率　upper cut-off frequency
相频特性　phase frequency characteristic
下限截止频率　lower cut-off frequency
瞬态响应　transient response
带宽　bandwidth
波特图　Bode diagram
反馈通路　feedback path
闭环增益　closed-loop gain
环路增益　loop gain
正反馈　positive feedback
负反馈　negative feedback
反馈网络　feedback network
反馈信号　feedback signal
运算电路　operational circuits
集成功放　integrated circuit power amplifier
电位器　resistance potentiometer

The AD574A, which is launched by the U. S. Digital Simulation (Analog) company is a complete 12-bit successive-approximation analog to digital converter. It is built-in bipolar hybrid integrated circuit chip conversion, with fewer external components, low power consumption, high accuracy, automatic correcting zero, and automatic polarity conversion function. So it only needs a small amount of external capacity of resistance to constitute a complete A/D converter.

AD574A是美国模拟数字公司(Analog)推出的单片高速12位逐次比较型A/D转换器,内置双极性电路构成的混合集成转换芯片,具有外接元件少、功耗低、精度高等特点,并且具有自动校零和自动极性转换功能,只需外接少量的阻容件即可构成一个完整的A/D转换器。

第三节 EDA应用设计
Section 3 Design of EDA Application

★ 电子设计自动化
electronic design automation (EDA)
★ 专用集成电路
application specific integrated circuit (ASIC)
硬件描述语言
hardware description language (HDL)
计算机辅助设计
computer aided design (CAD)
计算机辅助制造
computer aided manufacture (CAM)
计算机辅助测试
computer aided testing (CAT)
计算机辅助工程
computer aided engineering (CAE)
★ 自顶向下 top-down
★ 自下而上 bottom-up
封装和测试 package and test
工程 project
原理图编辑器 schematic editor
波形编辑器 waveform editor
综合 synthesis
仿真 simulate
编译 compiler
元件 symbol
功能设计 function design
超高速集成电路硬件描述语言
very high speed integrated circuit hardware description language (VHDL)
文本编辑器 text editor
实体 entity
结构体 architecture
★ 端口 port
进程 process
库 library
直接数字合成器
direct digital synthesizer (DDS)
起始位 start bit
数据位 data bit
校验位 parity bit
时钟使能 enable clock (EC)
多核 multicore
★ 时钟频率 clock frequency

A hardware debugging tool can be used to capture the logic levels (0 or 1) of dozens, or even hundreds, of electrical signals in real-time. Logic analyzers can be quite helpful for debugging hardware problems and complex processor-peripheral interactions.

一种硬件调试工具,能捕获实时电信号的许多逻辑电平(0或1),逻辑分析仪在调试硬件问题和复杂的处理外设交互时相当有用。

第四节 电子系统的抗干扰技术
Section 4 Anti-interference Technology of Electronic System

★ 信噪比 signal-to-noise ratio
过电压 over voltage
满量程 full scale
反向饱和电流 reverse saturation current
稳定判据 stability criterion
差模信号 difference-mode signal
共模信号 common-mode signal
恒流源 constant current source
★ 差分放大电路 differential amplifier
差模放大倍数 differential-mode gain
共模放大倍数 common-mode gain
共模抑制比 common-mode rejection ratio
场效应管差分放大电路 field effect transistor
失调电流 offset current
失调电压 offset voltage
保护电路 protecting circuit

过载断路器 overload circuit breaker
夹断电压 pinch off voltage
开启电压 threshold voltage
击穿电压 breakdown voltage
极间电容 interelectrode capacitance
扩散电容 diffusion capacitance
势垒电容 barrier capacitance
发射结电容 emitter junction capacitor
集电结电容 collector junction capacitor
★ 零点漂移 zero drift
校正措施 compensation method
稳定裕度 stability margin
相位裕度 phase margin
★ 超前校正 phase lead compensation
★ 滞后校正 phase lag compensation
校正措施 compensation method
自激振荡 self excited oscillation
★ 干扰 interference
★ 负反馈电路的自激振荡
self excited oscillation of feedback circuit
交越失真 cross over distortion
安全区保护 safety operating area protection
过热保护 thermal overload protection
滤波电容 filtering capacitance
电容滤波 capacitance filter
脉动系数 ripple factor
外特性 external characteristics
过流保护 current overload protection
基准源 reference
电磁干扰 electromagnetic interference
设计验证测试 design verification test
研究与开发 research and development

The error of instrument current transformer(TA) includes ratio error and phase error. The error of the measuring of TA or the accuracy of the calibration of TA usually applies differential measuring method.

电流互感器的误差包括比率误差和相位误差。电流互感器的测量误差和校准的准确性通常适用于微分测量方法。

第五节 应用系统举例
Section 5 Examples of Application System

电流一电压变换器 current to voltage convertor
电压一电流变换器 voltage to current convertor
频率/电压转换 frequency to voltage convertor
电压/频率转换 voltage to frequency convertor
智能功率模块 intelligent power module
红外辐射 infrared radiation
★ 光敏开关 light activated switch
★ 液晶显示器 liquid crystal display (LCD)
光敏电阻 light dependent resistor
发光二极管 light emitting diode
电动机 motor
麦克风 microphone
负温度系数 negative temperature coefficient
光通信系统 optical communication system
输出特性 output characteristics
分析方法 method of analysis
波形发生器 waveform generator
函数发生器 function generator
正弦波振荡器 sinusoidal oscillator
倍频器 frequency multiplier
波形变换器 wave form converter
方波发生器 square wave generator
三角波发生电路 triangular wave generator
锯齿波发生器 sawtooth wave generator
矩形波发生器 rectangular wave generator
★ 低通滤波器 low-pass filter
带通滤波器 band-pass filter
电压比较器 voltage comparators
★ 限幅 clipping
阈值电压 threshold voltage
带阻滤波器 band-reject filter
高通滤波器 high-pass filter
集成电压比较器 integrated voltage comparator
简单比较器 simple comparator
压控电压源 voltage-controlled voltage-source
通带电压放大倍数 pass-band voltage gain
★ 通带截止频率 cut-off frequency of pass-band
特征频率 characteristic frequency
分频器 frequency divider
混频器 mixer
信号转换电路 signal transfer circuit
选频网络 frequency-selective network
最大输出功率 maximum output power
散热 heat dissipation

热敏电阻
resistor with inherent variability dependent
电阻温度传感器 resistance temperature detector
开关组件 switching assembly
速度控制系统 speed control system
电源控制系统 supply control system
温度传感器 temperature sensor
应用软件 application software
汇编编译器 assembler
板卡支持包 board support package
编译器 compiler
计数信号 counting semaphore
★设备驱动程序 device driver
设备编程器 device programmer
嵌入式系统 embedded system
固件 firmware
闪存 flash memory
印刷电路板 printed circuit board

A microcontroller is very similar to a microprocessor. The main difference is that a microcontroller is designed specifically for use in embedded systems. Microcontrollers typically include a CPU, memory (a small amount of RAM and/or ROM), and other peripherals on the same chip.

微控制器很像微处理器。主要的差别在于微控制器被特殊设计用在嵌入式系统中。微控制器典型地包括 CPU、内存(很小的 RAM 和/或 ROM)以及其他的外设,它们在同一块芯片上。

第十九章　嵌入式操作系统及开发

Chapter 19　Embedded Operating System and Development

课程简介

随着技术的进步与发展，人们对于电子产品的要求也越来越高，速度快、功能强成为消费者的普遍追求，嵌入式系统的出现使这种追求成为可能。规模大、功能强的处理器为产品提供了一颗强劲的“心脏”；实时性好、移植方便的嵌入式操作系统为产品提供了灵活的“大脑”。

本课程主要围绕嵌入式实时操作系统 μC/OS-II 展开，介绍了 μC/OS-II 的任务、任务间通信与同步、信号量集、μC/OS-II 的中断和时钟、动态内存管理以及 μC/OS-II 在 ARM 上的移植。通过该课程的讲解，要求学生掌握嵌入式操作系统原理和使用方法，并能够将该系统移植到 ARM 平台上，实现多任务的操作。

Course Summary

With the progress and development of technology, people have more requirements for electronic products. Fast and strong functions become consumers' common pursuit. Embedded system just meets the demands. Its large scale and strong function of the processor provides a strong “heart” for electronic products. An embedded operation system which is perfectly real-time and convenient for transplant provides a flexible “brain” for products.

This course is focused on embedded real-time operating system named “μC/OS-II”, including the tasks in μC/OS-II, intertask communication and synchronization, semaphore set, interrupt and clock in μC/OS-II, dynamic memory management and transplanting μC/OS-II on ARM. With the course, the students are required to learn the principles and implementations of the embedded operating system, as well as transplanting the system to ARM platform to accomplish multitask operation.

第一节　概述

Section 1　Summary

操作系统　operating system
嵌入式系统　embedded system
★ 嵌入式操作系统　embedded operating system
★ 实时操作系统　real-time operating system
软实时系统　soft real-time system
硬实时系统　hard real-time system
逻辑正确　logically correct
时间正确　time is correct
★ 可剥夺型内核　preemptive kernel
不可剥夺型内核　non-preemptive kernel
应用程序接口　application programming interface
虚拟机　virtual machine
单片系统　system on chip
可裁剪　scalable
移植　porting

1 The following is the definition of embedded systems from the view of technical point: an application-oriented, computer technology-based special computer system, and its software and hardware can be cut to meet the stringent requirements of application functionality, reliability, cost, size, power consumption.

嵌入式系统从技术的角度定义：以应用为中心，以计算机技术为基础的专用计算机系统，该系统软硬件可改变以适应应用系统对功能、可靠性、成本、体积、功耗等严格要求。

2 μC/OS-II uses preemptive kernel. The highest priority task ready to run is always given control of the CPU. When a task makes a higher priority task ready to run, the current task is preempted or

suspended, and the higher priority task is immediately given control of the CPU.

μC/OS-II 使用的是可剥夺型内核，一旦有高优先级任务就绪，就马上会得到 CPU 的控制权，当一个运行着的任务使一个比它优先级高的任务就绪时，当前任务的 CPU 使用权就会被剥夺或者挂起，较高优先级的任务就会马上得到 CPU 的使用权。

第二节 μC/OS-II 中的任务

Section 2 Tasks in μC/OS-II

任务 task
程序代码 program code
★ 任务堆栈 task stack
★ 任务控制块 task control block (TCB)
用户任务 user task
系统任务 system task
空闲任务 idle task
统计任务 statistics task
任务优先级 task priority
睡眠状态 dormant state
就绪状态 ready state
运行状态 running state
等待状态 waiting state
中断服务状态 ISR state
链表 list
任务块链表 TCB list
空闲任务块链表 TCB free list
★ 就绪表 ready list
状态转换图 state transition diagram
任务组 task group
任务调度 task scheduling
★ 调度 scheduler
★ 任务切换 task switch
堆栈指针 stack pointer
就绪任务 ready task
锁定 lock
解锁 unlock
程序计数器 program counter
入栈 push stack
出栈 pop stack
创建任务 create task
挂起任务 suspend task
恢复任务 resume task
删除任务 delete task
查询任务 query task
初始化 initialization
数据结构 data structure

1 A task is a simple program that thinks it has the CPU all to itself. μC/OS-II can manage up to 64 tasks. The idle task must be created which is executed when none of the other tasks is ready to run. The idle task is always set to the lowest priority.

任务是一个简单的程序，在该任务中 CPU 完全属于自己使用。μC/OS-II 最多可以管理多达 64 个任务，其中空闲任务必须要创建，该任务在没有其他任务就绪时就会得到运行，并且该任务的优先级通常被设置为最低。

2 μC/OS-II always executes the highest priority task ready to run. The determination of which task has the highest priority and thus, which task will be next to run is determined by the scheduler. Task level scheduling is performed by OSSched(). ISR level scheduling is handled by function OSIntExit().

μC/OS-II 总运行优先级最高的就绪任务，哪个任务的优先级最高，接下来运行哪个任务都是由调度器来实现。任务级的调度由 OSSched()来执行，中断级的调度由函数 OSIntExit()来执行。

3 Each task that is ready to run is placed in a ready list consisting of two variables, OSRdyGrp and OSRdyTbl[]. Task priorities are grouped (8 tasks per group) in OSRdyGrp. Each bit in OSRdyGrp is used to indicate whenever any task in a group is ready to run. When a task is ready to run it also sets its corresponding bit in the ready table, OSRdyTbl[].

每个就绪的任务都被放在就绪表中的两个变量 OSRdyGrp 和 OSRdyTbl[]中。在 OSRdyGrp 中，任务按照优先级分组(每 8 个任务一组)，OSRdyGrp 中的各个位用来指示每一组中是否有任务处于就绪状态。如果有一个任务处于就绪状态时，对应的就绪表 OSRdyTbl[]上的相应位也要置高。

第三节 μC/OS-II 中的中断和时钟

Section 3 Interrupt and Clock in μC/OS-II

★ 中断 interrupt
时钟 clock
异步事件 asynchronous event
中断延迟 interrupt latency
中断响应 interrupt response
★ 中断服务子程序 interrupt service routine
中断向量 interrupt vector
中断嵌套 interrupt nesting
断点保护 breakpoint protection
★ 临界段 critical section
屏蔽中断 interrupt mask
时钟节拍 clock tick
时间管理 time management
时间期满 time specified expires
系统时间 system time
硬件计数器 hardware counter
★ 钩子函数 hook function

1 An interrupt is a hardware mechanism used to inform the CPU that an asynchronous event has occurred. When an interrupt is recognized, the CPU saves part (or all) of its context and jumps to a special subroutine called an interrupt service routine, or ISR. The ISR processes the event and upon completion of the ISR, the program returns to:

a) The background for a foreground/background system;

b) The interrupted task for a non-preemptive kernel;

c) The highest priority task ready-to-run for a preemptive kernel.

中断是一种硬件机制,主要用于当一个异步事件发生了之后告知 CPU。一旦中断被识别,CPU 就会保存部分(或者全部)现场并且跳转到专门的子程序,称之为中断服务程序(ISR)。中断服务子程序处理该事件,直到处理完了之后,程序会返回到:

a)在前/后台系统中,程序返回到后台;

b)在不可剥夺型内核中,程序返回被中断的任务;

c)在可剥夺型内核中,程序返回就绪的优先级最高的任务。

2 μC/OS-II requires that you provide a periodic interrupt to keep track of time delays and timeouts. This periodic time source is called a clock tick and should occur between 10 and 100 times per second. A clock tick is a special interrupt that occurs periodically. This interrupt can be viewed as the system's heartbeat.

μC/OS-II 需要提供一个周期性的中断去实现延时和超时控制,这个周期性的时钟源被称为时钟节拍,它应该每秒钟发生 10 到 100 次。时钟节拍是一个特殊的周期性中断,可以把它视为系统的心跳。

第四节 任务的同步与通信

Section 4 Intertask Synchronization & Communication

共享资源 shared resource
协调 coordination
制约 restriction
★ 同步 synchronization
通信 communication
事件 event
★ 事件控制块 event control block
★ 信号量 semaphore
消息 message
★ 消息邮箱 message mailbox
★ 消息队列 message queue
数据缓冲区 data buffer
标志 flag
互斥型信号量 mutual exclusion semaphore
指针数组 pointer array
等待任务表 wait list for task
创建信号量 create a semaphore
发送信号量 send a semaphore

请求信号量　get a semaphore
释放信号量　release a semaphore
查询信号量　query a semaphore
信号量有效　semaphore enable
信号量无效　semaphore disable
★优先级反转　priority inversion
消息缓冲区　message buffer
返回值　returned value
广播　broadcast
邮箱指针　mailbox pointer
队列控制块　queue control block
队列控制块链表　list of queue control block
消息邮箱数组　message mailbox array
可移动指针　movable pointer
常指针　constant pointer
循环队列　circular queue
先进先出　First-In-First-Out(FIFO)
后进先出　Last-In-First-Out (LIFO)
首地址　head address

1 A semaphore is a protocol mechanism offered by most multitasking kernels. Semaphores are mainly used to:
a)control access to a shared resource (mutual exclusion);
b)signal the occurrence of an event;
c)allow two tasks to synchronize their activities.
信号量作为一种约定机制广泛地使用在大多数多任务内核中。信号量主要用于：
a)控制获得共享资源(互斥条件下)；
b)作为一个事件发生的标志；
c)使两个任务之间行为同步。

2 A message mailbox is a μC/OS-II object that allows a task or an ISR to send a pointer size variable to another task. The pointer would typically be initialized to point to some application specific data structure containing a "message".
消息邮箱是μC/OS-II中允许一个任务或者中断服务程序向另外一个任务发送指针型变量的方式。该指针通常被初始化为指向一个包含了"消息"的特定数据结构。

3 There are three tasks, Task 1 has a higher priority than Task 2 which in turn has a higher priority than Task 3. Task 1 and Task 2 are both waiting for an event to occur, and Task 3 is executing. At some point, Task 3 acquires a semaphore that it needs before it can access a shared resource. Task 3 performs some operations on the acquired resource until it gets preempted by the high priority task, Task 1. Task 1 executes for a while until it also wants to access the resource. Because Task 3 owns the resource, Task 1 will have to wait until Task 3 releases the semaphore. As Task 1 tries to get the semaphore, the kernel notices that the semaphore is already owned and thus, Task 1 gets suspended and Task 3 is resumed. Task 3 continues execution until it gets preempted by Task 2 because the event that Task 2 was waiting for occurred. Task 2 handles the event and when it's done, Task 2 relinquishes the CPU back to Task 3. Task 3 finishes working with the resource and thus, releases the semaphore. At this point, the kernel knows that a higher priority task is waiting for the semaphore and, a context switch is done to resume Task 1. At this point, Task 1 has the semaphore and can thus access the shared resource.
From the above, the priority of Task 1 has been virtually reduced to that of Task 3's because it was waiting for the resource that Task 3 owned. The situation got aggravated when Task 2 preempted Task 3 which further delayed the execution of Task 1.
We can correct this situation by raising the priority of Task 3 (above the priority of the other tasks competing for the resource) when Task 3 is accessing the resource and restore the original priority level when the task is finished.
有三个任务,任务1的优先级高于任务2,任务2的优先级高于任务3。任务1和任务2都在等待事件的发生，而任务 3 处于运行状态。某一时刻，任务 3 要使用共享资源，但是使用之前需要先获得该资源的信号量，任务 3 获得了信号量并且得以使用该资源直到高优先级的任务 1 剥夺了任务 3 的 CPU 使用权。任务 1 运行着直到它也要访问该资源，但是由于任务 3 拥有该资源，所以任务 1 需要等待，直到任务 3 释放信号量。任务 1 试着去获得信号量，但是内核发现该信号量已经被使用，故任务 1 被挂起，任务 3 得以恢复运行。任务 3 继续运行，此时任务 2 等待的事件发生了，任务 3 又被剥夺了 CPU 使用权，任务 2 运行，直到任务 2 的事件全部完成才将 CPU 使用权归还给任务 3。任务 3 使用完该共享资源后释放了信号量，此刻内核得知高优先级的任务正在等待这个信号量，故进行任务的切换去运行任务 1。任务 1 获得了该信号量后自然也就得到了共享资源。

由上可知，任务 1 的优先级实际上已经降到了任务 3 的级别上，原因是由于任务 1 要使用任务 3 所拥有的资源。由于任务 2 剥夺了任务 3 的 CPU 使用权，使得这种情况进一步加剧，并且进一步延缓了任务 1 的运行。

我们可以通过将任务 3 的优先级提高到所有参与竞争该资源的任务中最高地位的办法去解决这一问题，并且在任务运行结束之后恢复该任务的初始优先级。

第五节 信号量集

Section 5 Semaphore Set

★ 信号量集 semaphore set
事件标志 event flag
★ 条件标志 conditions flag
组合逻辑 combinational logic
逻辑运算 logical operation
逻辑或 logic
逻辑与 logic
标志组 flag group
信号量值列表 semaphore value list
★ 信号过滤器 signal filter
信号量集指针 semaphore set pointer
逻辑运算类型 logic operation type
等待时间 waiting time
错误信息 error message
组合功能 combined function

1 Semaphore set are used when a task needs to synchronize with the occurrence of multiple events. The task can be synchronized when any of the events have occurred. This is called disjunctive synchronization (logic OR). A task can also be synchronized when all events have occurred. This is called conjunctive synchronization (logic). Kernels supporting event flags offer services to SET event flags, CLEAR event flags, and WAIT event flags。

信号量集用于任务中多事件之间的同步。当任务需要与任意事件之一产生同步时，这种同步称之为独立型同步(逻辑或)。当任务与事件中发生的所有事件产生同步时，这种同步称之为关联型同步(逻辑与)。内核支持事件标志，可以提供事件标志的置位、清零、等待。

2 Common events can be used to signal multiple tasks. Events are typically grouped. Tasks and ISRs can set or clear any event in a group. A task is resumed when all the events it requires are satisfied. The evaluation of which task will be resumed is performed when a new set of events occurs.

普通事件可以给多个任务发信号，事件通常成组使用。任务和中断服务程序可以设置或者清零该组的任意一个事件。当要求的所有事件都满足时，任务可以被继续执行。至于哪个任务被执行则在新的事件组发生时判断。

第六节 动态内存管理

Section 6 Dynamic Memory Management

动态 dynamic
内存空间 memory space
★ 动态分配 dynamic allocation
★ 内存分区 memory partition
内存块 memory block
内存碎片 memory fragment
★ 内存控制块 memory control block
空闲内存控制块 free memory control block
内存控制块链表 list of memory control block
分配动态内存 allocate dynamic memory

释放动态内存 free dynamic memory | 二维数组 two-dimensional array

1 Your application can allocate and free dynamic memory using any ANSIC compiler's malloc() and free() functions, respectively. However, using malloc() and free() in an embedded real-time system is dangerous because eventually, you may not be able to obtain a single contiguous memory area because of fragmentation. Fragmentation is the development of a large number of separate free areas (i. e. the total free memory is fragmented into small pieces). μC/OS-II provides an alternative to malloc() and free() by allowing your application to obtain fixed-sized memory blocks from a partition. More than one memory partition can exist and thus, you application can obtain memory blocks of different sizes. A specific memory block must, however, always be returned to the partition from which it came from. This type of memory management is not subject to fragmentation.

用户的应用程序可以通过 ANSIC 中 malloc()和 free()函数来实现动态的分配、释放内存,但是在嵌入式实时操作系统中使用 malloc()和 free()两个函数是非常危险的,多次这样做会把原来很大的一块连续内存区域逐渐地分割成许多非常小而且彼此又不相邻的内存区域,也就是内存碎片。由于这些碎片的大量存在,使得程序到后来连非常小的内存也分配不到。μC/OS-II 提供了一种改进型的 malloc()和 free()函数,使用该函数可以从内存分区中获得固定大小的内存块。一个系统中可以存在不止一个内存分区,这样,用户的应用程序就可以得到大小不同的内存块。但是,特定的内存块在释放时必须重新放回它以前所属的内存分区。采用这样的内存管理方式也就不会产生内存碎片的问题。

2 When your application is done using a memory block, it must return it to the appropriate partition. This is accomplished by calling OSMemPut(). You should note that OSMemPut() has no way of knowing whether the memory block returned to the partition belongs to that partition. In other words, if you allocated a memory block from a partition containing blocks of 32 bytes then you should not return this block to a memory partition containing blocks of 120 bytes. The next time an application request a block from the 120 bytes partition, it will actually get 32 "valid" bytes and the remaining 88 bytes may belong to some other task(s). This could certainly make your system crash.

当用户的应用程序使用了一个内存块,那么就必须在使用完之后归还到相应的分区中。这一操作由 OSMemPut()来完成。需要注意的是 OSMemPut()并不知道内存块是否回到了相应的分区。换句话说,假如你从一个包含 32 字节的内存分区中获得了一个内存块,释放的时候你就不能释放在包含 120 个字节的内存分区中。假如真的这么做了,下次你申请 120 字节分区中的内存块时,却只能申请到 32 个可用字节,剩下的 88 字节可能属于其他的任务。这样一来必然会导致系统崩溃。

第七节 移植 μC/OS-II
Section 7 Porting μC/OS-II

操作系统移植 OS porting
★ 可重入性函数 reentrant function
变量 variable
全局变量 global variable
指令集 instruction set
工作模式 working mode
软件中断 software interrupt
堆栈增长方式 stack growth
时钟节拍频率 tick rate
★ 堆栈结构 stack frame
中断级任务切换 interrupt level task switch
任务级任务切换 task level task switch
返回地址 return address
中断向量表 interrupt vector table
向量中断 vector interrupt
汇编语言 assembly language

1 A reentrant function is a function that can be used by more than one task without fear of data corruption. A reentrant function can be interrupted at any time and resumed at a later time without loss of data. Reentrant functions either use local variables (i. e., CPU registers or variables on the stack) or protect data when global variables are used.

可重入性函数指的是可以被多个任务使用并且不用担心数据被破坏的函数。该类型函数任何时间都可以被中断，过一段时间就可以恢复且任何数据都不会丢失。可重入性函数可以使用局部变量（即变量保存在 CPU 寄存器中或者堆栈中），也可以使用被保护的全局变量。

2 A task level context switch is accomplished by executing a software interrupt instruction on the ARM processor. The interrupt service routine must vector to OSCtxSw(). The sequence of events that leads μC/OS-II to vector to OSCtxSw() is as follows. The current task calls a service provided by μC/OS-II which causes a higher priority task to be ready-to-run. At the end of the service call, μC/OS-II calls the function OSSched() which concludes that the current task is no longer the most important task to run. OSSched() loads the address of the highest priority task into OSTCBHighRdy and then executes the software interrupt instruction by invoking the macro OS_TASK_SW(). Note that the variable OSTCBCur already contains a pointer to the current task's Task Control Block, OS_TCB.

在 ARM 处理器中，任务级的任务切换通常通过调用软件中断指令的方式来执行。中断的向量指向 OSCtxSw()。使 μC/OS-II 指向 OSCtxSw()的具体操作如下：当前任务调用 μC/OS-II 提供的函数，使得具有优先级最高的任务就绪。在函数的末尾会调用 OSSched()，如果现在执行的任务不是最重要的任务，则通过该函数将具有最高优先级的任务地址拷贝到 OSTCBHighRdy，然后通过宏 OS_TASK_SW()执行软件中断进行任务切换。需要注意的是，变量 OSTCBCur 始终包含一个指向当前运行任务的任务控制块 OS_TCB 的指针。

第二十章　通信原理

Chapter 20　Communication Principles

第一部分　通信原理

Part One: Communication Principles

课程简介

《通信原理》是通信工程、电子信息工程专业的一门专业核心课程。学习本课程的目的是使本专业学生掌握通信的理论和基本技术。本课程以模拟通信为基础，重点讲述数字通信原理。本课程大部分用于讲述数字通信，包括数字信号的转换、编码和传输，同时讲述了模拟信号的数字化过程。通过本课程的学习，要求学生掌握通信基本概念、模型及主要性能指标，掌握各种模拟和数字传输方式的基本原理和方法，掌握各种抗噪声性能的分析方法，为深入研究和设计新型通信系统打下坚实的基础。

Course Summary

Communication Principles is a core course of Communication Engineering and Electronic and Information Engineering. The purpose of this course is to help students master the professional communication theory and basic technology. On the basis of introducing the principles of analog communication, the course is focused on the principles of digital communication. The major part of this course is devoted to discussions of digital communication including transforming, encoding and transmission of digital signals, as well as the digitization of analog signals. By learning this course, the students will master the basic concepts, models and main performance indexes of communication; master the basic principles and methods of various analog and digital transmission; acquire skills to analyse various anti-noise performance. It will lay a solid foundation for further research and design of new communication system.

第一节　绪论

Section 1　Introduction

★ 模拟通信　analog communication
★ 数字通信系统　digital communication system
消息　message
信息　information
信息源　information source
发射机　transmitter
接收机　receiver
★ 调制　modulation
★ 解调　demodulation
信道　channel
噪声　noise
滤波器　filter
数据终端设备　data terminal equipment
模数转换器　analog-to-digital converter (A/D)
数模转换器　digital-to-analog converter (D/A)
压缩编码　compression coding
★ 基带信号　base band signal
信源编码　source coding
★ 频带信号　frequency signal
信源解码　source decoding
★ 单工通信　simplex communication
★ 半双工通信　half-duplex communication
★ 全双工通信　full-duplex communication
并行传输　parallel transmission
串行传输　serial transmission
信息量　information content
传信率　information transmission rate
误码率　bit error ratio (BER)
熵　entropy
信道解码　channel decoding

1 Entropy is a measure of the average information content per source symbol, and it depends only on the probabilities of the symbols in the alphabet of the source.
熵是每个信源符号包含的平均信息的度量，它只取决于信源字符集中符号的发生概率。

2 There are many kinds of digital communication systems, for instance, digital telephone systems, high-speed computer parallel data processing transmission systems and digital TV signal transmission systems, etc.
数字通信系统的种类很多,例如数字电话系统、高速计算机并行数据传输系统、数字电视信号传输系统等。

3 The purpose of channel coding is to improve the reliability of the signal transmission. The channel coding adds some redundant symbols in the signal after source coding in order to automatically detect or correct errors introduced during transmission. This process certainly increases the redundancy with the specific rule for error correcting.
信道编码的目的是提高信号传输的可靠性。信道编码是在信源编码后加入了一些冗余符号,目的是在传输中自动检错或者纠错。这个过程无疑会用特定的规则来增加冗余以实现检错功能。

4 Error probability is the main specification of measuring reliability. There are 3 different definitions for it:
(1)Symbol error probability: it is the ratio of the number of received code elements in error to the total number of the transmitted.
(2)Bit error probability: it is the ratio of the number of received bits in error to the total number of the transmitted bits.
(3)Word error probability: it is the ratio of the number of received words in error to the total number of the transmitted words.
差错率是衡量可靠性的主要指标,通常有三种不同的描述方式:
(1)误码率:是指错误接收的码元数在传输总码元数中所占的比例。
(2)误信率:是指错误接收的比特数在传输总比特数中所占的比例。
(3)误字率:是指错误接收的字数在传输总字数中所占的比例。

第二节 随机信号分析
Section 2 Random Signal Analysis

周期信号 periodic signal
非周期信号 non-periodic signal
★ 随机过程 random process
频谱密度 frequency spectrum density
能量信号 energy signal
★ 噪声 noise
时域 time domain
单位门函数 unit gate function
概率密度函数 probability density function
自相关 autocorrelation
广义平稳 generalized stationary
离散谱 discrete spectrum
★ 平稳随机过程 stationary random process
★ 功率谱密度 power spectra density
互相关 cross correlation
高斯过程 Gaussian process
随机变量 random variable
★ 窄带噪声 narrowband noise
分布函数 distribution function
★ 窄带干扰 narrowband interference
一维 one dimension
数学期望 mathematic expectation
加性高斯白噪声 additive white Gaussian noise
相关函数 correlation function
协方差函数 covariance function
正态随机过程 normal random process
线性时不变 linear time invariant
卷积 convolution
带限白噪声 band limited white noise
低通白噪声 lowpass white noise

1 If a Gaussian process X(t) is applied to a stable linear filter, then the random process Y(t) developed at the output of the filter is also Gaussian. If a Gaussian process is stationary, then the process is also strictly stationary.
如果高斯过程 X(t)应用于一个稳定线性滤波器,那么,滤波器的输出随机过程 Y(t)也是高斯型的。如果高斯过程是平稳的,那么这一过程也一定是严平稳的。

2 Signal and noise in communication systems are random, and usually called random signals. They may be regarded as random process varying with time *t*. This kind of process is a real function of time *t*, but its value observed at an arbitrary instant is a random variable.
通信系统中信号和噪声是随机的，通常被称为随机信号。它们可以被看成是随着时间 t 而变化的随机过程。这类过程是时间 t 的实函数，但是在任意时刻内它的值都可以被看成是一个随机变量。

3 In communication systems, the spectra of signals and noises are often limited to a narrow frequency band. In other words, if the bandwidth of the signal or noise is narrower than its "carrier" or central frequency, then it is called narrow band random process.
在通信系统中，信号谱或噪声谱通常被限制在窄带频率内，换句话说，如果信号或者噪声的带宽比它们的"载波"或者中心频率窄得多，那么就称之为窄带随机过程。

第三节 信道
Section 3 Channel

信道 channel
★ 无线信道 wireless channel
有线信道 wired channel
非时变信道 time invariant channel
电磁波 electromagnetic wave
★ 有限带宽信道 band-limited channel
★ 幅度畸变 amplitude distortion
包络 envelope
★ 幅频畸变 amplitude-frequency distortion
光波导 wave guide
调制信道 modulation channel
窄带信道 narrowband channel
散射 scatter
明线 open wire
光纤 optical fiber
对称电缆 symmetric cable
同轴电缆 coaxial-cable
地波 ground wave
中继器 repeater
视线 line of sight
上行线路 up line
下行线路 down line
天波 sky wave
同步卫星 synchronous satellite
寂静区 silent zone
卫星通信 satellite communication
卫星中继信道 satellite relay channel
平流层 stratosphere
对称电缆 symmetrical cable
同轴电缆 coaxial cable
★ 群迟延 group delay
★ 衰落 fading
★ 慢衰落 flat fading
衰减 attenuation
失真 distortion
多径效应 multipath effect
多径传播 multipath propagation
★ 离散信道 discrete channel
热噪声 thermal noise
★ 信道容量 channel capacity
★ 平均信息量 average amount of information
★ 帧 frame

1 Shannon's information capacity theorem: The capacity of an AWGN channel is defined by C=Blog2(1+SNR)b/s, where B is the channel bandwidth, and SNR denotes the signal-to-noise ratio measured at the channel output. It suffices to say that for a given SNR, we can transmit data over an AWGN channel of bandwidth B at the maximum rate of C bits per second with arbitrarily small probability of error, provided that we employ an encoding system of sufficiently high complexity.
香农信息容量定理：AWGN 信道容量定义为 C=Blog2(1+SNR)b/s，其中，B 为信道带宽，SNR 为信道输出端测得的信噪比。对于给定的信噪比，假设采用复杂度足够高的编码系统，就能够通过带宽为 B 的 AWGN 信道，以不超过 C bps 的速率和任意小的差错概率进行数据传输。

2 There are different definitions of channels for the discussion of communication system performance. Here the part from the output terminal of the modulator in the transmitter to the input terminal of the demodulator in the receiver is called channel. Amplifiers, frequency converters, and antennas may be included in it. In communication networks, exchange equipment may also be included in it because

there are several transmitting terminals and receiving terminals. It is convenient to use this definition in the performance research of different modulation systems. So, it is also called modulation channel.
对于讨论通信系统性能来说,信道有不同的定义。通常把发送部分中调制器的输出端到接收部分解调器的输入端统称信道,放大器、频率转换器和天线都被包含在内。在通信网络中,因为有多个发送终端和接收终端,交换设备通常也被包含其中。这么做是为了方便不同调制系统的性能研究,所以信道通常也被称为调制信道。

第四节 模拟调制系统

Section 4 Analog Modulation System

★ 模拟信号 analog signal
频域 frequency domain
★ 线性调制 linear modulation
调幅 amplitude modulation (AM)
双边带 double sideband (DSB)
双边带抑制载波
double sideband suppressed carrier
单边带 single sideband (SSB)
单边带一下边带
single sideband—lower sideband
单边带一上边带
single sideband—upper sideband
残留边带 vestigial sideband (VSB)
★ 频谱搬移 frequency translation
角度调制 angle modulation
包络检波 envelope detection
同步解调器 synchronous demodulator
希尔伯特变换 Hilbert transform
模型 model
滤波器 filter
频率调制 frequency modulation (FM)
★ 相位调制 phase modulation (PM)
★ 信噪比 signal-to-noise ratio (SNR)
调制指数 modulation index
低通滤波器 low-pass filter (LPF)
★ 衰减补偿 attenuation compensation
★ 限幅器 amplitude limiter
★ 鉴频器 discriminator
调制增益 modulation gain
调频立体声广播 FM stereo broadcasting
门限效应 threshold effect
预加重 pre-emphasis
去加重 de-emphasis
频分多路复用
frequency division multiplexing (FDM)
时分多路复用
time division multiplexing (TDM)
可用带宽 available bandwidth
基群 basic group
主群 master group
频带分割 band splitting
防护频带 guard band
防护间隔 guard spacing
多级调制 multilevel modulation
巨群 jumbo group
复用 multiplexing

1 A carrier has three parameters: amplitude, carrier angular frequency and initial phase. Modulation will enable a certain parameter of a carrier to vary with the signal, in other words, the value of signal from the source is represented by the value of a certain parameter of the carrier.
载频有三个参数:幅度、角频率和初始相位。调制能够使载频的其中一个参数随信号的变化而变化,换句话说,源信号的值是由载频的某一个参数来描述的。

2 The loss of a message in an envelope detector that operates at a low carrier-to-noise ratio is referred to as the threshold effect. By threshold we mean a value of the carrier-to-noise ratio below which the noise performance of a detector deteriorates much more rapidly than proportionately to the carrier-to-noise ratio. It is important to recognize that every nonlinear detector (e. g., envelope detector) exhibits a threshold effect. On the other hand, such an effect does not arise in a coherent detector.
在低载噪比的情况下包络检波器中消息的丢失称为门限效应。门限是一个载噪比值,当载噪比低于该值时,检测器的噪声性能将迅速恶化。每一个非线性检测器(如:检波器)都存在门限效应,但在相干检测中,并不存在门限效应。

3 Analog modulation can be classified into two kinds: linear modulation and nonlinear modulation.

Frequency spectrum structure of a linear modulated signal is the same as that of modulating signal. In other words, frequency spectrum of modulated signal is the result of displacement of modulating signal along frequency axis. Linear modulated signals include amplitude modulated signal, single-sideband signal, double-sideband signal, and vestigial side band signal. Nonlinear modulation is also called angle modulation. Frequency spectrum structure of a nonlinear modulated signal is much different from that of a modulating signal.
模拟调制根据特点分为两类:线性调制和非线性调制。线性调制信号的频谱结构和调制信号的一样。换句话说,线性调制只是调制信号的频谱在频率轴上的简单搬移。线性调制信号包括幅度调制、单边带调制、双边带调制和残留边带调制。非线性调制也称为角度调制,非线性调制信号的频谱结构和调制信号相比有很大的不同。

第五节 数字基带传输系统

Section 5 Digital Baseband Transmission System

★ 基带通信系统
baseband communication system
单极性波形 unipolar waveform
单极性不归零码
unipolar nonreturn-to-zero (NRZ)
双极性波形 bipolar waveform
双极性不归零码
bipolar nonreturn-to-zero (BRZ)
差分波形 differential waveform
单极性归零码
unipolar return-to-zero (RZ) code
双极性归零码
bipolar return-to-zero (BRZ) code
传号交替反转码
alternative mark inverse code (AMI)
三阶高密度双极性码
3rd order high density bipolar code (HDB3)
双相码 biphase code
密勒码 miller code
传号反转码 coded mark inversion (CMI) code
★ 序列 sequence
成对选择三进制码
paired selected ternary code
再生 regeneration

★ 加性干扰 additive interference
发送滤波器 transmitting filter
接收滤波器 receiving filter
抽样判决 sampling and decision
干扰 interference
★ 码间干扰 intersymbol interference (ISI)
★ 奈奎斯特准则 Nyquist's criterion
奈奎斯特速率 Nyquist rate
★ 冲激响应 impulse response
奈奎斯特带宽 Nyquist bandwidth
升余弦函数 raised cosine function
★ 滚降因子 rolloff factor
★ 预编码 precoding
★ 眼图 eye pattern
★ 示波器 oscillograph
★ 均衡器 equalizer
★ 相关编码 correlative coding
★ 部分响应 partial response
★ 加权 weight
★ 抽头 tap
★ 时域均衡 time domain equalization
迫零 zero forcing
自适应均衡器 adaptive equalization

1 Equation:

$$\sum_{n=-\infty}^{\infty} P(f-nR_b) = T_b$$

The Nyquist criterion for distortionless baseband transmission in the absence of noise: The frequency function P(f) eliminates intersymbol interference for samples taken at intervals T_b provided that it satisfies Equation. Note that P(f) refers to the overall system, incorporating the transform filter, the channel, and the receive filter in accordance with equation.
方程:

$$\sum_{n=-\infty}^{\infty} P(f-nR_b)=T_b$$

无噪声时的无失真基带奈奎斯特准则：如果频谱函数 P(f)满足前等式，那么就能消除以时间间隔 T_b 进行抽样的 ISI。P(f)对应的是整个系统，包括对应于等式的发射滤波器、信道和接收滤波器。

2 In the binary baseband signal transmission system, the decision device compares the sample of each received symbol at the sampling instant with a threshold level, and makes decision. For example, if the signal is a bipolar NRZ pulse, then the decision threshold should be 0 level; here, if the sample is positive, then the decision is a 1, if the sample is negative, then the decision is a 0.

在二进制基带信号传输系统中，判决设备将在采样时间收到的符号和门限值比较。例如，如果信号是双极性不归零码，则判决电平应该选为 0 电平；当采样值为正，则判为 1；当采样值为负，则判为 0。

3 The eye pattern introduced in this section is a method of practical observation of the received signal by using the oscilloscope. The eye pattern may display the influence of the limitation of the transmission system performance on the transmission of baseband digital signals.

本部分介绍的眼图是通过示波器实际观察接收信号波形的一种方法，通过观察眼图，可以评估基带信号传输性能，显示传输中受干扰的情况和传输系统的缺点。

第六节 数字带通传输系统
Section 6 Digital Band Pass Transmission System

★ 带通传输 band pass transmission
★ 正弦载波 sinusoidal carrier
数字调制 digital modulation
非线性调制 nonlinear modulation
数字解调 digital demodulation
通断键控 on-off keying (OOK)
★ 幅移键控 amplitude-shift keying (ASK)
★ 频移键控 frequency-shift keying (FSK)
★ 相移键控 phase-shift keying (PSK)
★ 同步检测 synchronous detection
差分检波 differential detection
非相干解调 noncoherent demodulation
相干解调 coherent demodulation
带宽 bandwidth
★ 主瓣 main lobe
带通滤波器 band-pass filter (BPF)
载波 carrier
连续相位 continuous phase
误码率 probability of error
功率谱 power spectra
相干检测 coherent detection
门限 threshold
过零点检测 zero-crossing point detection
恒定包络 constant envelop
分频器 frequency splitter
相位模糊 phase ambiguity
频偏 frequency deviation
灵敏度 sensitivity
非线性信道 nonlinear channel
幅度相位联合键控
amplitude-phase keying (APK)
差错概率 probability of error
★ 星座图 constellation
正交幅度调制
quadrature-amplitude modulation (QAM)
四相相移键控
quadriphase-shift keying (QPSK)
★ 失真 distortion
格雷码 Gray code
★ 最小频移键控 minimum shift keying
★ 相位网格图 phase trellis
幅度/相位混合调制
hybrid amplitude /phase modulation
欧氏距离 Euclidean distance
高斯滤波最小频移键控
Gaussian-filtered minimum shift keying
差分相移键控 differential phase-shift keying
移动通信 mobile communication
★ 压控振荡器
voltage-controlled oscillator (VCO)
★ 旁瓣 side lobe
★ 归一化 normalize

★ 同步 synchronization
★ 符号定时 symbol timing
★ 载波恢复 carrier recovery
调制调解器 modem
附加相位 append phase
轨迹 track

1 The generation of DPSK signals: the differential encoding process at the transmitter input starts with an arbitrary first bit, serving as reference. Let {dk} denote the differentially encoded sequence with this added reference bit. We now introduce the following definitions in the generation of this sequence:

If the incoming binary symbol bk is 1, leave the symbol dk with respect to the previous bit.

If the incoming binary symbol bk is 0, change the symbol dk with respect to the previous bit.

The differentially encoded sequence {dk} thus generated is used to phase-shift a carrier.

DPSK 信号的产生:在发射机输入端的差分编码过程中,选取任意一个比特作为起始参考。用{dk}表示加入了该参考比特的差分编码序列。下面介绍产生该序列过程中的一些约定:

如果输入二进制符号 bk 是 1,则保持符号 dk 与前一比特一致。

如果输入二进制符号 bk 是 0,则将符号 dk 改为与前一比特不同。

这样产生的差分编码序列{dk}用来对载波进行移相。

2 2FSK signal is extensively used in digital communication. ITU-T recommends that 2FSK system is used at bit rate 1200b/s and lower. 2FSK signal can be received by using noncoherent receiving method, and there is no need to use the phase information of the signal. Thus, in terrible channels, e. g. , the short wave radio wave channel, the phase of the received signal has random jittering and the amplitude also has random fluctuation, this kind of signal will be especially suitable for use.

2FSK 信号被广泛地应用在数字通信中,ITU-T 推荐 2FSK 系统的速率为 1200b/s 或者更低。2FSK 信号可以采用非相干方法接收,不需要使用信号的相位信息。这样,在某些恶劣信道环境下,如短波无线电信道,接收信号的相位可能有随机的抖动,幅度也会有随机的波动,这种频率信号可能更适合应用。

3 There are two generation methods of the 2PSK signal. The first method uses the binary baseband NRZ bipolar rectangular pulse to multiply the carrier, and two kinds of symbols with inverse phases are obtained. The second method uses the baseband signal to control a switching circuit, and the switching circuit selects the input signals.

有两种方法可以产生 2PSK 信号。第一种方法是使用二进制不归零双极性矩形脉冲和载波相乘,得到两种相位相反的信号;第二种方法是采用基带信号去控制开关电路,由开关电路选择输入信号。

第七节 模拟信号的数字传输
Section 7 Digital Transmission of Analog Signal

★ 抽样 sampling
★ 量化 quantization
★ 脉冲编码调制 pulse-code modulation (PCM)
奈奎斯特间隔 Nyquist interval
奈奎斯特采样速率 Nyquist sampling rate
重叠 superposition
★ 混叠 aliasing
脉冲 pulse
脉冲幅度调制
pulse-amplitude modulation (PAM)
脉宽调制 pulse-duration modulation (PDM)
脉冲相位调制
pulse-position modulation (PPM)
脉冲串 pulse train
抽样定理 sampling theorem
抽样速率 sampling rate
瞬时抽样 instantaneous sampling
★ 量化器 quantizer
★ 均匀量化器 uniform quantizer
量化阶梯 quantizing ladder
量化间隔 quantum step-size
量化步长 quantum step

压缩 compression
★ 非均匀量化器 nonuniform quantizer
对数 logarithm
因果律 the law of causation
★ 量化误差 quantization error
线性微分方程 linear differential equation
边界条件 boundary condition
压缩器 compressor
扩张 expansion
压扩器 compander
μ 律 μ-law
A 律 A-law
纵坐标 ordinate
横坐标 abscissa
扩张器 expander
★ 量化噪声 quantization noise
★ 矢量量化 vector quantization
★ 标量量化 scalar quantization
差分脉冲编码调制
differential pulse-code modulation
保持电路 holding circuit
自适应脉冲编码调制
adaptive differential pulse-code modulation
量化值 quantized value
固定量化 fixed quantization
预测值 prediction value
预测 prediction
预测编码 prediction coding
★ 动态范围 dynamic range
恒流源 constant current source
★ 增量调制 delta modulation
★ 斜率过载失真 slope-overloaded distortion
语音编码 speech coding
语音压缩 voice compression
图像信号 image signal
★ 线性预测 linear prediction
码激励线性预测
code excited linear prediction
线性预测编码器
linear predictive coding (LPC)
预测阶数 prediction order
预测系数 prediction coefficient
离散傅立叶变换 discrete Fourier transform
离散余弦变换 discrete cosine transform
★ 过载 overload
★ 时隙 time slot
国际标准化组织
international standard organization
共路信令 common channel signaling (CCS)
随路信令 channel associated signaling (CAS)
国际电信联盟
international telecommunication union
压缩编码 compressed coding
复接 multiple connection
分接 demultiple connection
准同步数字序列
plesiochronous digital hierarchy
同步数字序列 synchronous digital hierarchy
同步传送模块
synchronous transport module (STM)
段开销 section overhead
容器 container
虚容器 virtual container
双音多频 dual tone multi-frequency

The performance of a PCM system is influenced by two major sources of noise:

Channel noise, which is introduced anywhere between the transmitter output and the receiver input. Channel noise is always present, once the equipment is switched on.

Quantization noise, which is introduced in the transmitter and is carried all the way along to the receiver output. Unlike channel noise, quantization noise is signal dependent in the sense that it disappears when the massage signal is switched off.

Naturally, these two sources of noise appear simultaneously once the PCM system is in operation.

PCM 系统的性能主要受两个噪声源影响：

信道噪声。在发射机输出端和接收机输入端之间的任何位置均可引入。只要设备处于工作状态，就会存在信道噪声。

量化噪声。在发射机中产生，并一直被带到接收机的输出中。与信道噪声不同的是，量化噪声依赖于信号，即切断消息信号时，量化噪声将会消失。

只要系统处于工作状态，这两种噪声源就会同时出现。

2 Signal after quantization is a signal with discrete values. The next issue is how to encode a digital signal. The most often used code is to use the binary symbols representing discrete values, such as 0s and 1s. The basic process, from sampling the analog signal, the quantization, until it is converted to binary symbols, is usually called pulse code modulation (PCM).

量化后的信号是离散的。下一步骤是如何将其编码成数字信号。常用的编码方式是采用二进制来表示离散值，如 0 和 1。从对模拟信号进行抽样、量化，直到转换成二进制符号，整个过程被称为脉冲编码调制(PCM)。

3 PCM is the basic and often-used method of converting an analog signal to a binary signal. It is not only used in the area of communication, but also extensively used in many other areas, such as computer, remote control, telemetering, digital instrument, broadcasting, and TV. In these areas, it is sometimes called "analog/digital(A/D) conversion". In communication technology, this coding technology had been achieved in 1940s. It has been called PCM since then, because it was studied from the viewpoint of signal modulation. It is called A/D conversion later in computer science and other areas of data processing. Substantially PCM and A/D conversion are the same thing.

PCM 是将模拟信号转换成数字信号的基本和常用的方法，不光在通信领域，还在计算机、远端控制、遥测、数字仪器、广播和电视等许多其他的领域中都得到了广泛的应用。在这些领域中，它有时被称为模/数(A/D)转换。在通信技术中，这种编码技术从 20 世纪 40 年代就开始应用，从那时起，它就被称为 PCM，因为它是被从信号调制的角度来描述的。后来在计算机科学及其他领域里它又被称为 A/D 转换，实质上 PCM 和 A/D 转换就是一回事儿。

第八节 数字信号的最佳接收
Section 8 Optimum Receiving of Digital Signal

统计判决 statistical decision
★ 最佳 optimum
统计特性 statistical characteristics
最小差错概率意义下 optimum in the minimum probability of error sense
先验概率 prior probability
标准偏差 standard deviation
贝叶斯准则 Bayes' rule
最大似然准则 maximum likelihood rule
最大后验概率准则 maximum a posteriori probability rule
最佳接收 optimum reception
联合概率密度 joint probability density
最佳线性接收机 optimum linear receiver
相关接收 correlation reception
★ 最小均方误差 minimum-mean square error
区域 region
匹配滤波器 match filter
后验概率 posteriori probability
★ 最佳接收机 optimum receiver

1 We note that a filter, which is matched to a pulse signal g(t) of duration T, is characterized by an impulse response that is a time-reversed and delayed version of the input g(t), as shown by $Hopt(t)=kg(T-t)$. In other words, the impulse response Hopt(t) is uniquely defined, except for the delay T and the scaling factor k, by the waveform of the impulse signal g(t) to which the filter is matched. In the frequency domain, the matched filter is characterized by a frequency response that is, except for a delay factor, the complex conjugate of the Fourier transform of the input g(t), as shown by $Hopt(f)=k\times G(f)\times \exp(-j2\pi fT)$.

我们注意到，一个与持续时间为 T 的脉冲信号 g(t)相匹配的滤波器，其特性是冲激响应为输入 g(t)的时间反转和延迟，即 $Hopt(t)=kg(T-t)$。换言之，除了时延 T 及比例因子 k 之外，冲激响应 Hopt(t)仅由滤波器所匹配的脉冲信号 g(t)的波形决定。在频域里，除延迟因子之外，匹配滤波器的频率响应，是输入信号 g(t)的傅里叶变换的复共轭，即 $Hopt(f)=k\times G(f)\times \exp(-j2\pi fT)$。

第九节 差错控制编码
Section 9 Error-Control Coding

突发信道 burst channel
混合信道 mixed channel
★ 检错重发 error detection and retransmission
差错控制 error-control
★ 编码 coding
★ 译码 decoding
★ 前向纠错 forward error correction
信道编码器 channel encoder
★ 反馈信道 feedback channel
反馈校验 feedback checkout
★ 自动请求重发 automatic-repeat request
存储器 memory
纠错码 error-correcting codes
选择重发 selective repeat
检错 error detection
纠错 error correcting
混合纠错 hybrid error correct
分组长度 block length
★ 路径 path
★ 码率 code rate
线性分组码 linear block codes
循环码 cyclic codes
卷积码 convolutional codes
★ 有限状态 finite-state
分支 branch
分叉点 node
★ 冗余度 redundancy
冗余校验 redundancy check (RC)
代数译码器 algebraic decoder
★ 软判决 soft-decision
★ 重复码 repetition code
★ 硬判决 hard decision
二进制对称信道 binary symmetric channel (BSC)
校正子 syndrome
错误图样 error pattern
校验矩阵 parity-check matrix
最小距离 minimum distance
码重 code weight
汉明重量 Hamming weight
★ 汉明距离 Hamming distance
汉明码 Hamming codes
系统码 systematic code
BCH 码 Bose-Chaudhuri-Hocquenghem code
RS 码 Reed-Solomon code
生成矩阵 generator matrix
★ 生成多项式 generator polynomial
★ 奇偶校验 parity-check
移位寄存器 shift register
★ 约束长度 constraint length
编码器 encoder
突发错误 burst error
码树图 code tree diagram
★ 网格图 trellis diagram
★ 状态图 state diagram
维特比算法 the Viterbi algorithm
序贯解码 sequential decoding
自由距离 free distance
★ 幸存路径 survivor path
★ 度量 metric
链接码 concatenated code
网格编码调制 trellis-coded modulation (TCM)
分量码 component code
低密度奇偶校验码 low density parity check code (LDPC)

1 ARQ uses redundancy merely for the purpose of error detection. Upon the detection of an error in a transmitted code word, the receiver requests a repeat transmission of the corrupted code word, which necessitates the uses of a return path(i. e. , a feedback channel). As such, ARQ can be used only on half-duplex or full-duplex links. In a half-duplex link, data transmission over the link can be made in either direction but not simultaneously. On the other hand, in a full-duplex link, it is possible for data transmission to proceed over the link in both directions simultaneously.

ARQ 采用冗余的目的仅仅是为了误码检测。当在传输的码字中检测到错误时，接收机就要求重传错误的码字，这就需要使用一条返回路径(反馈信道)。因此，ARQ 只能用于半双工或全双工的链路。在半双工链路上，链路可以在任一方向上传送数据，但不能同时进行两个方向上的数据传输。另一方面，在全双工链路上，数据可以在两个方向上同时传送。

2 In the block code, the number of "1" in the codeblock is called the weight of the codeblock, or code weight for short; and the number of bits which have different values in the corresponding location of two codeblock is called the distance of the codeblock, or code distance for short. Code distance is also called Hamming distance.

在分组码中，把码组中"1"的个数称为码组的重量，简称码重。把两个码组中对应位上数字不同的位数称为码组的距离，简称码距。码距又称汉明距离。

3 An important subclass of linear block codes is called cyclic codes. Cyclic codes are developed on the basis of rigorous modern algebraic theory. The coding and decoding equipment of these codes is not complex, and their error detecting and correcting abilities are very strong. In addition to the general properties of linear codes, cyclic codes have cyclicity. Cyclicity is designated in a way that any codeblock obtained by an end-around shift of a codeblock in a code is also a codeblock in this code. Here "end-around shift" is designated in a way that the rightmost symbol shifts to the left end; or contrarily, and the leftmost symbol shifts to the right end.

在线性分组码中，有一种重要的码叫作循环码，这种码是在严谨的现代代数理论基础上发展起来的。这种码的编码和解码都不复杂，但是它的检错和纠错能力很强。除了线性分组码的一般特性，循环码还具有循环性。循环性是指任一码组经过循环移位后仍是该码中的一个码组。这里"循环移位"是指最右边的符号移位到最左边，或者最左边的移位到最右边。

4 The definition of spread-spectrum modulation may be stated in two parts:

Spread spectrum is a means of transmission in which the data sequence occupies a bandwidth in excess of the minimum bandwidth necessary to send it.

The spectrum spreading is accomplished before transmission through the use of a code that is independent of the data sequence. The same code is used in the receiver (operating in synchronism with the transmitter) to despread the received signal so that the original data sequence may be recovered.

扩频调制的定义可以表述为两部分：

扩频是一种使数据序列所占带宽超过发送它所需最小带宽的传输方法。

扩频是在传输之前通过使用独立于数据序列的编码来完成。同样的编码用于接收机(已经与发射机进行了同步)以对接收信号进行解扩，从而恢复原始数据序列。

第十节 同步原理

Section 10 Synchronization

★ 同步 synchronization
载波同步 carrier synchronization
码元同步 symbol synchronization
位同步 bit synchronization
群同步 group synchronization
网同步 network synchronization
位定时 bit timing
★ 帧同步 frame synchronization
★ 通信网 communication network
字符同步 character synchronization
辅助导频 pilot-aided
频偏 frequency shift
载波提取 carrier abstraction
相偏 phase shift
★ 锁相环 phase-locked loop (PLL)
无辅助导频 non-pilot aided
帧定时脉冲 frame timing pulse
帧传输 frame transmission
开环 open loop
闭环 closed loop
帧速率 frame rate
捕获 capture

跟踪 tracking
流程图 flow chart
同步位 sync bits
假同步 false synchronization
漏同步 miss synchronization
★ 同步保持 synchrolock
同步保护 synchronize protection
分频器 frequency divider
起止式同步 start stop synchronization
同步调整 synchronization adjustment

1 There are two basic approaches for dealing with carrier synchronization at the receiver. One is to multiplex, usually in frequency, a special signal, called a pilot signal, that allows the receiver to extract and, thus, to synchronize its local oscillator to synchronize its local oscillator to the carrier frequency and phase of the received signal. The second approach, which appears to be more prevalent in practice, is to derive the carrier phase estimate directly from the modulated signal.
在接收机中,有两种基本的方法处理载波同步。一种是复用法,通常在频域采用一个称为导频的特殊信号,这种方法使接收机提取导频,并使本地振荡器与接收信号的载波频率和相位同步。第二种方法是从已调信号直接导出载波相位的估计值,在实践中这种方法更为普遍。

2 When receiving or demodulation of the signal is discussed, synchronization is often involved, especially digital signal, although it is not often mentioned during previous discussion on digital signal demodulation. Several synchronization issues are involved in a digital communication system. For example, during the coherent demodulation of a PSK signal, a local carrier with the same frequency and the same phase as that of the received signal is necessary to be generated in the receiver for multiplication with the received PSK signal. Hence, the frequency and the phase information of the local carrier must come from the received signal; or in other words, it is necessary to extract the carrier synchronization information from the received signal. The synchronization issue of the local carrier with the received signal carrier is called carrier synchronization.
当讨论信号尤其是数字信号的接收或者解调时,尽管在前面数字信号解调的讨论中不经常提及,但同步是必不可少的。数字通信系统中涉及几种同步方式,例如,在 PSK 信号的相干解调时,在接收本地必须产生一个和接收信号同频同相的载频信号来和 PSK 信号相乘。因此,当地载波信号的频率和相位必须来自于接收信号;换句话说,必须从接收信号中提取出载波同步信息。从接收信号中恢复当地载波的同步方式称为载波同步。

第二部分 实验

Part Two: Experiment

第××章 通信原理实验

Section ×× Principles of Communications Experiment

Lab1: AMI/HDB3 encoding and decoding
Type: verification
The experiment date: ×× ×× ×××× Place: ××
Professional Class: ×× Name: ××
Student No.: ×× Instructed by: ×× Term: ××

1. Objectives

(1) To master the encoding rules of AMI and HDB3.
(2) To observe the characteristics of AMI/HDB3 waveform.

2. Equipments and Components Needed

Communication experiment box, digital oscilloscope, etc.

3. Tasks and Procedure (Including schematic diagram)

(1) To connect the circuit according to the principle.

(2) To observe the waveform of AMI and HDB3 code through digital oscilloscope.

The full term for AMI code is the Alternate Mark Inversion code. Its coding rule is that 1 in message symbols will be converted into +1 and −1 alternatively, and 0 in message symbols will keep 0. For example:

Message symbol: 0 1 1 0 0 0 0 0 0 0 1 1 0 0 1 1 …

AMI code: 0 −1 +1 0 0 0 0 0 0 0 −1 +1 0 0 −1 +1 …

The HDB3's encoding and decoding schematic diagram is showed in Fig 1.

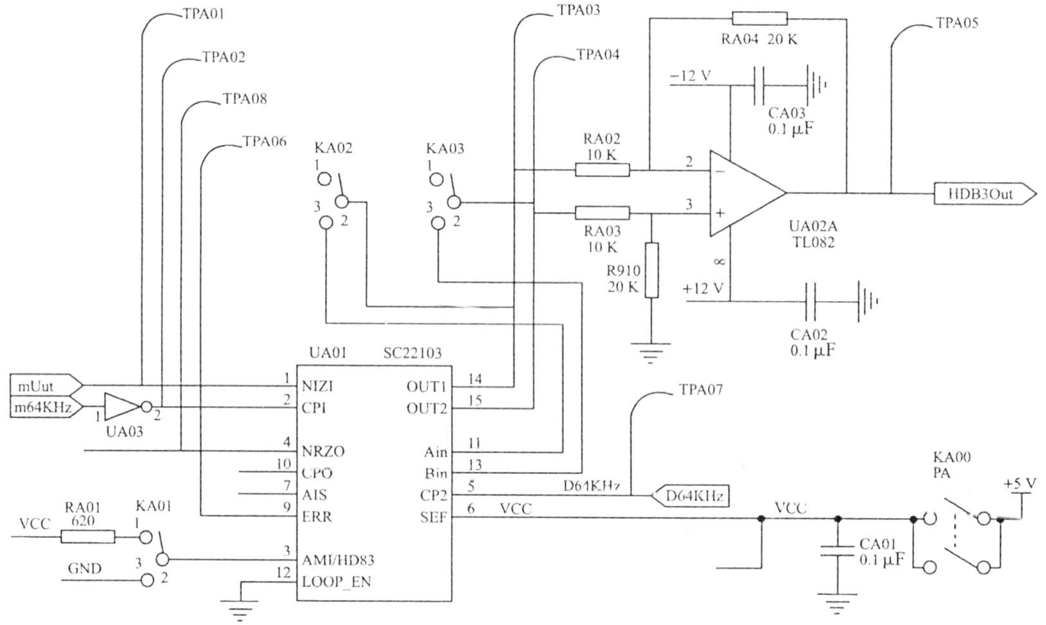

Figure 1. HDB3's encoding and decoding schematic diagram

In digital communication, it is very important for transmitting quality. HDB3 is the abbreviation of 3rd High Density Bipolar code. It's used in digital transmission, the code rule of HDB3 yard is: firstly the message symbol is converted into AMI code, and then the continuous 0s in AMI code are checked. When there are no more 4 (including 4) continuous 0s, no change will be made, and AMI code is just HDB3 code. When 4 or more than 4 continuous 0s appear, the fourth 0 will be converted into a symbol which has the same polarity of the previous non - 0(+1 or −1) symbol. Obviously, the result of the process will violate the "polarity alternatively inverse" rule of AMT code. Hence, this symbol is called "violation symbol", and is denoted by a V, i. e. +V represents +1, and −V represents −1. If V violates the "polarity alternatively inverse" rule for the following sequence, then D. C. component will appear. However, when there are even non - 0 symbols between the adjacent Vs, the requirement of the "polarity alternatively inverse" cannot be satisfied. To solve this problem, it is necessary to convert the first 0 of the continuous 0 string into a +B or a −B. The sign of B is the inverse of the previous non - 0 symbol; and the sign of the following non - 0 symbol begins to alternatively change from symbol V, for example:

Message symbol: 1 0 0 0 0　1 0 0 0 0　1　1 0 0 0 0 0 0 0 0　1　1
AMI code: −1 0 0 0 0 +　1 0 0 0 0　−1　+1 0 0 0 0 0 0 0 0　−1　+1
HDB code: −1 0 0 0 − V + 1 0 0 0 + V − 1 + 1 − B 0 0 − V + B 0 0 + V　−1　+1

4. The Record of the Experiment Form:

Fig. 2 shows the waveform for the AMI/HDB3 coding and decoding.

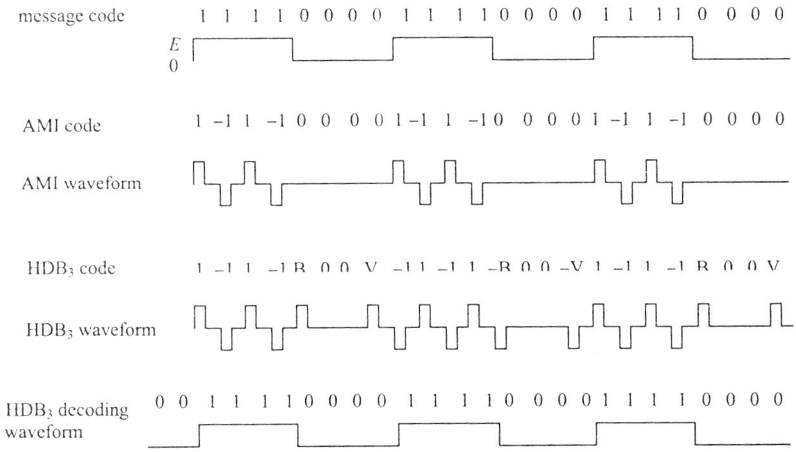

Figure2. AMI/HDB3 coding and decoding waveform

5. Waveform Analysis

From the waveform, we know the rule of HDB3. As can be seen from the above waveform, the polarity of a violation symbol is always the same as that of the previous non - 0 symbol (including the B), and so violation symbol is very easy to be found from the received sequence. Therefore it is known that the V and its previous 3 continuous symbols must be continuous 0s, then 4 continuous 0s may be restored.

6. Answer the Questions

What is the coding characteristic of the HDB3?

Answer: According to the rule of HDB3, its coding characteristic is that there are at most 3 continuous 0s.

第二十一章　计算机控制技术

Chapter 21　Computer Control Techniques

课程简介

本课程是电气类本科生的一门重要的专业课。课程介绍了计算机控制系统的基本概念和原理，主要内容包括：模拟量输入输出通道接口技术，人机接口技术，通用的控制程序设计，总线接口技术，过程控制的数据处理，数字 PID 算法，直接数字控制算法模糊控制技术，微型计算机控制系统设计等。通过学习本课程，学生可以掌握计算机控制技术的基础知识，提高应用计算机控制技术的能力。

Course Summary

This course is an important professional course for electrical engineering undergraduate students. Conceptual framework and principle of the computer control techniques are introduced in the course. Main topics included are: interface technology for analog input/output channel, man-machine interface technology, universal control program design, bus interface technology, data processing methods for the process control, digital PID algorithm, direct digital control algorithm, fuzzy control technology, microcomputer controlled system design, etc.. Having studied this course, students can get the abcs of the computer control techniques and improve their application ability in this domain.

第一节　微机控制系统概述

Section 1　Introduction to the Microcomputer Controlled Systems

微型计算机　microcomputer
★ 计算机控制系统　computer controlled systems
计算机控制技术　computer control techniques
总线工业控制机　bus industrial control computer
外部通用设备　exterior universal device
工业生产对象　industrial production object
工业控制系统　industrial process-control systems
工业自动化系统　industrial automation systems
★ 被测参数　measured parameters
★ 传感器　sensor
★ 变送器　transmitter
智能仪表　intelligent instrument/smart instrument
标准电信号　standard electric signal
标准总线　standard bus
主机　host
数字信号　digital signal
模拟信号　analog signal
★ 检测元件　detector
热电偶　thermocouple
电阻　resistance
★ 生产过程　production process
★ 误差　error
电动　electro-motion
气动　pneumatic
★ 设定值控制　set-point control
最优化　optimization
系统辨识　system-identification
中断设备　interrupt devices
操作站　operator stations
工程站　engineering stations
★ 实时　real-time
自动整定　automatic tuning
★ 监控管理程序　supervisory control management program
操作指导　operator guide
★ 直接数字控制　direct digital control (DDC)
计算机监督控制　supervisory computer control (SCC)
★ 集散控制系统　distributed control systems (DCS)
多级计算机控制　hierarchical computer control
管理信息系统　management information system
★ 计算机集成制造系统　computer integrated manufacturing system
可编程逻辑控制器　programmable logic controller

智能控制系统 intelligent control system
学习控制系统 learning control system
专家控制系统 expert control system
模糊控制系统 fuzzy control system
★ 现场总线控制系统 field bus control systems
开放式控制系统 open control system
★ 自适应控制 adaptive control
★ 平均无故障时间 mean time between failures (MTBF)

1 DCS systems generally consist of process stations, which control the process; operator stations, where process operators monitor activities; and various auxiliary stations.
分布式控制系统通常包括控制过程的过程站、过程操作员监控过程运行的操作站和各种辅助的站点。

2 Based on the dramatic developments in the past, it is tempting to speculate about the future. There are four areas that are important for the development of computer process control.

- Process knowledge
- Measurement technology
- Computer technology
- Control theory

在已有的引人注目的发展基础上，展望未来，前景诱人。要发展计算机过程控制，以下四个领域非常重要。

- 过程知识
- 测量技术
- 计算机技术
- 控制理论

第二节 模拟量输入输出通道接口技术

Section 2 Interface Technology for Analog Input/Output Channel

★ 通道与接口 channel and interface
数字量输入通道 digital input channel
数字量输出通道 digital output channel
模拟量输入通道 analog input channel
模拟量输出通道 analog output channel
★ 采样定理 sampling theorem
★ 采样/保持 sampling/hold
★ 采样周期 sampling period/sampling time
采样频率 sampling frequency
周期采样 periodic sampling
多速率采样 multirate sampling
随机采样 random sampling
解码网络 decoding network
★ 放大器 amplifier
模数转换 analog to digital conversion (ADC)
数模转换 digital to analog conversion (DAC)
★ 中断方式 interrupting mode
查询方式 query mode
软件延时方式 software delay mode
参考电平 reference voltage
数字地 digital earth
模拟地 analog earth
直接存储器存取 direct memory access
★ 采样保持电路 sampling-and-hold circuit
连续时间系统 continuous-time system
离散时间系统 discrete-time system

1 In the context of control and communication, sampling means that a continuous-time signal is replaced by a sequence of numbers, which represent the values of the signal at certain times.
在控制和通信领域，采样则意味着一连续时间信号由一个数值序列所代替，这个数值序列代表了某些特定时刻的信号值。

2 Shannon's sampling theorem: A continuous-time signal with a Fourier transform that is zero outside the interval $(-\omega_0, \omega_0)$ is given uniquely by its values in equidistant points if the sampling frequency is higher than $2\omega_0$. The continuous-time signal can be computed from the sampled signal by the

interpolation formula

$$f(t)=\sum_{k=-\infty}^{\infty}f(kh)\frac{\sin(\omega_s(t-kh)/2)}{\omega_s(t-kh)/2}$$
$$=\sum_{k=-\infty}^{\infty}f(kh)\operatorname{sinc}\frac{\omega_s(t-kh)}{2}$$

where ω_s is the sampling angular frequency in radians per second (rad/s).

香农采样定理：如果一个连续时间信号的傅立叶变换在($-\omega_0$，ω_0)之外等于零，那么当采样频率大于 $2\omega_0$ 时，该信号可由它的等时间距离点上的值所唯一确定。这时应用插值公式：

$$f(t)=\sum_{k=-\infty}^{\infty}f(kh)\frac{\sin(\omega_s(t-kh)/2)}{\omega_s(t-kh)/2}$$
$$=\sum_{k=-\infty}^{\infty}f(kh)\operatorname{sinc}\frac{\omega_s(t-kh)}{2}$$

就能由采样信号算出这个连续时间信号。式中 ω_s 是采样角频率，单位为弧度/秒(rad/s)。

3 Mass markets such as automotive electronics have also led to the development of special-purpose computers, called microcontrollers, in which a standard computer chip has been augmented with A-D and D-A converters, registers, and other features that make it easy to interface with physical equipment.

巨大的市场(比如汽车电子)需求使得一些称为微控制器的特殊用途计算机得到了发展。在这些微控制器中，一块标准的计算机芯片已增添了模数转换器和数模转换器、寄存器以及其他特性，使微控制器可以方便地与物理设备接口。

4 It is also possible to use different sampling periods for different loops in a system. This is called multirate sampling.

在一个系统的不同的回路中，同样可采用不同的采样周期，这种采样称为多速率采样。

第三节　人机接口技术
Section 3　Man-machine Interface Technology

★ 键盘　keyboard
★ 抖动　dithering
重击　repeating hit
连击　double hit
矩阵键盘　matrix keyboard
描述法　describing method
★ 功能键　function key
★ 显示仪表　displaying instrument
★ 记录仪表　recording instrument
数码管　digital displaying diode
★ 发光二极管　light emitting diode (LED)
★ 动态显示　dynamic display
★ 静态显示　static display
硬件译码　hardware coding
光柱显示器　light columniation display
★ 液晶显示器　liquid crystal display (LCD)
★ 点阵式显示器　matrix display

1 Man-machine interface, the region where a human being comes in contact with a machine, viz. the relationship between a man and a machine. One must ensure that the interface is designed properly for the capabilities and limitations of the users.

人机接口是人和机器接触的区域，也是人和机器之间的联系。必须保证接口的设计要恰当地满足用户的接受能力和局限性。

2 It becomes clear that process control puts special demands on computers. The need to respond quickly to demands from the process leads to the development of the interruption feature, which is a special hardware device that allows an external event to interrupt the computer in its current work so that it can respond to more urgent process tasks.

显然，过程控制对计算机提出了许多特殊的需求。对各种过程命令做出迅速响应的需求导致中断设备的发展。中断设备是一种特殊的硬件装置，它允许外部事件中断计算机的当前工作，以便计算机能够对更紧迫的过程任务做出响应。

第四节 通用的控制程序设计
Section 4 Universal Control Program Design

报警程序设计 alarm program design
★ 越限报警 beyond range alarm
★ 开关量 switch variable
★ 光电隔离 photoelectric isolation
继电器 relay
★ 固态继电器 solid state relay
直流继电器 direct current relay
交流继电器 alternating current relay
★ 大功率场效应管 high-power field effect transistor
可控硅接口技术 controlled silicon interface technology
单向可控硅 unilateral controlled silicon
★ 双向可控硅 triac
★ 电磁阀 electro-magnetic valve
小功率直流电动机 low-power direct current motor
★ 脉冲宽度调制 pulse width modulation (PWM)
平均速度 average speed
★ 占空比 duty cycle/duty ratio
驱动器 driver
电子开关 electronic switch
专用接口芯片 special interface chip
软件延时法 software delay method
专用接口板 special interface board
计数法 counting method
闭环脉冲宽度调速系统 closed-loop pulse width speed regulation system
★ 测速发电机 speed indicating generator
数字式转速传感器 digital rotate speed sensor
交流电动机 alternating motor
方向控制 directional control
★ 正向转动 forward directional turn
★ 反向转动 reverse directional turn
变速控制 shift gear control
★ 定时器 timer

例 Pulse width modulation, abbreviated as PWM, is a method of transmitting information on a series of pulses. The data being transmitted are encoded on the width of these pulses to control the amount of power being sent to a load.
脉冲宽度调制（简写 PWM），是以串行脉冲的方式传递信息的一种方法。传递的数据被编码为脉冲的宽度来控制传递给负载的能量。

例 Pulse width modulation is a modulation technique for generating variable width pulses to represent the amplitude of an input analog signal or wave. The popular applications of pulse width modulation are in power delivery, voltage regulation and amplification and audio effects.
脉冲宽度调制是一种调制技术，产生可变宽度的脉冲，描述输入模拟信号或波形的幅度。脉冲宽度调制广泛应用在电力传输、电压调制、电压放大和音频效果方面。

例 Industrial automation systems traditionally have two components, controllers and relay logic. Relays are used to sequence operations such as startup and shutdown. They are also used to ensure safety of the operations by providing interlocks.
工业自动化系统在传统上有两个部分：控制器和继电器逻辑电路。继电电路通常用于顺序操作，如开和关，同时，它通过提供连锁来保护操作的安全。

第五节 总线接口技术
Section 5 Bus Interface Technology

模块式结构 modularization structure
★ 串行总线 serial bus
并行总线 parallel bus
数据总线 data bus
地址总线 address bus
控制总线 control bus

刷新 refresh
定时控制 timing control
总线响应 bus response
★ 总线请求 bus request
中断响应 interrupt response
中断请求 interrupt request
等待请求 waiting request
★ 地址锁存允许 address locking enable
串行通信 serial communication
数据传送方式 data transfer mode
★ 单工方式 simplex mode
半双工方式 half duplex mode
全双工方式 full duplex mode
波特率 baud rate
★ 异步通信 asynchronous communication
★ 同步通信 synchronous communication
★ 协议 protocol
★ 信号调制 signal modulation
频移键控法 frequency shift key
相移键控法 phase shift key
幅移键控法 amplitude shift key
★ 差错控制技术 error control technology
自动重发控制 automatic repeat request
前向纠错方式 forward error correction
混合纠错 hybrid error correction
纠错编码 error correction coding
★ 奇偶校验 parity check
循环冗余校验 cyclic redundancy check
★ 串行通信标准总线 serial communication standard bus
选择接口控制 selection interface control
电平转换芯片 electric level conversion chip
★ 数据终端设备 data terminal equipment
★ 数据通信设备 data communication equipment
电气特性 electric performance
机械特性 mechanical performance
发送数据 transmitting data
接收数据 receiving data
★ 请求发送 request to send
★ 清除发送 clear to send
★ 数据准备就绪 data set ready
★ 数据终端就绪 data terminal ready
数据载波检测 data carrier detect
振铃指示 ring indication
自动化技术 automation technology
★ 工艺流程 production process
仪表装置 instrument equipment
★ 智能变送器 intelligent transducer
智能现场设备 intelligent field device
★ 网络 network
★ 现场总线基金会 fieldbus foundation (FF)
开放系统互连参考模型
open system interconnection reference model
控制器局域网络 controller area network
局部操作网络 local operating network
★ 神经元 neuron
★ 国际标准化组织
International Standard Organization (ISO)
★ 国际电工委员会
International Electrical Committee (IEC)
过程现场总线 process fieldbus
可寻址远程传感器数据通路通信协议
highway addressable remote transducer
神经元专用芯片 neuron special chip
★ 路由器 router
载波侦听多路访问/介质访问控制 carrier sense multiple access / medium access control

1 Fieldbus is a generic-term which describes a new digital communications network which will be used in industry to replace the existing 4～20 mA analogue signal.
现场总线是一个描述新型数字通信网络的常用术语，可以用在工业上取代现有的 4～20 mA 模拟信号。

2 Fieldbus is a digital, bi-directional, multidrop, serial-bus, communications network used to link isolated field devices, such as controllers, transducers, actuators and sensors. Each field device has low cost computing power installed in it, making each device a "smart" device.
现场总线是一个数字化的、双向的、多节点的、串行总线的通信网络，用于连接分散的现场设备，如控制器、变送器、执行器和传感器。每个现场设备内部都有运算单元，使其成为智能设备。

3 Each device will be able to execute simple functions on its own such as diagnostic, control, and

maintenance functions as well as providing bi-directional communication capabilities. With these devices not only will the engineers be able to access the field devices, but they are also able to communicate with other field devices.
每个设备都能执行简单的功能,如诊断、控制、维护以及双向的通信能力。使用这些设备,工程师不仅能访问现场设备,而且能与其他的现场设备通信。

4 In essence, fieldbus will replace centralized control networks with distributed-control networks. Therefore, fieldbus is much more than a replacement for the 4～20 mA analogue standard.
本质上,现场总线将用分散化的网络取代集中化的网络。因此,现场总线不仅仅替代了 4～20 mA 模拟信号标准。

第六节　过程控制的数据处理
Section 6　Data Processing Methods for the Process Control

智能化仪器　intellectualized instrument
数据处理　data processing
★ 容错技术　fault tolerant technology
★ 工业控制组态软件
industrial control configuration software
查表技术　checking list technology
顺序查表法　sequential look up table method
计算查表法　computing look up table method
对分查表法　bisection look up table method
★ 数字滤波　digital filtering
模拟滤波　analog filtering
程序判断滤波　program judge filtering
限幅滤波　clipped filtering
限速滤波　velocity limiting filtering
★ 中值滤波　median filtering
算术平均滤波　arithmetic average filtering
加权平均滤波　weighted average filtering
★ 滑动平均滤波　moving average filtering
★ 低通数字滤波　low pass digital filtering
复合数字滤波　compound digital filtering
量程自动转换　span automatic conversion
★ 标度转换　scale conversion
★ 可编程增益放大器
programmable gain amplifier
非线性参数　nonlinear parameters
自动校正　self tuning

1 A low-pass filter blocks high frequencies and passes low frequencies. It would be most desirable if a low-pass filter had a characteristic such that all signals with frequency above some critical value are simply rejected. A high-pass filter passes high frequencies (no rejection) and blocks (rejects) low frequencies.
低通滤波器使低频信号通过而阻断高频信号。理想的低通滤波器能够使超过某个转折频率的所有频率信号截止。高通滤波器使高频信号通过,并阻止低频信号通过。

2 Using computers to implement controller has great advantages. Many of the difficulties with analog implementation can be avoided. For example, there are no problems with accuracy or drift of the components. It is very easy to have sophisticated calculations in the control law, including logic and nonlinear functions.
用计算机做控制器有很多优点,可以克服一些模拟控制器的困难,如没有精度或者元件的漂移问题。也很容易在控制规律中完成精密的计算,包括逻辑的和非线性的函数。

3 The ideal filters pass all signals in the passband with a gain of unity and completely reject all signals in the stopband. The cutoff frequencies are typically defined by the points where the magnitude drops to $1/\sqrt{2}$. In real filters, the magnitude can not change discontinuously, so there is some transition band between the passband and the stopband.
理想的滤波器在通频带中以同一增益通过所有的信号,在衰减带中禁止所有的信号通过。剪切频率定义在幅值下降为 $1/\sqrt{2}$ 处。实际的滤波器中,幅值不能间断地变化,所以在通频带和衰减带之间有一个过渡带。

第七节　数字 PID 算法

Section 7　Digital PID Algorithm

数字控制算法　digital control algorithm

★ 被测参数　controlled parameter

★ 过阻尼　overdamped

★ 欠阻尼　underdamped

温度　temperature

压力　pressure

流量　flow rate

成分　ingredient

液位　liquid level

★ 传感器　sensor

★ 调节器　adjustor

★ 给定值　reference value/set point

★ 测量值　measured value

差值　difference value

★ 比例增益　proportional gain

★ 积分时间　integration time or reset time

★ 微分时间　derivative time

调节过程　control process

★ 控制阀　control valves

★ 执行机构　actuator

程序和顺序控制　programmable and sequential control

最优控制　optimum control

★ 位置算法　position algorithm

★ 增量算法　incremental algorithm

★ 无扰动切换　bumpless transfer

★ 自动控制　automatic control

★ 手动控制　manual control

连续控制系统　continuous-time control systems

离散控制系统　discrete-time control systems

★ 静态误差　steady-state error

被控对象　controlled object

速度控制　velocity control

★ 正作用　positive action

反作用　negative action

★ 积分饱和　integral saturation

采样周期　sampling period /sampling interval

采样定理　sampling theorem

控制回路　controlled loop

控制方式　control modes

参数整定　parameter tuning

★ 拉普拉斯变换　Laplace transforms

流程图　flowchart

★ z 变换　z transform

★ s 平面　s-plane

z 平面　z-plane

拉普拉斯逆变换　inverse Laplace transforms

★ 传递函数　transfer function

例1 A pure derivative cannot, and should not be, implemented, because it will give a very large amplification of measurement noise. The gain of the derivative must thus be limited. This can be done by approximating the transfer function as follows:

$$sT_d \approx \frac{sT_d}{1+sT_d/N}$$

The transfer function on the right approximates the derivative well at low frequencies but the gain is limited to N at high frequencies. N is typically in the range of 3 to 20.

一个纯微分无法实现,或者最好不要被实现,因为它将导致噪声被大幅度地放大。因此微分增益必须受到限制。为此可把传递函数近似为:

$$sT_d \approx \frac{sT_d}{1+sT_d/N}$$

上式右边的传递函数在低频段内能很好地近似微分,而在高频段就把增益限制到 N,N 的范围通常在 3 到 20 之内。

例2 Many practical control problems are solved by PID-controller. The "textbook" version of the PID-controller can be described by the following equation:

$$u(t) = K\left(e(t) + \frac{1}{T_i}\int_0^t e(s)\,ds + T_d\frac{de(t)}{dt}\right)$$

where error e is the difference between command signals u_c (the set point) and process output y (the measured variable). K is the *gain* or *proportional gain* of the controller, T_i the *integration time* or *reset time*, and T_d the *derivative time*.

采用 PID 控制器解决了许多实际控制问题。标准的"教科书"版本中可以用方程:

$$u(t) = K\left(e(t) + \frac{1}{T_i}\int_0^t e(s)ds + T_d \frac{de(t)}{dt}\right)$$

来描述 PID 控制器,其中 e 是指令信号 u_c(设定值)和过程输出 y(实测变量)之间的差,K 是增益,即控制器的比例增益,T_i 是积分时间或重调时间,T_d 是微分时间。

第八节 直接数字控制算法

Section 8 Direct Digital Control Algorithm

采样数据系统 sampled-data systems
★ 数据采集系统 date acquisition systems
★ 最少拍控制 deadbeat control
随动系统 follow system
离散系统 discrete-time system
自动跟踪 self tracking
★ 脉冲传递函数 impulse transfer function
★ 零阶保持器 zero-order hold
一阶保持器 first-order hold
高阶保持器 high-order hold
广义对象 general object
★ 控制规律 control law
★ 单位阶跃信号 unit step signal
单位速度信号 unit velocity signal
单位加速度信号 unit acceleration signal
★ 数字控制器 digital controller
响应曲线 response curve
★ 零点和极点 zeros and poles
★ 波纹 intersample ripple/hidden oscillations
采样开关 sampling switch
大林算法 dahlin algorithm
超调 overshoot
停滞 dead time
★ 一阶惯性环节 first-order lag process
二阶惯性环节 second-order lag process
时间常数 time constant
振铃现象 ringing phenomena
采样频率 sampling frequency
输出幅度 output amplitude
初值定理 initial-value theorem
★ 终值定理 final-value theorem
直接程序设计法 direct program design method
串行程序设计法 serial program design method
并行程序设计法 parallel program design method
★ 差分方程 difference equation

This strategy has the property that it will drive all the states to zero with least sampling periods after an impulse disturbance in the process state. The control strategy is called deadbeat control.

当系统受到脉冲扰动时,使系统达到稳定时所需要的采样周期最少,这种控制策略称为最少拍控制。

A special type of controller, called a deadbeat controller, responds quickly to the control input and settles out with zero error in minimum finite time. A deadbeat controller can be designed in the z-domain by replacing the closed-loop poles of the system with poses at the origin of the z-domain.

被称为特殊控制器的最少拍控制器,对控制输入响应快速,且输出在最短的有限时间内达到稳定。最少拍控制器能在 z 域内设计,用 z 域原点处的极点替代系统的闭环极点。

This type of controller design is actually a special case of the direct design. Deadbeat controllers, then, suffer from all the problems and constraints that need consideration when doing direct design. In addition, the controllers resulting from this design procedure tend to be highly sensitive to parameter variations within the system.

此类控制器设计,实际上是直接设计的一个特例。而在进行直接设计时,最少拍控制器要考虑各种问题和约束。此外,按此程序设计的控制器可能对系统内部的参数变化非常敏感。

Deadbeat design presents an optimal kind of design (optimal in the sense of minimal settling time) and

is often useful for comparison purposes.
最少拍设计是一类最优的设计(最小过渡过程时间意义上的最优),通常用于比较的目的。

第九节 模糊控制技术

Section 9 Fuzzy Control Technology

★ 模糊控制 fuzzy control
单变量系统 single variable system
多变量系统 multi-variables system
非线性复杂系统 nonlinear complex systems
★ 经典控制理论 classical control theory
★ 现代控制理论 modern control theory
自适应控制 adaptive control
专家模糊控制 expert fuzzy control
多变量模糊控制 multi-variables fuzzy control
自学习 self learning
★ 神经网络 neuron network
★ 数学模型 mathematics model
模糊控制算法 fuzzy control algorithm
★ 控制规则 control rule
★ 模糊关系 fuzzy relation
单输入单输出 single-input and single-output
双输入单输出 double-input and single-output
多输入单输出 multi-input and single-output
★ 模糊条件语句 fuzzy condition clause
★ 语言变量 language variable
模糊数学模型 fuzzy mathematics model
模糊语言 fuzzy language

1 Fuzzy logic is a way of interfacing inherently analog processes, which moves through a continuous range of values, to a digital computer to perform tasks, based on abstracted values, as if they were well-defined discrete numeric values.
模糊逻辑是基于抽象的值,将在一定范围内变化的固有的模拟过程和数字计算机进行接口执行任务,就好像他们是定义好的数字值一样。

2 The input variables in a fuzzy control system are in general mapped into by sets of membership functions similar to this, known as "fuzzy sets". The process of converting a crisp input value to a fuzzy value is called "fuzzification".
通常将模糊控制系统的输入变量映射成与之相似的成员函数的集合,即模糊集。将输入值变成模糊值的过程称为模糊化。

3 The fuzzy controller is composed of the following four elements:
(1)A rule-base (a set of IF-THEN rules), which contains a fuzzy logic quantification of the expert's linguistic description of how to achieve good control.
(2)An inference mechanism (also called an "inference engine" or "fuzzy inference" module), which emulates the expert's decision making in interpreting and applying knowledge about how to best control the plant.
(3) A fuzzification interface, which converts controller inputs into information that the inference mechanism can easily use to activate and apply rules.
(4)A defuzzification interface, which converts the conclusions of the inference mechanism into actual inputs for the process.
模糊控制器由下面四部分组成:
(1)规则库(如果—那么规则集),包含取得良好控制的专家语言描述的模糊逻辑量化。
(2)推理机构(又称推理机或模糊推理模块),模仿专家制定决策,解释和应用知识以便更好地控制设备。
(3)模糊化接口,将控制器的输入转换为推理机构易于应用的信息,激活或者应用规则。
(4)去模糊化接口,将推理机构的结论转换为过程的实际输入。

第十节 微型计算机控制系统设计

Section 10 Microcomputer Controlled System Design

系统设计 system design
调试及实验 debugging and testing
★ 控制方案 control scheme
★ 原理图 principle map
工业控制机 industrial process computer
★ 单片机系统 single chip system
★ 程序流程图 program flow chart
软件开发过程 software development process
★ 硬件调试 hardware debugging
软件调试 software debugging
★ 离线 off-line
★ 在线 on-line

1 The design of control system is a specific example of engineering design. Again, the goal of control engineering design is to obtain the configuration, specifications, and identification of the key parameters of a proposed system to meet an actual need.
控制系统设计是工程设计的特定例子。也可以说，控制工程设计的目标是获得被提议系统关键参数的结构、规格及确定，以满足实际的需要。

2 The first step in the design process is to establish the system goals. For example, we may state that our goal is to control the velocity of a motor accurately. The second step is to identify the variables we desire to control (for example, the velocity of the motor). The third step is to write the specification in terms of the accuracy we must attain. This required accuracy of control will then lead to the identification of a sensor to measure the controlled variable.
设计过程的第一步是建立系统的目标。例如，可以声明控制的目标是精确地控制电机的速度。第二步是确定期望控制的变量(如电机的速度)。第三步写出关于必须达到的精度规格。依据这个要求的控制精度，就可以确定测量被调变量的传感器。

第二十二章　数字图像处理
Chapter 22　Digital Image Processing

课程简介

数字图像处理是一门迅速发展的新兴学科，它的目的是在计算机上实现和强化人的视觉以及人对视觉信息的加工处理能力。学生通过这门课程的学习，能够掌握数字图像处理中的基本概念、基本方法和系统的知识，对图像的数学、视觉、光学以及二维变换等基本理论有一定的了解，并能使用经典的方法实现图像的增强、复原和投影重建，对图像的压缩、分割、描述和理解都有较深的认识。数字图像处理技术是 20 世纪 60 年代发展起来的一门新兴学科。近 30 多年来，由于大规模集成电路技术和计算机技术的迅猛发展，离散数学理论的创立和完善，以及军事、医学和工业等方面应用需求的不断增长，数字图像处理的理论和方法进一步完善，使得数字图像处理技术在宇宙探测、遥感、生物医学、工农业生产、军事、公安、办公自动化、视频和多媒体系统等领域得到了广泛应用，并显示出广阔的应用前景，成为计算机科学、信息科学、生物学、医学等学科研究的热点。先修课程：计算机程序设计基础、高级程序设计、线性代数、数字信号处理、MATLAB 语言基础、高等数学。教材：数字图像处理学，阮秋琦编著，电子工业出版社，2007 年。

Course Summary

As a new subject, digital image processing has developed rapidly. The subject focuses on the realization and enhancement of human vision through computer, and the improvement of pictorial information for human interpretation. Students will master the basic concepts, methods and system etic knowledge of digital image processing through this course, learn the basic theories such as image mathematics, human vision, optics and two-dimensional transform, and understand image compression, image segmentation, image description and image understanding. The students will be able to use classic methods to realize image enhancement, image restoration and reconstruct image from projections. Digital image processing techniques were developed in the 1960s. In more than 30 years, with the rapid development of large scale integration and computer science, the establishment and improvement of discrete mathematics, the increasing application demands on military, medicine and industry, and the improvement of digital image processing theory and methods, the digital image processing technology has penetrated into every field of knowledge such as space exploration, remote sensing, biomedicine, industrial production, agricultural production, military, office automation, public security, video system and multimedia system. Preparatory Courses: Computer Programming, High-level Programming Design, Linear Algebra, Digital Signal Processing, MATLAB Language, Advanced Mathematics. Text book: ***Digital Image Processing***, Qiuqi Ruan, Publishing house of Electronics Industry, 2007.

第一节　绪论
Section 1　Introduction

★ 图像　image
★ 图形　graphic
图像处理　image processing
模拟图像处理　analog image processing
★ 数字图像处理　digital image processing
★ 计算机图像处理　computer image processing
计算机图形学　computer graphics
计算机视觉　computer vision
数字化　digitizing
景物　scene
★ 像素　pixel
★ 灰度　gray level
★ 亮度　intensity level
电磁波谱　electromagnetic spectrum
可视波段　visual band
★ 图像获取　image acquisition
★ 图像存储　image storage
★ 图像表示　image representation

★ 图像传送　image transmission
★ 图像表现　image presentation
伽马射线　gamma
超声波　ultrasound
电子显微镜　electron microscopy
人工智能　artificial intelligence (AI)

An image may be continuous with respect to the x and y coordinates, and also in amplitude. Converting such an image to digital form requires that the coordinate, as well as the amplitude be digitized. Digitizing the coordinate values is called sampling; digitizing the amplitude values is called quantization. Thus, when x, y, and the amplitude values of g are all finite, discrete quantities, we call the image a digital image.
一幅图像的 x 和 y 坐标以及振幅可能是连续的。要将这样的一幅图像转换成数字形式,就要求数字化坐标和振幅。将坐标数字化称为采样;将振幅数字化称为量化。因此,当 g 的 x,y 分量和振幅都是有限且离散的量时,称该图像为数字图像。

A digital image is defined as a two-dimensional function, $f(x, y)$, where x and y are plane coordinates, and the amplitude of f at a pair of coordinates (x, y) is called the intensity or gray level of the digital image at that point, where x, y and the values of f are all finite, discrete quantities.
数字图像可由一个二维函数 $f(x, y)$ 定义。其中,x 和 y 是平面坐标,任意坐标点 (x, y) 的幅度值 f 称为该点的亮度或者灰度,其中,x,y 和 f 都是有限的离散量。

第二节　图像、图像系统与视觉系统
Section 2　Image, Image System and Visual System

人类视觉系统　human visual system
图像成像　image formation
亮度适应　brightness adaptation
光线　light
电磁波谱　electromagnetic spectrum
成像特性　image characteristics
★ 发光强度　intensity
★ 照度　illumination
★ 静止图像　still image
吉布森效应　Gibson effect
图像残效　figural residual effect

Liquid crystals (LCs) are a state of matter that have properties between those of a conventional liquid and those of a solid crystal. For instance, an LC may flow like a liquid, but its molecules may be oriented in a crystal-like way.
液晶是物质的一种状态,其特性介于通常的液体与固体之间。例如,液晶能够像液体一样流动,但是其分子却能够像晶体一样排列。

The function $f(x, y)$ contains two components: (1) the amount of source illumination incident on the scene being viewed; (2) the amount of illumination reflected by the objectives in the scene. The two components are called illumination and reflectance components respectively, and are denoted by $i(x, y)$ and $r(x, y)$ appropriately. The two functions combine as a product to form $f(x, y)$:

$$f(x, y) = i(x, y) \cdot r(x, y)$$

where

$$0 < i(x, y) < \infty$$

and

$$0 < r(x, y) < 1$$

The last equation indicates that reflectance is bounded by 0, which means total absorption, and 1, which means total reflectance.
函数 $f(x, y)$ 包含两个分量:(1)照射到观察场景的光源的光照总量;(2)观察场景中物体反射光的总量。这两个分量分别被称为照射分量和反射分量,相应地用 $i(x, y)$ 和 $r(x, y)$ 表示。这两个函数的乘积就是函数 $f(x, y)$。$f(x, y)=i(x,y) \cdot r(x,y)$

其中 $0< i(x, y)<\infty$,并且 $0< r(x, y)<1$。后一个公式指出反射分量的范围在 0 到 1 之间。0 表示全吸收,1 表示全反射。

第三节 图像的正交变换
Section 3 Image Orthogonal Transforms

共轭 conjugate
复共轭运算符 complex conjugate operator
变换系数 transform coefficients
相角 phase angle
★ 复数 complex numbers
傅里叶级数 Fourier series
★ 傅里叶变换 Fourier transform
★ 离散傅里叶变换 discrete Fourier transform
卷积 convolution
采样定理 the sampling theorem
混叠 aliasing
★ 平移特性 translation
★ 可分离性 separability
旋转特性 rotation
周期性 periodicity
对称性 symmetry
★ 离散余弦变换 discrete cosine transform
★ 沃尔什变换 Walsh transform
★ 拉德梅克函数 Rademacher function
★ 格雷码 Gray code
列率 sequency
离散沃尔什哈达玛变换
discrete Walsh Hadamard transform
★ 正变换核 forward transformation kernels
★ 反变换核 inverse transformation kernels
★ 尺度可变性 scalability
正交基 orthogonal basis
双正交基 biorthogonal basis
★ 多分辨率 multiple resolutions
余弦变换 cosine transform
小波变换 wavelet transform
★ 离散小波变换 discrete wavelet transform
★ 快速小波变换 fast wavelet transform
母小波 mother wavelet

1 Multiresolution compatibility. The 1-D scaling function satisfies the following requirements of multiresolution analysis:

(1) The set of functions that can be represented as a series expansion of $\varphi_{j,k}$ at low scales or resolutions are contained within those that can be represented at higher scales.

(2) $\varphi_{j,k}$ is orthogonal to its integer translations.

(3) Any function can be represented with arbitrary precision as $j \to \infty$.

(4) The only function that can be represented at every scale is $g(x)=0$.

When these conditions are met, there is a companion wavelet $\psi_{j,k}$ that, together with its integer translations and binary scalings, spans - that is, can represent - the difference between any two sets of $\varphi_{j,k}$- representable functions at adjust scales.

多分辨率的一致性。一维尺度函数满足多分辨率分析的如下要求：

(1)在低尺度或低分辨率下可表示为一系列 $\varphi_{j,k}$ 的展开的一组函数，包含在可以以更高尺度表示的那些函数中。

(2) $\varphi_{j,k}$ 与其整数平移正交。

(3)当 $j \to \infty$ 时，可用任何精度来表示任何函数。

(4)唯一可以以任意尺度表示的函数是 $g(x)=0$。

当这些条件满足时，就存在一个伴随小波 $\psi_{j,k}$ 及其整数平移和二进制尺度，其变化范围是在邻接尺度上可表示的任意两组函数 $\varphi_{j,k}$ 之间的差。

2 If a function $x(t)$ contains no frequencies higher than B hertz, it is completely determined by giving its ordinates at a series of points spaced 1/(2B) seconds apart.

若函数 $x(t)$ 所包含的频率不超过 B 赫兹，则该函数可由间隔为 1/(2B) 秒采样的坐标序列确定。

3 The Fourier transform of a continuous function $f(t)$ of a continuous variable, t, denoted $F(u)$, is defined by the equation

$$F(u)=\int_{-\infty}^{\infty} f(t)e^{-j2\pi ut}dt \tag{1}$$

where u is also a continuous variable.

Conversely, given $F(u)$, we can obtain $f(t)$ back using the inverse Fourier transform, written as

$$f(t)=\int_{-\infty}^{\infty}F(u)e^{j2\pi ut}du \quad (2)$$

Equations (1) and (2) comprise the so-called Fourier transform pair.
对连续变量 t 构成的连续函数 $f(t)$ 的傅里叶变换记作 $F(u)$，由公式(1)定义。

$$F(u)=\int_{-\infty}^{\infty}f(t)e^{-j2\pi ut}dt \quad (1)$$

其中 u 是一个连续变量。相应地，可给定 $F(u)$，通过傅里叶反变换获得 $f(t)$。

$$f(t)=\int_{-\infty}^{\infty}F(u)e^{j2\pi ut}du \quad (2)$$

公式(1)和(2)组成了一对傅里叶变换对。

4 The discrete cosine transform is similar to the discrete Fourier transform, but has following features: (1) the discrete cosine transform coefficients are purely real numbers; (2) the discrete cosine transform is the nearest optimal property for energy compaction; (3) the discrete cosine transformer has fast computing algorithm.
离散余弦变换与离散傅里叶变换相似，但是具有以下特性：(1)离散余弦变换的系数是实数；(2)离散余弦变换最接近最佳的能量集中；(3)离散余弦变换具有快速算法。

第四节 图像的增强
Section 4 Image Enhancement

★ 空间域 spatial domain
★ 频率域 frequency domain
★ 亮度变换 intensity transformation
★ 对比度扩展 contrast stretching
★ 灰度级变换 grayscale transformation
★ 图像反转 image negatives
★ 对数变换 log transformation
★ 幂次变换 power-law transformation
削波 clipping
阈值化 thresholding
★ 直方图 histogram
阈值二值图像 threshold binary image
★ 直方图均衡化 histogram equalization
累计分布函数 cumulative distribution function
★ 直方图匹配 histogram matching
★ 直方图规定化 histogram specification
★ 模糊图像 blurring image
★ 平滑图像 smoothing image
滤波掩模 filter mask
★ 低通滤波器 lowpass filter
★ 高通滤波器 highpass filter
★ 理想低通滤波器 ideal lowpass filter
★ 巴特沃斯低通滤波器 Butterworth lowpass filter
★ 指数低通滤波器 exponential lowpass filter
★ 梯形低通滤波器 trapezoid lowpass filter
★ 图像锐化 image sharpening
★ 梯度 gradient
★ 罗伯特梯度法 Robert gradient
★ LOG 算法 Laplacian of Gaussian algorithm
★ Sobel 算子 Sobel operators
★ Canny 算子 Canny operators
★ Prewitt 算子 Prewitt operators
★ Kirsh 算子 Krish operators
★ 同态滤波 homomorphic filtering
★ 彩色图像处理 color image processing
★ 亮度 brightness
★ 色调 hue
★ 饱和度 saturation
★ 色度 chromaticity
★ 彩色模型 color models
★ 伪彩色 pseudocolor
灰度分割 intensity slicing

1 A grayscale transformation is often called a point operation, because $T(f(n_1, n_2))$ only depends on the value of the intensity at the point (n_1, n_2). A linear transformation will in general not be a point operation. The output usually depends on the value of the intensity in a neighborhood around the point (n_1, n_2).
灰度级变换通常称为点运算，因为点 (n_1, n_2) 处的灰度级变换 $T(f(n_1, n_2))$ 仅与该点的灰度值有关。线性变换通常不是点运算。其输出通常与点 (n_1, n_2) 邻域的灰度值有关。

2 Histogram equalization produces a transformation function that is adaptive. Histogram equalization

achieves enhancement by spreading the levels of the input image over a wider range of the intensity scale. Histogram matching or histogram specification is the method used to generate a processed image that has a specified histogram.

直方图均衡化生成了自适应的变换函数。直方图均衡化通过扩展输入图像的灰度级到较宽灰度尺度的范围来实现图像增强。生成具有指定直方图的图像的方法称为直方图匹配或直方图规定化。

3 Definition : an edge is a boundary between two regions of relatively uniform intensity, indicated by a strong gradient or a discontinuity in the intensity function.

定义:边缘就是两个具有相对均匀亮度的区域之间的边界,表现为较大的梯度或亮度函数的不连续。

第五节 图像编码

Section 5 Image Coding

★ 编码冗余 coding redundancy

★ 像素间冗余 interpixel redundancy

★ 心理视觉冗余 psychovisual redundancy

★ 图像熵 image entropy

编码效率 coding efficiency

★ 压缩比 compression ratio

霍夫曼编码 Huffman encoding

霍夫曼解码 Huffman decoding

★ 游程长度编码 run length encoding

★ 算术编码 arithmetic encoding

离散哈达玛变换

discrete Hadamard transform (DHT)

★ 联合图像专家组

joint picture expert group (JPEG)

★ 活动图像专家组

moving picture expert group (MPEG)

多媒体内容描述接口

multimedia content description interface

重新同步标记 resync marker

预测器 predictor

预测编码 predictive encoding

★ 脉冲调制编码 pulse encoding modulation

统计编码 Statistical encoding

有损压缩 lossy compression

无损压缩 lossless compression

★ 香农—费诺码 Shannon-Fano encoding

★ 增量调制编码 delta modulation

★ 差分脉冲编码调制编码 differential pulse code modulation (DPCM) encoding

★ 音视频编码标准

audio video coding standard(AVS)

1 When coding the gray levels of an image or the output of a gray level mapping operation, Huffman codes contain the smallest possible number of code symbols per source symbol subject to the constraint that the source symbols are coded one at a time.

当对一幅图像的灰度级或一个灰度级映射操作的输出进行编码时,在每次编码一个源符号的限制条件下,对于每个源符号,霍夫曼码包含了最小可能的代码符号数。

2 The first step in Huffman's approach is to create a series of source reductions by ordering the probabilities of the symbols into a single symbol that replaces them in the next source reduction.

The second step in Huffman's procedure is to code each reduced source, starting with the smallest source and working back to the original source. The minimal length binary code for a two-symbol source, of course, consists of the symbols 0 and 1.

霍夫曼方法的第一步是,通过对符号的概率排序并将最低概率符号组合为下一次约简时替代这些符号的单个符号,来建立一个源约简序列。

霍夫曼方法的第二步是对每个约简的源编码,编码从最小的源开始一直到原始源。两个符号的最短二进制码就是 0 和 1。

3 Differential pulse code modulation (DPCM) is a signal encoder that uses the baseline of pulse code modulation (PCM) but adds some functionalities based on the prediction of the samples of the signal. The input can be an analog signal or a digital signal. If the input is a continuous time analog signal, it needs to be sampled first so that a discrete time signal is the input to the DPCM encoder.

差分脉冲调制编码是一种采用脉冲调制原理,并加入对信号采样的预测等功能的编码器。其输入可以是模拟信号也可以是数字信号。如果输入是连续时间的模拟信号，则需要先通过采样变成离散时间信号再输入到差分脉冲调制编码器。

第六节　图像的复原

Section 6　Image Restoration

★ 数据通信系统　data communication system
数据电路　data circuit
★ 数据交换机　data switching exchange (DSE)
★ 本地网　local network
★ 通信子网　communication subnet
复用器　multiplexer
通信控制器　communication controller
前置处理机　pre-processor
★ 数字数据网　digital data network
编码　encode
解码　decode
★ 分组交换网　packet switching network
计算机网　computer network
★ 中继网　relay net
异步转移交换网
asynchronous transfer switching network
工作速率　working speed
符号速率　character rate
信息传输速率　information transmission rate
频带利用率　frequency band capacity factor
误码率　code error rate
中国公用分组数据交换数据网　China packet data switching network (CHINAPAN)
中国公用数字数据网
China digital data network (CHINADDN)
中国公用帧中继网
China frame relaying network (CHINAFRN)
中国公用计算机互联网
China computer inter-network (CHINANET)
中国公用传真存储转发网
China fax store and forward network (CHINAFAX)
中国公用电子信箱网
China electronic mail network (CHINAMAIL)
中国公用无线数据网
China wireless data network
中国公用电子数据交换网
China electronic data interchange (CHINAEDI)
★ 节点交换机　node switching exchange
数据终端　data terminal
★ 分组拆装设备
packet assembly and disassembly (PAD)
远程集中器　remote concentrator
网络管理　network management center (NMC)
传输线路　transport line
调制解调器　modem
虚呼叫　virtual call
★ 永久虚电路　permanent virtual circuit (PVC)
永久虚连接　permanent virtual connection (PVC)
数字交叉技术　digital cross technology
数字交叉连接　digital cross connection (DCC)
数字通道　digital path
网络设备　network equipment
★ 网络管理系统
network management system (NMS)
本地传输系统　local transport system
资源共享　resource sharing
分布式处理　distributed processing
均衡　equalization
局域网　local area network (LAN)
高速局部网　high-speed local network (HSLN)
计算机化分支交换网
computerized branch exchange (CBX)
双绞线　twisted-pair
载波监听多址访问/冲突检测
carrier sense multiple access/collision detection (CSMA/CD)
令牌　token
★ 城域网　metropolitan area network (MAN)
★ 广域网　wide area network (WAN)
★ 网桥　bridge
交换虚电路　switched virtual circuit (SVC)
虚拟专用网　virtual private network (VPN)
点到点协议　point-point protocol (PPP)
国际电信联盟
international telecommunications union (ITU)
★ 宽带综合业务数字网
broadband integrated services digital network (B-ISDN)
异步时分　asynchronous time division (ATD)

★ 异步转移模式
asynchronous transfer mode (ATM)
★ 信元　cell
定长信元　fixed length cell
变长信元　variable length cell
回波抵消器　echo canceller
网络一节点接口　network-node interface (NNI)
用户网络接口　user network interface (UNI)
虚路径　virtual path (VP)
虚通道　virtual channel (VC)
视频会议　video conferencing
视频点播　video on demand (VOD)
远程医疗　long distance medical treatment
因特网络电话　internet phone (IP)
因特网络协议　internet protocol (IP)
★ 网关　gateway
★ 网闸　gatekeeper
★ 多点控制单元　multipoint control unit (MCU)
互联网电话网关　internet telephone gateway (ITG)
★ 退化模型　degradation model
★ 逆滤波　inverse filtering
★ 最小二乘方滤波
minimum mean square error filtering
★ 去卷积　de-convolution
★ 中值滤波　median filtering

1 Digital images often suffer from systematic distortions and addition of noise. Distortions can be caused by the defocusing of a camera or by the blurring caused by the imperfection of the optical system.
数字图像常受到系统畸变以及噪声的影响。系统畸变的成因可能为摄像器材不聚焦，或者是光学系统的不完善。

2 The typical approach when attempting inverse filtering is to form the ratio $\hat{G}(u,v)=F(u,v)/M(u,v)$ and then limit the frequency range for obtaining the inverse, to frequencies "near the origin". The idea is that zeros in $M(u,v)$ are less likely to occur near the origin because the magnitude of the transform typically is at its highest value in that region. There are numerous variations of this basic theme, in which special treatment is given at values of (u,v) for which M is zero or near zero. This type of approach sometimes is called pseudo inverse filtering.
采用逆滤波时，典型的方法是形成比率 $\hat{G}(u,v)=F(u,v)/M(u,v)$，然后，为了得到逆，将频率的范围限制在接近原点的频率。概念是 $M(u,v)$ 中的零不太可能在接近原点的地方出现，因为变换数值通常是该区域中的最高值。这个基本主题有很多变化，其中，使 M 为零或接近零的 (u,v) 值被特殊对待。这种方法有时称为伪逆滤波。

3 Let $x_0, x_1, \cdots, x_{N-1}$ be a sequence of N numbers. We first rank the sequence x_k. Let $k_0, k_1, \cdots, k_{N-1}$ be the indices of x_k once they are ordered as

$$x_{k_0} \le x_{k_1} \le \cdots \le x_{k_{N-1}}$$

The median of the sequence is defined as

$$\begin{cases} x_{k_n} & if \quad N = 2n-1 \\ \frac{1}{2}(x_{k_{n-1}} + x_{k_n}) & if \quad N = 2n \end{cases}$$

In other words, the median is the number x_k that lies in the middle of the sequence, after all numbers have been ranked.
令 $x_0, x_1, \cdots, x_{N_{-1}}$ 为 N 个数字组成的序列。我们首先对序列 x_k 排序。令 $k_0, k_1, \cdots, k_{N_{-1}}$ 标志 x_k。按从小到大排序的指数。则该序列的中值定义为：

$$\begin{cases} x_{k_n} & if \quad N = 2n-1 \\ \frac{1}{2}(x_{k_{n-1}} + x_{k_n}) & if \quad N = 2n \end{cases}$$

也就是说，序列 x_k 的中值就是序列中所有数排序后处于中间位置的数字。

第七节 图像分析
Section 7 Image Analysis

★ 图像分割 image segmentation
★ 边缘检测 edge detection
索引图像 index image
遥感图像 remote sensing image
全局阈值处理 global thresholding
局部阈值处理 local thresholding
★ 区域生长 region growing
邻域像素 neighboring pixel
纹理特性 texture character
★ 区域分割 region segmentation
★ 区域分离 region splitting
★ 区域合并 region merging
分水岭变换 watershed transform
★ 样板匹配 template matching
★ 描绘 description
★ 区域描绘子 regional descriptors
★ 矩描绘子 moments descriptors
拓扑描绘子 toplogical descriptors

1 In image processing, the Laplacian of a 2 - D function $g(x,y)$ is formed from second-order derivatives as follows:

$$\nabla^2 g(x,y) = \frac{\partial^2 g(x,y)}{\partial x^2} + \frac{\partial^2 g(x,y)}{\partial y^2}$$

在图像处理中，二维函数 $f(x,y)$ 的拉普拉斯由二阶导数形成，如下式所示：

$$\nabla^2 g(x,y) = \frac{\partial^2 g(x,y)}{\partial x^2} + \frac{\partial^2 g(x,y)}{\partial y^2}$$

2 The Laplacian is seldom used by itself for edge detection because, as a second-order derivative, it is unacceptably sensitive to noise, its magnitude produces double edges, and it is unable to detect edge direction. However, the Laplacian can be a powerful complement when used in combination with other edge-detection techniques. For example, although its double edges make it unsuitable for edge detection directly, this property can be used for edge location.
拉普拉斯算子自身很少被直接用做边缘检测，因为二阶导数对噪声具有无法接受的敏感性，它的幅度会产生双边缘，而且它不能检测边缘的方向。然而，当与其他边缘检测技术组合使用时，拉普拉斯算子是一种有效的补充方法。例如虽然它的双边缘使得它不适合直接用于边缘检测，但该性质可用于边缘定位。

3 The basic idea behind edge detection is to find places in an image where the intensity changes rapidly, using one of the two general criteria:
(1)Find places where the second derivative of the intensity has a zero crossing.
(2)Find places where the first derivative of the intensity is greater in magnitude than a specified threshold.
边缘检测的基本意图是使用如下两个基本原则之一在图像中找到亮度快速变化的地方：
(1)找到亮度的二阶导数有零交叉的地方。
(2)找到亮度的一阶导数在幅度上比指定的阈值大的地方。

4 Basically, representing a region involves two choices: (1) we can represent the region in terms of its external characteristics (its boundary), (2) we can represent the region in terms of its internal characteristics (the pixel comprising the region). An external representation is chosen when the primary focus is on shape characteristics. An internal representation is chosen when the primary focus is on regional properties, such as color and texture.
基本上，表示一个区域有两种选择：(1)用其外部特性来表示区域(如它的边界)；(2)用其内部特性来表示区域(如组成区域的像素)。当主要关注的是区域的形状特征时，选择外部特性来表示区域；当主要关注的是区域的内部性质时，如颜色和纹理，选择内部特性来表示区域。

5 Most of the segmentation algorithms are based on one of two basic properties of intensity values: discontinuity and similarity. In the first category, the approach is to partition an image based on abrupt changes in intensity, such as edges. The principal approaches in the second category are based

on partitioning an image into regions that are similar according to a set of predefined criteria. Thresholding, region growing and region splitting and merging are examples of methods in this category.

大多数图像分割算法是基于亮度的两个基本特性之一:不连续性和相似性。第1类方法基于亮度的不连续变化分割图像,比如图像的边缘。第2类方法依据事先制定的准则将图像分为相似的区域。门限法、区域生长和区域分离和聚合都是第2类方法的例子。

第二十三章　数字语音处理

Chapter 23　Digital Speech Processing

课程简介

数字语音处理是电子信息工程和通信工程专业的一门重要的专业方向选修课。通过本课程的学习，学生可以具有信号处理及分析能力，掌握先进的信号处理方法及其在语音信号处理方面的应用。本课程主要介绍一些要用到的语音学和数字信号处理的基础知识，以及汉语语音学有关内容。还介绍了作为语音信号处理的基础技术的各种分析方法和关键技术。

Course Summary

Digital speech processing is one of the important electives to students majoring in electronic and information engineering and communication engineering. The course may enable students the abilities of signal processing and analysis. Students may acquire the advanced signal processing methods and the application of speech signal processing. The course mainly introduces the basic knowledge about digital signal processing, phonetics and Chinese phonetics to the students. The course also talks about analysis methods and key technologies for phonetic signal processing.

第一节　绪论

Section 1　Introduction

★ 语音信号　speech signal
★ 语音编码　speech code
★ 语音质量　speech quality
数码率　data rate
★ 语音识别　speech recognition
★ 语音合成　speech synthesis
★ 说话人识别　speaker recognition
★ 说话人确认　speaker verification
★ 语音增强　speech enhancement
★ 语音压缩　speech compression
语音理解　speech understanding
★ 语言编码　language code
数字信号处理　digital signal processing
激励参数　excitation parameter
声道参数　vocal track parameter

1. In order to understand the nature of speech signal, we should know how communication technologies, and information theory are used to deal with problems in practical application.
要理解语音信号的本质，还要理解通信技术、信息理论技术如何被用来解决各种实际应用中存在的问题。

2. For the sake of uncovering various mathematical or practical properties of the speech signal, converting one type of speech signal representation to another can help solve both fundamental and deep problems of interest.
为了揭示语音信号的各种精确的实际特性，把语音信号从一种表现形式转换为另一种形式，可以解决很多我们所关心的有关语音信号的基本问题和更深奥的问题。

第二节　语音信号处理基础

Section 2　Fundamental of Speech Signal Processing

★ 时变特性
properties of speech change with time
语音波形　speech waveform
★ 语音频谱　speech spectra
语音帧　speech frame
发声器官　vocal apparatus
★ 清音　unvoiced speech
★ 浊音　voiced speech
★ 爆破音　plosive speech
元音　vowel
半元音　semivowel
辅音　consonant

摩擦音 fricative

★ 基音周期 pitch period

★ 共振峰 formant

★ 语谱图 sound spectrogram

★ 音素 phoneme

音节 syllable

外耳 outer ear

内耳 inner ear

中耳 middle ear

★ 响度 loudness level

★ 听阈 threshold of hearing

★ 痛阈 threshold of pain

★ 音调 pitch

★ 听觉隐蔽效应 auditory masking

1 The range of human hearing is intervenient between threshold of hearing and threshold of pain. Threshold of hearing is the lowest limit of Brownian motion of air particles in the inner ear, and threshold of pain is from 10^{12} to 10^{16} greater than the threshold of hearing in intensity.

人类听觉范围介于听阈和痛阈之间，所谓听阈就是内耳所能感受到的空气颗粒布朗运动的最低限度，而痛阈则是听阈的 10^{12} 到10^{16} 倍强度。

2 Human hearing can perceive both sound frequency and sound direction, and also detect weak components of speech spectrum in strong broadband noise.

人类的听觉能够感知声音的频率和声音的方向，同时能够在强的宽带噪声下检测到微弱的语音频谱成分。

3 Masking is the phenomenon whereby one loud sound makes another softer sound inaudible when... Masking is used to hide quantizer noise by methods of spectral shaping.

当两种响度不同的声音作用于人耳时，响度大的声音将会使响度小的声音听不到，这种现象称为隐蔽效应。隐蔽效应通常能够通过频谱的修整隐蔽量化器噪声。

第三节 语音信号的时域分析

Section 3 Time Domain Analysis of Speech Signals

窗函数 windows function

★ 时域 time domain

★ 频域 frequency domain

★ 短时能量 shot-time energy

★ 短时幅度 shot-time magnitude

★ 短时平均过零率

shot-time average zero crossing rate

★ 短时自相关 short-time autocorrelation

★ 端点检测 endpoint detection

★ 基音周期估计 pitch period estimation

倍频 frequency doubling

半频 frequency halving

★ 短时平均幅度差函数

short-time average magnitude difference function

中心削波 center clipping

★ 三电平削波 3-level center clipper

声道传输函数 vocal tract transfer function

线性平滑 linear smoothing

非线性平滑 non-linear smoothing

★ 基音周期平滑 pitch period smoothing

★ 浊音清音检测 voiced-unvoiced detection

★ 时域波形 time domain waveform

周期信号 periodic signal

Properties of the speech signal change relatively slowly with time (5～10 sounds per second).

—over very short (5～20 msec) intervals => uncertainty due to small amount of data, varying pitch, varying amplitude;

—over medium length (20～100 msec) intervals => uncertainty due to changes in sound quality, transitions between sounds, rapid transients in speech;

—over long (100～500 msec) intervals => uncertainty due to large amount of sound changes;

There is always uncertainty in short time measurements and estimates from speech signals.

语音信号的各种特性在每秒 5～10 个声音单位内变化相对缓慢。

—非常短的间隔(5～20 毫秒)内存在不确定性，这是因为语音数据、基音周期的变化以及语音幅度的变化都很小。

—在中等长间隔内(20～100 毫秒)存在不确定性，这是因为声音的品质在声音转换的快速瞬间发生了变化。

—在很长的时间间隔内(100～500 毫秒)也存在不确定性,因为这时候大量的语音数据发生了变化。

在短时间内衡量和估计语音信号总是存在不确定性。

第四节 语音信号的变换域分析
Section 4 Transform Domain Analysis of Speech Signals

★ 频域分析 frequency domain analysis
★ 短时傅里叶变换 short-time Fourier transform
★ 频谱特性 spectra representations
线性滤波 linear filtering
★ 频域处理 frequency domain processing
信号恢复 signal recovery
短时功率谱密度函数
short-time power speetrum density function
语音重构 speech reconstruction
平滑 smoothing
频谱分辨率 spectral frequency resolution
★ 低通滤波器 low pass filter
时间分辨率 time resolution
冲激响应 impulse response
★ 调制 modulation
★ 解调 demodulation
带通滤波器 band pass filter
★ 采样 sampling
★ 采样率 sampling rate
★ 同态声码器 homomorphic vocoder
倒谱共振峰估计
cepstrum formant estimation
线性处理 linear processing
非线性处理 non-linear processing
小波变换 wavelet transform
★ 量化 quantizing
同态语音处理
homomorphic speech processing
卷积 convolution
解卷积 de-convolution
★ 复倒谱 complex cepstrum
★ 倒谱 cepstrum

例1 Time-dependent complex cepstrum retains all the information of the time-dependent Fourier transform =>exact representation of speech signal.
依赖于时间的复倒谱保留了依赖于时间的傅里叶变换所反映的特征信息,而这些特征信息很好地体现了语音信号。

例2 Time-dependent real cepstrum loses phase information => not an exact representation of speech signal. Quantization of cepstrum parameters also loses information.
依赖于时间的倒谱丢失了相位信息,这样就不能完全描述语音信号。量化倒谱参数也会丢失信息。

例3 Cepstrum gives good estimates of pitch, voicing and formants which can build homomorphic vocoder.
倒谱能够很好地进行基音周期、浊音和共振峰的估计,利用这些参数就能够构成同态声码器。

第五节 语音信号线性预测分析
Section 5 Linear Prediction Analyzing of Speech Signals

★ 线性预测 linear prediction
★ 预测系数 prediction coefficient
预测波形 prediction waveform
★ 声道模型 vocal track model
最小均方误差 minimum mean-squared error
协方差 covariance
最大似然法 maximum likelihood
传输函数 transfer function
差分方程 difference equation
逆滤波器表达 inverse filter formulation
高斯白噪声 Gauss white noise
★ 预测误差 prediction error
无损声道模型 lossless tube models
杜宾算法 Durbin algorithm
格型算法 Lattice algorithm
舒尔算法 Schur algorithm
★ 增益 gain
★ 线谱对 line-spectrum pair (LSP)
线谱频率 line-spectrum frequency (LSF)
★ 频谱估计 spectral estimation

例1 LPC methods are the most widely used in speech coding, speech synthesis, speech recognition, speaker recognition and verification, speech storage, etc..

线性预测编码方法广泛地应用于语音编码、语音合成、语音识别、说话者识别和确认以及语音存储等方面。

LPC methods provide extremely accurate estimates of speech parameters, with great efficiency.
线性预测编码方法使语音特征参数得以精确估计,而且极其有效。

Basic idea of linear prediction: current speech sample can be closely approximated as a linear combination of the past samples.
线性预测的基本思想:当前的语音采样值能够由过去的多个采样值线性逼近合成。

LP is based on speech production and synthesis models. Speech can be modeled as the output of a linear, time-varying system, excited by either quasi-periodic pulses or ramdom noise signal. LP provides a robust, reliable and accurate method for estimating the parameters of the linear system. We have already seen linear predictive techniques in speech coding as part of a differential quantization scheme, concentrated on finding an adaptive predictor in DPCM to reduce the variance of the difference signal.
线性预测基于语音的产生和合成模型。语音可以由线性时变系统模型产生,激励源由准周期脉冲信号或者随机噪声信号构成。线性预测为线性系统的各种参数的估计提供了稳健、可靠和精确的方法。我们已经把预测技术作为差分量化方案的一部分应用在语音编码中;目的是在差分脉冲编码调制中寻找一种自适应预测器来减少差分信号的变化。

第六节 矢量量化
Section 6 Vector Quantization

★ 矢量 vector
★ 标量 scalar
★ 量化速率 quantization rate
★ 维数 dimension
关联 correlation
冗余 redundance
信源 resource
★ 量化器 quantizer
★ 编码器 encoder
★ 译码器 decoder
★ 码书 codebook
★ 码字 codeword
无记忆矢量量化器
non-memory vector quantizer
记忆矢量量化器 memory vector quantizer
预测矢量量化 predictive vector quantization
自适应矢量量化 adaptive vector quantization
分段量化 segmental quantization
边带信息 side information
Mel 频率倒谱系数
Mel frequency cepstrum coefficient
★ 胞腔 voronoi cell
欧氏失真 Euclidean distortion
最邻近准则 nearest neighbor rule (NNR)

Instantaneous Quantization:
- separate the A/D conversion of speech signal into the processes of sampling and quantization.
- assume $x(n)$ obtained by sampling a band - limited signal at a rate at or above the Nyquist rate.
- assume $x(n)$ is known to infinite precision in amplitude.
- quantize $x(n)$ in some suitable manner.

瞬时量化:
- 把语音信号的模数变换分成采样和量化两个部分。
- 假定在大于或等于奈奎斯特采样率的采样速率下对带限信号采样得到 $x(n)$。
- 假定 $x(n)$在幅度上精度是无限的。
- 用适当的方法对 $x(n)$进行量化。

第七节 语音编码
Section 7 Speech Coding

★ 传输 transmission
★ 存储 storage
信道 channel
★ 模拟语音 analog speech

自适应增益 adaptative gain
差分编码 differential coding
自适应编码 adaptive coding
★ 波形编码 waveform coding
熵编码 entropy coding
自适应变换编码 adaptive transform coding
★ 编码速率 coding rate
★ 语音质量 speech quality
可懂度 intelligibility
自然度 naturalness
编码质量估计 coding quality evaluation
★ 脉冲编码调制 pulse code modulation (PCM)
★ 电平 level
自适应脉冲编码调制
adaptive pulse code modulation (APCM)
差分脉冲编码调制
differential pulse code modulation (DPCM)
增量调制 delta modulation (△M)
★ 线性增量编码 linear delta coding
自适应增量编码调制
adaptive delta modulation (ADM)
★ 同步 synchronization
自适应量化 adaptive quantization (AQ)
前向自适应量化
forward adaptive quantization (FAQ)
后向自适应量化
backward adaptive quantization (BAQ)
★ 子带编码 sub-band coding (SBC)
短时预测误差滤波器
short term prediction error filter
混合激励线性预测编码
mixed excitation LPC (MELP)
合成分析法 analysis by synthesis (ABS)
多带激励 multi-band excitation (MBE)
主观质量评价 subjective quality evaluation
客观质量评价 objective quality evaluation

例1 Another waveform following method, called either code excited linear prediction (CELP) or multi-pulse excitation (MPE), contains both a formant tracking filter and a pitch tracking filter. Formant tracking filter is also known as a short-time predictor, and pitch tracking filter is also known as a long-term prediction filter or an adaptive codebook.
另一种波形跟随方法,称为码激励线性预测(CELP)或多脉冲激励(MPE),包括共振峰跟踪滤波器和基音跟踪滤波器。共振峰跟踪滤波器又称为短时预测器,基音跟踪滤波器又称为长时预测器或自适应码书。

例2 Although this coding rate is more than acceptable for telecommunications, it limits the quality of the speech, which is called telephone-quality speech. Therefore, it affects the performance of not only speech coder, but also speech recognition systems.
虽然此编码速率超过了电信的要求,但它限制了语音(我们称之为电话质量语音)质量,因此不仅影响了语音编码器的性能,还影响了语音识别系统的性能。

第八节 语音识别

Section 8 Speech Recognition

★ 动态时间规整
dynamic time warping (DTW)
★ 大词汇表 large vocabulary table
★ 小词汇表 little vocabulary table
★ 中词汇表 middle vocabulary table
★ 孤立词识别 isolated word recognition (IWR)
连接词识别 connected word recognition (CWR)
协同发音 co-articulation
★ 特定人识别 speaker dependant recognition (SDR)
★ 非特定人识别
speaker independent recognition (SIR)
关键词确认技术 keyword spotting
语义信息 semantic information
语用信息 pragmatic information
★ 隐马尔可夫模型 hidden Markov model (HMM)
期望最大化算法
expectation maximum algorithm (EMA)
最大似然估计 maximum likelihood estimation (MLE)
最小分类误差 minimum classification error (MCE)
最大互信息 maximum mutual information (MMI)
最大后验概率
maximum aposterior probability (MAP)
参数平滑 parameter smoothing

消除内插 deleted interpolation
互相验证 cross-validation
连续语音识别 continuous speech recognition
堆栈解码 stack decoding

Recognition and understanding of speech can realize human-machine communications by voice.

—Command and control applications, e. g. control of look and feel of desktop, control of fonts and styles in word processing, simple commands for spreadsheets and presentation graphics;

—Voice dictation to create letters, memos and other documents;

—Natural language voice dialogues with machines to enable help desks and call centers;

—Voice dialing for cell-phones and from PDA's and other small devices;

—Agent services such as calendar entry and update, address list modification and entry, etc..

语音识别和语音理解能够通过语音实现人机通信：

—命令控制应用，比如，电脑桌面的感观控制，文字处理中字体和风格的控制处理，电子表格和图表的简单控制；

—语音控制写信、备忘录以及其他文档处理；

—用自然的人类语言与机器进行对话，可以产生呼救或和呼叫中心通信；

—用手机、个人数字助手及其他小型设备完成语音拨号；

—诸如日历登录和更新、地址簿的修改和记录这样的语音服务中心。

第九节 语音合成
Section 9 Speech Synthesis

★ 文本语音合成 text-to-speech (TTS)
概念语音合成
concept-to-speech (CTS)
意向语音合成
intention-to-speech (ITS)
★ 基音同步叠加法
pitch synchronous overlap and add (PSOLA)
参数合成 articulatory synthesis
★ 线性预测合成 linear prediction synthesis
★ 共振峰合成 formant synthesis
波形拼接合成 wave splice synthesis
概念层次网络 hierarchical network of concept
缩减 reduction
二元文法 di-grammar method
三元文法 tri-grammar method
神经网络法 neural network method
多带重合叠加 multi-band re-synthesis overlap and add
★ 韵律 prosody
★ 停顿 pause
★ 时长 duration

Synthesis of speech for effective human-machine communications:

—Reading email messages over a telephone;

—Telematics feedback in automobiles;

—Talking agents for completion of transactions;

—Call center, help desks and customer care;

—Handhold devices such as foreign language phrasebooks, dictionaries and crossword puzzle helpers;

—Automated guided machines provide things like stock quotes, airline schedules, updates of arrivals and departures of flights.

语音合成有效地应用在人机通信方面：

—通过电话可以阅读电子邮件；

—在汽车上实现远程反馈信息的处理；

—与代理商语音通信完成交易；

—完成呼救和消费者的服务；

—诸如外语词汇书、字典、字谜助手等掌上语音设备；

—可以提供股票行情、航班时间表以及航班起飞和到达时间的更新等功能的自动导航机器。

第十节 语音增强
Section 10 Speech Enhancing

★ 背景噪声 background noise
★ 平均意见得分 mean opinion score (MOS)
★ 判断韵字测试 diagnostic rhyme test (DRT)
★ 判断满意度测量
diagnostic acceptability measure (DAM)
★ 信噪比 signal noise rate (SNR)
★ 识别率 recognition rate
★ 颗粒噪声 granular noise
自适应滤波器 adaptive filter
最小均方误差 minimum mean square error (MMSE)

Speech enhancement is used in noisy environment to align voices with video segments, to eliminate echo, to speed-up or slow-down prerecorded speech and to change voice qualities, e. g. rapid review of material, careful scrutinizing of spoken material and talking books,etc..

语音增强用在噪声环境中来拼接视频片断、消除回声、快放或慢放事先录音、改善语音质量,例如资料的快速回顾、仔细扫描口语材料、有声读物等。

第十一节 语音通信应用中的关键技术
Section 11 Pivotal Technologies in Speech Communication Application

语音通信 speech communication
★ 声码器 vocoder
★ 不连续传输 discontinuous transmission (DTX)
★ 语音激活检测 voice activity detection (VAD)
拖尾延迟 hangover delay
舒适噪声 comfort noise
★ 回波抵消 echo return loss
前向纠错 forward error correcting (FEC)
纠错码 error correcting code

Since characters which have lower frequency components pass at a different speed from data characters with high frequency components, it is possible in higher-speed circuits for portions of one character to enter or remain in the time slot allocated to other characters.

由于低频率分量的字符与高频率分量字符的传输速度不同,可能会使高速电路中的一个字符进入或停留在其他字符的时隙中。

第十二节 语音处理的实时实现
Section 12 Real-time Implementing of Speech Processing

数字信号处理 digital signal processing (DSP)
★ 微处理器 microprocessor
★ 代码调式器 code composer studio (CCS)
模拟器 simulator
高速缓存器 cache
★ 集成开发环境 integrated developing environment (IDE)
基本输入输出系统 basic input and output system (BIOS)
★ 应用程序接口 application program interface (API)
实时数据交换 real time data exchange (RTDX)
★ 编译器 assembler
★ 连接器 linker
★ 汇编器 compiler
文档管理器 archiver
汇编翻译工具 assembler translation assistant
★ 工程 project
并行调试管理器 parallel debug manager

TMS320C20 is a complete series of processors similar to the TMS320C10, but with larger data and program memory units and the ability to perform multiply and accumulate operations in a single cycle.

TMS320C20 是与 TMS320C10 相似的一套完整系列处理器,但具有更大的数据和程序存储器,并能在单个周期内完成乘加运算。

第二十四章　软件工程
Chapter 24　Software Engineering

课程简介

《软件工程》是计算学科的一门核心课程，是指导计算机软件开发与维护的一门综合性课程。通过本课程的学习，使学生掌握软件工程的基本原理和技术，掌握现代化的软件开发方法和步骤，为将来从事软件开发提供方法上的指导。本课程以软件生命周期的主要活动为主线，从软件及软件工程的历史和发展、软件开发过程、需求分析、软件设计、程序编码、软件测试、软件维护等方面全面介绍软件工程的基本理论、方法、技术和工具。

Course Summary

Software Engineering is a core curriculum in the computing discipline. It is a comprehensive course that is aimed to guide the development of computer software and its maintenance. Learning it enables the students to master the basic principles and techniques of software engineering and the development methods and procedures of modern software. It also provides methodological guidance for those engage in software development in the future. This course is based on the main activities of the software life cycle, including the history and development of software and software engineering, software development process, requirements analysis, software design, program encoding, software testing, and software maintenance, so as to give a comprehensive introduction to the primary theory, methods, technologies and tools of software engineering.

第一节　概述
Section 1　Introduction

★ 软件危机　software crisis
开发案例　development case
开发流程　development process
文档　document
文档编制、文档管理　documentation
文档说明　document description
文档模板　document template
零起点开发　green-field development
生命周期　life cycle
★ 生命周期模型　life-cycle model
模式　pattern
产品需求文档
product requirements document (PRD)
质量保证　quality assurance (QA)
复审　review
复用、重用　reuse
软件架构　software architecture
★ 软件生命周期　software life cycle
★ 计算机辅助软件工程
computer-assisted software engineering (CASE)
结构化设计模式　structured design pattern
遗产软件　legacy software

Software: It is computer program and associated documentation. Software products may be developed for a particular customer or may be developed for a general market.
软件是指计算机程序及其相关文档。软件产品可以分为专用和通用两类。

Software engineering (SE) : Software engineering is an engineering discipline which is concerned with all aspects of software production. Software engineering is the profession concerned with creating and maintaining software applications by applying computer science (CS), project management (PM), domain knowledge (DK), and other skills and technologies.
Software engineering is used with at least three distinct meanings: (1) As the usual contemporary term for the broad range of activities that was formerly called programming or systems analysis; (2) As the broad term for the technical analysis of all aspects of the practice, as opposed to the theory of computer programming; (3) As the term for an engineering profession rather than an art or a craft,

and the codification of recommended practices in the form of software engineering methodologies.
软件工程是一门涉及软件开发的所有问题的工程学科。其所涉及的领域包括应用计算机科学知识开发和维护应用软件、项目管理知识、软件相关应用领域的背景知识以及其他技术知识。
软件工程至少有三种不同的解释：(1) 传统意义上的程序设计或系统分析；(2) 有别于计算机程序设计的、包含软件开发实践的所有方面的技术分析；(3) 把软件开发看作工程实践而非技艺的软件工程方法学。

- Software process: A software process is a set of activities and associated results which lead to the production of a software product. These activities include software specification, software development, software validation, and software evolution.
  Software specification defines the functionality of the software and constraints on its operation.
  Software development refers to that the software meeting the specification must be produced.
  Software validation refers to that the software must be validated to ensure that it does what the customer wants.
  Software evolution refers to that the software must evolve to meet changing customer needs.
  软件过程是软件开发过程中所有相关活动及其结果的集合，这些活动包括软件规格描述、软件开发、软件验证和软件演化。
  软件规格描述定义了软件功能及其运行限制。
  软件开发是指开发满足规格描述所定义的软件。
  软件验证是指软件必须经过验证以确保其满足客户需求。
  软件演化是指软件必须不断演化以满足变化的客户需求。
- Software process model: A software process model is a simplified description of a software process which is presented from a particular perspective. It may include activities which are part of the software process, software products and the roles of people involved in software engineering.
  Workflow model shows the sequence of activities in the process along with their inputs, outputs and dependencies. The activities in this model represent human actions.
  Data-flow or activity model represents the process as a set of activities each of which carries out some data transformation. It shows how the input to the process such as a specification is transformed to an output such as a design. The activities here may represent transformations carried out by people or by computers.
  Role/action model represents the roles of the people involved in the software process and the activities for which they are responsible.
  软件过程模型是一种从特定的角度对软件过程的简化描述，它可以包含软件过程、软件产品及相关开发人员的信息。工作流模型描述了过程中活动的次序以及它们的输入、输出及其制约关系。在这个模型中活动表示了人的行为。
  数据流/活动模型将过程描述为一组活动，每一个活动执行某种数据转换。它表示对某个过程(例如一个规格说明)的输入如何转换为输出(例如一个设计)。这里，活动可以表示由人或计算机执行的转换。
  角色/活动模型描述了软件过程相关人员的角色及其所负责的活动。
- Milestone: It is the event that signifies the accomplishment or completion of major deliverables during a project.
  里程碑是项目进行期间标识主要交付成果完成的事件。
- Rapid application development (RAD): It is a kind of technique that emphasizes extensive user involvement in the rapid and evolutionary construction of working prototypes of a system to accelerate the system development process.
  快速应用开发是一种系统开发策略，该策略强调用户深入地参与到一系列系统工作原型的快速进化和构造过程中，以加速系统的开发过程。

第二节 需求分析
Section 2 Requirements Analysis

★ 可行性分析 feasibility analysis
需求工程 requirements engineering
★ 需求获取 requirements discovery
联合需求计划 joint requirements planning (JRP)
程序描述语言 program description language (PDL)
软件设计规格说明 software design specification
★ 软件需求规格说明
software requirements specifications (SRS)
★ 需求分析 requirements analysis
功能需求 functional requirements
接口需求 interface requirements
需求属性 requirements attribute
需求管理 requirements management
需求跟踪 requirements tracing
需求类型 requirements type
软件需求规格复审
software specification review (SSR)
需求验证 requirements verification
需求确认 requirements validation
说明、描述 specification
系统需求复审 system requirements review (SRR)
分析 analysis
分析与设计 analysis and design
分析模式 analysis pattern
★ 结构化分析 structured analysis
快速架构分析 rapid architecture analysis
模型驱动分析 model-driven analysis
业务实体 business entity
业务对象模型 business object model
业务建模 business modeling
业务流程 business process
业务重建 business re-engineering
业务规则 business rule
核心工作流程 core workflow
★ 数据流图 data flow chart
★ 数据字典 data dictionary
工作流程 workflow
实体 entity
实体关系图 entity relationship diagram (ERD)
需求工程过程 requirements engineering processes

1 Requirements engineering: Requirements engineering is a process that involves all of the activities required to create and maintain a system requirements document. These activities include the system feasibility study, the elicitation and analysis of requirements, the specification of requirements and the validation of the requirements.
需求工程是一个涉及建立和维护系统需求描述文档所需的全部活动的过程。这些活动包括:可行性研究、需求导出及分析、需求规格描述和需求验证。

2 User requirements: It refers to the statements, in a natural language plus diagrams, of what services the system is expected to provide and the constraints under which it must operate.
用户需求是指用自然语言及图表所描述的、说明软件系统所应提供的功能及限制条件的陈述性文本。

3 System requirements: It is used to set out the system services and constraints in detail. The system requirements document, which is sometimes called a functional specification, should be precise. It may serve as a contract between the system buyer and software developer.
系统需求用于详细定义系统功能及其限制条件。系统需求文档一般也叫功能规格描述,它必须是准确的。系统需求文档可以作为开发者和用户之间的合约。

4 Technical feasibility: It is a measure of the practicality of a specific technical solution and the availability of technical resources and expertise.
技术可行性是对一种专门技术方案的现实性以及技术资源和专门知识可用性的度量。

5 Economic feasibility: It is a measure of the cost-effectiveness of a project or solution. This is often called a cost-benefit analysis.
经济可行性是对一个项目或解决方案的成本效益的度量,通常叫作成本效益分析。

6 Operational feasibility: It is a measure of how well the solution will fulfill the users' requirements. It is also a measure of how people feel about the system/project.
操作可行性是对解决方案满足用户需求情况如何的程度度量。它也是对人们如何探明系统或项目的度量。

Fact-finding(or information gathering): It is a classical set of techniques used to collect information about system problems, opportunities, solution requirements and priorities.
调查研究(或信息收集)是用于收集有关系统问题、机会、方案需求和优先权的一套典型方法。

第三节 软件设计
Section 3 Software Design

事件驱动系统 event-driven system
实时系统 real-time system
模块 module
★ 模块分解 modular decomposition
模块强度 module strength
功能独立性 functional independence
重构 refactoring
★ 内聚度 cohesion
★ 耦合度 coupling
客户端 client
客户机/服务器 client/server
组件对象模型 component object model (COM)
分布式组件对象模型 distributed component object model (DCOM)
公共网关接口 common gateway interface (CGI)
公用对象请求代理体系结构 common object request broker architecture (CORBA)
关键设计复审 critical design review (CDR)
设计 design
设计期 design time
设计机制 design mechanism
设计模型 design model
设计包 design package
★ 设计模式 design pattern
结构化设计 structured design
模型驱动设计 model-driven design
设计子系统 design subsystem
★ 详细设计 detailed design
★ 程序流程图 program flow chart (PFC)
★ 问题分析图 problem analysis diagram (PAD)
★ 盒式图(或 N-S 图) Nassi-Shneiderman Diagram
★ 判定表 decision table
★ 判定树 decision tree
过程设计语言 procedure design language (PDL)
分布式计算环境 distributed computing environment
分布式系统结构 distributed system architecture
分布式处理 distributed processing
环境 environment
框架 framework
体系结构描述语言 architecture description language
★ 概要设计 preliminary design
自顶向下设计 top-down design
自底向上设计 bottom-up design
概要设计复审 preliminary design review (PDR)
伪码 pseudo code
吞吐量 throughput
形式语言 formal language
体系结构,架构 architecture

Architectural design: Large systems are always decomposed into sub-systems that provide some related set of services. The initial design process of identifying these sub-systems and establishing a framework for sub-system control and communication is called architectural design and the output of this design process is a description of the software architecture.
大型软件系统一般都分解为若干子系统,并由这些子系统提供某种服务。所谓系统结构设计就是确定这些子系统并建立这些子系统的控制以及通信的框架。系统结构设计的结果就是对软件体系结构的描述。

Architectural design process: The architectural design process is concerned with establishing a basic structural framework for a system. It involves identifying the major components of the system and the communications between these components.
系统结构设计过程主要是为系统建立一个基本的结构框架。其内容包括区分软件系统的各主要组成部分及其相互间的通信联系。

Prototype: It is a smaller-scale, representative or working model of the users' requirements or a proposed design for an information system.

它是一个小规模的、有代表性的或者可工作的模型，这个模型反映了信息系统的用户需求或建议设计。

4 Prototyping: It is a technique for quickly building a functioning, but incomplete model of the information system using rapid application development tools.
它是一种使用快速应用开发工具快速地构造一个可工作的、但是不完整的信息系统模型的方法。

第四节 编码
Section 4 Coding

版本 version
代码 code
编程 programming
编程语言 programming language
编辑程序(编辑器) editor
模块化程序设计 modular programming
面向对象程序设计 object-oriented programming (OOP)
源代码组织 source code organization
★ 源程序 source program
子程序 subprogram, subroutine
命名规则 naming convention
程序保护 program protection
程序变异 program mutation
程序段 program segment
程序块 program block
程序库 program library
程序扩展 program extension
★ 程序设计语言 programming language
程序设计支撑环境 programming support environment
★ 程序正确性 program correctness
程序支持库 program support library
★ 代码审查 code inspection
代码生成器 code generator
递归例程 recursive routine
地址空间 address space
注释 comment
提交 commit
面向应用的语言 application-oriented language
★ 目标程序 object program
★ 目标语言 target language
执行程序 executive program
组件 component
组件图 component diagram
组件模型 component model
基于组件的开发 component-based development (CBD)
并行、并发 concurrency
动态链接库 dynamic link library (DLL)
★ 集成开发环境 integrated development environment (IDE)
集成 integration
集成构建计划 integration built plan
储存库 repository
资源文件 resource file
软件编码 software coding

1 Coding: It is a process of programming which leads to the implementation of the software design specification.
编码是指用计算机语言编写程序的过程，它具体实现了软件设计的规格说明。

2 Portability: It means that a source program file can be compiled and executed on different machines.
可移植性是指一个源程序可以在不同的机器上被编译并执行。

第五节 测试
Section 5 Testing

★ 测试用例 test case
桩模块 stub module
测试覆盖 test coverage
★ 测试数据 test data
测试驱动程序 test driver
测试项 test item
测试日志 test log
测试阶段 test phase
测试计划 test plan
测试过程 test procedure
测试可重复性 test repeatability
★ 测试报告 test report

测试有效性 test validity
验收测试 acceptance testing
★ 黑盒测试 black-box testing
边界值分析 boundary value analysis (BVA)
★ 白盒测试 white-box testing
结构测试 structural testing
路径测试 path testing
Beta 测试 Beta testing
面向对象测试 object-oriented testing
对象类测试 object class testing
正式测试 formal testing
正确性证明 correctness proof
错误测试 defect testing
组件测试 component testing
集成测试 integration testing
接口测试 interface testing
间歇性错误 intermittent failure
合格性测试 qualification testing
回归测试 regression testing
★ 软件测试 software testing
可测试性 testability
运行测试 operational testing
运行可靠性 operational reliability
★ 调试 debug
代码走查 code walk-through

Testing: It is a process to verify if a system conforms to its specifications.

Unit testing refers to that each component is tested to ensure that it operates correctly. Each component is tested independently, without other system components.

Module testing refers to that each module encapsulates related components, it can be tested independently, without other system components.

Sub-system testing involves testing collections of modules which have been integrated into sub-systems.

The sub-systems are integrated to make up the system. System testing is concerned with finding errors that result from unanticipated interactions between sub-systems and sub-system interface problems.

Acceptance testing refers to that the system is tested with data supplied by the system customer rather than simulated test data. Acceptance testing may reveal errors and omissions in the system requirements definition.

测试是验证软件是否满足需求规格的过程。

单元测试是测试每个组件，以保证它正确运行。不需要其他组件，每个组件单独地进行测试。

模块测试是指每个模块封装若干个相关组件，不需要其他模块，每个模块可以单独地进行测试。

子系统测试涉及组成子系统的各个模块的测试集合。

整个系统由若干子系统组合而成。系统测试主要是发现子系统间的交互操作产生预料之外的错误以及子系统的接口问题。

验收测试是使用客户提供的数据而不是模拟的数据来进行测试。验收测试可以发现系统需求定义中的错误和疏漏。

第六节 面向对象方法
Section 6 Object-Oriented Approach

统一建模语言 unified modeling language (UML)
★ 面向对象分析 object-oriented analysis (OOA)
★ 面向对象设计 object-oriented design (OOD)
抽象 abstraction
抽象操作 abstract operation
活动类 active class
活动对象 active object
类分层结构 class hierarchy
类库 class library
类方法 class method
构造函数 constructor
容器 container
容器分层结构 containment hierarchy
元类 metaclass
用例 use case
用例实例 use-case instance
用例模型 use-case model
用例包 use-case package

用例实现 use-case realization
用例视图 use-case view
★ 协作图 collaboration diagram
★ 构件图 component diagram
★ 部署图 deployment diagram
元模型 metamodel
元一元模型 meta-metamodel
元对象 metaobject
方法 method
方法调用 method call
★ 可重用性 reusability

1 Object-oriented approach: Object-oriented approach is a development strategy where system designers think in terms of "thing" instead of operations or functions. The executing system is made up of interacting objects that maintain their own local state and provide operations on that state information.
面向对象方法是一种开发策略,系统开发者考虑问题的角度是实体而不是操作或功能。最终的软件由一些相互作用的对象构成,这些对象保持其状态信息并实现基于这些信息的操作。

2 Use-case diagram: It graphically depicts the interactions between the system and external systems and users. In other words, it graphically describes who will use the system and in what ways the user expects to interact with the system.
用例图是以图形方式描述系统与其他外部系统以及用户之间的交互作用。换句话说,用例图以图形方式描述了谁将使用系统、用户希望以什么方式与系统交互。

3 Class diagram: It depicts the system's object structure. They show object classes that the system is composed of as well as the relationships between those object classes.
类图描述了系统的对象结构,显示了构成系统的对象类,以及这些对象类之间的关系。

4 State diagram: It is used to model the dynamic behavior of a particular object. It illustrates the various states in an object's life cycle that an object can assume and the events that cause the object to transit from one state to another.
状态图用于对某个对象的动态行为进行建模。它描述了一个对象在生命周期里呈现的各种状态以及引起该对象从一种状态变迁为另一种状态的各种事件。

5 Activity diagram: It graphically depicts the sequential flow of activities of either a business process or a use case.
活动图是以图形方式描述业务过程或用例中活动的顺序流程。

6 Sequence diagram: It graphically depicts how objects interact with each other via messages in the execution of a use case or operation.
顺序图是以图形方式来描述在用例子或操作的执行当中对象之间是如何通过消息来进行交互的。

第七节 软件维护

Section 7 Software Maintenance

改正性维护 corrective maintenance
完善性维护 perfective maintenance
适应性维护 adaptive maintenance
数据再工程 data re-engineering
★ 维护 maintenance
维护阶段 maintenance phase
维护计划 maintenance plan
维护请求 maintenance request
维护者 maintainer
★ 可维护性 maintainability
可扩展性 scalability
可移植性 portability
可用性 availability
可重复性 repeatability
程序升级 program evolution
正向工程 forward engineering
逆向工程 reverse engineering
平均无故障时间 mean time to failure (MTTF)
平均无故障间隔时间
mean time between failure (MTBF)

1 Software maintenance: Changes to the software are made in response to changed requirements but the fundamental structure of the software remains stable.

There are three different types of software maintenance: (1) Maintenance to repair software faults. (2) Maintenance to adapt the software to a different operating environment. (3) Maintenance to add to or modify the system's functionality.
软件维护:为满足需求对软件进行修改,但软件的基本结构保持不变。
软件维护有三种类型:(1) 修改错误;(2)由于操作系统环境改变而做出的适应性修改;(3)修改或增加系统功能。

Software re-engineering: The system is modified to make it easier to understand and change. It may involve some structural modifications but does not usually involve major architectural change.
There are five different activities in software re-engineering process. They include source code translation, reverse engineering, program structure improvement, program modularization, and data re-engineering.
Source code translation refers to that the program is converted from an old programming language to a more modern version of the same language or to a different language.
Reverse engineering refers to that the program is analyzed and information is extracted from it, which helps to document its organization and functionality.
Program structure improvement refers to that the control structure of the program is analyzed and modified to make it easier to read and understand.
Data re-engineering refers to that data processed by the program is changed to reflect program changes.
软件再工程:系统被修改以使其更易于理解和变化。它可能涉及某些结构的修改,但通常体系结构会保持不变。
软件再工程过程包含五种不同的活动,它们包括:源代码翻译、逆向工程、程序结构改进、模块化和数据再工程。
源代码翻译是将源程序从一种旧的程序设计语言转换为更新版本的同一种语言或一种不同的语言。
逆向工程就是分析程序、提取信息,以便对程序组织结构和功能进行文档化。
程序结构改进指分析并修改程序的控制结构以使其更易于阅读和理解。
数据再工程是指对程序所处理的数据进行修改,以反映程序的改变。

第二十五章　电子线路设计与测试

Chapter 25　Design and Experiments on Electronic Circuits

Labl: The Transistor Common-Emitter Amplifier

Type: verification

The experiment date: ××　××　××××　　Place: ××

Professional Class: ××　　Name: ××

Student No. : ××　Instructed by: ××　　Term: ××

1. Objectives

(1)To learn the debugging method of amplifier quiescent point.

(2)To master the testing method of voltage gain, input resistance, output resistance and maximum output voltage without distortion.

(3)Be familiar with common electronic instruments and analog circuit.

2. Equipments and Components Needed

+12V DC power, function generator, oscilloscope, AC voltmeter, DC voltmeter, AC milliammeter, frequency meter, potentiometer, capacitor, etc..

3. Tasks and Procedure (Including schematic diagram)

According to Figure 2-1, to connect the electronic instrument, to avoid interference, the common terminal of the instrument must be set together, and the signal source, AC milliammeter and oscilloscope must use special cable or shielded wire.

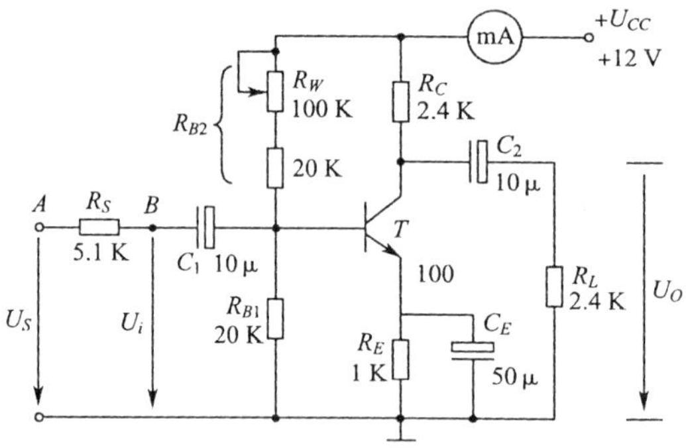

Figure 2-1　circuit diagram

(1)Debugging quiescent point

Before connecting the DC power, adjust R_w to make it maximum, and make the function generator switch to zero. Connect +12V power and adjust R_w to make $Ic=2.0mA(U_E=2.0V)$, and use DC voltmeter to measure U_B, U_C, U_E, and use multimeter to measure R_{B2}. Fill in the Table 2-1.

(2)Measuring voltage gain

Add 1KHZ sinusoidal signal to the input end of the amplifier, and adjust the function generator output to make amplifier input voltage $U_i=10mV$, in the same time, to observe the output waveform Uo with the oscilloscope. Use AC milliammeter to measure U_o Fill Table 2-2.

(3)Observing quiescent point's influence on voltage gain

Make $R_C=2.4K\Omega$, $R_L=\infty$, adjust U_i, use oscilloscope to observe the output voltage waveform, under the condition of undistortion, measure U_E and U_o without distortion, and fill in the Table 2-3.

(4) Observing quiescent point's influence on waveform distortion.

Make $R_C=2.4K\Omega$, $R_L=2.4K\Omega$, $U_i=0$, adjust R_w to make $Ic=2.0mA$, and measure U_{CE}, and increase input signal progressively, to make output voltage large enough but not distortion. Then maintain the same input signal, and respectively increase and decrease R_w, make wave shape distortion, and draw the waveform of U_o, and measure I_c and U_{CE} during distortion, and fill in the Table 2-4.

(5) Measuring maximum output voltage without distortion.

Make $R_C=2.4K\Omega$, $R_L=2.4K\Omega$, according to the experiment principle 2.4, in the same time, adjust input signal range and resistance R_w, use oscilloscope and AC milliammeter to measure U_{opp} and U_o. Fill in the Table 2-5.

(6) Measuring input resistance and output resistance

Make $R_c=2.4K\Omega$, $R_L=2.4K\Omega$, $I_c=2.0mA$. Input the sinusoidal signal with $f=1KH_Z$, use AC milliammeter to measure U_s, U_i and U_L without distortion. Fill in the Table 2-6.

4. The Record of the Experiment Form

Table 2-1:

Measured Value				Calculated Value		
U_B(V)	U_E(V)	U_C(V)	R_{B2}(KΩ)	U_{BE}(V)	U_{CE}(V)	Ue(mV)
2.71	2.00	7.92	50.02	0.71	5.92	2

Table 2-2:

R_c(KΩ)	R_L(KΩ)	Uo(V)	Av
2.4	∞	0.217	-21.7
1.2	∞	0.107	-10.7
2.4	2.4	0.108	-10.8

Table 2-3:

U_E(V)	1.0	1.5	2.0	2.5	3.0
Uo(V)	0.11	0.15	0.217	0.25	0.30
Av	10	15	20	25	30

Table 2-4:

U_E(V)	U_{CE}(V)	Output Waveform	BJT Operating region
1.0	8.87	Cutoff distortion	Cutoff region
2.0	5.78	Active	Active region
3.5	1.12	Saturation distortion	Saturation region

5. Data Analysis

(1) According to Figure 2-1, when circuit flow into R_{B1} and R_{B2} is bigger than I_B, then the quiescent point can be calculated by:

$$U_B \approx \frac{R_{B1}}{R_{B1}+R_{B2}} \approx U_{CC} \qquad I_E \approx \frac{U_B - U_{BE}}{R_E} \approx I_C$$

$$U_{CE} = U_{CC} - I_C(R_C + R_E)$$

Voltage amplification factor:

$$Av = \frac{\beta(R_C \mathbin{//} R_L)}{r_{be}}$$

Input resistance:　　　　Output resistance:

$$Ri = R_{B1} // R_{B2} // r_{be} \qquad Ro \approx Rc$$

(2) The measurement of IC

$$I_C \approx I_E = \frac{U_E}{R_E} \quad \text{or} \quad I_C = \frac{U_{CC} - U_C}{R_C}$$

(3) The measurement of Av

$$Av = \frac{U_o}{U_i}$$

(4) The measurement of output resistance

$$U_L = \frac{R_L}{R_O + R_L} U_{CC} \qquad R_O = \left(\frac{U_O}{U_L} - 1\right) R_L$$

6. Answer the Questions

(1) How to measure the value of R_{B2}?

We must transfer the switch to disconnect stote first.

(2) When measure Av, R_i and Ro, how to choose the size and frequency of the input signal?

You must ensure the output signal were not the distortion.

第二十六章 随机信号分析

Chapter 26 Random Signal Analysis

课程简介

《随机信号分析》是一门学科专业基础必修课，是电气信息类专业后续课程的基础课。本课程介绍随机过程的基本概念、平稳随机过程和遍历随机过程的概念、随机过程的统计特性概念和计算方法、随机过程相关函数、功率谱密度的概念和计算方法、随机过程通过线性系统的统计特性分析方法。

通过本课程的学习，使学生建立明确的统计信号的基本概念和必要的基础知识，掌握随机过程通过线性系统和窄带随机过程的分析方法，掌握窄带随机过程的概念、窄带随机过程的表示方法及窄带随机过程的性质。具有解决实际问题的能力。先修课程有《信号与系统》《概率论》和《电路原理》等。为后续课程《数字语音信号处理》《信号检测与估值》等奠定基础。

Course Summary

Random Signal Analysis is a basic compulsory course and it's the basic course for the electronic information engineering majors. This course introduces the basic concepts of random process, stationary random process and ergodic process, the statistical characteristics and calculation methods of random processes, the relation function of random process, power spectrum density concept and calculation and the statistical characteristics analysis of random process passing a linear system.

Students can establish the basic concepts and necessary basic knowledge of statistical signals from the course, grasp the analysis method of random process passing through linear system and narrow-band random process, grasp the narrow-band random process concepts, denotation and properties and solve the practical problems. The previous courses are: *signals and systems*, *probability theory and circuit theory*. The following courses can be *digital audio signal process*, *the detection and estimation of signals*, etc..

第一节 随机信号基础

Section 1 Basis of Random Signal

随机 random
随机信号 random signal
★随机变量 random variable (RV)
确定信号 definite signal
概率 probability
概率论 probability theory
随机试验 random experiment
试验结果 experiment outcomes
样本空间 sample space
分布律 distribution law
可能取值 possible value
概率分布函数 probability distribution function
累积分布函数 cumulative distribution function
离散随机变量 discrete random variable
连续随机变量 continuous random variable
非减函数 non-decreasing function
右连续 continuous to the right
★概率密度函数 probability density function (PDF)
一维随机变量 one-dimensional random variable
多维随机变量 multidimensional random variables
二维概率密度函数 two-dimensional probability density function (two-dimensional PDF)
联合概率分布函数 joint probability distribution function
联合概率密度函数 joint probability density function
边缘概率密度函数 marginal probability density function
边缘概率分布函数 marginal probability distribution function
独立 independence
相互独立 mutually independent
相互统计独立 mutual independence in the probabilistic sense
条件概率 conditional probability

条件概率分布函数　conditional probability distribution function
★ 均值　mean value/ mean
★ 数学期望　expectation
★ 方差　variance
标准差　standard deviation
矩　moments
中心矩　central moments
n 阶中心矩　central moments of order n
偏态系数　skewness
峰态系数　kurtosis
矩函数　moment function
★ 高斯分布　Gaussian distribution
★ 相关　correlation
★ 协方差　covariance
★ 相关系数　correlation coefficient
★ 相关函数　correlation function
随机变量的函数变换　functions transformation of random variables
中心极限定理　central limit theorem
★ 特征函数　characteristic function
矩生成函数　moment-generating function
傅里叶变换　Fourier transformation
麦克劳林展开　McLaurin expansion
第二特征函数　second characteristic function
特征函数的对数　log characteristic function
单调的　monotonic
单调函数　monotonic function
非单调　non-monotone
二项式(的)　binomial
二项式分布　binomial distribution
泊松分布　Poisson distribution
★ 均匀分布　uniform distribution
★ 正态分布　normal distribution
χ^2 分布　Chi-squared distribution
n 个自由度的 χ^2 分布　Chi-squared distribution with n degrees of freedom
瑞利分布　Rayleigh distribution
莱斯分布　Rice distribution
零均值　zero mean
协方差阵　covariance matrix

1 The distribution function $F_X(x)=P(X\leqslant x)$ of the random variable X is given by

$$F_X(x)=P(X\leqslant x)$$

Where $P(X\leqslant x)$ is the probability that the value taken by the random variable X, which is less than or equal to a real number x.

随机变量 X 的分布函数 $F_X(x)$ 是这样定义的：

$$F_X(x)=P(X\leqslant x)$$

其中 $P(X\leqslant x)$ 是随机变量 X 的取值小于或者等于实数 x 的概率。

2 The variance of X is also denoted as σ_X^2, and its square root, σ_X, is called the standard deviation of X. Variance is a measure of the "randomness" of the random variable X. By specifying the variance of a random variable, we are constraining the width of its probability density function. The variance and the mean-square value are related by

$$\sigma_X^2=E\{X^2\}-m_X^2$$

Thus, the variance is equal to the difference between the mean-square value and the square of the mean.

X 的方差也被表示为 σ_X^2，其平方根 σ_X 被称为 X 的标准差。方差是随机变量 X 的随机性的度量。通过指定随机变量的方差，我们限制了概率密度函数的宽度。方差与均值的关系是：

$$\sigma_X^2=E\{X_2\}-m_X^2$$

因此，方差等于均方值与均值平方的差。

3 Problem: X and Y are independent and identically distributed normal random variables with zero mean and variance σ^2. Define

$$U=\frac{X^2-Y^2}{\sqrt{X^2+Y^2}}\quad V=\frac{XY}{\sqrt{X^2+Y^2}}$$

(a) Find the joint PDF $f_{uv}(u,v)$ of the random variables U and V.

(b) Show that U and V are independent normal random variables.

(c)Show that $[(X-Y)^2-2Y^2]/\sqrt{X^2+Y^2}$ is also a normal random variable.

习题:随机变量 X 和 Y 互相独立,且具有相同的分布,都服从均值为零、方差为 σ^2 的正态分布。现定义随机变量 U 和 V:

$$U=\frac{X^2-Y^2}{\sqrt{X^2+Y^2}} \quad V=\frac{XY}{\sqrt{X^2+Y^2}}$$

(a)求随机变量 U 和 V 的联合概率密度 $f_{uv}(u,v)$。

(b)证明 U 和 V 是相互独立的正态随机变量。

(c)证明随机变量$[(X-Y)^2-2Y^2]/\sqrt{X^2+Y^2}$也服从正态分布。

第二节 随机过程和随机序列
Section 2 Random Processes and Random Sequences

实函数 real functions
实随机过程 real random process /real stochastic process
★ 随机过程 random processes/ stochastic processes
时间序列 time sequence
统计特性 statistical properties
噪声源 noise sources
映射 map
随机变量序列 sequence of random variables
随机过程的分布 random process distribution
总体 ensemble
总体平均 ensemble average
常数 constant
协方差函数 covariance function
自协方差函数 autocovariance function
互协方差函数 crosscovariance function
★ 自相关函数 autocorrelation function
★ 互相关函数 crosscorrelation function
样本平均 sample average
收敛 convergence
依均方收敛 convergence in mean square
依概率收敛 convergence in probability
均方收敛 mean square convergence
平方的 quadratic
以概率 1 收敛 convergence with probability one
分布收敛 convergence in distribution
弱收敛 weak form of convergence
强收敛 strong form of convergence
连续 continuity
不连续的 discontinuous
均方连续 mean square continuity
导数 derivation
微分 differentiability
均方导数 mean square derivation
均方微分 mean square differentiability
均方极限 mean square limit
均方积分 mean square integral
★ 相关时间 correlation time
高阶矩 higher-order moments
平稳的 stationary
★ 平稳随机过程 stationary random processes
严平稳过程 strict-sense stationarity
一阶平稳 first-order stationarity
一阶平稳过程 first-order stationary processes
二阶矩 second-order moments
二阶平稳 second-order stationarity
★ 宽平稳 wide-sense stationarity/stationary in the wide sense
二阶平稳随机过程 second-order stationary random processes
随机相位 random phase
随机频率 random frequency
n 阶平稳 nth-order stationarity
★ 高斯过程 Gaussian processes
高斯随机过程 Gaussian random processes
★ 各态历经性(遍历性) ergodicity
★ 各态历经过程 ergodic process
瞬时平均功率 instantaneous mean power
时间平均 time average
时间平均功率 time-average power
功率谱 power spectrum
★ 功率谱密度 power spectral density
谱分布函数 spectral distribution function
谱线 spectral lines
正交的 orthogonal
★ 正交性 orthogonality
时域 time domain
频域 frequency domain

★ 联合平稳 jointly stationary
★ 联合各态历经 jointly ergodic
维纳—辛钦定理 Wierer-Khintchine Theorem
归一化 normalized/uniform
噪声 noise
★ 白噪声 white noise
单位白噪声 unit white noise
限带白噪声 limited-band white noise
高阶谱 higher-order spectra

1 A random process $X(A,t)$ can be viewed as a function of two variables: an event A and time. For a specific event A_j, we have a single time function $X(A_j,t)=X_j(t)$ (i. e., a sample function). The totality of all sample functions is called an ensemble. For a specific time t_k, $X(A,t_k)$ is a random variable $X(t_k)$ whose value depends on the event. Finally, for a specific event, $A=A_j$ and a specific time $t=t_k$, $X(A_j,t_k)$ is simply a number.

随机过程 $X(A,t)$可以看作两个变量:事件 A 与时间的函数。对特定事件 A_j,可得到一个时间函数 $X(A_j,t)=X_j(t)$(即一个样本函数)。所有样本函数的整体叫作整体。对于特定时间 t_k,$X(A,t_k)$是一个随机变量 $X(t_k)$,其值取决于事件。最后,对于特定事件 $A=A_j$ 与特定时间 $t=t_k$,$X(A_j,t_k)$仅是一个简单的数值。

2 A stochastic process $X(t)$ is called strict-sense stationary (abbreviated SSS) if its statistical properties are invariant to a shift of the origin. This means that the processes $X(t)$ and $X(t+c)$ have the same statistics for any c.

如果随机过程 $X(t)$的统计特性不随时间的起点不同而变化,就称该随机过程 $X(t)$为严平稳过程(缩写为 SSS)。也就是说,严平稳过程 $X(t)$对于任意的 c 都存在 $X(t)$与 $X(t+c)$具有相同的统计特性。

3 Testing for the ergodicity of a random process is usually very difficult. A reasonable assumption in the analysis of most signals is that the random waveforms are ergodic in the mean and the autocorrelation function. Since time averages equal ensemble averages for ergodic processes, fundamental electrical engineering parameters, such as dc value, rms value, and average power can be related to the moments of an ergodic random process.

测试随机过程是否是各态历经通常是非常困难的。分析大多数信号时的一个合理的假设是随机波形的均值和自相关函数是各态历经。由于各态历经过程的时间均值等于统计均值,基本的电子工程参数,例如直流值、均方值和平均功率都可以认为是各态历经的随机过程。

4 Definition. The power spectrum (or spectral density) of a WSS process $X(t)$, real or complex, is the Fourier transform $S(\omega)$ of its autocorrelation $R(\tau)=E[X(t+\tau)X^*(t)]$:

$$S(\omega)=\int_{-\infty}^{\infty}R(\tau)e^{-j\omega\tau}d\tau$$

Since $R(-\tau)=R^*(\tau)$ it follows that $S(\omega)$ is a real function of ω.

定义。对于宽平稳过程 $X(t)$,不论是实随机过程或复随机过程,其功率谱(或谱密度)是其自相关函数 $R(\tau)=E[X(t+\tau)X^*(t)]$的傅里叶变换 $S(\omega)$:

$$S(\omega)=\int_{-\infty}^{\infty}R(\tau)e^{-j\omega\tau}d\tau$$

由于 $R(-\tau)=R^*(\tau)$,所以 $S(\omega)$是 ω 的实函数。

第三节 系统对随机信号的响应

Section 3 System Response to Random Signals

线性系统 linear systems
线性时不变系统 linear time-invariant system
冲激响应 impulse response
卷积 convolution
输入输出关系 input-output relationship
拉普拉斯变换 Laplace transformation
确定函数 deterministic function
★ 输出的自相关函数 output autocorrelation
输出的概率分布 output probability distribution
★ 输出的互相关函数 output cross-correlation function
★ 输出的功率谱密度 output power spectral density

低通 low-pass
★ RC 低通滤波器 RC low-pass filter
带宽 bandwidth
3dB 带宽 3-dB bandwidth
绝对带宽 absolute bandwidth
等效带宽 equivalent bandwidth
带通 bandpass
理想低通系统 ideal low-pass system
理想带通系统 ideal band-pass system
理想线性系统 ideal linear system
实际线性系统 practical linear system
单边功率谱 one-sided power spectrum
★ 平均功率 average power
非线性系统 nonlinear system
动态系统 dynamic system

例1 The primary spectral characteristic of thermal noise is that its power spectral density is the same for all frequencies of interest in most systems; in other words, a thermal noise source emanates an equal amount of noise power per unit bandwidth at all frequencies - from dc to about 10^{12} Hz. Therefore, a simple model for thermal noise assumes that its power spectral density is flat for all frequencies. When the noise power has such a uniform spectral density we refer to it as white noise.

温度噪声的主要频谱特性是在多数系统中，它的功率谱密度在所有频率处的取值都一样；换句话说，温度噪声源在所有频带范围内(从直流到大约 10^{12} Hz)每单位带宽释放出等量的噪声功率。因此温度噪声的一个简单模型就是假设它的功率谱密度对于所有频率都是平坦的。当噪声功率具有这种唯一谱密度时，我们就将其称为白噪声。

例2 Suppose that the input to a memoryless system is an SSS process $X(t)$, we can show that the resulting output $Y(t)$ is also SSS.

假设无记忆系统的输入为严平稳过程 $X(t)$，我们可以证明该系统所得到的输出 $Y(t)$ 也是严平稳过程。

例3 If a random process forms the input to a time-invariant linear system, the output will also be a random process. That is, each sample function of the input process yields a sample function of the output process. The input power spectral density $G_X(f)$ and the output power spectral density $G_Y(f)$ are related as follows:

$$G_Y(f)=G_X(f)|H(f)^2|$$

如果线性时不变系统的输入是随机过程，系统输出也将是一个随机过程。即，输入过程的每个样本函数都产生输出过程的一个样本函数。输入功率谱密度 $G_X(f)$ 与输出功率谱密度 $G_Y(f)$ 的关系是：

$$G_Y(f)=G_X(f)|H(f)^2|$$

第四节 窄带随机过程

Section 4 Narrow-band Random Processes

频率特性 frequency properties
解析信号 analytic signal
实信号 real signal
实随机信号 real random signals
★ 希尔伯特变换 Hilbert transformation
实部 real part
虚部 imaginary part
正交信号 quadrature signal
移相 phaseshift
★ 理想移相器 ideal phase-shift
角频率 angular frequency
复随机过程 complex random processes
复随机变量 complex random variables
窄带 narrow-band
窄带信号 narrow-band signals
窄带系统 narrow-band systems
窄带随机过程 narrow-band random processes
实窄带随机过程 real narrow-band random processes
★ 中心频率 central frequency
有限频带 limited frequency band
确定性窄带信号 deterministic narrow-band signal
幅度调制信号 amplitude-modulated signal
包络 envelope
包络调制信号 envelope-modulated signal

相位调制信号 phase-modulated signal
载频 carrier frequency
限带信号 band-limited signals
★ 窄带随机过程的特点 properties of narrow-band random processes
瞬时包络 instantaneous envelope
瞬时相位 instantaneous phase
瞬时频率 instantaneous frequency
包络检波器 envelope detector

1 Any narrow-band process may be represented by $v(t)=x(t)\cos\omega_c t-y(t)\sin\omega_c t$ or $v(t)=A(t)\cos[\omega_c t+\theta(t)]$. Where $A(t)$ is the real envelope, $\theta(t)$ is the phase, and $x(t)$ and $y(t)$ are the quadrature components.

任何窄带过程均可表示为：

$$v(t)=x(t)\cos\omega_c t-y(t)\sin\omega_c t \text{ 或 } v(t)=A(t)\cos[\omega_c t+\theta(t)]。$$

其中，$A(t)$是实包络，$\theta(t)$是相位，$x(t)$和 $y(t)$是正交分量。

2 Since the impulse response $h(t)$ doesn't vanish for $t<0$, the Hilbert transform is a non-causal linear operator. If $x(t)$ is an even (alternatively, odd) function then $\hat{x}(t)$ is an odd (alternatively, even) function. This claim follows easily from Fourier transform theory.

由于 $t<0$ 时，$h(t)$不会消失，所以希尔伯特变换是一个非因果线性运算符。如果 $x(t)$是偶函数(奇函数)，那么 $\hat{x}(t)$是奇函数(偶函数)。从傅里叶变换理论不难得到这一结论。

3 A system with the system function $H(\omega)=-j\text{sgn}(\omega)=\begin{cases}-j & \omega>0\\ j & \omega<0\end{cases}$ is called a quadrature filter. The corresponding impulse response equals $1/\pi t$. Thus $H(\omega)$ is all-pass with $-90°$ phase shift; hence its response to $\cos(\omega t)$ equals $\cos(\omega t-90°)=\sin(\omega t)$ and its response to $\sin(\omega t)$ equals $\sin(\omega t-90°)=-\cos(\omega t)$.

The response of a quadrature filter to a real process $X(t)$ is showed by $\overline{X}(t)$ and is called the Hilbert transform of $X(t)$. Thus

$$\overline{X}(t) = X(t) * \frac{1}{\pi t} = \frac{1}{\pi}\int_{-\infty}^{\infty} \frac{X(\alpha)}{t-\alpha}d\alpha$$

具有系统函数为 $H(\omega)=-j\text{sgn}(\omega)=\begin{cases}-j & \omega>0\\ j & \omega<0\end{cases}$ 的系统称为正交滤波器，其对应的冲激响应为 $\frac{1}{\pi t}$。因此，$H(\omega)$是一个带有$-90°$相移的全通网络；所以它对 $\cos(\omega t)$的响应为 $\cos(\omega t-90°)=\sin(\omega t)$，对 $\sin(\omega t)$的响应为 $\sin(\omega t-90°)=-\cos(\omega t)$。

正交滤波器对实随机过程 $X(t)$的响应可以用 $\overline{X}(t)$来表示，$\overline{X}(t)$就称为 $X(t)$的希尔伯特变换。因此有：

$$\overline{X}(t) = X(t) * \frac{1}{\pi t} = \frac{1}{\pi}\int_{-\infty}^{\infty} \frac{X(\alpha)}{t-\alpha}d\alpha$$

4 The envelope of a narrow-band Gaussian process follows a Rayleigh distribution and the phase follows a uniform distribution in $(0,2\pi)$.

窄带高斯过程的包络服从瑞利分布，相位服从$(0,2\pi)$上的均匀分布。

第二十七章　电子技术课程设计

Chapter 27　Electronic Technique Practice

Objectives

Students will design, install and debug the analog electronic circuits, digital electronic circuits and the analog and digital integrated circuits according to the previously learned theories in Analog Electronic Technique and Digital Electronic Technique.

The integrated training of electronic technique practice makes students further understand the basic theory of electronic techniques. The design process trains them for the designing ideas and skills, debugging and experimental techniques. At the same time, it is favorable for improving students ability of self-studying and solving practical engineering problems by using the basic theory. It lays a solid foundation for future electronic system design.

教学目的

根据所学模拟电子技术、数字电子技术的理论，对模拟电子线路、数字电子线路以及模拟与数字综合电子线路进行设计、安装与调试。

通过电子技术课程设计的综合训练，使学生加深对电子技术基础理论的理解，通过设计过程使学生受到设计思想、设计技能、调试技能与实验研究技能的训练，同时有利于提高学生的自学能力和运用基础理论去解决工程实际问题的能力，为电子技术系统设计打下坚实的基础。

Basic Requirements:

1. To be familiar with the usage and testing methods of common electronic devices;

2. To master how to access to relevant references;

3. To acquire proficiency in computer-software-aided circuit design and perform circuit design and the printed circuit board(PCB) fabrication by using Protel and Workbench;

4. To know well in related electronic circuit engineering standards and technical performance indexes of the normal electronic elements;

5. To study the installing and debugging skills for electronic systems;

6. To open minds in the application fields of electronic circuits and complete the task of circuit design with satisfying some performance indexes or possessing specific functions;

7. To foster serious work styles and build conscientious and careful engineering and technology concepts;

8. To train the ability in engineering practice, creative and integrated design.

基本要求

1. 熟悉常用电子仪器的操作使用和测试方法；

2. 掌握查阅相关参考文献的方法；

3. 熟练掌握计算机软件辅助电路设计方法，能熟练应用 Protel、Workbench 进行电路设计和印刷电路板的设计制作；

4. 掌握相关电子线路工程技术规范以及常规电子元器件的性能技术指标；

5. 学习电子系统电路的安装调试技术；

6. 拓展电子电路的应用领域，能设计、制作出满足一定性能指标或特定功能的电子电路；

7. 培养严肃认真的工作作风与科学态度，建立严谨的工程技术观念；

8. 培养工程实践能力、创新能力和综合设计能力。

Contents:

• Design procedures

1. The subject can be selected by student himself or from prepared reference titles;

2. The references related to assigned subject must be self-studied;

3. The process of circuit design by using related software should be studied within the specified time;

4. Based on the requirement for the design subject, students can access to some relevant references, propose its design scheme and procedures, and perform initial design process;

5. The installation, debugging and soldering of designed circuits will be finished in the laboratory;

6. The design report will be written in detail;

7. The promptly guide and FAQ will be provided by teachers in the process;

8. The common problems in the design process should be instructed appropriately.

• Design content

The design, installation and debugging for the analog electronic circuits, digital electronic circuits and the both integrated circuits should be made according to the studied knowledge.

• Time schedules

The collection of related references and scheme demonstration will be performed according to the subject's requirements, including ① system design of external characteristics; ② system design of internal characteristics; ③ a list of system components. (3 days)

The circuit design will be made, including ① specific circuit design and related calculation; ② the preliminary design of the circuit is simulated using EWB tools. (3 days)

The circuit assembly will be made, including ① the selection and test for the system components used; ② the soldering and assembly of the circuit; ③ the unit testing of the circuit (if not enough conditions, it should be made in the experimental box). (3 days)

The whole set debugging will be made, including ① the entire system's debugging; ② with the requirements of technical indicators in the task book, the quantitative measurements should be made one by one, according to the measurement results to determine whether they meet the demands of the task book; ③the related circuit adjustment needs to be made for not meeting the requirements of the technical indicators in the task book. (4 days)

The design report will be written and the defense will be performed. (2 days)

Note: the time slot can be adjusted according to different subjects.

教学内容

设计步骤：

1.学生可自拟或从参考设计题目中选定设计题目；

2.学生自学与指定设计题目有关的参考资料；

3.在规定时间内学习使用有关电路设计软件进行电路设计的方法；

4.学生针对实验课题的要求，查找资料提出设计方案，写出设计步骤，并进行初步设计；

5.在实验室安装电路、调试和焊接电路；

6.写出完整的课程设计报告；

7.教师在课内外给予及时指导和答疑；

8.设计过程中出现的普遍问题，应适当讲授。

设计内容：

用所学知识对模拟电子线路、数字电子线路以及模拟与数字综合电子线路进行设计、安装与调试。

时间安排：

根据题目要求收集有关文献资料，进行方案论证。要求：① 完成系统的外部特性设计；② 完成系统的内部特性设计；③ 列出构成系统的元、器件清单。(3天)

电路设计。要求：① 完成具体电路的设计和相关计算；② 对初步设计的电路用EWB进行仿真验证及修正。(3天)

电路组装。① 完成对系统所用元器件的挑选和检测；② 完成电路的焊接组装；③ 完成电路的单元调试(如果条件不足，应该在实验箱上进行单元电路的调试)。(3天)

整机调试。① 完成系统的整机调试；②对照任务书中各项技术指标的要求，逐一进行定量的测量，根据测量结果判断是否满足任务书的要求；③ 对不能满足任务书要求的技术指标做相关的电路调整。(4天)

写设计报告、准备答辩。(2天)

注：根据选题的不同，可以适当增减以上项目和调整时间。

Appendix: Reference Titles

• Analog circuit part

1. OCL and BTL audio frequency power amplifier
2. Adjustable direct current voltage stabilizing power supply
3. Functional signal generator
4. Electronic control system on water temperature
5. Amplifier circuit on speech
6. Integrated differential amplifier circuit (single, double, triple operational differential amplifier)
7. Square wave and triangle wave generator
8. Voltage control oscillator(LM324, LM331, LM566)
9. Display circuit of round inspect on multiple data

• Digital circuit part

1. Digital frequency meter
2. Digital voltage meter
3. Digital timer
4. Taxi meter
5. Digital electronic scale
6. Digital revolution meter using inferred
7. Digital temperature meter
8. Digital measure meter on capacitor
9. Measure meter on large current
10. Operational circuit on Add and Subtraction
11. Digital responder with timer and acoustical & optical alarm
12. High speed and parallel A/D transformer system
13. Driver circuit of dynamic scrolling on four LED
14. Digital automatic adjust circuit
15. Digital pulse control circuit on direct current motor

• High frequency circuit part

1. Soldering and debugging on Amplitude Modulation receiver
2. Design and experiment on LC sinusoidal oscillator
3. 50W power amplifier with high frequency and broad band

4. CATV relay amplifier
5. Design and experiment on frequency synthesizer
6. Design and experiment on AM high frequency transmitter with small power
7. Design on the machine with receiving, recording, playing and amplifying functions
• Synthesized circuit part
1. Amplifier with measure
2. Multi-function meter with digital effective value
3. Device with measuring frequency property
4. Digital speech storage and playback system
5. Audio power amplifier with high efficiency
6. Simple intelligent motor
7. Device with monitoring fluid dropping rate
8. Voltage-controlled LC oscillator
9. Intelligent modulation receiver
附录:参考设计内容:
(一)模拟电路课程设计内容
课程设计 1. OCL 和 BTL 音频功放的设计
课程设计 2. 可调式直流稳压电源的设计
课程设计 3. 函数信号发生器的设计
课程设计 4. 水温电子控制系统设计
课程设计 5. 语音放大电路设计
课程设计 6. 集成差分放大电路(单运放差分放大器、双运放差分放大器、三运放差分放大器)的设计
课程设计 7. 方波和三角波发生器的设计
课程设计 8. 压控振荡器(VCO)的设计(LM324、LM331、LM566)
课程设计 9. 多路数据巡回检测显示电路的设计
(二)数字电路课程设计内容
课题设计 1. 数字频率计
课题设计 2. 数字电压表
课题设计 3. 数字时钟
课题设计 4. 出租汽车里程计价表
课题设计 5. 数字电子秤
课题设计 6. 红外线数字转速表
课题设计 7. 数字温度计
课题设计 8. 电容数字测量仪
课题设计 9. 大电流测量仪
课题设计 10. 加/减法运算电路
课题设计 11. 数字定时声光报警抢答器的设计
课题设计 12. 高速并行 A/D 转换系统
课题设计 13. 四位 LED 显示器动态扫描驱动电路的设计
课题设计 14. 数字式自动调节电路的设计
课题设计 15. 直流电机的数字脉冲控制电路设计
(三)高频电路课程设计
课程设计 1. 调幅接收机的焊接与调试

课程设计 2. LC 正弦振荡器的设计与实验
课程设计 3. 50W 高频宽带功率放大器的设计
课程设计 4. CATV 中继放大器设计
课程设计 5. 频率合成器的设计与实验
课程设计 6. 小功率调幅高频发射机的设计与实验
课程设计 7. 收、录/放、扩四位一体机的设计
(四)综合电路设计
课程设计 1. 测量放大器设计
课程设计 2. 数字式工频有效值多用表设计
课程设计 3. 频率特性测试仪设计
课程设计 4. 数字化语音存储与回放系统
课程设计 5. 高效率音频功率放大器设计
课程设计 6. 简易智能电动车设计
课程设计 7. 液体点滴速度监控装置设计
课程设计 8. 电压控制 LC 振荡器设计
课程设计 9. 智能调制接收机设计

第二十八章　单片机系统课程设计

Chapter 28　Single-chip Computer System Practice

Objectives

This course offers a further teaching stage for *Microcomputer Principle* and *Interface and Single Chip Computer Application Courses*, and is also the integration and complement for the course's theories and experiments. Its goal is to further enhance the student's ability in computer knowledge, and enable them to have an thorough understanding for designing a microcomputer or single chip computer system and intelligent instrument with a core of single chip system. This stage is to foster the student's ability in the analysis of and solution to the practical problems. It plays a significant role in helping the students understand the theories and improve practical operation abilities and creative abilities.

教学目的

本课程设计为《微型计算机原理与接口技术》和《单片机应用技术》课程的后续教学环节，是对课程理论和课程实验的综合和补充，目的是进一步加强学生在计算机方面所学知识和能力，使学生对微型计算机（单片机）的系统设计及以单片机为核心的智能化仪表有完整的了解。本环节主要培养学生分析和解决实际问题的能力，对加深课程理论的理解、提高学生的实践动手能力和创新能力具有重要意义。

Basic Requirements:

From this teaching stage the methods for designing the minimum single chip computer system should be mastered. The students can start to make an independent task design, to learn the design, use and management for the microcomputer common ports, and to understand some basic skills such as the design, printing, installing, soldering, debugging of electronic circuits and so on. It requires the students to firstly master the skills of managing hardware by using compile language and programming skills. These skills include the design of interrupt, sampling, keying, display and other hardware management program.

基本要求

通过此教学环节，使学生掌握单片机最小系统的设计方法，具备初步的独立设计能力；理解微机常用通道的设计、使用及管理方法，并对电子线路的设计、制版、安装、焊接、调试等基本技能有基本的了解。初步掌握用汇编语言和程序来管理硬件的方法及程序设计技巧，包括中断、采样、键盘、显示等硬件设备管理程序的设计。

Contents:

The titles in this course should be of small type of electronic products or systems with the core of single chip computer, including minimum system of single chip computer, man-machine interface and I/O port etc.. The reference titles are as follows:

1. Electronic calendar
2. Digital number displayer
3. Standard current signal generator
4. Time indicator
5. Resistor measurement device
6. Taxi meter
7. Traffic light controller
8. Cipher lock controller
9. Multifunctional contest responder
10. Lattice LED character display

11. Electronic table tennis
12. Simple calculator

Time Schedule:

1. Design block diagram of system (1 day)
2. Design and drawing of the system's diagram (3 days)
3. Drawing the plot of a printed circuit board (2 days)
4. System installation and debugging (2 days)
5. Software programming and debugging (5 days)
6. Make the system specification(including hardware and software) (1 day)
7. Defense (1 day)

教学内容

设计题目应该是以单片机为核心的小型电子产品或系统。设计中应包含单片机最小系统、人机接口及输入输出通道等内容。参考题目如下：

1. 电子日历牌
2. 数显表
3. 标准电流信号发生器
4. 报时器
5. 电阻检测装置
6. 出租车计价器
7. 交通灯控制器
8. 密码锁控制器设计
9. 多功能竞赛抢答器
10. 点阵 LED 字符显示器
11. 电子乒乓球
12. 简易计算器

学时分配：

1. 设计系统框图。(1 天)
2. 设计并绘制系统原理图。(3 天)
3. 按原理图绘制印刷电路板图。(2 天)
4. 系统安装调试。(2 天)
5. 编制程序并调试。(5 天)
6. 编写系统说明书(包括软件和硬件)。(1 天)
7. 答辩。(1 天)

第二十九章　生产实习
Chapter 29　Production Practice

教学目的

生产实习是在专业基础课和专业课之后进行的理论联系实际的实践性教学环节。通过生产实习，使学生接触实际的生产、科研和企业管理，其主要目的有：

1. 让学生了解与本专业相关的现代工业生产组织形式、管理方式、工艺过程及现代工艺技术方法。
2. 进一步培养学生的基本操作技能。
3. 培养学生理论联系实际、从实际出发分析问题、研究问题和解决问题的能力。
4. 培养学生热爱劳动的工作作风，激发学生自主学习的热情。

Objectives

Production Practice is a practical teaching link to combine the theory with practice after the study of basic courses and special courses. It exposes the students to practical production, research and enterprise management. The goals are to:

1. Enable students to learn the organization mode, management mode, technological process and method of modern industrial production with the specialty related;
2. Further train students' basic operational skills;
3. Train students' ability in integrating theory with practice and analysing, studying and solving problems from a practical point of view;
4. Foster the students' love for their work and stimulate their desire to study independently.

基本要求

1. 了解典型的电子信息类企业的生产流程及工艺特点。
2. 理解典型电子系统产品的现代加工制造方法以及组装调试过程。
3. 理解电子系统产品的加工制造设备的组成、结构特点、工作方式和工作原理。
4. 通过参与电子类产品的生产、装配和调试过程，掌握现代的电子产品的生产流程、制作工艺和调试方法。

Basic Requirements:

1. To learn the production process and characteristics of a typical electronic information enterprises.
2. To understand the modern manufacturing method and assembly debugging process of typical electronic system products.
3. To comprehend the composition, structure characteristics, working style and working principle of equipment for manufacturing the electronic system products.
4. To master the production process, fabrication and debugging methods for a modern electronic product through the participation in the production, assembly and debugging of electronic products.

教学内容

1. 观看典型电子类企业生产过程的录像、相关专题讲座；企业内部实习。（2 周）
2. 在校内实习基地完成实际系统的电路设计、焊接、组装、调试等整套生产工艺流程。（1 周）

Contents:

1. Watch production processing videos for a typical electronic enterprise and lecture with related topic and get training in enterprise. (two weeks)
2. Fulfill the entire production process in the school's practice base including the design, soldering, assembly and debugging of a practical system circuit. (one week)

第三十章　专业综合课程设计
Chapter 30　Synthesized Specialized Practice

教学目的

专业综合课程设计，其目的是综合利用本专业所学过的各种专业知识，将模拟电子技术、数字电子技术、微机原理与单片机、数字信号处理、通信等技术与现代电子设计自动化(EDA)相结合，通过电子设计自动化手段对系统加以实现，使学生掌握电子设计自动化的设计原理、设计过程、实现手段以及硬件调试方法，同时使学生真正懂得现代电子技术设计的前沿和设计方法，从而提高本专业学生利用单片机、EDA 等先进设计工具解决相关问题的能力以及综合利用本专业所学专业知识解决实际问题的能力。

该课程设计是电子信息工程专业教学中极为重要的实践性教学环节，它不但起着提高本课程教学质量、水平和检验学生对课程内容掌握程度的作用，而且还将起到从理论过渡到实践的桥梁作用。

Objectives

The goal of this course is to synthetically use the previously learned knowledge in this field, and integrate the analog electronic technology, digital electronic technology, microcomputer principle and single-chip system, digital signal processing, communication technology, etc. with modern electronic design automation (EDA) technology. The system will be completed by using EDA tools. It enables students to master the EDA's design principle, design procedure and hardware debugging. At the same time, it enables students to fully understand the leading edge and methods of modern electronic technology design. Thus it will improve the students' professional ability in solving the related problems by using single chip computer and EDA tools, and in solving a practical problem by synthetically using the professional knowledge acquired in the courses.

The practicum is a very important practical teaching link in the professional education of electronic information engineering. It not only plays the role of improving the teaching quality and level, and testing the student's mastery degree for the course content, but also plays the role of being a bridge in the transition from theory to practice.

基本要求

1. 方案设计：根据设计课题的技术指标和给定条件，能够独立而正确地进行方案论证，要求概念清楚、方案合理、方法正确、步骤完整。
2. 实现技术：运用以 EDA、单片机等设计工具完成系统的设计、编码、仿真。
3. 制作与调试：针对相应的解决方案和实现技术完成系统的制作与调试。
4. 通过专业综合课程设计中的方案选择和论证，了解、熟悉以及进一步掌握电子信息工程及通信工程专业设计的特点、思路以及具体的方法和步骤，以提高独立工程设计的能力。
5. 通过专业综合课程设计中的设计计算、软件编制、产品图纸和系统线路的绘制与制作，提高计算机软硬件设计、工程计算和工程制图的能力。
6. 要求掌握相关资料检索的能力。

Basic Requirements:

1. Scheme design: The scheme demonstration can be made independently and correctly based on the technical indexes and the given condition of the subject, with the requirements of clear concept, reasonable plan, correct method and complete procedure.
2. Implementation technology: The system's design, encoding and simulation must be finished by EDA and single-chip computer and other tools.
3. Fabrication and debugging: These should be fulfilled according to the corresponding solution and the implementation technology.

4. From the scheme selection and demonstration in this practice, the students can understand and further master the design's characteristics, thoughts as well as the specific methods and steps, so as to improve the ability in independent engineering design.

5. Through the design calculation, software programming, product drawings and system circuit drawing and making, the students can enhance the ability in the computer hardware and software design, engineering calculation and engineering drawing.

6. The students are required to master the ability in relevant information retrieval.

教学内容

1. 选定相关的设计课题,确定相应的解决方案。明确设计任务,收集相关资料,包括参考书、手册和图表等,为设计工作做好准备。根据设计内容完成方案设计。(1/2 周)

2. 运用 EDA、单片机等设计工具完成系统的设计、编码、仿真和调试。(2 周)

3. 对得到的结果进行分析,完成设计报告。(1/2 周)

Contents:

1. The related design subjects must be selected and the corresponding solution scheme should be determined. The students make clear of the design task and collect relevant references including reference books, manuals and diagrams for the preparation of the design work. The entire design scheme should be finished based on the design requirements. (half week)

2. The system's design, encoding, simulation and debugging must be completed through the application of EDA tools and single-chip computer and other design tools. (two weeks)

3. The design report must be finished with the analysis of results obtained. (half week)

第三十一章　毕业设计

Chapter 31　Graduation Design

教学目的

电子信息工程专业毕业设计体现了毕业生的专业教育的最高标准。毕业设计是本科教育的高峰，给毕业生提供运用和开发其所学全部知识和兴趣的机会。毕业设计选题的范围很广，包括理论和实践等课题，来源可以是教研组自拟题目，也可以是一个学生独立选择的课题。在毕业设计中，要求学生能够展示其独立确定及开发 IT 问题的能力，确定解决问题的适当范围和完全根据题目要求解决问题的能力。

Objectives

Graduation Design exemplies the highest demands for students majoring in Electronic and Information Engineering upon their gradation. This project represents the culmination of the undergraduate education, providing students with the opportunity to draw upon and develop their total knowledge and interests. Topics explored may range from theoretical to practical design issues and may come from a faculty set topic or an independent topic. Students are required to demonstrate their ability to define and develop a complete IT problem, to address a range of scales appropriate to the design and to competently resolve the problem as defined.

正文是毕业设计(论文)的主体，要着重反映本科生自己的工作，要突出新的见解，例如新观点、新研究方法、新结果等。正文一般可包括:理论分析;试验装置和测试方法;对试验结果的分析讨论及理论计算结果的比较等。正文要求文字图表清晰整齐，计算单位采用国际单位制。利用别人研究成果必须附加说明。引用前人材料必须引证原著文字。论文要注意语句通顺，达到科技论文所必须具备的“正确、准确、明确”的要求。

Main Text Format Instruction

The main text of a thesis is the principal part for the graduation design. It mainly focuses on the graduates'own work, such as new ideas, new methods and new results. The body of a thesis composes of theoretical analysis, test apparatus, test methods, analysis and discussion of the test results, and comparisons. The words, figures and tables in the body must be clear and formatted. Authors should use SI as primary units. Authors should cite the references of other papers during paper submission. Authors should pay attention to the statements' fluency to achieve the requirements of accuracy correctness and sanity of scientific papers.

Thesis Structure

论文结构

The general structure of a thesis is as follows:

毕业论文的一般结构如下:

论文题目:Title
摘要:Abstract
关键词:Keywords
目录:Content
绪论:Introduction
主体:Body
结论:Conclusions
参考文献:References
附录:Appendix
致谢:Acknowledgement

Thesis Format

论文格式

1 The main title (on the first page) should be in Times New Roman 3-point, boldface type, centered capitalize the first letter of nouns, pronouns, verbs, adjectives and adverbs; do not capitalize articles, coordinate conjunctions, or prepositions (unless the title begins with such a word).

首页是论文题目,采用 Times New Roman 3 号字体,加粗,居中。论文题目中的名词、代词、动词、形容词和副词需首字母大写。除非论文题目是以冠词、并列连词和介词开头,否则上述词不需首字母大写。

2 The abstract contains the purpose and scope of the paper, the method of study or experiment, a brief summary of the results, conclusions and recommendations. The abstract is below the author information. Use the word Abstract as the title, in Heiti SC, 15-point, centered relative to the column, initially capitalized. The abstract is to be in Stzhongs, 12-point, and 1.25 spaced type. All manuscripts must be in Chinese and English.

摘要的内容包括论文涉及的范围、写作目的、试验研究方法以及结果、结论或建议。摘要在作者信息之后,用单词 Abstract 作为标题,黑体,小三,居中,首字母大写。摘要正文宋体,小四号,1.25 倍行距。摘要要采用中文和英文两种语言对照书写。

3 The keywords are below the abstract, in Heiti SC, 12-point, centered.

关键词在摘要后,黑体,小四,居中。

4 The introduction states the exact nature of the problem, the significance of this work, the purpose of the work, the background of the problem, the previous work on it, and the method which the author will be used. The body of a thesis is organized by the author. The information should be presented in some logical way, the major points emphasized with suitable illustrations. Type your main text in 12-point Stzhongs, 1.25 spaced. Do not use double-spacing. Be sure your text is fully justified—that is, flush left and flush right. Figure and table captions should be 10.5-point Stzhong. Figures and tables must be numbered separately. Figure captions are to be below the figures. Table titles are to be centered above the tables.

论文的绪论部分说明了问题的本质、研究工作的意义和目的、问题的背景、前人的工作以及作者将要采用的研究方法。论文正文的组织由作者决定。论文涉及的信息要以符合逻辑的方式呈现。主要的观点应加以强调并辅以适当的说明。论文正文采用宋体,小四,1.25 倍行距,两端对齐。请不要使用双倍行距。图表的标题 5 号宋体。图和表的编号需独立。图题应该在图的下方居中。表头需在表格的上方居中。

5 The conclusion summaries and evaluates the research results, the significance and advantages over previous work, the gaps and limitations in the work, and directs for the future work and its applications.

结论对研究结果、本文工作的意义和优缺点加以总结和评价,并为未来的研究和应用指明方向。

Some Common Mistakes

常见错误

1 The word "data" is plural, not singular.

单词 data 表示复数,不是单数。

2 The subscript for the common scientific constants, is zero with subscript formatting, not a lowercase letter "o".

通常数据量的脚标是从 0 开始的,而不是英文小写字母"o"。

3 A graph within a graph is an "inset", not an "insert". The word alternatively is preferred to the word "alternately" (unless you really mean something that alternates).

图中插入的图用 inset 而不是 insert。表示交替的意思用单词 alternately,表示二者选一用 alternatively。

4. Do not use the word "essentially" to mean "approximately" or "effectively".
   单词 essentially 表示本质上的，approximately 表示大概、近似，effectively 表示有效地。不要混淆。
5. In your paper title, if the words "that uses" can accurately replace the word "using", capitalize the "u"; if not, keep using lower-cased.
   若论文题目中的英文"that use"可代替"using"，则用大写字母"U"；若不能代替，仍用小写字母"u"。
6. Be aware of the different meanings of the homophones "affect" and "effect", "complement" and "compliment", "discreet" and "discrete", "principal" and "principle".
   注意形近字 affect 和 effect，complement 和 compliment，discreet 和 discrete，principal 和 principle 的区别。
7. Do not confuse "imply" and "infer".
   注意 imply 和 infer 的区别。
8. The prefix "non" is not a word; it should be joined to the word it modifies, usually with a hyphen.
   前缀 non 不是单词，和单词一起使用时用于修饰，通常带有连字符。
9. There is no period after the "et" in the Latin abbreviation "et al.".
   拉丁文缩写"et al."中"et"后面没有"."号。
10. The abbreviation "i. e." means "that is", and the abbreviation "e. g." means "for example".
   省略语 i. e. 意为"也就是"，e. g. 意为"举例来说"。

参考文献

References

[1]王兆安.电力电子技术.北京:机械工业出版社,2003.

[2]Jai P. Agrawal. Power Electronic Systems Theory and Design. 北京:清华大学出版社,2001.

[3]Timothy J. Maloney. Modern Industrial Electronics. 北京:科学出版社,2002.

[4]胡保生.便携英汉电工技术词典.北京:机械工业出版社,2003.

[5]新稳.微波技术与天线.北京:电子工业出版社,2003.

[6]R. E. Collin. Foundations for Microwave Engineering. 北京:人民邮电出版社,2001.

[7]R S. Elliott. Modern Antenna Theory and Design. 北京:科学出版社,2002.

[8]刘学观.微波技术与天线.西安:西安电子科技大学出版社,2001.

[9]汉英科技辞典编辑组.汉英科技辞典.北京:国防工业出版社,2004.

[10]汉英科技辞典编辑组.英汉科学技术辞典.北京:国防工业出版社,2014.

[11]Behzad Razavi.射频微电子.北京:清华大学出版社,2003.

[12]William Stallings.数据与计算机通信.北京:高等教育出版社,2001.

[13]Douglas E Comer.计算机网络与因特网.北京:清华大学出版社,2002.

[14]James Bignell &Robert Donovan. Digital Electronics. 4th edition. 北京:机械工业出版社,2003.

[15]M. Morris Mano &Charles R. Kine. Logic and Computer Design Fundamentals. Second edition Update. 北京:电子工业出版社,2002.

[16]康华光.电子技术基础(数字部分).北京:高等教育出版社,2001.

[17]数字信号处理系统分析与设计.北京:电子工业出版,2002.

[18]Panlo S. R. Diniz. Digital Signal Processing System Analysis and Design. Eduardo A. B. da Silva. Sergio L. Netto

[19]丁玉美.数字信号处理.西安:西安电子科技出版社,2001.

[20]Michael B. Pursley. Random Processes in Linear Systems. Prentice Hall, 2002.

[21]魏东兴.现代通信技术.北京:机械工业出版社,2003.

[22]LeeWCY. Mobile Communication Engineering. McGraw-Hill, 1982.

[23]Sibley M J N. Optical Communication. McGraw-Hill, 1990.

[24]James R. Armstrong, F. Gail Gray. VHDL 设计、表示和综合.北京:机械工业出版社, 2002.

[25]JamesR. Armstrong,F. Gail Gray. VHDL Design Representation and Synthesis. 北京:机械工业出版社,2003.

[26]潘松,黄继业. EDA 技术实用教程.北京:科学出版社, 2002.

[27]曾繁泰.可编程器件应用导论.北京:清华大学出版社,2001.

[28]邱关源.电路.北京:高等教育出版社,1999.

[29]James W. Nilsson. Susan A. Riedel. Electric Circuits (Sixth Edition). 北京:科学出版社,2003.

[30]李发海.电机与拖动基础.2版.北京:清华大学出版社,1998.
[31]Theodore Wildi. Electrical Machines Fifth Edition. Drives and Power Systems. 2002.
[32]潘新民.微型计算机控制技术.北京:高等教育出版社,2004.
[33]李锡雄,等.微型计算机控制技术.北京:科学出版社,1999.
[34]冯培悌.计算机控制技术.北京:浙江大学出版社,1994.
[35]俞优昀.计算机控制技术.北京:电子工业出版社,1998.
[36]K. J. Astrom&B. Wittenmark. Computer-Controlled Systems-Theory and Desige. 北京:清华大学出版社,2002.
[37]Brian Roffel. John E. Rijnsdorp. Process Dynamics. Control and Protection, Butterworths, Ltd., 1982.
[38]Charles L. Philips. H. Troy Nagle. JR. Digital Control System Analysis and Design, Prentice-Hall. INC. Englewood Cliffs, N. J., 1984.
[39]周明德.微型计算机系统原理及应用.北京:清华大学出版社.
[40]陈伯石.电力拖动自动控制系统.3版.北京:机械工业出版社,2003.
[41]Gerd Keiser.光纤通信.北京:电子工业出版社,2002.
[42]Bhag Singh Guru.电磁场与电磁波.北京:机械工业出版社,2004.
[43]樊昌信.通信原理.北京:国防工业出版社,2001.
[44]赵淑清.电子信息与通信专业英语.哈尔滨:哈尔滨工业大学出版社,2000.
[45]Leon W. Couch Ⅱ. Digital and Analog Communication Systems(Sixth Edition).北京:科学出版社,2003.
[46]Simon Haykin,等. Communication Systems (Fourth Edition).北京:电子工业出版社,2003.
[47]胡传国.英汉袖珍通信词典.上海:上海科学普及出版社,2003.
[48]夏华,等.英汉信息技术词典.北京:机械工业出版社,2002.
[49]Theodore S. Rappaport. Wireless Communications Principles and Practice.北京:电子工业出版社,2004.
[50]冯晓敏.英汉移动通信缩略语词典.北京:人民邮电出版社,2003.
[51]郭梯云,等.移动通信(修订版).西安:西安电子科技大学出版社,2000.
[52]张敏瑞,张红.通信与电子信息科技英语:北京:邮电大学出版社,2003.
[53]曾兴文,等.扩展频谱通信及其多址技术.西安:西安电子科技大学出版社,2004.
[54]Simon Haykin. Communication Systems.北京:电子工业出版社,2003.
[55]上海市通信管理局.电信技术实用大典.北京:人民邮电出版社,2002.
[56]A. Bruce Carlson, Paul B. Crilly, Janet C. Rutledge. Communication Systems.北京:高等教育出版社,2002.
[57]厦华,等.英汉信息技术词典.北京:机械工业出版社,2002.
[58]John G. Proakis, Masoud Salehi. Communication Systems Engineering.北京:电子工业出版社,2004.
[59] Wayne Wolf.现代VLSI电路设计——芯片系统设计(英文影印版).北京:科学出版社,2003.

[60] 韦恩. 沃尔夫. 现代 VLSI 电路设计——芯片系统设计(翻译版). 北京:科学出版社, 2004.
[61]M. Morris Mano, Charles R. Kime. 数字逻辑与计算机硬件设计基础(英文影印版). 北京:电子工业出版社,2002.
[62]Wayne Wolf. 现代 VLSI 电路设计(英文影印版). 北京:科学出版社,2003.
[63]Francis H. Raven. Automatic Control Engineering. 3rd edition. McGraw-Hill Book Company, 1978.
[64]Palm William John, Control systems engineering copyright by John Wiley & Sons, Inc. , 1986.
[65]Kenneth R. Castleman. Digital Image Processing. 北京:清华大学出版社,2003.
[66]Rafacl C. Gonzalesz. Digitat Image Processing Using Matlab. 北京:电子工业出版社, 2004.
[67]李朝晖. 数字图像处理及应用. 北京:机械工业出版社, 2004.
[68]Thomas L. Floyd. Digital Fundamentals. 北京:科学出版社,2002.
[69]Thomas L. Floyd. 数字基础. 李晔,等译. 北京:清华大学出版社,2005.
[70]康华光,陈大钦,张林. 电子技术基础模拟部分. 5 版. 北京:高等教育出版社, 2009.
[71]Allan R. Hambley. 电子技术基础(英文改编版). 北京:电子工业出版社,2007.
[72]郑君里,应启珩. 信号与系统. 北京:高等教育出版社,2011.
[73]奥本海姆. 信号与系统(英文版). 北京:电子工业出版社,2002.
[74]赵淑清,郑薇. 随机信号分析. 哈尔滨:哈尔滨工业大学出版社,2007.
[75]普罗科斯. 数字通信. 北京:电子工业出版社,2011.
[76]张肃文,陆兆熊. 高频电子线路. 3 版. 北京:高等教育出版社,1993.
[77]王卫东,傅佑麟. 高频电子线路. 北京:电子工业出版社,2004.
[78]曾兴雯,刘乃安,陈健. 通信电子线路,西安:西安电子科技大学出版社,2010.
[79]Behrouz A. Forouzan. 数据通信与网络. 北京:机械工业出版社,2006.
[80]William Stallings. 数据域计算机通信. 北京:电子工业出版社,2004.
[81]William A. Shay. 数据通信与网络教程. 北京:机械工业出版社,2003.
[82]Kay A. Robbins, Steven Robbins. UNIX 系统编程. 北京:人民邮电出版社,2006.
[83]高传善,毛迪林,曹袖. 数据通信与计算机网络. 北京:高等教育出版社,2004.
[84]Mark Zwolinski. VHDL 数字系统设计 Digital System Design with VHDL(英文版). 北京:电子工业出版社,2002.
[85]Mark Zwolinski. VHDL 数字系统设计 Digital System Design with VHDL. 2 版. 李仁发,凌纯清,等译. 北京:电子工业出版社,2004.
[86]任哲. 嵌入式实时操作系统 μC/OS-II 原理及应用. 北京:北京航空航天大学出版社,2009.
[87]Jean J. Labrosse. 嵌入式实时操作系统 μC/OS-II. 邵贝贝,等译. 北京:北京航空航天大学出版社,2003.
[88]阮秋琦. 数字图像处理学. 2 版. 北京:电子工业出版社,2007.
[89]Rafael C. Gonzalez, Richard E. Woods. 数字图像处理. 3 版. 北京:电子工业出版社,2007.
[90]Tamal Bose. 数字信号与图像处理. 北京:高等教育出版社,2004.
[91]瞿少成,吴军其. 电子信息工程专业英语导论. 北京:清华大学出版社,2008.

[92]朱一纶.电子技术专业英语.3版.北京:电子工业出版社,2009.

[93]Duane A. Bailey. Data Structures in Java for the Principled Programmer. WCB/McGraw-Hill.北京:清华大学出版社,1999.

[94]William Ford, William Topp. Data Structures With C++. Prentice Hall.北京:清华大学出版社,1997.

[95]严蔚敏,陈文博. 数据结构及应用算法教程.北京:清华大学出版社,2001.

[96]Sartaj Sahni.数据结构、算法与应用——C++语言描述.汪诗林,刘晓东,等译.北京:机械工业出版社,2000.

[97]Ian Sommerville. Software Engineering, 6th Odition. Pearson Education Limited,2001.

[98]Eric J. Braude. Software Engineering: An Object-Oriented Perspective. John Wiley & Sons, Inc., 2001.

[99]陈松乔,等. 现代软件工程. 北京:北方交通大学出版社, 2002.

[100]冯玉琳,等. 网络分布计算和软件工程. 北京:科学出版社, 2003.

[101]张海藩. 软件工程. 北京:人民邮电出版社, 2002.